Dialogues on Verbal Behavior

Series Editors

The International Institute
on Verbal Relations

Linda J. Hayes
Steven C. Hayes
University of Nevada, Reno

Dialogues on Verbal Behavior

The First International Institute on Verbal Relations

Edited by

Linda J. Hayes
University of Nevada, Reno
Philip N. Chase
West Virginia University

CONTEXT PRESS
Reno, Nevada

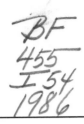
Dialogues on Verbal Behavior: The First International Institute on Verbal Relations /
edited by Linda J. Hayes and Philip N. Chase

Paperback. 308 pp. Includes bibliographies.

Library of Congress Catalog Card Number: 90-62178

ISBN 1-878978-00-4

© 1991 CONTEXT PRESS
933 Gear Street, Reno, NV 89503-2729

Printed in the United States of America

To our parents

Fred and Rose
John and June

Contributors

Paul Andronis, *The University of Chicago*

Philip N. Chase, *West Virginia University*

Jeff Danforth, *West Virginia University*

John W. Donahoe, *University of Massachusetts*

Maria Emma Garcia, *Western Michigan University*

Helga Guckel, *German Behavior Academy*

Cloyd M. Hyten, *University of North Texas*

Linda J. Hayes, *University of Nevada, Reno*

Steven C. Hayes, *University of Nevada, Reno*

T. V. Joe Layng, *The University of Chicago*

Jan LeFrancois, *Converse College*

Richard W. Malott, *Western Michigan University*

Jack Marr, *Georgia Institute of Technology*

Laura L. Methot, *Surrey Place Center, Toronto*

Paulo Moderato, *University of Palermo*

David C. Palmer, *University of Massachusetts*

Ullin T. Place, *University College of North Wales*

Hayne W. Reese, *West Virginia University*

Emilio Ribes Inesta, *Universidad Nacional Autonoma de Mexico*

Kurt Salzinger, *New York Polytechnic University and New York Psychiatric Institute*

Simon M. H. Starbuck, *St. Mary's University*

Ernest Vargas, *West Virginia University*

Julie S. Vargas, *West Virginia University*

Preface

The idea for a summer institute on verbal relations came to us one afternoon in Siena. We had been arguing about the role of reference in verbal interaction when the idea of continuing our discussion with a small group of others in an unusual context occurred to us. With the help of Claus Thierman and Thomas Skutella of the German Behavior Academy, we set to work making it happen. This volume is an edited record of the proceedings of the First International Institute on Verbal Relations, held in Bad Kreuznach, West Germany in June of 1986.

The chapters and related discussions are partitioned into five sections. In the first of these, Behavioral Theories, are three chapters addressing fundamental issues of definition and basic process in the language area. In chapter 1, Linda Hayes argues for an analysis of the verbal action of the listener in terms of substitution and reference. The argument is interbehavioral in kind. A emphasis on listener behavior is also apparent in the second chapter by Steven Hayes. Hayes proposes a relational control theory of stimulus equivalence, demonstrating how listener behavior may be described in terms of arbitrarily applicable relational responding and that stimulus equivalence is a special case of this type of responding. The last chapter in this section, by Emilio Ribes, also of an interbehavioral sort, argues that linguistic action involves not mere substitution of function but substitution of contingencies.

In Part 2, empirical methods for language study are discussed. Hyten and Chase show how approval and disapproval by a listener control the speaker's editing of overt verbal behavior in Chapter 4. In the following chapter, Place explains how conversational behavior studies through techniques adapted from sociolinguists is interpretable from a behavior analytic perspective.

The next three chapters, by Donahoe, Reese, and Salzinger, focus on analytic traditions other than behavior analysis and together make up Part 3. Donahoe's chapter outlines a world view, selectionism in which behavior analysis is subsumed. The chapter then demonstrates how a number of neuropsychology and cognitive science findings can be addressed from a selectionist perspective. In Chapter 7, Reese shows how the problems addressed by mentalists might have a bearing on the work of behavior analysts. In chapter 8, Salzinger argues that a behavioral approach to the problems addressed by cognitivists might help to solve them.

In the forth part of the book, listener activities again become the issue, although in this section the emphasis is on listener behavior is the form of rule governance in particular. Chase and Danforth, in chapter 9, review the findings of the rule governance literature and provide ties to problems in concept formation and conceptual behavior. Malott and Malott consider relations among public and private verbal stimuli in chapter 10, pointing to the role of private stimuli in the control of rule following.

The last section of the book is devoted to related topics, including memory in one case and artificial intelligence in the other. In chapter 11, Palmer argues convincingly for the usefulness of interpretation and then uses interpretive techniques to provide an analysis of memory. In the final chapter Vargas examines the significance of artificial intelligence work as it relates to whether or not computers are speakers in the Skinnerian sense, concluding that they are not.

Following each chapter is a brief discussion, based in part of the discussion pertaining to that chapter when delivered as an address at the institute, and in part on the discussant's further considerations of the chapter as it appears in the present form. We have included these discussions because they best illustrate the dialogue and debate that was so critical to the success of the institute. For us, it is these dialogues that make the book a vital part of the changing field of behavior analysis.

In ending we would like to thank a number of people who assisted us in the activities that eventuated in this book. Those involved in the planning and implementation of the Institute included: Claus Thierman, Thomas Skutella, Helga Guckel, Jorge Rade, Petra Schopf and the students of the German Behavior Academy. Amile and Rosemarie Schopf, the proprietors of the Birkenhof Hotel in Bad Kreuznach, provided the hospitality, good food and cool drink that helped us concentrate on our work. Finally we would like to acknowledge the staff of CONTEXT PRESS.

Linda J. Hayes
Philip N. Chase
May, 1990

About the Series

Three International Institutes on Verbal Relations have been held. The first was held in Bad Kreuznach, West Germany in June of 1986, the second in Tequesquitengo, Mexico in June 1988 and the third in Aguas de Lindoia, Brazil in January 1989. Additional Institutes are planned. The structure of the Institutes has been roughly the same. About 10-12 psychologists from around the world have been asked to participate as primary speakers, including several from the host country. About 15-20 other psychologists and students serve as observers and discussants. The Institute extends over a period of about five days. Each day, two to three talks are given in the morning. In the afternoon, each talk is discussed by the entire group, lead by a discussion leader. Discussion then extends into the wee hours of the morning.

Proceedings of each of the Institutes are being published by CONTEXT PRESS. Linda J. Hayes and Steven C. Hayes are editors of the series. For further information or to order these volumes contact CONTEXT PRESS, Box 50172, Reno, NV 89513.

Table of Contents

Part 5 - Related Topics

Chapter 11

David C. Palmer, *University of Massachusetts*

Discussion: Paulo Moderato, *University of Palermo*

Chapter 12

Ernest Vargas, *West Virginia University*

Discussion: Linda J. Hayes, *University of Nevada, Reno*

Part 1

Behavioral Theories

Chapter 1

Substitution and Reference

Linda J. Hayes[1]
University of Nevada, Reno

For some time now I have been arguing that an important concept is missing from Skinner's treatment of verbal behavior (Parrott, 1984; 1986a; 1987). That concept is reference, and its omission is deliberate. Historical interpretations of reference arose under the auspices of mentalism, and as it was Skinner's intention to provide a non-mentalistic account of verbal behavior, reference was legislated out of consideration. Or at least so it would seem. In actual fact, a concept of reference is so central to the analysis of verbal behavior that even Skinner was not able to abandon it completely. And it is not a concept that can be abandoned if we are to understand this subject matter. It does require reinterpretation, however; and when reinterpreted, its place in the analysis of verbal behavior becomes evident, and its omission an inadequacy.

My purpose in this chapter, then, is to provide an alternative treatment of the concept of reference -- one that I believe is not wholly incompatible with the postulational basis of Radical Behaviorism -- and to show how this concept may improve our understanding of linguistic interaction. I will begin by considering Skinner's objections to traditional concepts of reference, what Skinner's analysis lacks in the absence of such a concept, and how reference has worked its way back into his analysis, albeit unwittingly and without adequate articulation. Having completed this portion of my address, I will move on to an alternative interpretation of reference, along with issues of association and substitution upon which it depends.

Skinner's Position
Problems of Correspondence and Reference

Skinner's objection to the concept of reference is, more accurately, an objection to traditional theories of meaning in which this concept is invoked. From a traditional perspective, meaning is an issue of correspondence between verbal utterances on one side, and things and events of the nonverbal world on the other. The meaning of an utterance is some thing or event of the nonverbal world with which it corresponds and to which it refers. The meaning of the word cup, for example, is the object cup; and the word is said "to refer to" or "stand for" the object. There are two issues here, really, one being correspondence, the other reference. How do verbal utterances correspond to the things that are their meanings, and what is the nature of the relation between them called "reference?"

Correspondence. With regard to the issue of correspondence, Skinner's argument takes the following form: If verbal responses correspond to the things that are their meanings, then it must be possible to identify the things to which verbal responses correspond on every instance of their occurrence, and this is not, in fact, possible to do. In the first place, he argues, not all verbal utterances may be said to correspond to things of the nonverbal world. What can we identify as the referent for a response such as "please" or "therefore?" Secondly, when a correspondence of this sort **might** obtain, as in the case of the tact, there is always an element of abstraction. In his words: "We cannot point to a single chair which is the referent for the response chair" (Skinner, 1957, p. 117). And were we willing, for the sake of argument, to suggest that the referent for this abstract tact were certain properties common to all chairs, we would still be left with the problem of identifying those properties in physical terms. Now while this may not seem particularly difficult to do in the present case of chairness, Skinner (1957, p. 112) invites us to consider the problem of describing -- in physical terms -- the referents for an abstract tact such as "pyramidality" or "justice." So insurmountable seems the problem in these cases that an interpretation of correspondence among verbal utterances and things of the nonverbal world is rendered useless by Skinner.

I would argue, at this point, that the referent for a verbal utterance need not have substantive structure -- it need not be a thing of the material world, and its characteristics need not be identified in physical terms. The referent for a verbal utterance, that is, the "thing" to which it corresponds, may be an event, relation, or other verbal utterance.

Reference. With the issue of correspondence out of the way, Skinner goes on to relations of reference. Two arguments are relevant here, one applying to reference from the standpoint of the speaker and one from the standpoint of the listener.

With regard to the speaker, Skinner objects to traditional views of reference because they implicate the involvement of mental or psychic events (1957, pp. 5-9). Traditional views hold that words symbolize psychic events called "ideas" and are used by speakers as a means of conjuring up those ideas in the minds of listeners. It is a familiar argument, although not a very sophisticated one, as even Skinner admits that the term "idea" might be revived for use through operational definition (1957, p. 128).

From an operational standpoint, an idea amounts to the reactional component of a history of contact with stimuli or relations among them sharing certain properties in common. Such actions, while derived from previous specific circumstances, are no longer attached to those circumstances. They are, rather, abstracted and standardized reactions that substitute for and sum up a person's experiences in a form useful for present purposes. They are a person's reactional history with respect to events having common properties, configured at a moment in time. For Skinner, though, the threat of traditional implication seems too great, and for this reason he rejects the concept of reference as it applies to the behavior of the speaker.

As for referential relations and the listener's behavior, Skinner's argument is as follows: If a verbal utterance can be said to "stand for" or "refer to" some thing or event of the nonverbal world, then the listener's reaction to the utterance and to the thing must be the same. The problem is that our reactions to verbal stimuli and to the things they are said to stand for are not the same. He explains his position with a fox hunting example, arguing that one "turns and looks" under the control of the **word** fox, while one "rides after" an **actual** fox (1957, pp. 87-88). Skinner does acknowledge that a verbal stimulus and its referent may elicit similar behaviors of the respondent type, among which might be included conditioned seeing and other perceptual acts. However, a verbal stimulus does not stand for a thing as far as the operant behavior of the speaker is concerned, and with that assertion, the concept of reference is abandoned -- at least officially.

I would point out that the operant or effectual behavior of a speaker, while not wholly irrelevant to the issue of reference, is not the repertoire of principle interest in this context. The interesting repertoire is, in fact, the very perceptual activities that Skinner acknowledges to be the same in the presence of verbal stimuli and their referents. I will return to this issue.

Continuing Problems of Correspondence and Reference

One wonders why traditional theorists, who are no doubt not totally inept, have clung to an interpretation of linguistic events involving concepts of correspondence and reference if these concepts are as useless as Skinner believes them to be. Of what service are these concepts in traditional theory? And does Skinner's interpretation of verbal behavior provide these services in other more satisfying ways?

Utility of correspondence and reference in traditional theory. Let us deal with the utility of these concepts in traditional theory first. In these theories, correspondence and relations of reference explain the listener's ability to act with respect to things and events of the nonverbal world upon being confronted with verbal stimuli alone. The listener reaches for, grasps, and passes the salt upon being confronted with auditory verbal stimulation of the form "please pass the salt." To reiterate, reference, as an analytical tool, is used to explain the control over **nonverbal** behavior by **nonverbal** stimuli as a function of prior **verbal** stimulation. It is, among other things, the substance of traditional theories of listening and understanding. Beyond this service, reference and its companion processes of association and substitution, constitute an explanation for the ability of both speakers and listeners to respond to things and events in their absence. It is referential activity that enables us to act with respect to the past, the future, the remote and the nonexistent.

While it is true that traditional theorists have explained these events in traditional ways, that is, by inventing psychic processes with mystical powers of causality, they have nonetheless identified significant problems of verbal interaction that cannot be overlooked if an analysis of this subject matter is to be complete. How has Skinner dealt with these issues? What does Skinner say about listening and understanding? And how has he dealt with responding to things and events in their absence?

Listening from Skinner's perspective. Listening is most often discussed by Skinner in the general context of perception (for example, 1969, pp. 251-253; 1974, pp. 82-86). In this context, listening is conceptualized as operant behavior maintained by the consequence "what is heard." Seeing and other perceptual activities are similarly analyzed. In the context of verbal behavior, however, the listener's behavior is not explained by appeal to consequences of this sort. Rather, an explanation for the listener's behavior is to be found in the subsequent behavior of the speaker, which may take the form of gratitude, approval or threat withdrawal (1957, pp. 38-39, pp. 84-85).

This discrepancy is owing to the fact the Skinner is not dealing with the behavior of listening in the book *Verbal Behavior*. He is dealing the listener behaviors occurring **after** listening has taken place, namely those involved in mediating reinforcement for the speaker's behavior. Little is said, and none of it systematic, about the behavior of listening per se (see Parrott, 1984, for further discussion).

Understanding from Skinner's perspective. The act of understanding, as a contemporaneous segment of behavior, is similarly not addressed by Skinner in the context of verbal behavior. From Skinner's perspective, understanding is a construction, not an event. It refers to a repertoire of behavior and its potential for occurrence on given occasions of suitable stimulation (Skinner, 1957, p. 363). Accordingly, from Skinner's standpoint, "to know about" or "to understand" is really nothing at all until it eventuates in some form of overt behavior (see Parrott, 1983a for further discussion). That is, from an event standpoint, understanding amounts to whatever it is a listener does in response to verbal stimulation, and the only activity of the listener mentioned in this context is constituted of mediating reinforcement for a speaker's behavior.

It is obvious nonetheless that mediating reinforcement is not the **only** activity going on under such conditions. The fact that a listener may listen but not understand and understand but not mediate reinforcement suggests the need for conceptual specification of these events as well.

In summary, neither listening nor understanding are conceptualized as actions of a listener in their own right and it would seem to me that there is little chance of explaining how a listener's nonverbal behavior comes under the control of nonverbal stimuli as a function of prior verbal stimulation if no attempt is made to understand the listener's contact with the prior verbal stimulation. What is it that the listener is **doing** when he confronts verbal stimulation of the form "please pass the salt"? And how is it that whatever he is doing at this moment evolves into a manipulation of the salt shaker? Skinner has not asked these questions.

Rule Governed Behavior

Not asking questions does not prevent one from answering them inadvertently, however, and this is precisely what has happened. Skinner's answers to these questions surface in his analysis of rule governed behavior; and concepts of correspondence and reference are implicit in this analysis. Let me explain.

Generally speaking, behavior is interpreted as rule governed when it appears to occur despite "defective" contingencies of reinforcement, the most often cited defect being the absence of immediate consequences for the behavior in question (Skinner, 1969, pp. 166-171; 1974, pp. 125-128). In addition to maintenance despite defective contingencies of reinforcement, rule governed behaviors are behaviors occurring under the control of contingency specifications called rules, a complete rule being a description of the behavior to be executed, the circumstances under which it is to be executed, and its likely consequences. So far, so good.

A problem arises, however, when an attempt is made to explain **how** rules govern behavior. The temporal relations of rules to the behaviors they govern suggest that rules may be operating as discriminative stimuli -- except for the fact that the discriminative functions of stimuli are established when behaviors are reinforced in the presence of those stimuli. In short, to understand how rules -- interpreted as discriminative stimuli -- govern behavior, we must be prepared to conceptualize rule governed behavior as contingency shaped behavior. But if we conceptualize rule governed behavior as contingency shaped behavior, we must be prepared to identify the effective consequences for such behavior and it was the absence of effective consequences that gave rise to the category of rule governance in the first place.

Skinner solves this problem by conceptualizing rule governance as a operant of which individual instances of rule following may be considered members (1969, p. 148). We follow a rule because we have been reinforced for following rules in the past. The only problem with this solution is that it raises another problem, namely, if rule governance is just another operant and operants are contingency shaped, why the rule governed-contingency shaped dichotomy? How do these two **operants** differ?

Skinner does attempt to deal with this issue. In doing so, however, he completely overlooks his previous argument. He compares contingency shaped operants or classes of action not with the operant rule governance, but rather with individual instances of rule following. He argues, for example that instances of rule governed behavior occur under conditions that do not allow for contingency shaping, implying that rule governed behaviors are not products of contingency shaping (1974, pp. 123-128). This is a statement made with respect to an **instance** of rule following, and even here it is not entirely accurate. He means, essentially, that the consequences specified in rules are not immediate enough to maintain the behaviors specified in rules. The consequences specified in rules are not the consequences responsible for the maintenance of rule governed behaviors though. The effective consequences for rule governed behaviors can only be identified at the level of the operant class, rule governance. At this level the consequences responsible for the maintenance of rule governed behaviors are the generalized consequences of following rules.

Moreover, upon looking further into Skinner's comparisons of rule governed and contingency shaped behaviors, it becomes obvious that all of the distinguishing characteristics of rule governance cited by him, including differences in response topography and motivational circumstances, are peculiarities of specific **instances** of rule following. They are not class characteristics. The only real difference between rule governed and contingency shaped operants is that the antecedent stimuli in the former case are always verbal in nature (see Parrott, 1987, for further discussion).

How can we account for Skinner's logic in this context? What point is he trying to make by comparing instances of rule governed behavior with contingency shaped operants? And, given that he is making comparisons of this sort, on what grounds are examples of each selected for comparison?

Rule Governed and Contingency Shaped Behaviors Compared

Instances of rule governed behavior and contingency shaped operants are selected for comparison by Skinner on the basis of a concept of **correspondence:** Rules describe contingencies and because they do a rule governed counterpart of a contingency shaped operant may be identified for the purposes of their comparison. Further, the relation existing between corresponding patterns of verbal stimulation (i.e., rules) and occurrences of behavior under particular circumstances producing particular consequences (i.e., contingency shaped behaviors) is one of **reference.** A rule is said to "describe" (Skinner, 1974, p. 125) or to "specify" (Skinner, 1969, p. 147) a contingency of reinforcement.

Perhaps I am missing something here, but this sounds an awful lot like a referential analysis to me. At least we may agree that Skinner's theory is not without inconsistency if on one hand he identifies the rule governed counterpart of a contingency shaped operant by way of a referential interpretation of the relation between verbal and nonverbal events, while on the other hand argues that verbal behavior, including the tact, does not refer to anything.

Summary

I will conclude this section of my address by returning to the reasons for it. I wondered why traditional theorists continued to invoke concepts of correspondence and reference in their analyses of listening, understanding, and responding to things and events in their absence if these concepts were as useless as Skinner believed them to be; and set out to discover how Skinner dealt with listener activities of these types without invoking them.

The analysis of rule governed behavior is Skinner's analysis of the listener's behavior. It falls short of providing an account of such listener activities as listening and understanding, however. Consider the substance of Skinner's account: A listener confronts a verbal stimulus in the form of a rule. Sometime later, in the absence of the rule, the listener engages in the behavior specified in the rule. What the listener is doing when he confronts the rule escapes analysis altogether. And how we get from this episode to the events of rule following at a later date is analyzed in no further detail than to suggest that the listener "does what the rule told him to do". This does not constitute a system-specific, technical analysis of listener behavior. It is nothing more than a lay description of a readily observable sequence of activity.

The best we can say about Skinner's analysis of listener activity, as attempted in his discussions of rule governance, is that it is referential in kind. And the best we can say about our own analyses, as witnessed over these proceedings of the International Institute on Verbal Relations, is that it has something to do with verbal stimulation. Perhaps if we put these two together, and took in enough air to talk about speaking and listening in the same breath, we might have something!

An Alternative Formulation of Reference

We are ready now to consider an alternative and, I believe, a thoroughly naturalistic treatment of the concept of reference as it applies to both speaker and listener. We leave traditional interpretation, although not traditional purpose, behind us at this point. I would like to begin by saying that referential speech, and I use the term speech in the generic sense, is one of two classes of linguistic action identified by J. R. Kantor in his 1936 and 1977 treatments of this subject matter. The other class, symbolic action, is closer to the events that have been discussed in the context of stimulus equivalence than is referential action, although I believe the equivalence paradigm is very well suited to the study of both classes. I will, however, restrict my comments to the referential type of linguistic action.

Distinguishing Mediational Acts from Implicit fields

The analysis to follow will entail a discussion of "implicit action" (Kantor, 1924). In my experience, this concept poses some difficulty for behavioral psychologists. It is misinterpreted as an intervening variable with objectionable structural as well as functional properties. Hence, I would like to offer some clarification as to the nature of implicit behavior before going on to the concept of reference.

Mediating activity. The objection to formulations of reference in terms of implicit behavior is really an objection to the concept of mediating activity. It is an argument about the admissability of unobservables in our descriptions of observable behavior-environment relations. As unobservable events, mediating activities may be invented at will to solve whatever problems of accounting for relations among observable factors we are otherwise unable to solve. The inclusion of such activities in our analyses threatens the integrity of the behavior analytic system, harking back as it does to earlier learning formulations in which intervening variables carried a heavy burden.

Beyond this, the argument amounts to: "so what if the organism engages in unobservable activities--what can we legitimately say or do about such events--of what consequence are they to our analyses--what good are they to us?" I will deal with this argument toward the end of the chapter. For now, let me attempt to explain the differences between mediating events, when conceptualized as intervening variables, and the category of implicit behavior involved in my analysis of reference.

Implicit fields. Unlike mediating activity, the response phases of implicit events are not necessarily nor even typically unobservable. The term implicit refers to a type of interbehavioral field -- one in which a response is occurring with respect to a stimulus not present in that field, through the operation of another stimulus. It is a way of speaking about the transfer of stimulus functions from one object to another as a result of their partial identity in form or function, or their having been encountered in contiguous relation (spatial or temporal) at some previous time in the reactional history of a given organism (see Parrott, 1986b for further discussion).

We may speak of relations of these sorts among physical objects as **conditions** of association. Association, itself, may be regarded as the occurrence of proximal reactions with respect to stimuli related in these ways (Kantor, 1924). A stimulus acquiring functional properties by these means is designated a substitute stimulus, and a field of interaction characterized by the operation of substitute stimuli is called an implicit field. As such, it is typically the stimulus phase of implicit action that presents problems of observation, not the response phase. Responding with respect to substitute stimulation may be readily observable. Contorting the face at the mention of a gruesome accident or kissing a photograph of a lover, both examples of implicit action, are by no means unobservable.

Moreover, regardless of how readily observable the response phase of an implicit field may be on a given occasion of its occurrence, it is never "private" in the sense of occurring in the deep dark recesses behind the skin (Parrott, 1983b). That the response factor involved may be subtle and thereby difficult to observe is not a comment on where such activity is taking place. It is a comment on observational strategy. Implicit events are relations between the responding of an organism and the stimulating of an environment, and all such relations are understood in terms of their origins and histories of development. Implicit events are no exception. Their observation is achieved by way of a study of their histories (see Parrott, 1986b, for further discussion.)

Implicit events differ from mediational activities in another way as well: **They play no causal role in the occurrence of subsequent events**. As such, they are not as "useful" in the objectionable sense of an intervening variable.

Skinner (1969) has by no means neglected events of this type. It is his willingness to include them that warrants the "radical" of Radical Behaviorism. His analysis appears in his book *Contingencies of Reinforcement,* among other places. It is restricted to operant and respondent perceptual activities for the most part, to "seeing in the absence of the thing seen", "hearing in the absence of the thing heard", and other events of a similar sort. Unfortunately, these analyses have never been fully integrated with his formulations of verbal behavior nor of rule governance, and it is responding to events in their absence that is the essence of what is meant by the concepts of substitution and reference.

Referential Behavior

Three characteristics of referential behavior may be identified, two of which are not shared by other types of activity. We may deal with each of these in turn, beginning with shared characteristics.

Conventionality of response form. Referential behaviors are conventional forms of responding, acquired under the auspices of group circumstances (Kantor, 1982). They are responses coordinated with stimulus functions of things which groups of particular persons have **bestowed upon** such things during the evolution of social control over group members. More specifically, verbal response forms are not conditioned by the natural properties of stimulus objects. The form of the response "book" is not determined in a mechanical way by the physical properties of the object book. Verbal response topographies are, in this sense, arbitrary, while at the same time, conventional from the standpoint of a particular group. Likewise the listener, being a member of the same group, responds in conventional ways to the stimulus products of referential speech.

Nonverbal responding bears a different relation to stimulus objects. The natural properties of stimulus objects, including their size, shape, weight, etc., do determine what forms of nonverbal behaviors will be effective in handling such objects, and the forms of action are thereby conditioned by these properties. The topographical features of nonverbal responding of these varieties are, therefore, not arbitrary.

Conventionality of response form is not a property of verbal action exclusively. Much of our behavior is conventional. However, verbal behavior does differ from other kinds of behavior in this regard in that **every** instance of verbal behavior shows this property, while particular instances of other response classes may exemplify nonconventional responding. This feature of verbal action affords possibilities for great variation in form, an issue to which I will return (see Parrott, 1986a for further discussion.)

Bistimulational interaction. Secondly, while in other classes of interbehavior a function may be regarded as the relation between a single stimulus and a single response, referential functions may be interpreted as involving two stimulus functions operating simultaneously. Referential responding is thereby described as bistimulational (Kantor, 1936, 1977). The two stimulus functions operating in a referential episode typically have their sources in two different objects, one being another person, the other being the thing or event spoken of, in other words, the referent. Speakers may, of course, speak of themselves to themselves, in which case the two stimulus functions as well as the response function involved all have their sources in the same object, namely, the speaker.

A listener's response to referential speech is also bistimulational, with one stimulus function having its source in the speaker, the other in the thing spoken of. From Kantor's (1936; 1977) perspective, it is only referential conduct that has the property of bistimulation. All other interbehaviors, including symbolic activities, are unistimulational in character. The significance of this feature of referential conduct will become apparent when we consider what it is that listeners are **doing** in their confrontation with verbal stimulation, and how these activities eventuate in confrontations with the nonverbal environment, as is required for the mediation of reinforcement.

Indirectness of action. Thirdly, referential behavior may be regarded as a type of indirect interaction with the environment. I will explain what I mean by indirect action after first describing direct action.

When responding operates directly upon the stimulus coordinated with it, such as to produce some change in the source object -- its location in space, for example -- we may call the action **direct**. I am interacting directly with the coffee cup when I pick it up.

Much of our nonverbal behavior is direct in this sense, although not all of it. Feeling reactions, for example, effect changes not in the stimulus objects with which they are coordinated, but rather in the responding organism. Further, many nonverbal responses do not operate directly upon stimulus objects such as to effect changes or modifications in them because the objects originally coordinated with those actions are not immediately present (Kantor, 1924.) A direct interaction is necessarily one in which action with respect to a source of stimulation occurs in the absence of substitution by another object, person, or event.

Actions occurring with respect to absent stimulus objects, through the operation of substitute stimulus functions inhering other objects, are, therefore, interactions of the **indirect** variety. We are speaking now of nonverbal implicit behaviors, of such things as seeing in the absence of the thing seen, hearing in the absence of the thing heard, clenching one's jaw upon hearing the name of one's rival, and so on. Likewise, verbal interactions may be indirect in this sense, as when one speaks of things in their absence.

Unlike other kinds of action though, verbal interactions have an indirect character even when they are occurring with respect to immediately present stimulus objects. This is the case because verbal action is always ineffectual with respect to one of the sources of stimulation participating in its occurrence, namely, the thing spoken of. The speaker's request of a listener for coffee may be effectual with respect to the listener, but it is never effectual with respect to the coffee and it is this indirectness of contact with the referent that gives verbal behavior its distinctive character. (See Parrott, 1986a for further discussion.)

Stimulus Products of Referential Behavior

Two characteristics of referential behavior just mentioned, conventionality of response form and indirectness of contact with the referent, combine to give verbal stimuli a unique character. And when this characteristic of verbal stimuli is understood in the context of the third characteristic of referential behavior, namely bistimulation, the concept of reference may be fully articulated. Let us begin with the character of verbal stimuli.

Verbal stimuli acquire the functions of other stimuli more readily than do nonverbal stimuli, and as a result they serve to extend both the speaker's and listener's contact with the environment beyond its object-bound stimulational capacity at a given moment (see Parrott, 1984, for further discussion). A verbal repertoire is a substitutive repertoire, and it is by means of verbal substitution that we are able to act in a **highly specific** way to events in their absence. There are two reasons for the relatively greater serviceability of verbal over nonverbal stimuli as substitutive events.

Conjunctive occurrence. The first has to do with the indirect character of verbal action. Because verbal responding is ineffectual with respect to the referent, its execution does not interfere with the execution of nonverbal behavior with respect to that referent as much as would other nonverbal behavior. We can, for example, **say** "shoes" while tying our shoes more readily than we can **polish** our shoes while tying them. As a result, verbal action occurs in conjunction with other response events more often than does nonverbal action coordinated with the same stimulus.

Further, because perceptual activities are inevitable components of **all** nonverbal behaviors, verbal responses occur in conjunction with perceptual activities more often than with any other type of nonverbal activity. In other words, saying shoe is likely to have occurred more often in conjunction with seeing a shoe than with tying a shoe, or polishing a shoe, or any other nonverbal behavior with respect to shoes. This is the case because seeing a shoe is involved in each of these activities and occurs as well in the absence of any of them.

Frequent conjunctive occurrence of verbal and perceptual responding has important implications. Namely, whenever different types of responding occur in conjunction or close temporal proximity with sufficient frequency, the subsequent occurrence of one type of activity may give rise to reactions of the other type. For example, upon saying shoe or hearing it said, one may have a tendency to see a shoe even if there is no shoe to be seen in the immediate situation. Further, upon seeing a shoe, one may have a tendency to say shoe despite the absence of an appropriate social context for this response. While this process is not peculiar to conjunctions of verbal and perceptual action, it is more prevalent in the verbal field because of the ineffectual character of verbal action and its resulting lack of interference with the occurrence of other behavior.

Variability of response form. The second reason for the greater serviceability of verbal over nonverbal stimuli as substitutes may be traced to the conventionality of verbal response forms. The conventional character of verbal responding allows for actions with respect to things and events in their absence to be especially precise and differentiated. Verbal responding, not being conditioned by the natural properties of stimuli, is possible of wide variation in form and this variation allows for a greater degree of specificity of correspondence with aspects of the nonverbal world. As a result, upon saying coffee, we may see or smell or taste coffee in its absence with unusual clarity. On the contrary, were we to attempt to produce coffee-seeing activity on the part of another person by way of fanciful drinking responses, seeing coffee may be no more likely than seeing tea, or some other beverage.

In summary, we are able to engage in actions with respect to things and events in their absence, among them perceptual actions, and to do so in a highly specific way by means of verbal stimulation. Stimulation of other sorts employed for this purpose cannot produce such highly differentiated action and is less effective as substitute stimulation for this reason.

The referential function of language. Combining these features of verbal stimulation with the fact that verbal interactions are bistimulational, the concept of reference may be understood as follows: When a speaker produces verbal stimulation for a listener, the listener's response is not mere audient activity. Audient activity occurs with respect to the natural properties of verbal stimulation, of course. But verbal stimuli have substitutional functions as well, and these functions bring to bear the listener's reactional history with respect to the things spoken of. In other words, verbal stimulation allows the listener to react in a characteristic way to the **referent.**

If the referent is present in the immediate situation, the effect of verbal stimulation is to orient the listener toward that thing in a direct manner. Verbal stimulation, in such cases, circumscribes the scanning activities of listeners through which they eventually make contact with the things spoken of. If, on the other hand, the things spoken of are not immediately present, the listener may react to those things indirectly by means of historically associated perceptual and other types of action. It is this **orientation of the listener with respect to the things spoken of** that is meant by the concept of reference, and it is only by way of verbal stimulation that it can come about with any degree of efficiency. In short, referential speaking is the act of bringing the listener into contact with stimulus objects **other than** the stimulus products of the speaking act itself.

In summary, nonverbal interbehaviors involve coordinations of single stimulus and single response functions. Such responses typically have an effectual character, producing some change in the source of stimulation coordinated with them. They may also occur in the absence of the stimuli originally coordinated with them through the operation of historically associated stimuli. Nonverbal behaviors do not have referential function, though, which is to say, they do not have the effect of orienting another person to stimuli other than the stimulus products of the nonverbal act itself.

Verbal interbehaviors, on the other hand, are bistimulational functions. Such behavior is always ineffectual with respect to one of the stimuli coordinated with it, specifically, the thing spoken of. Hence, in order for verbal responding to effect change in the referent, and thereby have utility for the speaker, it must operate to bring the listener into effectual contact with the referent. It is the production of listener responses with respect to the things spoken of, by way of the substitutional functions of verbal stimulation, that I am calling the referential function of language.

A note on referents. Before closing, I would like to make one additional point about referents themselves. I have been speaking of nonverbal referents and, moreover, thing-like nonverbal referents. Not all referents have this character. The "thing spoken of" may not be an object having substantive structure. An event, process, situation, person, or relation among things or events may constitute the referent for a particular verbal response. The referent of verbal behavior in the form of a rule, for example, is a probable temporal relation among events in context.

Further, not all referents are usefully described as features of the nonverbal world, however substantive. Rather, the referent of a given verbal response may be other verbal stimuli, each of which may or may not have a referent in the nonverbal world. The relation to the nonverbal world is simply more removed in such cases. An abstract tact is an example. I would argue nonetheless that a relation to the nonverbal world, while perhaps very distantly removed, is a part of the history of referential responding at least from the standpoint of a given verbal community, if not the individual speaker. The ineffectual character of verbal responding makes this necessary to postulate.

Why Concern Ourselves with Inapparent Events?

Now as for the issue of what good it does to talk about events that present problems of observation -- the "so what" argument -- I will attempt two brief responses.

First, few would assert that our momentary actions consist of simple muscle movements to be understood wholly in the context of momentary circumstances. We are complex organisms living in complex environments accumulating complex histories, considerable portions of which have always and always will present problems of direct observation. The difficulty posed by subtle forms of action is not reason to ignore such action altogether, though. Quite the contrary, the identification and analysis of subtle events is our biggest challenge.

Moreover, if we conceptualize our subject matter as consisting of **relations** obtaining between responding and stimulating, the difficulties posed by inapparent stimuli and responses may be overcome, at least in part. Specifically, the topographical characteristics of response events and the physical features of stimulus objects are of less immediate concern than are their actions with respect to one another, that is, their functional properties. And the functional properties of any event, however apparent or inapparent its sources, are understood in terms of their origins and histories of development. To understand even the "simplest", most apparent form of interaction, we must understand its history. Inapparent, implicit actions may be understood in the same way. The study of their development is simply the only study possible in such cases.

To study inapparent implicit action, we begin by observing an organism's apparent action with respect to immediately present stimulus objects, embedded in a setting consisting of many other factors. The next step is to observe apparent action under changing circumstances of stimulation and setting conditions, through which the development of the substitutional functions of particular stimulus objects may become known. The final step is, admittedly, inferential, although not freely so. It consists of inferring the occurrence of inapparent action on the basis of related and very possibly similar sorts of apparent action, occurring with respect to the known substitutional functions of immediately present stimulus objects.

This sort of inferential practice is, as such, relatively well controlled. Moreover, the inference itself is subject to validation, at least to some degree. Validation may be achieved by arranging circumstances wherein the subsequent occurrence of particular forms of apparent action depends in some way on particular forms of inapparent action having previously occurred, such that the occurrence of a given apparent act indicates the previous occurrence of a given inapparent act.

In short, the action of an organism must be understood as a point in the evolution of its history of contact with its environment: We **are** our histories. And since no one would deny that subtle events such as thinking, imagining, and remembering are a part of that history, we must see it as our task to understand the nature and operation of these events as well, and to do so by whatever means are available to us. We must attempt to provide a more complete account of behavior than we have become accustomed to providing, and these discussions of association, substitution, implicit behavior, and reference have been such an attempt.

Secondly, the "so what" argument is an argument arising out of practical considerations. Not all of the business of science has an immediate practical aim, nor are all of the products of science put to immediate use. Sometimes the practical utility of a finding, a technique, or an analysis is not immediately obvious. This does not mean that those findings, techniques and analyses are without value. To suggest as much would be to argue that the value of scientific achievement is defined solely in terms of the imagination of the practitioner. This attitude ignores, as well, the fact that science is a cumulative enterprise, and that understanding is accomplished as bits and pieces of scientific knowledge, collected at different points in time, are put together.

Furthermore, **theoretical** science, of which this paper may be considered an instance, always has a not-immediately-practical character because verbal behavior, which is its principle means and mode of operation, carries us beyond the present moment of utility. This is what verbal behavior is all about.

References

Kantor, J. R. (1924). *Principles of psychology,* Vol 1. Chicago: The Principia Press.

Kantor, J. R. (1936). *An objective psychology of grammar.* Chicago: The Principia Press.

Kantor, J. R. (1977). *Psychological linguistics.* Chicago: The Principia Press.

Kantor, J. R. (1982). *Cultural psychology.* Chicago: The Principia Press.

Parrott, L. J. (1983a). Perspectives on knowing and knowledge. *The Psychological Record, 33,* 171-184.

Parrott, L. J. (1983b). Systemic foundations for the concept of private events: A critique. In N. W. Smith, P. T. Mountjoy & D. H. Ruben (Eds.). *Reassessment in psychology: The interbehavioral alternative.* Washington, D.C.: University Press of America

Parrott, L. J. (1984). Listening and understanding. *The Behavior Analyst, 7,* 29-39.

Parrott, L. J. (1986a). On the difference between social and verbal behaviors. In P. N. Chase & L. J. Parrott (Eds.). *Psychological aspects of language: The West Virginia lectures.* Springhill, IL: Charles C. Thomas.

Parrott, L. J. (1986b). On the role of postulation in the analysis of inapparent events. In H. W. Reese & L.J. Parrott (Eds.), *Behavior science: Philosophical, methodological and empirical advances.* Hillsdale, New Jersey: Erlbaum.

Parrott, L. J. (1987). Rule governed behavior: An implicit analysis of reference. In S. Modgil & C. Modgil (Eds.), *B.F. Skinner: Consensus and controversy.* Barcomb, UK: Falmer Press.

Skinner, B. F. (1957). *Verbal behavior.* New York: Appleton-Century-Crofts.

Skinner, B. F. (1969). *Contingencies of reinforcement: A theoretical analysis.* New York: Appleton-Century-Crofts.

Skinner, B. F. (1974). *About behaviorism.* New York: Knopf.

A Discussion of Chapter 1

Pointing the Finger at Reference

Jack Marr
Georgia Institute of Technology

It is always a pleasure to comment on Linda Hayes's work. It bristles with challenging and novel ideas as it energetically wrestles with the most difficult problems of behavior analysis. Her work also brings into the light the formidable contributions of J. R. Kantor that otherwise might remain in a *Nebelheim* of obscurity.

The place of reference in meaning and understanding has a long and distinguished history-- from Plato's essences to Augustine's ostention and association to Frege's *Sinn* and *Bedeutung*, to Russell's logical atoms and to Wittgenstein's propositions and pictures in the *Tractatus*. All of these approaches embody some notion of **reference** and Hayes's paper pays homage to this concept (and its history) by asserting the value, nay, the necessity, of reference in the understanding of verbal behavior from a behaviorist perspective. To carry this program through it is presumably necessary to unlock and cast aside the shackles of mentalism that are said to bind concepts like "reference", "idea", "understanding", etc. to their long philosophical traditions. At the same time, it is necessary to show that the radical behaviorist's (e.g., Skinner) generally negative positions on these notions are inadequate to the task of accounting for anything useful in verbal behavior and are inconsistent and incoherent. It is the thesis of this brief discussion that Hayes's reinterpretation of "reference" is actually a case of putting old wine into old bottles and further, that criticisms of inadequacy, inconsistency and incoherence can be leveled as well against this reinterpretation.

Hayes begins with a discussion of Skinner's criticisms of the concept of reference. To review, basically there are four: (l) There are words for which one can not point to a particular object or property of an object as a "referent" or "correspondent." Indeed, outside what are commonly termed concrete objects and some ostensible properties such as "red", few words could function as "names" or "labels." (2) As a corollary to this, Skinner emphasizes that even for concrete objects, there is always an element of abstraction such that no particular object possesses all aspects that could embody a correspondence between a word and its referent. (3) Ambiguity about the referents of words leads to a doctrine of ideas, namely that behind words and their combinations into sentences lie "ideas"--presumably the referents for the words and sentences. Since, at least traditionally, "idea" smacks of mentalism, this approach is rejected. (4) To the extent to which the word "stands for" or corresponds with or substitutes for the object, responses to the word and to the referent should be similar. Yet, with perhaps some exceptions (to be elaborated on below), this is clearly not the case (e.g., we neither pet "cat" nor drink from "cup").

Delaying for a moment a discussion of how Hayes comes to define reference, I wish to comment on her rejoinders to the above criticisms. The first three actually are closely related-- lack of corresponding "object", necessary abstraction, and "idea." Hayes asserts that reference need not involve an object or property of an object, but "an event, relation, other verbal utterance." This would seem not only to dilute to vanishing the concept of reference, but to lead to incoherence. Events may be distinguished from objects by the character of temporal relief in the former and the relative temporal independence of the latter. Events seem to lie outside of ostention--that is, one would have difficulty pointing to "Christmas", but not to "Christmas tree." As such, this use of reference is certainly unconventional. Relations and verbal utterances offer even more difficulties. Relations are generally object-independent abstractions (e.g., "larger than"). As such there can only be instances and never a referent. To extend the notion of referent to verbal utterances and to other examples of verbal behavior leaves us either chasing our tails or falling into a black hole of infinite regress--if the referent of a verbal utterance is a verbal utterance and the referent of that verbal utterance is another verbal utterance, and so on. The traditional Augustinian notion of naming by ostention was a last refuge from supplying a meaning to a word merely by giving other words. But, as we have seen, ostention is often not possible. Here is another example: "There are infinitely many prime numbers." Now, point to the referents! Perhaps one might inject the notion of "idea" here. Presumably, standing behind the words of the above theorem are ideas of "number", "primeness", "infinity", etc. I cannot apply Hayes's operational definition of idea here except to agree that to respond appropriately would depend upon a special history with respect to the verbal behavior we call mathematics. However, to say that one possesses a repertoire of mathematical ideas solves no problems, since the "ideas" are themselves verbal. Language is sometimes naively defined as the means by which we express ideas. But, in what form are the ideas before they are being so expressed? Try grasping the "idea" of **this** sentence **nonverbally** and then putting it into words! What then is the "referent" for **this** sentence? One might want to say that the application of the notion of reference to verbal behavior is justified since verbal behavior begins with the nonverbal world--the things we learn to talk about. Ultimately, then, we could reach back through whatever verbiage to ostensible objects or properties of objects as the referents. Even allowing for that possibility, the chain may be so long and the links so weak, that no effective control could ever be demonstrated. For example, by the age of five or six most children engage in counting independently of the objects counted. This seemingly "natural" verbal behavior is, in fact, extraordinarily abstract and was not "discovered" until relatively recently in human history. There are yet places in the world where it is unknown. To say somehow that humankind **discovered** a state of affairs in Nature--"five"--and then gave it a name (in whatever language) seems nonsensical. The evolution of counting depended upon an already established verbal repertoire--a "mastery of a technique" to use Wittgenstein's phrase. Wittgenstein, at the beginning of *The Philosophical Investigations,* provides an extensive criticism of the concept of reference as fundamentally exemplified by Augustine's notion of meaning established through ostention. Any notion of reference can be reduced to ostention, but as Wittgenstein points out, ostention is already **part** of the language game and, as such, cannot be used to **explain** meaning. What is more, naming is but one of many, many functions of language. This was recognized by Skinner in that he carefully distinguished different classes of verbal operants by the contingencies controlling their emission. He, as well, considered problems of combination and context to yield the verbal episode and its "meaning."

There is an additional criticism of reference not mentioned by Hayes or Skinner, but which I will add to the pile. Words and phrases that are said to have the same "referent" are not always mutually substitutable in a sentence. For example: "Last night I saw the Morning Star." Or consider the following: "I want to be Linda Hayes."; "I want to be the most famous Kantorian from Canada."; "I want to be the wife of Steve Hayes." These are clearly not equivalent, yet they have the same "referent."

In emphasizing reference--even if it could be put into good order--Hayes is functionally restricting the richness of verbal behavior--reducing it to a "Me Tarzan, you Jane" level of interaction. This is further exemplified by her response to Skinner's fourth criticism of reference, that of correspondent reaction to a word and its referent. What sort of "reactions" comprise the correspondence? If we do not pet "cat", what then do we do when "cat" is uttered? In the absence of any details of context and history, **nothing** useful can be said about this. Hayes seems to want to focus on perceptual activities, those that might be acquired through some Pavlovian paradigm. Certainly the doctrine of association by contiguity has a heavy loading in her analysis. This Pavlovian perspective incorporates a theory of stimulus substitution. (Pavlov himself espoused this idea and further the notion of language as a "second-signal system.") In any case, the above criticisms of reference still stand regardless of mechanism--whether one speaks of ideation, mediation, indirectness, association, etc.

The concept of reference as meaning has not been advocated since at least late Wittgensteinby many of those calling themselves linguists or, more recently, psycho-linguists. So Hayes's point about traditional theorists not being totally inept in clinging to some concept of reference could apply only to a bygone era. That reference was so compelling a notion to have been espoused for ages by very clever people is, considering a similar status of some other unfortunate and even dangerous ideas, more a mark of suspicion than validity. In sum, it is difficult to see Hayes's effort as a reformulation or reinterpretation of reference; it is more like a resurrection.

Putting all the above issues aside, what can reference do for us? What problems does it solve? If I understand Hayes's argument, a primary problem solved by "correspondent reaction" involving a substitutive repertoire is the ability to talk about things in their absence. A related problem, sometimes said to lie at the foundations of the split between cognitive psychology and behaviorism, is that the "same" stimulus can control different behaviors. What Hayes seems to argue is that verbal behaviors reach back via indirect links from present stimulation to perhaps even remote "referents", objects, events or other verbal behaviors. What is involved here is no less than the whole problem of memory, but especially recall memory, i.e., remembering in the absence of explicit "cues". Following in the associationist tradition (which, in fact, cognitive psychology shares with methodological behaviorism), some form of causal link **must** be hypothesized to bridge action at a temporal distance; otherwise how could past events control present behavior? Radical behaviorism places enormous burdens on "history" for its analysis of behavior. Part of the reason for this is that the effects of different histories generated in the laboratory, clinic, and classroom, are seen in subsequent behaviors. History is, of course, the source of the construct of "repertoire". **How** history can exert its effects in a given context is a question behaviorists tend to leave to physiologists. Typically not concerned with action at a temporal distance, behaviorists have been satisfied with what Russell calls "mnemic causality". That is to say, given a particular history, a context, various initial and boundary conditions, and an appropriate set of functional relations, then present behavior is predictable, at least in a stochastic sense. Skinner expresses this by asserting that the individual comprises a locus of interacting variables. The mechanisms underlying functional relations are not part of the theory, much like classical thermodynamics. Hayes is providing a mechanism which involves speculating not in physiology, but in stimulus links. What is puzzling to me, however, is her statement that "Implicit events...play **no causal role** in the occurrence of subsequent events" (emphasis mine). If they play no causal role, then what are we talking about? Why involve them? I believe I'm missing something vital here.

Hayes's example of kissing a lover's photograph might be understood on the basis of stimulus generalization. Here one might invoke causal (i.e., functional) relations between common stimulus properties and certain classes of responses. But one might kiss an article of clothing belonging to the lover, an object sharing no obvious common properties with the lover.

Nevertheless, in Hayes's terms, these objects would certainly be linked by association. Perhaps this is closer to the kind of implicit or indirect relation she is invoking, but the **causal** role of this class of events is clear.

There is a major difference in approach between Hayes and Skinner that accounts for their contrasting views on the notion of reference. Unlike Hayes, Skinner makes a primary distinction between discriminative and eliciting functions of stimuli. This distinction, I believe, provides a far richer field for growth and maintenance of verbal behavior than variations on Pavlov's theme of the "second-signal system". Discriminative stimuli do not have to bear the burden of being surrogates for anything. However, it can be reasonably argued, as Hayes does, how far one might want or need to extend the burden of discriminative stimuli into other areas, e.g., rules as S^D's.

I'm not sure Hayes does justice to Skinner's distinction between contingency-controlled and rule-governed behavior. Aside from questions of what consequences maintain what behaviors, under what contingencies, Hayes believes the referent for a rule is the contingency it describes. Whether or not Skinner believes this is not so relevant as the fact that this rule-as-referent notion would then be subject to all the criticisms of reference outlined by Skinner and others. "Rule" is obviously a family resemblance term, but one member of that family is embodied in what Skinner calls a tact. One kind of rule tacts (or, more commonly, describes) a contingency. To the extent to which this holds, then the notion of reference, for reasons already pointed out, raises more problems than it solves. I don't wish to go into further detail here on the lively topic of rules. As readers of this volume will have discovered, "rule-governed behavior" is a very slippery notion.

Hayes discusses in some detail what she calls "characteristics of referential behavior", namely, conventionality of response form, bistimulational interaction, and indirectness of action. These kinds of special characteristics have been invoked for verbal behavior or language by a number of theorists, including Skinner. However, to assign them to "referential behavior" is begging the question since at least one of these theorists apparently did not require a notion of reference.

I think the issue of conventionality needs more careful treatment. Hayes asserts that ". . . verbal response forms are not conditioned by the natural properties of stimulus objects." First, just what are the natural properties of stimulus objects? If this question is asked, say, about an apple, one is tempted to respond "round", "red", and so on. But one forgets that these **properties** are **bestowed** on the apple. "What color is this apple?" It is our language that has taught us to ask this kind of question. Moreover, in the evolution of language, conventionality is a result, not a cause. It is extremely unlikely that "apple" was **bestowed** on apple. If Hayes is searching for the distal links to referents, they stretch back--as our German hosts might say-- *im grauen Vorzeit.*

Chapter 2

A Relational Control Theory of Stimulus Equivalence

Steven C. Hayes
University of Nevada, Reno

When humans are taught a series of related conditional discriminations, the stimuli that enter into these discriminations can often become connected to each other in new ways, not explicitly taught in training. The phenomena involved are typically investigated in a matching to sample format. One particularly interesting way in which the stimuli involved can become connected is revealed by the following illustration. Suppose a person is taught, given the presence of a particular unfamiliar visual form (the sample), to choose another particular unfamiliar visual form from an array of three or four such forms (the comparisons). We could say that the person learns "given A1 pick B1" where "A1" and "B1" represent different visual forms. The person is then taught to select another unfamiliar visual form from another array of forms, given the same sample, or "given A1 pick C1." To control for a history of reinforcement for selecting particular stimuli, the incorrect comparison forms will be correct in the presence of other samples. With this kind of training, it is likely that, given the opportunity, the person will, without additional training, select A1 from an array of comparisons, given B1 or given C1 as samples. The person is also likely to select B1 given C1 as a sample and C1 given B1 as a sample (e.g., Sidman, 1971; Sidman, Cresson, & Willson-Morris, 1974). This set of phenomena is called "stimulus equivalence."

An equivalence class is said to exist if the stimuli in the class show the three defining relations of reflexivity, symmetry, and transitivity (Sidman & Tailby, 1982). This definition has some notable difficulties, but we will adopt it as a point of departure. In matching-to-sample procedures, reflexivity is identity matching. For example, given A1 the person picks A1 from an array. Symmetry refers to the functional reversibility of the conditional discrimination: the trained discrimination "given A1 pick B1" leads to the derived discrimination "given B1 pick A1." This reversibility must be demonstrated in the absence of direct reinforcement to be considered symmetry (Sidman, Rauzin, Lazar, Cunningham, Tailby & Carrigan, 1982). To demonstrate transitivity, at least three stimuli are required. If after the discriminations "given A1 pick B1" and "given B1 pick C1" have been taught, "given A1 pick C1" emerges without additional training, transitivity has been demonstrated.

The reason stimulus equivalence has captured the imagination of behavioral researchers is two-fold. A major source of interest is the apparent correspondence between the stimulus equivalence phenomenon and language phenomena. If a child of sufficient verbal abilities is taught to point to a particular object given a particular written word, the child may point to the word given the object without specific training to do so. In naming tasks, symmetry and transitivity between written words, spoken words, pictures, and objects is commonplace. Several studies on stimulus equivalence have used naming-like preparations using auditory and visual stimuli (e.g., Dixon & Spradlin, 1976; Sidman, 1971; Sidman & Tailby, 1982; Sidman, Kirk, & Willson-Morris, 1985; Spradlin & Dixon, 1976). Behaviorists are excited at the possibility that the equivalence phenomenon may provide a new avenue for the empirical investigation of language.

The second reason for interest is that the phenomenon is unexpected. It would not be readily predicted from a three term contingency formulation. If an organism learns to pick B1 given A1, we can think of this as a conditional discrimination. The probability of reinforcement for selecting B1 is greater in the presence of A1 than in the presence of, say, A2. We would say that A1 is functioning as a conditional discriminative stimulus in the presence of which B1 is functioning as a discriminative stimulus for a selection response.

This does not mean, however, that the probability of reinforcement for selecting A1 is greater in the presence of B1 than in its absence. Consider a natural example. A primate may learn to hide in a thicket given the presence of a lion. We could think of this as a conditional discrimination: given lion select a thicket over open savanna. The lion is a conditional discriminative stimulus, in the presence of which the thicket is a discriminative stimulus for an approach response such as running toward it. Such a contingency arrangement provides no grounds to suppose that reversing the functions of the stimuli involved will be reinforced. The value of approaching a thicket given a lion does not imply the value of approaching a lion given a thicket. "Given thicket approach lion" makes little sense.

In the natural environment, the contingencies supporting conditional discriminations rarely seem to be symmetrically arranged in this sense. The functions of a conditional stimulus and discriminative stimulus, established in a given context, will not simply reverse. Most commonly, if the functions **were** reversed the consequences seemingly would either be extinction or, as in the example of the lion, notable punishment.

Despite this fact, humans readily display stimulus equivalence: the functions do in fact reverse. Even children as young as two years old will display such performances without explicit experimental training (Devany, Hayes, & Nelson, 1986). The interchangability of functions characteristic of stimulus equivalence are not readily shown in most contexts or with most organisms, however. To date, not a single demonstration of stimulus equivalence in non-humans has been shown (D'Amato, Salmon, Loukas, & Tomie, 1985; Kendall, 1983; Sidman et al., 1982).[1] A theoretical explanation for stimulus equivalence that makes sense of these various finds seems needed.

While the early work in the area attempted mediational explanations for the phenomenon (e.g., Spradlin, Cotter, & Baxley, 1973) researchers have gradually turned away from these interpretations (e.g., Sidman & Tailby, 1982). Mediated learning has a long tradition (Peters, 1935; Jenkins, 1963), but no well defined mediational model seems to be capable of encompassing the existing equivalence data (Steele, 1987).

Sidman (1986) has attempted to explain stimulus equivalence by appealing to the concept of a four and five term contingency. As noted, in arbitrary matching to sample, the sample can be thought of as a conditional stimulus; the correct comparison as a discriminative stimulus. We can think of the conditional discriminative stimulus as the "fourth term" of a contingency and the discriminative stimulus as the third. If the selection of a particular comparison given a particular sample is reinforced only in a particular context, and not others, then this contextual stimulus may be thought of as a conditional/conditional stimulus, or the fifth term of a contingency. An unlimited number of terms can be generated in this fashion.

Sidman views stimulus equivalence as a basic behavioral phenomenon that emerges in humans given a four-term contingency. Conditional stimulus equivalence emerges given a five-term contingency. In his view, discriminative and conditional discriminative stimuli can enter into the same stimulus class for humans. The third and fourth terms of the contingency become functionally reversible because subjects are choosing comparisons that are members of the same class as the sample.

Sidman's model is quite useful in describing the kinds of conditionalities involved in stimulus equivalence. As an explanatory model, however, it has certain difficulties. First, it does not explain why the phenomenon is seen only in humans, or why it is seen only in particular kinds of humans. Equivalence has been shown to be language related. Humans without any spontaneous productive use of signs or symbols do not demonstrate equivalence relations, even when the underlying conditional discriminations are thoroughly learned (Devany et al, 1986). Because these conditional discriminations are instances of what Sidman would call a four-term contingency, something other than a four-term contingency seems to be required for the development of equivalence, as Sidman himself points out (1986, p. 233).

Second, Sidman's model suggests that the third and fourth terms of a contingency enter into the same class. It is important to Sidman's logic, however, that fifth and greater terms **not** enter into equivalence classes. Consider the following discriminations:

Context		Sample		Comparison
5th term		**4th term**		**3rd term**
Given X	&	Given A1	pick	B1
Given X	&	Given A2	pick	B2
Given Y	&	Given A1	pick	B2
Given Y	&	Given A2	pick	B1

If the discriminations represented above are trained, the subject may show derived symmetry and pick A1, given B1, in context X, but A2, given B1, in context Y, and so on. Conditional equivalence classes of this kind have been demonstrated in humans (Wulfert & Hayes, 1988). Sidman's explanation is that in that A1 and B1 have entered into the same class in context X. As Sidman points out, if X also entered into the class, the distinct equivalence classes would necessarily break down. This is because X would now be in a class with A1 and B1, but the next trained discrimination ("given X and A2 pick B2") would mean that X would be in a class with A2 and B2. By virtue of transitivity, all stimuli would be in one equivalence class. As an empirical matter (Wulfert & Hayes, 1988) this is not what in fact happens. An explanation seems to be needed as to why fifth and greater terms do not enter into equivalence relations.

Third, if we argue that symmetrical responding occurs because the sample and comparison are in the same class, we are left with a need to explain why equivalence classes operate unlike other stimulus classes. Pigeons, for example, have yet to show generalized identity matching. When a stimulus acquires a function (e.g., becomes a discriminative stimulus), identical stimuli are presumably now in the same functional stimulus class. Yet the failure to show identity matching means that the functions of the sample and comparison are not interchangable between these stimuli even though a functional stimulus class obviously exists. Apparently a functional stimulus class does not operate like an equivalence class (though there is evidence that it can in humans, Shipley, 1935). A stimulus classes explanation of equivalence thus begs the question -- why do these stimulus classes operate in the fashion that they do?

Finally, and most importantly for our present purposes, for equivalence classes to have advantages for organisms, equivalence formation itself must be under conditional control. Many normal actions can be interpreted as conditional discriminations. Without contextual control over "equivalencing" itself, all stimuli would gradually enter into larger and larger equivalence classes, as they entered into more and more conditonal discriminations. Eventually this would have severe consequences for an organism that formed equivalence classes whenever a four-term contingency was encountered. Why do some conditional discriminations in verbally competent humans lead to stimulus equivalence, and some do not?

The purpose of the present chapter is to attempt to explain the phenomena shown in stimulus equivalence in another way. Much as in the historical case of generalized imitation (Gewirtz & Stengle, 1968), a solution will be proposed in terms of a higher order type of responding. Stimulus equivalence will be interpreted as a special case of arbitrarily applicable relational responding. The explanation of this kind of responding will be given in terms of the history that can give rise to it.

Relations

What is a relation? More to the point for our purposes, what is an arbitrarily applicable relation? The terms do not lend themselves to direct or simple definition. The dictionary defines relations in terms of connections, comparisons, associations, and so forth, but as these terms are themselves defined, we find ourselves quickly turning in circles. Perhaps the best course is to put off a frontal attack on the terms and to nibble around their edges, so to speak.

At least three characteristics can be identified that seem central to the concept of relation as it applies to those that are arbitrarily applicable: mutual entailment, combinatorial mutual entailment, and transfer of control. The first two characteristics are both logically and psychologically relevant aspects. The last characteristic is purely psychological.

Mutual Entailment

We will first consider the logical elements of a relation. In the abstract, a relation between two events involves responding to the one event in terms of the other and vice versa. A relation in this sense is necessarily mutual. If A is related to B, then B is related to A. The specific relations involved need not be literally identical. If A is better than B, then B is worse than A. In its abstract sense, however, better implies worse and vice versa -- they are different aspects of an overall relation. We may term this quality of relation "mutual entailment." We will write it this way:

Mutual Entailment

1.1 $$A \; r_x \; B \; ||| \; B \; r_y \; A$$

where "r" stands for "relation," the subscripts "x" and "y" stand for the specific aspects of the relation relevant to the stimuli involved, "A" and "B" stand for the events in the relation, and "|||" is a symbol for entailment.

The logical requirement of mutual entailment has its psychological counterpart. When applied to relational responding, mutual entailment means that if a person is responding relationally to A and B, then the person is also responding relationally to B and A. If a response to one stimulus is an aspect of such relational responding, a response to the other stimulus must be another aspect. In terms of the diagram above, if a response to B is part of an "r_x" response, then a response to A must be available as part of a "r_y" response. As an example, if a person is responding to an object because of its **relation** to a word, the person must also be able to respond to the word because of its relation to the object.

Combinatorial Entailment

Logically, relations must not only be mutual, they must be combinatorially mutual. That is, relations be sensitive not only to a single instantiation, but to combinations of relations. If A is related in a particular way to B and B is also related to C, then some kind of relation must be entailed between A and C. This entailed relation, as with all relations in the abstract, must itself be mutual. We will term this property "combinatorial entailment" and will represent it in this manner:

Combinatorial Entailment

2.1 $\qquad$ $A \ r_x \ B \ \text{and} \ B \ r_x \ C \ ||| \ A \ r_p \ C \ \text{and} \ C \ r_q \ A$

It may seem at first blush that this is merely a repetition or simple elaboration of the earlier concept of mutual entailment. It is not, because the nature of the entailed relation may be different in combinatorial entailment. In mutual entailment, the entailed aspect of the relation is always specified to the same degree as the specified aspect. Specifying "better" entails "worse" and both are equally specific. In combinatorial entailment, the relations that are entailed may not be specific.

Consider the case in which a given relation is specified between A and B and between B and C. The relations between C and B and between B and A must also be specified. The relation between A and C and between C and A, however, may not be specified, or not to the same degree. For example, if A is different than B and B is different than C, we cannot say what the relation is between A and C and between C and A. This lack of a specified relation, however, is itself specified by the nature of the relation of "difference." It is entailed, not simply left open. We cannot say what the mutual relation is between A and C but we can say that we cannot say.

Examples are much more common when the specified relation between A and B is different than that between B and C. If A is faster than B and B is better than C, what are the entailed mutual relations between A and C? Without additional information, we cannot say. Such examples are even the basis of verbal games we play with young children. We may say such things as "If Harry is bigger than Sam, and Sam is faster than Joe, who is prettier, Harry or Joe?" The humor in such talk is based both on the child's growing ability to respond relationally, and the lack of specified entailed relations in this example of combinatorial mutual entailment.

As this logical characteristic of relations applies to the psychological phenomenon of arbitrarily applicable relational responding, combinatorial entailment means that if we are responding relationally to A and B, and to B and C, we must be able to respond relationally to A and C. If a response to one stimulus is an aspect of such relational responding, a response to the other stimuli must be available as another aspect. In terms of the diagram above, if a response to B is part of an "r_x" response, and a response to C is part of a "r_x" response, then a response to C must be available as part of a "r_p" response, and a response to A must be available as part of a "r_q" response. To take a language example, if we are responding to the words "five cents" based on its relation to "one cent", and we are responding to "ten cents" based in part on its relation to "five cents", then we must be able to respond to "one cent" in terms of its relation to "ten cents" and vice versa.

Transfer of Functions

Relations between stimulus events would be of little importance to psychologists if the functions of these events could not themselves be moderated by these relations. As a psychological matter, we are interested in stimuli not as objects, but as events that have psychological functions. Thus, for the concept of relational responding to be psychologically relevant, it must be shown that such responding is relevant to the modification of various stimulus functions. We will term this modification "transfer of functions" and will write it this way:

Transfer of Functions

3.1   Given 1.1 and 2.1 above, A f ||| B fr and C fr

where "f" refers to a psychologically relevant stimulus function, and "r" refers to the type of relational responding occurring. We can say it this way: given mutual entailment and combinatorial entailment between A, B, and C, a given psychological function of A entails functions of B and C in terms of the underlying relations. For example, suppose A is specified as smaller than B, and B is smaller than C. Suppose that A is given conditioned reinforcement functions and that these functions are relevant to the relation of size between A, B, and C. We might expect that B and C will have ordinally more value as conditioned reinforcers than A, to the degree that a response to B or C is an aspect of a relational response to A, B, and C. As a practical example, consider a child who has learned to work for pennies. Pennies are now conditioned reinforcers. As the child learns to relate events in terms of the abstract relation of amount, the child will work harder when promised a nickel or a dime than a penny without direct experience of getting paid with nickels or dimes.

The transfer of stimulus functions includes not just discriminative or reinforcement functions, but also such things as perceptual functions. As a network of relational events becomes organized, the person may, for example, see one stimulus given another. Consider the following phase and do what it says: "Picture a car." Many readers presumably did in fact see a car. This perceptual event can be thought of as a transfer of the visual functions of cars to the verbal name symmetrically related to it. Such transfer provides a model of mutual entailment and combinatorial entailment, as will be discussed later.

Arbitrarily Applicable Relational Responding

The three characteristics of relational responding -- mutual entailment, combinatorial entailment, and transfer of functions -- are relevant to all forms of psychologically relevant relations. They do not yet form the basis of an explanation of stimulus equivalence, however. For that we must distinguish relational responding that is arbitrarily applicable from relational responding that is based on the non-arbitrary characteristics of the stimuli involved.

The dictionary tells us that the word "arbitrary" means that something is dependent upon the discretion of a judge (originally an "arbiter" -- literally "one who goes to see"). It is a matter of opinion or preference. Thus, "arbitrarily applicable relations" are specified socially (the events the dictionary refers to -- judgement, opinion, or preference -- are all clearly social acts). We might say that the relation applies on the basis of convention.

A non-arbitrary form of relational responding is based on the physical form of the stimuli that are related. If one object is larger than another, and the relation of size that obtains between the two is based on that fact, the relation is not arbitrary. It is not merely a matter of convention. To take an example used earlier, a young child will typically work harder for a nickel than a dime because a nickel is larger. An older child will work harder for the dime, because the dime is larger. The relation of size in the first instance is non-arbitrary; in the second, however, it is arbitrary. There is nothing in the physical form of the dime that requires the convention that a dime is worth two nickels.

As a psychological matter, the distinction between arbitrary and non-arbitrary forms of relational responding is crucial. Most living organisms show relational responding based on non-arbitrary characteristics of the stimuli involved. This was considered to be a crucial finding in the middle part of this century, in part because traditional S-R learning theory seemed to have a difficult time explaining the findings. Responding in terms of relations is clearly shown, for example, in the transposition literature (Reese, 1968). Although the details of the methods involved differ, the typical transposition problem is as follows: subjects are given a history of responding to stimuli that differ from others presented along some physical dimension (e.g., a long and a short line, a large and a small square, a light and a dark chamber, etc.). After a history of this sort, subjects are presented with a choice between a stimulus that has previously been correct and another stimulus that is now the correct one if the subjects are responding in terms of a trained relation. For example, after a history of choosing the longer of two lines, the subjects are given a choice between the previously long line and an even longer line. In a wide variety of organisms, including humans, birds, non-human mammals, and fish, subjects will choose the stimulus that is correct in terms of the trained relation (e.g., the even longer line) over specific stimuli that have a history of reinforcement for their selection (Reese, 1968).

Non-arbitrary relational responding of this kind is based entirely upon the formal characteristics of stimuli. A darker chamber, for example, is actually a darker chamber (discounting the special case of sensory illusions). The relation between, say, a larger and smaller square is every bit as physical and formal as the squares themselves.

Arbitrarily applicable relational responding, since it is not based on the form of the relatae, must be brought to bear on the relatae by events other than the relatae themselves. This kind of relational responding, in short, must be under contextual control. Contextual specification of the relation is necessary because it is not specified by the form of the relatae themselves. It is the very generality of non-arbitrary forms of relational responding that shows its non-arbitrary characteristics. For an organism to respond to the relative size of two objects, the two objects need only be seen. If the relation were arbitrary, this alone would not be enough. The relation itself would have to be specified. Suppose a person is asked whether "a" is taller than "b." In a non-arbitrary sense (the size of the letters) the answer is presumably that "b" is slightly taller. If "a" and "b" are merely symbols, as they might be in algebra, they first have to be defined before the question can be answered.

What is brought to bear in a given instance of arbitrarily applicable relational responding is a history applicable to the given situation. At a minimum, the historical conditions that seem necessary to establish arbitrarily applicable relational responding are the following: a) discriminations that would prevail as the outcome of mutual entailment, combinatorial entailment, and transfer of functions are **directly** trained, b) responding relationally is advantaged, and c) "a" and "b" above occur in particular contexts.

Consider the simplest kind of relation. There is only one type of relation in which all the derived relations are the same as the specified relations. In the language we have used in the formulae above, there is only one relation in which r_x, r_y, r_p, and r_q are always the same: that is the relation of sameness. If it is specified that A is the same as B, and that B is the same as C, then all of the derived relations are also the relation of sameness. B is the same as A, C is the same as B, and so on.

Take the case of a young child learning the name "Daddy." Such a learning experience usually includes such elements as the following. The child is oriented toward Daddy and asked "who's that?" If the child says "Daddy" celebration ensues. If not, the child may again be prompted "Is that your Daddy?" If the child shows any sign of acknowledgement (e.g., a smile when the name is given), the child is fussed over. Even before the child can speak, parents can to some degree assess whether Daddy has control over the word "Daddy". The child may be oriented toward Daddy and asked "Who's that? Is that your Mommy?" If the child makes a face that indicates agreement, the child may be tickled or playfully shaken and told "No, that's right, that's your Daddy!" The child, in other words, is taught to pick the sound "Daddy" (and later to produce it) in the presence of Daddy. We could say that the child has learned "given A1 pick B1."

The relevant learning history includes trained responding that would be produced were mutual entailment present. In this example, symmetrical responding will be trained. The child will be asked "where's Daddy" while Daddy is not immediately in the child's view. Yound children will be carried around the room to face various persons and objects. Given the question, signs of recognition when the child is oriented toward Daddy are followed by parental signs of excitement. Signs of recognition elsewhere are followed by retraining: "No, that's not Daddy, that's the doggie!" Later the child will have to search the room visually without assistance, or for a more mobile child may have to look behind objects, to find Daddy given the question "where's Daddy?" We can say that the child is taught "given B1 pick A1."

But such a history is not going on just with Daddy. It is being established deliberately with doggie, Mommy, Grandma, dolls, and a host of animate and inanimate objects. It is also occurring incidentally in the child extensive exposure to a natural language community.

We can think of the training history this way:

Trained	$A \dashrightarrow B$;	$B \dashrightarrow A$;	Given Af, Bf;	Given Bf, Af
	$C \dashrightarrow D$;	$D \dashrightarrow C$;	Given Cf, Df;	Given Df, Cf
	$E \dashrightarrow F$;	$F \dashrightarrow E$;	Given Ef, Ff;	Given Ff, Ef
	$G \dashrightarrow H$;	$H \dashrightarrow G$;	Given Gf, Hf;	Given Hf, Gf
Derived	$X \dashrightarrow Y$;	**$Y \dashrightarrow X$;**	Given Xf, **Yf;**	Given Yf, **Xf**

In short, with enough examples of specifically trained symmetrical responding, and transfer of functions in terms of that, a more general form of responding may emerge. The three major aspects of the history can be seen in the "Daddy naming" example. First, the types of derived responses that would be present were relational responding occurring are specifically trained. In the example, that included summetrical responding and transfer of functions. It is probably also important that similar non-arbitrary relations are trained. Most obvious forms of arbitrarily applicable relations have parallels in non-arbitrary relations that can be found in the natural environment. Thus the relation of, say, largeness exists in both arbitrarily applicable forms (e.g., "a > b") and non-arbitrary forms (e.g., xxxxxxxx > x). Training in the latter may aid with acquisition of the former. Not all arbitrarily applicable relations have similarities to non-arbitrary relations, however. There are many arbitrary relations with no parallels in the world of common sense. We will return to this point later. Second, the child is immediately advantaged if relational responding does begin to occur. The child may, for example, be able to respond to a name in terms of an object, when only the object-name function has been trained. Finally, all of this occurs in a particular context -- in this case a linguistic context of naming -- in which bringing these aspects of one's history to bear will be reinforced.

This kind of history is arbitrarily applicable because at least under some conditions it does not depend on the form of the events related. Suppose a child is shown a pea and told "this is called a pea." An organism without established verbal abilities may have to learn explicitly that if this object is called a "pea," that a "pea" is also this object. As was discussed earlier, there is nothing in normal processes of stimulus control which would dictate a symmetrical relation between the pea and the word "pea." The child told "this is a pea," however, does not arrive in this situation as a tabula rasa. Various contextual cues (e.g., the word "is", or pointing to an object and speaking) may indicate that this is a situation in which responding in terms of the relation of sameness would be reinforced.

Arbitrarily applicable relational responding must to some degree be under conditional control. If relational responding can be applied arbitrarily, and if it is not under conditional control, nothing would prevent all types of relational responding from occurring with regard to all events. For example, if stimulus equivalence occurred automatically whenever conditional discriminations were encountered, eventually the great variety of conditional discriminations in normal life would yeild stimulus equivalence among virtually all stimuli. Everything would be in one gigantic class. This obviously does not happen, and it is contextual control that prevents it from happening.

This point requires a modification of each of our defining characteristics of relational responding as it applies to the arbitrarily applicable variety. Mutual entailment must be under conditional control of a context relevant to the relation of interest. We can now write the final definition of mutual entailment this way:

Mutual Entailment

2.1 $$C_{rel} \{ A \ r_x \ B \ ||| \ B \ r_y \ A \}$$

where "C_{rel}" symbolizes a context in which a particular history of relational responding is brought to bear on the current situation.

Similarly, both combinatorial entailment and transfer of functions must be redefined in the same way:

Combinatorial Entailment

2.2 $$C_{rel} \{ A \ r_x \ B \ \text{and} \ B \ r_x \ C \ ||| \ A \ r_p \ C \ \text{and} \ C \ r_q \ A \}$$

Transfer of Functions

2.3 $$C_{rel} \{ A_f \ ||| \ Bfr \ \text{and} \ Cfr \}$$

A final modification is also required. A given stimulus (e.g., "A" above) always has many functions. If **all** functions of a stimulus transferred to another, there would no longer be two separate stimuli in a psychological sense, by definition. Distinctions between stimuli require distinct functions in at least some areas. Thus, which functions transfer must be under contextual control. We can write the final version of transfer of functions this way:

Transfer of Functions

3.3 $$\text{(Given 2.1 and 2.2)} \ C_{func} [\ C_{rel} \{ Af_1 \ ||| \ Bf_2 r \ \text{and} \ Cf_3 r \} \ ]$$

where "C_{func}" symbolizes the contextual stimuli that select the particular stimulus functions that transfer in a given situation, while the subscripts refer to the specific functions involved.

The integrity of the concept of arbitrarily applicable relations requires that distinctions between the perspective of observer and that of subject must be rigidly observed. Virtually any two events can be connected verbally, and thus be "related" to each other, from the standpoint of a verbal observer. That does not mean that all sets of events have the quality of mutual entailment from the standpoint of the subject. For example, one event may be different than another. An observer may note that difference. The observer may be responding in terms of a relation of difference. That does not mean that the subject necessarily is responding to each event in terms of the relation of difference with another.

Arbitrarily Applicable Versus Arbitrarily Applied

It is my view that all truly verbal events, whether those of speakers or listeners, involve arbitrarily applicable relational responding. It is not my point, however, that all verbal relations are arbitrary. To the contrary, the use of linguistic relations in the natural environment requires the discrimination of relevant formal properties of relatae. The participation of formal properties in the application of a given instances of relational responding does not alone indicate that the relation is not arbitrarily applicable. Rather, the question is "was the act of relation an act that could be brought to bear on relatae regardless of form." If so, the relation is arbitrarily applicable, even if it is not arbitrarily applied.

For example, a scientist may state that Saturn is larger than the moon. From the earth Saturn appears smaller, and thus the relation of size is clearly not formal in a simple sense. But the form of the satelittes involved participated in the relation that was derived: this is part of what we mean when we say that the observation was a scientific one. The relation may have been in part an arbitrarily applicable relation of relative size, but it was surely not arbitrarily applied. That the relation is arbitrarily applicable could be shown by replacing Saturn and the moon with purely symbolic events. The scientist could be asked, for example, to consider the relative size of two satelittes x and y, given that x is 1,000 time larger. The scientist, or even the schoolboy, would have no trouble deriving mutual relations from this specified relation, despite the lack of formal support in the relatae. Thus, even when the formal properties do align with the relation, as when the scientist says that the moon is larger than an asteroid, we cannot say if the relation is non-arbitrary or arbitrarily applicable without further examination.

Relational Frames and Verbal Construction

It is cumbersome to discuss types of relational behavior using the phase "arbitrarily applicable relational responding." We will use two simpler terms to describe this kind of responding. When speaking of specific kinds of arbitrarily applicable relational responding we will call them *relational frames*. It is, of course, dangerous to turn actions into nouns, but the convenience this allows seems worth the risk. We mean this noun to be used much as nouns referring to behavior (or even the word "behavior" itself) are used: as semantically convenient descriptions of particular interactions between the organism and the environment. A verb form might be "framing relationally." The metaphor of a "frame" is used to emphasize the idea that this type of relational responding is not based on the specific stimuli that are related. A picture frame can be empty. Any picture can be placed in it. In much the same way, arbitrarily applicable relational responding can brought to bear on any set of stimuli whenever appropriate contextual events bring the relevant history of relational responding to bear.

In the case of non-arbitrary relational responding, there is no need for the metaphor of a frame, because the relation is not "empty." That is, the relation involved can only be specified by the stimuli themselves.

We shall define a relational frame as responding that shows the contextually controlled qualities of mutual entailment, combinatorial entailment, and transfer of functions; is due to a history of relational responding relevant to the contextual cues involved; and is not based on direct non-relational training with regard to the particular stimuli of interest, nor solely to non-arbitrary characteristics of either the stimuli or the relation between them.

A second term we will use is the term "construction" or, at other times, verbal construction. We will use this when speaking of the general process of relating events in this fashion, without regard to the specific kinds of relational acts that are possible.

Types of Relational Frames

Our purpose in this section is not to list all possible kinds of relational frames. There are undoubtedly many different kinds possible and subtle subtypes within each. Rather we wish to use some of the major kinds to demonstrate the ways that frames can combine to establish various classes of events.

Some of the kinds of possible relational frames, and diagrammatic symbols for each, are shown in Figure 1.

Coordination

Undoubtedly the most fundamental type of relational responding is that encompassed by the frame we will call "coordination." The relation is one of identity, sameness, or similarity: this is that. Much of the earliest language training received by children seems to be of this kind and thus a relational frame of coordination is probably the first to be abstracted sufficiently that its application becomes arbitrary. The kind of history involved in teaching such relational responding was described in the example of learning the word for Daddy. A frame of coordination is one that is central to those types of verbal relations termed "referential." This relational frame is thus one of the most important types and we will discuss it more extensively in the context of our analysis of stimulus equivalence.

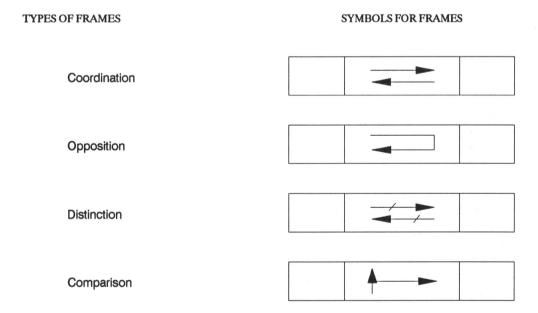

Figure 1. *Some major types of relational frames and symbols for each type.*

Opposition

Another kind of relational frame is that of opposition. In most practical instances this kind of relational responding is organized around some dimension along which events can be ordered. With regard to some point of reference, and an event that differs from that point in one direction along the continuum involved, an opposite differs in the other direction and to about the same degree. So, for example, cool is the opposite of warm, and cold is the opposite of hot. The reference point often seems to be anthropocentric --in this case the temperature of the human body. The relational frame of opposition typically specifies the dimenion of relevance (e.g., pretty is the opposite of ugly is relevant only to appearance), but as an arbitrarily applicable frame it can be applied even when no physical dimension of relevance has been specified. For example, I may simply say "a is the opposite of b." When stripped of a relevant dimension, the frame of opposition collapses into the logician's "logical not." The relatae in the frame entail the complete converse of each other. It is this quality that permits a logician to say "a is not not b" to mean "a is b."

The derived stimulus functions -- transfer of functions -- based on opposition are somewhat unusual. The relation of opposition implies that a behavior reinforced with regard to one stimulus placed in the relation, may be unlikely to be reinforced with regard to the other, particularly if the dimension distinguishing the two is relevant to the contingencies controlling the behavior. For example, if drinking cold water would be reinforced, and if the temperature of the water is relevant to that contingency, then a person is likely to avoid drinking from the hot water tap if "hot" is framed as the opposite of "cold" (as is likely to be the case with a verbal English-speaking adult). This kind of control need not involve a history of punishment for actually drinking hot water in the past -- the relational frame itself implies the avoidance through a transfer of functions.

Distinction

Another relational frame is that of distinction. It involve responding to one event in terms of its difference from another, typically along some specified dimension. Like a frame of opposition, this implies that responses to one event are unlikely to be reinforced to the other, but unlike opposition, the nature of the reinforcement contingency is typically not specified. If I am told only that "this is not warm water" I do not know if the water is ice cold or boiling.

Comparison

The frame of comparison is involved whenever one event is responded to in terms of a known non-equal and non-opposite quantitative or qualitative relation along a specified dimension (e.g., faster, larger, better). Many specific sub-types of comparison exist. Although each may require their own history, the family resemblance may allow the more rapid learning of successive members.

Some of the members of this family of relations are not obvious. For example, hierarchical class membership is a particularly important sub-type of a frame of comparison. "A is a member of B," is the general form of this frame. If the nature of B is clear, this may determine responses to A. For example, "John is a man" may permit appropriate responding to John to the degree that the class "man" is relevant. This is superficially quite different from the relation "A is better than B", but as will become clear when we talk about networks of relations, all frames of comparison yeild a common characteristic network.

Relational Networks

The implications of the major types of relational frames can best be seen by constructing relational networks of the same particular relational frame. In each sample case we will construct a four-member relational network, of stimuli A, B, C, and D (see Figure 2). The following relations will be taught: from A to B, from A to C, and from C to D. We will then examine the implications of various relational frames for the following relations: from A to A, from B to A, from B to C, from B to D, and from A to D. This particular network (which we will call an "archetypal relational network") is useful because it reveals most of the important differences between the major types of relational responding.

Archetypal Relational Network

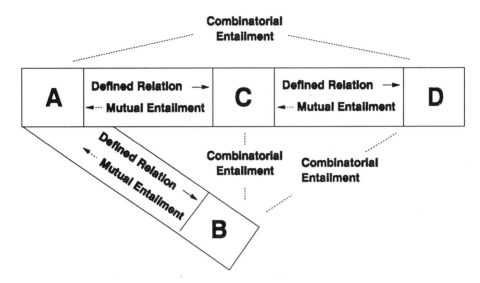

Figure 2. A relational network between four stimuli that will be used to describe some major types of relational frames.

Coordination - The Case of Stimulus Equivalence

The frame of coordination yields an equivalence class when combined in an archetypal network (see Figure 3). With regard to the relation involved, all possible combinations of stimuli can be included in the same relation. A is the same as A, B is the same as A, B is the same as C, and so on. With a four-member class, the three defined relations establish nine undefined relations (13 if relational reflexivity is included).

The simplest equivalence class can be thought of as the product of two instances of relational responding. For example, picking B given A may be sufficient to place A and B into the coordination frame "____ = ____" and thus "A = B." The same with A-C matching. Given the combination of these two instances of a coordination frame ("A = B" and "A = C"), the two defined relations may produce four undefined symmetrical and transitive relations ("B pick A," "C pick A," "B pick C," and "C pick B"). In the present analysis, symmetry is viewed as fundamental to stimulus equivalence because mutual entailment is the basis for the other aspects of relational responding (combinatorial entailment and transfer of functions). The kind of symmetry described in the equivalence literature is a specific instance of mutual entailment.

Combinatorial entailment is a more complex aspect of relational responding. It can be thought of as the generic case of transitivity. A relational control view of stimulus equivalence suggests that mutual transitivity cannot occur without symmetry. There are no published reports of a lack of transitivity given symmetrical responding.

There is a report of transitivity without symmetry, but it contains an instructive issue. D'Amato et al (1985) found that non-human primates would show some degree of A to C transitivity, given A to B and B to C training. No symmetrical responding was found. The difference between transitivity and combinatorial entailment, however, is that the latter must be

Archetypal Coordination Network

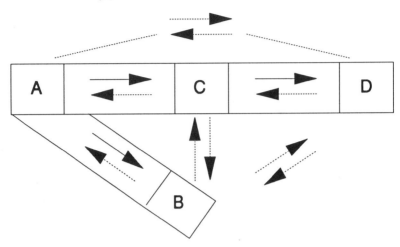

*Figure 3. The archetypal coordination network. Solid lines indicate
defined relations, dotted lines are derived relations.*

mutual. Because of its linkage to mathematics, transitivity has typically been talked about
linearly: A to B and B to C implies A to C. There are non-relational forms of responding that
may show transitivity in this sense (e.g., higher order classical conditioning). Combinatorial
entailment suggests that not just A to C responding, but also C to A relations are required. No
such "reverse transitivity" was found by D'Amato et al. No available data suggests that **mutual**
transitivity will occur without symmetry.

What about the issue of reflexivity? Where does this characteristic of equivalence classes
fit into an interpretation based on frames of coordination?

In a non-relational sense, reflexivity is a background basis for all forms of stimulus control
and thus of relational responding. It is necessary to recognize an event has itself in order to
respond to that event in terms of derived relations. For example, if an event when viewed as a
sample was seen as different than when it was viewed as a comparison, mutual entailment could
not occur. Reflexivity can thus always be interpreted in terms of a non-arbitrary relation of
sameness. Two instances of the same physical form is involved. As I argued earlier, however,
the issue is more complex because we must first determine whether the instance of relational
responding can be arbitrarily applied.

If a subject is responding solely in terms of the specified relation, reflexivity will be seen only
in classes built on a coordination frame -- that is, in equivalence classes. Responding in terms
of a frame of opposition, for example, will not show reflexivity, even though it assumes that the
subject can respond to the same stimulus as being the same. "A" is not the opposite of "A" but
one must respond to "A" as "A" in order to respond relationally at all. Thus, *relational reflexivity*
is implied by equivalence and *relational irreflexivity* by all other relational frames.

The relational control perspective suggests that stimulus equivalence can be interpreted as
a special case of a network of relational frames. In this way of thinking equivalence is not a
unique phenomenon -- only the most common and fundamental type of verbal construction.
Equivalence is just the beginning.

Opposition

The archetypal network yields different results when a frame of opposition is involved (see Figure 4). If A is the opposite of B, and the opposite of C, and if C is the opposite of D, then the undefined relations implied are as follows. Mutual entailment yields symmetrical relations because B is the opposite of A. Combinatorial entailment yields both frames of opposition and coordination. The derived relations in the archetypal network specify that B is the same as C, A is the same as D, and B is the opposite of D. The rule is that is two stimuli are separated by an even number of instances of frames of opposition, they are the same; if it is odd they are opposite.

Distinction

In an archetypal network (see Figure 5) symmetrical mutual entailment is observed (e.g., B is different than A), but any kind of combinatorial entailment is indeterminant. We cannot say what the relation is between B and C, A and D, or B and D. Any relation is possible. For example, if a car is different from an elephant, and also different from a house, the relation between house and elephant is undefined. In this case, they are different, but if the word "abode" is substituted for "elephant," they would be the same.

Archetypal Opposition Network

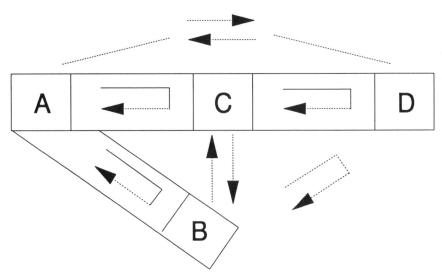

Figure 4. The archetypal opposition network. Solid lines indicate defined relations, dotted lines are derived relations.

Comparison

Frames of comparison are perhaps better viewed as a family of frames because there are numerous types of comparisons that are possible. Mutual entailment in frames of comparison imply inverse derived relations. If A is better than B, B is worse than A. Combinatorial entailment is sensitive to the exact sequence of frames of comparison. Frames of comparison in a sense are like an electrical diode: the defined relation always moves in one direction.

Archetypal Distinction Network

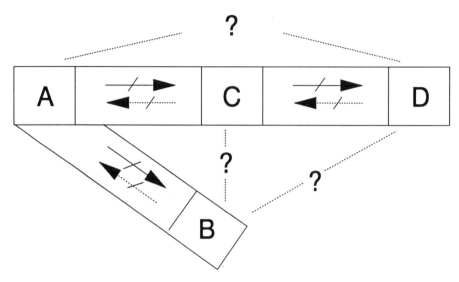

Figure 5. The archetypal distinction network. Solid lines indicate defined relations, dotted lines are derived relations.

Archetypal Comparison Network

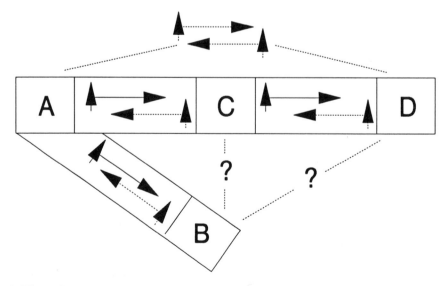

Figure 6. The archetypal comparison network. Solid lines indicate defined relations, dotted lines are derived relations.

Derived relations can move in the opposite directions, but if a linear progression is broken the derived relation remains unspecified. Consider an archetypal network with, say, the comparison of "greater than" (see Figure 6). The relations A is greater than D, and D less than A are derived. The relations specified by mutual entailment will also hold for all ordinal comparisons, so long as a linear progression is maintained. If it is broken, the entailed relations are indeterminant. In Figure 6, the mutual relations between B and C or B and D is not known, for example.

Complex Relational Networks

It is quite possible to create relational networks from mixtures of various relational frames and to relate entire relational classes with other relational classes. For example, if one equivalence class is the opposite of another equivalence class then each member of the first class is the opposite of all members of the second and vice versa. This can continue, presumably, to virtually any level of complexity. For example, consider that relations that surround a given word, such as "car." It is a part of many hierarchical classes, such as the class "noun," or the class "vehicles." Other terms are in a hierarchical relation with it, such as "windsheild" or "wheel." It enters into many comparisons. It is faster than a snail, or bigger than a bread box. It is the same as "automobile," but different than a house. And so on. The participation of the word "car" in these relations is part of the training required for the verbal community to use the stimulus "car" in the way that it does.

Note that the concept of "class" does not apply very easily to much of this. There has been a tendency for some to view stimulus equivalence as just another way to form stimulus classes. This is a mistake. Sometimes stimulus classes will result, and sometimes they will not. Even when they do, the transfer of new functions through these classes seem to distinguish them from other types of stimulus classes (e.g., functional stimulus classes) where such transfer is weak or non-existant. Consider the following relational network: A is better than B is better than C is the same as D. Where is the "class" here? C and D could be said to be in a class, but the not A and B, either alone or in combination with C and D. We have a relational network that sometimes gives rise to classes, but often does not.

When very complex relational networks are considered, it is especially important to remember that the relations we speak of when we invoke the concept of a relational frame are relations in the environment/organism interaction. They are stimulus functions that are coordinated with characteristic kinds of behavior and behavior coordinated with characteristic kind of stimulus functions. Relations do not exist "in" the person (at least not any more than any bit of stimulus control is in the person). Nor, in an arbitrarily applicable sense, are relations "in" the environment. They exist in behavior/environment interactions.

Are Relational Frames Logical?

It is tempting for a verbal organism (such as the reader of this paper) to treat the kind of relation we have been discussing as if they were "logical" or "common sense." This too is a mistake. Arbitrarily applicable relational responding is not due to logic; it is not caused by logic; it is not based on logic. This point cannot be overemphasized. Rather, this kind of relational responding is due to a characteristic history, and is itself the substance of or the basis of the kind of responding we call logical.

We call verbal constructions "logical" based on the kinds of relational frames taught to us by the verbal community. Logic is not a thing in the non-social world -- an object that can make other things happen. It is social behavior. As such, it is up to behavioral scientists to explain logic, not to appeal to it as an explanation of psychological events.

When people appeal to logic as an explanation they usually seem to be appealing to particular kinds of relational responding based on everyday interactions with the environment. Common sense, we might call it. But there are types of relations that do not fit with common sense or everyday logic. They therefore cannot be caused by common sense or logic. Consider the kinds of relations dealt with by verbal sub-communities, such as mathematicians or cosmologists. Mathematical or cosmological relational systems may lead to conclusions (e.g., that straight lines are curved, or that space has ten dimensions) that are inherently "illogical" for most people, but bear an elegant correspondence to a set of verbal constructions. They are not at all common sense.

Are Verbal Relations Referential?

Skinner, among others, have strongly criticized referential theories of meaning. The present framework looks superficially like a referential theory when it is only stimulus equivalence or frames of coordination that are considered. Etymologically, reference means "to carry back" -- presumably an appeal to the kind of symmetry inherent in frames of coordination. But other relations are equally verbal even if not relations of sameness. For example, the statement "hot is the opposite of cold" is verbal but cold does not *refer* to hot nor hot to cold. The theory proposed here encompasses the phenomena described by "relations of reference," but it is not a referential theory and does not view verbal constructions as pictures or copies of a "real world."

Evidence for a Relational Control Theory of Stimulus Equivalence

The space limits of the present chapter preclude an examination of the implications of the present argument, and the evidence for it can only be described very briefly. We will point to three major findings of relevance to this point of view.

Improvement in Testing

It is well known that significant improvements occur during the testing of equivalence relations, even without feedback on performance. This improvement in performance during testing has been seen in several studies (Lazar, Davis-Lang, & Sanchez, 1984; Sidman et al., 1985) even without additional conditional discrimination training interspersed between test trials (Devany et al, 1986). It has been suggested (Sidman et al., 1985) that this improvement occurs because the equivalence test itself provides a context in which the equivalence class is formed. This is an important observation, and one that would be embraced by a relational control perspective. The equivalence test can be interpreted as a contextual source of control over relational responding. In the formulae above, C_{func} applies to such factors. Conditional discrimination training will not by itself produce equivalence unless or until a relational response is made with regard to the components of those discriminations. The present perspective does suggest, however, that there are ways other than testing to bring to bear a relational frame on conditional discriminations.

This has been tested in our laboratory (Devany & Hayes, 1987). In a group of normal college students, we first trained a set of conditional discriminations and tested for equivalence. Equivalence emerged over the period of the test. Then we trained a second set of discriminations and tested for equivalence. This time equivalence classes were demonstrated more rapidly -- in many subjects they were immediately present. An interpretation could be made that equivalence was now beginning to form during the conditional discrimination training itself, not the test, because the earlier training and testing was sufficient to establish relational responding during conditional discrimination training. This was tested in the following fashion. The same subjects were given a third set of conditional discriminations. During the test, however, on half of the test trials a comparision stimulus could not be selected on the basis of equivalence. For example, only stimuli in the same class were used in a given set of comparisons. We reasoned that these "disrupter" trials would constitute a contextual cue for **not** responding in terms of the relation of coordination. They should, therefore, disrupt the formation of the third set of equivalence classes if that class was forming during the test. If the third class had already formed before the test, however, we reasoned that the disrupters would disrupt not the third set of equivalence classes, but the next set to be trained. Thus, a fourth set of discriminations was trained. The equivalence test used for the fourth set did not contain any of the disrupter items used in the third set. The results showed that about half of the subjects revealed notable disruption of equivalence class formation given the disrupter test items. The disruption, however, was shown in the fourth class, learned **after** the disruption trials. This seemingly shows that equivalence classes can form before testing, given a proper context.

The stimuli placed into a relational frame do not themselves determine the relation, by definition. Therefore, additional stimuli must be present to establish the particular relation between the particular stimuli. The present analysis holds that the combination of the contextual stimuli controlling relational responding and the stimuli to be related produce the results seen. Thus, a wide variety of procedures may establish arbitrary relations between events. For example, two stimuli are simply shown together, as in the recent work on compound stimuli and equivalence (Stromer, 1986). If there are contextual cues indicating that they should be related in a particular way, this kind of concurrent presentation may alone be enough to place them into a relational frame.

Transfer of Functions

The perspective presented suggest that transfer of functions should occur between elements of an equivalence class. Several studies in our laboratory have documented this effect. Discriminative control will transfer both through elements of an equivalence class (Hayes, Brownstein, Devany, Kohlenberg, & Shelby, 1987), and a conditional equivalence class (Wulfert & Hayes, 1988). Conditioned reinforcement functions will also transfer through equivalence classes (Hayes et al., 1987).

Additional Relations

The strongest support as yet for a relational control theory of stimulus equivalence is the demonstration that subjects with a proper pretraining history will respond in arbitrary matching-to-sample tasks in ways that fit perfectly with the frames of coordination, distinction, and opposition as described earlier (Steele, 1987). The basic procedure was as follows. Normal teenagers were first trained to select non-arbitrary stimuli in different ways. In the presence of a contextual cue consisting of an unfamiliar visual form, subjects learned to choose a long line from an array of lines of varying lengths, given a long line as a sample. Through many such examples they learned, in the presence of the contextual cue, to pick thick given thick, many given many, short given short, few given few, and so on. In similar fashion, in the presence of another unfamiliar visual form, to pick many given few, thin given thick, short given long, and so on. Finally, in the presence of yet another unfamiliar visual form they learned to pick anything other than the sample, given any sample. We may say that the subjects could now pick same, opposite and different given any set of non-arbitrarily related materials, and that these selections were under contextual control.

Subjects were now presented with an elaborate network of conditional discriminations in an arbitrary matching-to-sample task. Selections were made in the presence of the various contextual cues established during pretraining. Testing could then be done in the presence of these same contextual cues. The results corresponded perfectly to the patterns described earlier in the archetypal networks section.

To get a sense of what was done, consider the following two training trials: #1: O A1 (B1 or B2) #2: O A1 (C1 or C2). The letter "O" stands for the visual form that had been established in pretraining as a contextual cue for opposite, A1 is the sample, and the events in parentheses were the comparisons. Selecting the underlined form was reinforced. That is, given A1 they learned to pick B2 from an array; given A1 they picked C2. A relevant test trials was the following: O B2 (C1 or C2). If an equivalence class had formed, subjects would choose C2 because they had selected B2 and C2, given A1. If the O stimulus controlled non-relational responding they would also choose C2, because C2 choices had been reinforced in the presence of the stimulus O (trial #2). In fact, subjects chose C1. If A1 is the opposite of B2 and also the opposite of C2, then B2 and C2 are the same. In the presence of the symbol for opposite, the subjects have to chose C1 in the test trial if they are responding in terms of a frame of opposition.

Pretraining with regard to relational responding (same, opposite, and different) lead to three different kinds of performance. In the presence of the stimulus for "same", equivalence was readily shown. In the presence of "opposite" or "different" the responses predicted from a relational network were revealled. Thus, relational responding could be arbitrarily applied to various stimuli. This supports the view that stimulus equivalence is but one of a whole class of phenomena that can be derived based on relational frames. None of the available data seem to contradict a relational control theory of stimulus equivalence, and the studies conducted to test it have been universally supportive.

Summary

The excitement underlying the work in stimulus equivalence is based in part upon the apparent relevance of this phenomenon to language. The present analysis suggests that language may, as various non-behavioral theorists have argued, in fact involve a different kind of responding, but it is one that is still interpretable in terms of context and history. An analysis of language in terms of its context and history has been largely overwhelmed by structuralistic and mentalistic analyses. In part this may be because naturalistic analyses of language have relied too much on forms of responding that are not relational in the sense used here. As a result, analyses have seemed strained, and no robust empirical traditions adequate to the complexities of language have emerged within behavioral and other non-mentalistic traditions. The present analysis may provide another point of entry into the study of language as a natural phenomenon (Hayes & Hayes, 1989).

Does Verbal Construction Involve New Behavioral Principles?

It is in the area of transfer of functions that the evidence for new a new behavioral principle is provided. Behavior analysts are used to distinguishing between learned and unlearned phenomenon. A conditioned reinforcer is learned. It is considered to be different from an unconditioned reinforcer that is not learned, or at least not in the same way. Unconditioned reinforcers require only a normal biological structure and a normal developmental history for their effectiveness.

The transfer of stimulus functions can occur through classical conditioning, pairing, and other means. The specific functions must be learned, but the process itself is "unlearned" (in the epigenetic sense above). This is not what we find with verbal construction. Here the method or mode of stimulus function transfer must be learned. I am arguing that it is not enough to learn A pick B and A pick C to transfer functions from B to C without training. One must also have previously learned to form frames of coordination. Verbal construction involves a **learned**

pattern of the transformation and derivation of stimulus functions. While there are other behavioral principles involving the learning of stimulus functions, there are none where **the method of acquisition itself** need be learned. Relational frames are, therefore, something new. The derivation of relational frames seems to be based on existing principles (though not all species seem to be capable of this kind of act) but at the point of their acquisition their effects deserve then to be treated as a new phenomenon involving a new principle.

References

D'Amato, M. R., Salmon, D. P., Loukas, E., & Tomie, A. (1985). Symmetry and transitivity of conditional relations in monkeys (**Cebus apella**) and pigeons (**Columba livia**). *Journal of the Experimental Analysis of Behavior, 44,* 35-47.

Devany, J. M., Hayes, S. C., & Nelson, R. O. (1986). Equivalence class formation in language-able and language-disabled children. *Journal of the Experimental Analysis of Behavior, 46,* 243-257.

Devany, J. M. & Hayes, S. C. (May, 1987). *Irrelevant testing can disrupt equivalence: Implications for underlying processes.* Paper presented at the meeting of the Association for Behavior Analysis, Nashville, TN.

Dixon, M. H. & Spradlin, J. E. (1976). Establishing stimulus equivalences among retarded adolescents. *Journal of Experimental Child Psychology, 21,* 144-164.

Gewirtz, J. L. & Stengle, K. G. (1968). Learning of generalized imitation as the basis for identification. *Psychological Review, 5,* 374-397.

Hayes, S. C. (1989). Non-humans have not yet shown stimulus equivalence. *Journal of the Experimental Analysis of Behavior, 51,* 585-592.

Hayes, S. C., Brownstein, A., Devany, J. M., Kohlenberg, B. & Shelby, J. (1987). Stimulus equivalence and the symbolic control of behavior. *Mexican Journal of Behavior Analysis, 13,* 361-374.

Hayes, S. C. & Hayes, L. J. (1989). The verbal action of the listener as a basis for rule-governance. In S. C. Hayes (Ed.). *Rule-governed behavior: Cognition, contingencies, and instructional control.* (pp. 153-190). New York: Plenum.

Jenkins, J. J. (1963). Mediated association: Paradigms and situations. In C. N. Cofer and B. S. Musgrave (Eds.). *Verbal behavior and verbal learning.* New York: McGraw-Hill, pp. 210-245.

Kendall, S. B. (1983). Tests for mediated transfer in pigeons. *Psychological Record, 33,* 245-256.

Lazar, R., Davis-Lang, D. & Sanchez, L. (1984). The formation of visual stimulus equivalences in children. *Journal of the Experimental Analysis of Behavior, 41,* 251--266.

Peters, H. N. (1935). Mediate association. *Journal of Experimental Psychology, 18,* 20-48.

Reese, H. W. (1968). *The perception of stimulus relations: Discrimination learning and transposition.* New York: Academic Press.

Shipley, W. C. (1935). Indirect conditioning. *Journal of General Psychology, 12,* 337-357.

Sidman, M. (1971). Reading and auditory-visual equivalences. *Journal of Speech and Hearing Research, 14,* 5-13.

Sidman, M. (1986). Functional analyses of emergent verbal classes. In T. Thompson & M. D. Zeiler (Eds.). *Analysis and integration of behavioral units* (pp. 213-245). Hillsdale, New Jersey: Erlbaum.

Sidman, M., Cresson, O., & Willson-Morris, M. (1974). Acquisition of matching-to-sample via mediated transfer. *Journal of the Experimental Analysis of Behavior, 22,* 261-273.

Sidman, M., Kirk, B.,& Willson-Morris, M. (1985). Six-member stimulus classes generated by conditional-discrimination procedures. *Journal of the Experimental Analysis of Behavior, 43,* 21-42.

Sidman, M., Rauzin, R., Lazar, R., Cunningham, S., Tailby, W., & Carrigan, P. (1982). A search for symmetry in the conditional discriminations of rhesus monkeys, baboons and children. *Journal of the Experimental Analysis of Behavior, 37,* 23-44.

Sidman, M. & Tailby, W. (1982). Conditional discrimination versus matching to sample: An expansion of the testing paradigm. *Journal of the Experimental Analysis of Behavior, 37,* 5-22.

Spradlin, J. E., Cotter, V. W. & Baxley, N. (1973). Establishing a conditional discrimination without direct training: A study of transfer with retarded adolescents. *American Journal of Mental Deficiency, 77,* 556-566.

Spradlin, J. E. & Dixon, M. (1976). Establishing a conditional discrimination without direct training: Stimulus classes and labels. *American Journal of Mental Deficiency, 80,* 555-561.

Steele, D. L. (1987). Unpublished doctoral dissertation. Department of Psychology, University of North Carolina at Greensboro.

Wulfert, E. & Hayes, S. C. (1988). Transfer of conditional sequencing through conditional equivalence classes. *Journal of the Experimental Analysis of Behavior, 50,* 125-144.

Footnotes

Requests for reprints should be addressed to Steven C. Hayes, Department of Psychology, University of Nevada, Reno, NV 89557-0062. The line of thinking that is reflected in this chapter was heavily influenced by the late Aaron Brownstein [Hayes, S. C. & Brownstein, A. J. (1985). *Verbal behavior, equivalence classes and rules: New definitions, data and directions.* Paper presented at the meeting of the Association for Behavior Analysis]. I am not listing Aaron as a co-author on the latest manuscripts that have resulted from this line of work because the specific points have changed and I am not sure my late friend and colleague would still approve in all details. Nevetheless, I would like to ackowledge my great debt to Aaron in this and so many other areas of my professional work.

1. A few investigators have recently claimed to find stimulus equivalence in animals but their claims do not seem credible. See Hayes, 1989.

A Discussion of Chapter 2

Equivalence and Relational Frames

Richard W. Malott
Western Michigan University

Sniping at the Snipe Hunters

The history of learning theory is littered with the burned-out corpses of previously hot research topics, those originally thought to embarrass behaviorism (e.g., latent learning, insight learning, relational learning). Researchers on both sides of the fence fill our journals with the results of their quest for the mythical, crucial experiment. And then we move on. Will history deal as harshly with the current hot topics, those thought to be an embarrassment to our beloved three-term contingency (cue, response, and behavioral consequence)? What will become of the research on learned helplessness, constraints on learning, automaintenance, and the replication of schedule effects in human beings? More to the point, what will become of the research on stimulus equivalence?

Hayes says, "A major source of interest [in stimulus equivalence] is the apparent correspondence between the stimulus equivalence phenomenon and language phenomena....The second reason for interest is that the phenomenon is unexpected. It would not be readily predicted from a three-term contingency formulation."

But the embarrassment stimulus equivalence causes the three-term contingency causes me to lose interest. That embarrassment causes me to think, watch out now or we'll get sucked into another latent-learning type wild-goose chase. Psychology's closet is already sufficiently full of sky hooks, left-handed monkey wrenches, and snipes.

Furthermore, the apparent prerequisite of language skills, for the demonstration of stimulus equivalence, suggests that stimulus equivalence may not be a basic behavioral phenomenon but rather a cultural artifact of our linguistic history. Thus the stimulus equivalence phenomenon may shed little light on basic behavioral processes. However, the problem of stimulus equivalence can tie up the time of many of our best theoreticians and researchers until they do manage to explain it in terms of our basic principles and the three-term contingency. In general, we seem to be straying from Skinner's (1950) recommendation that we study topics of intrinsic interest and value, not those selected because they will prove one theory superior to another, not those that will be of little interest after the heat of the controversy cools down.

In the mean time, some use stimulus equivalence in an attempt to explain other cultural and language-based behavioral phenomena--for example, the control of rules describing contingencies that are too delayed to reinforce the behavior being controlled.

Those are my concerns; but then what can you expect from a man who predicted that long-playing records, stereophonic music, jogging, and personal computers were all fads. Yes, I've been wrong before.

On the Other Hand

With the assumption that I now have your attention, let me qualify slightly the preceding overstatement. My point is not that stimulus equivalence is necessarily a wild-goose chase. Rather, I am suggesting that for it to deserve the notice it is getting, stimulus equivalence should have some theoretical and practical import for the understanding and control of human behavior, independent of its potential for embarrassing the status quo.

I believe Steven Hayes' chapter makes a major contribution to such an understanding of human behavior, in general, and to an understanding of stimulus equivalence, especially because his careful, thorough, thoughtful, clearly presented analysis coincides with my own biases. Hayes' analysis represents a parsimonious effort to explain as much as possible with as little as possible. His analysis assumes no more than the three-term contingency and the standard short list of principles of behavior, a list to which I am reluctant to add. In other words, Hayes uses no new principles to deal with stimulus equivalence.

As I interpret his chapter, Hayes accomplishes three objectives: (a) He develops a general logical framework within which he places stimulus equivalence. (b) He presents a speculative account of the behavioral history needed for the occurrence of stimulus equivalence and related phenomena. (c) He shows that those phenomena do, in fact, occur.

Relational Frames as a Descriptive System

Hayes describes, as a conditional discrimination, the stimulus control involved in stimulus equivalence. In other words, the discriminative control exerted by one stimulus depends on the concurrent presence or value of another stimulus. For example, the discriminative control exerted by a plate of potatoes over the passing response depends on the request, "Pass the potatoes, please."

He also describes this stimulus control of stimulus equivalence as relational. Roughly, a set of stimuli are relational if a complex set of dependencies exists among them affecting the possible control they might exert. For example, "A potato has fewer calories than a Hostess Twinkie cupcake which in turn has fewer calories than a fudge sundae. So select the food, a potato or a sundae, that has fewer calories." (I'm inserting the cumbersome select mand, in an effort to show how the example relates to stimulus control.)

Hayes then enumerates some of the various forms of *possible* relational stimulus control that logically follow from the existence of a set of relational stimuli. For example, "A potato is a stimulus that tastes good. So select the potato, if it is not a stimulus that tastes bad."

He then calls this kind of relational stimulus control a *relational frame*. Relational frame refers to the fact that many, different, arbitrarily selected stimuli could be involved in each of the various forms of relational stimulus control. In other words, each form is a frame that may determine the stimulus control exerted by whatever set of stimuli are involved at the moment. Stimulus equivalence, then, is just one of several types of relational stimulus control or relational frames. The oppositional frame involving, for example, taste and potatoes is another type. And, because opposition is a general frame, we can, for instance, substitute watermelons for potatoes and size for taste.

Anti-rationalism. Hayes points out that it is a mistake "to treat the kind of relations we have been discussing as if they were 'logical' or 'common sense.'...It is up to behavioral scientists to explain logic, not to appeal to it as an explanation of psychological events." In other words, when we are trying to explain a behavioral phenomenon, we should not be satisfied with saying that it is simply rational, or logical, or common sense for people to behave in that way. We must still explain why they behave in a rational, logical, sensible manner. Rationality is more a phenomenon to explain rather than a final explanation itself. Our field might profit from placing as much emphasis on understanding the rational, the sensible, the normal, as it does on understanding and controlling the irrational, the senseless, the abnormal.

Stimulus Equivalence as a New Principle

Hayes says, "Some authors . . . have tended to see stimulus equivalence as a fundamental behavioral phenomenon, perhaps even a new behavioral principle." However, Hayes suggests that we need no new principles to account for stimulus equivalence. To support his suggestion, he speculates about how verbal human beings might acquire the repertoire needed for relations such as stimulus equivalence to exert stimulus control over their behavior. He speculates about the acquisition of relational stimulus control in young children. He starts with symbolic matching to sample like "Is that your Daddy?" and goes on to the search for Daddy, in the presence of the cue "Daddy has your dolly." Thus Hayes accounts, in what I consider to be a plausible manner for relational stimulus control--relational frames.

The Existence of Relational Frames

Finally, Hayes briefly presents experimental data suggesting that, in fact, relational stimulus control does exist. He summarizes data from a sort of complex Harlow-type learning-to-learn or discrimination-reversal design. These data exemplify relational stimulus control. In addition, he mentions data showing that "conditioned reinforcement functions will also transfer through equivalence classes." And he describes data showing a higher-order conditional discrimination that supported generalized, symbolic matching to sample, matching to the opposite, and oddity matching. The particular form of matching depended on which of three values of the higher-order conditional stimulus was present. These data also show the existence of relational stimulus control--relational frames.

The Importance of Relational Frames

I suggested earlier that the work on stimulus equivalence phenomena might not have much staying power, if its chief *raison d'etre* was to prove the limitations or generality of the three-term contingency. However, there may be other justifications for this work, as well as the more general work on relational stimulus functions--relational frames. Those justifications involve the analysis of verbal and logical control of human behavior.

Language. Hayes says, "The present analysis may provide another point of entry into the study of language as a natural phenomenon." Unfortunately, it is not clear from this chapter just how relational frames will allow us to enter into the study of language. Fortunately, however, this is no idle promise, as Hayes (1989) has clearly shown the relationship elsewhere.

Logic. In addition, relational stimulus control may be an important form of stimulus control in our everyday life, worthy of study, regardless of its implications for the three-term contingency. We would interact with the world much less effectively, if our behavior were not controlled by logical relations such as those involving similarity, difference, and greater than.

Quibbles

I would feel I had betrayed my graduate training, if I didn't have a few quibbles, so:

The Thin Ice Covering Reification

Hayes carefully defines *relational frame* so that it refers to "interactions between the organism and the environment." But its noun form tempts us toward reification, toward saying, "the person has a relational frame, but the pigeon doesn't" or "the girl's relational frame caused her to point to the word *cat* when you pointed to the picture of the cat." I fear that those less behaviorally adept than Hayes will succumb to that temptation. So I would be more comfortable talking in terms of *relational stimulus control, relational control, relational framing,* or even *framing relationally.* (See Hineline, 1980, for a thoughtful analysis of the problems of nouns.)

Latent Mentalisms

I start itching a little, whenever I hear *learn;* and I start itching a lot, whenever I hear *learn to.* For example: "The person *learns* 'given A1 pick B1.'" "A primate may *learn to* hide." "The child *learns to* relate events." We might better avoid falling through the thin ice that covers reification and drowning in the slimy depths of cognitivism if we stuck to the more awkward but safer data language: "The response of picking B1 in the presence of A1 becomes more likely." "The likelihood of the primate's entering the thicket increases." "The relation between events comes to exert control over the child's behavior."

I have a similar problem, when I read that "Discriminations can often become *connected* to each other." Only with great effort do I refrain from looking for the mind that holds those connected discriminations.

The Shy Primate

Hayes considers the primate that hides in the thicket, on sight of the lion. He says, "The lion is a conditional discriminative stimulus, in the presence of which the thicket is a discriminative stimulus for an approach response." If so, what reinforcement process maintains that approach response? This is like saying electric shock, in a Skinner box, is a conditional discriminative stimulus, in the presence of which the lever is a discriminative stimulus for an approach response. I think, instead, the shock is an aversive stimulus whose termination reinforces approaching and pressing the lever. And the sight of the lion is an aversive stimulus whose termination reinforces approaching and entering the thicket. Here I am not quibbling with the concept of conditional discriminative stimulus, just with the example.

Conclusions

I see this chapter as consisting of three main parts: One part is the description of relational frames. This is an atheoretical, logical analysis, amenable to evaluation only in terms of its logical consistency and comprehensiveness. A second part is the description of plausible mechanisms for acquiring the prerequisites to relational-frame control. This is a theoretical analysis amenable to future empirical evaluation. And a third part is an empirical demonstration of the existence of relational-frame control. This demonstration supports the utility of describing some types of behavioral control in terms of relational framing. I found all three parts of this chapter to be persuasive. I think Hayes provides an excellent framework within which to view stimulus equivalence, an excellent and testable account of the acquisition of relational framing, a convincing demonstration of the existence of relational framing, and a strong platform from which we can extend our understanding and control of human behavior.

References

Hayes, S. C. (1989). *Rule-governed behavior: Cognition, contingencies, and instructional control.* New York: Plenum.

Hineline, P. N. (1980). The language of behavior analysis: Its community, its functions, and its limitations. *Behaviorism, 8,* 67-86.

Skinner, B. F. (1950). Are theories of learning necessary? *Psychological Review, 57,* 193-216.

A Discussion of Chapter 2

Stimulus, Response, or Interbehavior?

Linda J. Hayes
University of Nevada, Reno
Laura L. Methot
Saint Mary's University

Attributing psychological occurrences to mysterious processes of "emergence," as is sometimes done in the context of stimulus equivalence, has never been very popular with thorough-going behaviorists. It smacks of internal causality at worst. At best it is imprecise. Steven Hayes' concept of arbitrarily applicable relational responding is not articulated as a product of emergent processes. On the contrary, it is held to be a product of abstraction from a history of stimulus-bound relational responding. The analysis is worthy of note for this reason alone.

Steven Hayes' analysis lacks precision on certain key issues, however, detracting from its usefulness. The aim of this brief comment is to draw attention to a couple of those issues, although not for the purpose of solving the problems they raise. They are very complex issues. Rather, our intent is to add them to the analytic agenda, and to offer some suggestions for the course of their analysis.

To begin, then, specificity is lacking in the account of the abstraction process by which arbitrarily applicable relational responding comes about. How one proceeds from a stimulus-bound history to a **first instance** of stimulus-free relational responding is not explained. It is as though the first instance of stimulus-free relational responding "emerges" out of a relevant stimulus-bound history -- an argument he has tried to avoid. To be tackled at this juncture, then, is the process of abstraction. Can abstraction be understood as an event -- as something an organism does, subtle though it may be? Or is it a construct built upon other constructs and bearing, at best, only a very distant relation to actual behavior?

Secondly, a given instance of arbitrarily applicable relational responding, when it occurs, can be assumed to be taking place with respect to the specific configuration of stimuli present at the time of its occurrence. In other words, responding implies stimulating and can be understood only in relation to such stimulating. As a contextualist, Hayes would agree. However, if responding implies stimulating, relational responding implies relations among stimuli. As such, to understand arbitrarily applicable relational responding, more than a characterization of the response event is required: It becomes necessary also to identify the stimulus event with respect to which such a response is occurring. Despite the analytical obligation here, neither response event nor stimulus event is adequately described in Steven Hayes' treatment.

His problem seems to be one of indecision as to whether relational framing is a stimulus event or a response event. As a response event, it is described as "organizing" or, more aptly, as "an organizing," neither of which have any measure of precision. When pushed as to the nature of organizing as a response event, attention shifts to the stimulating features of the framing situation, to relations of coordination or opposition among **stimuli**, for example.

Alternatively, when an attempt is made to pin down the stimulus event of a relational frame, the response factor is emphasized. In this vein, an arbitrarily applicable relational response is said to occur **because** of a history, not **to** a stimulus, making it appear unnecessary to identify the immediate stimulating circumstance. A particular response cannot simply be said to occur because of a history, though. While the response may be a product of historical circumstances, when the response **is occurring**, its history is no longer relevant. What is relevant -- not to responding per se but to **this** response occurring at **this** moment -- is the stimulus coordinated with it.

In summary, Steven Hayes acknowledges the complexity of the arbitrarily applicable relational response, the fact that it is coordinated with relations among stimuli, and that these relations, as well as the responses coordinated with them, develop historically. This is a good beginning. From here, it would seem useful to ask: If relational responding is to be conceptualized as organizing activity, what is it organizing? This, we may assume, would lead to a more detailed consideration of coordinated relational **stimulation**.

In more general terms, we offer two suggestions for the course of analysis from this point on. First, because concentrating on either stimulating or responding in isolation has tended to steer the analysis away from an event perspective, we would suggest adopting **relations between responding and stimulating** -- interbehavior -- as the relevant analytic unit in this domain. Second, we would suggest an attempt to describe in detail the nature and operation of one specific unit of this type. Obviously, the detail will speak only to that particular unit. The exercise may have broader utility though: It may give meaning to the critical concepts of "abstracting" and "organizing" invoked here to overcome the difficulties involved in characterizing what are without question very complex relational events.

Chapter 3

Language as Contingency Substitution Behavior

Emilio Ribes Inesta
Universidad National Autonoma de Mexico

"And to imagine a language means to imagine a
form of life"

Ludwig Wittgenstein
Philosophical Investigations (1953, p. 8)

A functional analysis of language as behavior may be accomplished if: a) problems of individuals interacting while speaking, writing, reading or gesturing are not confounded with those that derive from morphological or structural analysis of the behavior products, for example, written materials, test composition, phonetic patterns in taped speech, etc.; and b) the functional properties of interactions which are to be identified as qualitatively different from those not considered as linguistic are spelled out; otherwise the distinction between language and non-language behaviors is without value.

Several problems arise in this context, some of them conceptual, and some methodological in nature. Among the conceptual issues, two are outstanding: 1) the definition of language as behavior in terms accurate enough to distinguish it from behavioral processes shared with prelinguistic events; and 2) the conception of language behavior as a developmental process embracing transitions in the qualitative complexity of interactions among the individual and his or her environment. Among the methodological issues, the following seem to be the most relevant: 1) the development of functional categories that allow for the identification of interactive units which include both linguistic and non-linguistic response morphologies; and 2) the comparability of data obtained under experimentally contrived, longitudinal, and comparative methods.

Three basic assumptions provide the rationale for this approach to language behavior:

First, morphology is not a sufficient condition to allow for distinctions among language behavior and other simpler behavior;

Second, current categories in behavior theory, based upon the operant-respondent distinction, are not adequate to formulate a taxonomy of behavior including language behavior[1];

Third, the explanation of language behavior must take into account the functional specificity of conventional properties of stimulus and response events as compared to those only deploying physico-chemical dimensions.

Although language as behavior share many of the morphological features of language products as things (Kantor, 1963), it deserves a special treatment to the extent that it consists of an episodic relation always involving variables additional to the utterance or writing by a speaker or writer. Language as behavior represents a particular class of interaction, which is possible of classification in terms of its conventional morphology, but is not restricted to the morphological features of the actions themselves. We shall examine the concepts necessary to provide an adequate definition of language as behavior: conventional reactional systems, functional detachment of responses, and substitutional contingencies.

Language and Conventional Reactional Systems

Human language is social in nature. Its social character does not mean only that language appears in individuals living in groups, but that the morphological and functional features of language do not depend upon biological, individual or species-specific conditions. On the contrary, human language, as qualitatively different from animal paralanguages, has evolved as a conventional system of relations among individuals and environment events. The conventional character of human language is reflected both in its morphology and functionality. The conventional character of human language, although implying regularities among individuals, does not necessarily require explicit rules or norms regulating the uniformities in the conventional action of individuals. Conventions represent social agreement, but the establishment of social agreements does not follow from supraordinate explicit rules concerning them. The formulation of such rules or norms is a further step in the evolution of conventions, not an initial and or necessary condition for their development. Conventions develop as tacit practices among individuals, and rules describing these practices are sometimes formally expressed by society as laws or norms. The formulation of these rules does not necessarily entail that they regulate corresponding practices. The preminence of practices in relation to rules, is shown by the history of grammar, law, religion, and morals to the extent that rules are changed from time to time to adjust them to actual practices of individuals in society, practices that on occasion are verbal practices "expressing" rules.

The view that conventional behavior and actions are rule-following processes, arises out of the assumptions of dualistic thinking, namely, the postulate of existing ideal entities, in the form of rules, laws or similar stuff, inferred from invariances in conventional practices. Not only is the existence of these devices asserted, but also that conventions as events, that is, as interactions among individuals and the environment, are regulated or determined by such rules.

According to this view, actions and sayings are the effect or reflection of events taking place in an internal world. Nevertheless, as Ryle (1949) has claimed, to know or to say something, does not imply a two-stage causal process in which first takes place what is known or is going to be said and afterwards it is done or uttered. To know and to say, even when there are non-apparent or silent actions involved, is a single process or occurrence. When speaking or knowing about one's actions is an additional occurrence, although descriptive of self-deeds, it is a separate action in and of itself. In this regard, to know or to speak in advance about what is going to be done or said, is a consequence of previous actions or doings and not the proof of these being caused or ruled by separate knowing or internal speaking episodes.

This is specially relevant in the analysis of language as behavior. Since mankind developed writing, linguistic practices could be transcribed and perpetuated from generation to generation. These transcriptions were not identical to the original linguistic interactions. Transcriptions were linguistic products and therefore derived from actions, but not actions themselves. Thus, the various grammars developed as the description of transcribed and written practices, and grammatical rules were abstracted from those descriptions as ideal, universal invariances.

To summarize, rules were abstracted from descriptions of linguistic actions which, in turn, were abstracted from linguistic action itself. Lost in the process of abstraction is the heterogeneus and constantly changing character of linguistic practices.

Since grammar represents a formal description of speaking and writing practices, it cannot be postulated as a property of the same behavior of speaking and writing, and even less in those cases in which language involves gestural and arbitrary movements which are not "verbal."

When individuals speak, write or engage in some other kind of language as an interactive episode, they are not following rules of grammar, even when their behavior may adjust to what grammarians would describe as "correct language use." Most people cannot identify the rules of grammar that describe their own behavior when speaking or writing, and even in individuals able to do so, they do not first identify the rules to be followed and then speak or write in accordance with them. To "edit" speech or writing while at the same time engage in language action is **impossible.**

Conventional behavior, therefore, does not entail any prior social or individual rule-following process. It consists in socially functional interactions with arbitrary morphologies in regard to the physico-chemical and biological dimensions of events and response. To the extent that these interactions are shared by individuals in a group, interacting among them and events in the environment. Because of this, we may find as many sets of conventions as functional uses of arbitrary morphologies.[2]

The important feature of language as conventional behavior is that it is difficult to identify a single human interaction in which a linguistic component is not present as an essential functional dimension of the situation, and it would be proper to add that these linguistic components are not necessarily equated with utterances or graphisms, but with socially transmitted conventional properties of events, actions and relations. The human environment, as the outcome of social history, is mainly a cultural environment. That is, it is formed by objects and practices built up during the evolution of mankind, and because of this, even things and nature are in a sense humanized. Nature and things have been created or transformed by mankind in the course of history and have become meaningful to the extent that we individually interact with them in terms of *social practices* or *conventions*. Language, either as gestures, speech or writing, originated as conventions, and has been the medium of production, reproduction and transformation of conventions. If man and woman are to be identified, in a Aristotelian sense, as intelligent beings, this is due, as Ryle (1949) keenly describes, to didactic speech, that is to the capacity to transform the individual experience into social practices, and viceversa. This is possible only because of language as conventional behavior.

Human individuals, from the very moment they are born, become part of a field of interactions functionally mediated and contextualized by linguistic events. Although objects, actions and relations in the environment are contacted directly or through the interaction with other individuals, their functional properties as meaningful social events also depend upon conventions made possible by linguistic exchange and transmission. Because of this, I propose that the human environment is a linguistic environment, even when dealing with objects and things that are not linguistic in morphology.

Along the same reasoning, linguistic behavior as conventional interaction includes not only actions with a verbal morphology, but also any action that is part of an interaction mediated by linguistic events. Because of this, the distinction between verbal and non-verbal behavior, as based on morphological grounds, is not a sound distinction. Behavior must be viewed as part of interactional episodes; and from this perspective, although episodes always involve morphologically linguistic components on the parts of some of the participating individuals, only under special circumstances can the action of the speaker, gesturer or writer be considered truly linguistic. Further on, in examining substitutional behavior, I'll discuss about the circumstances that qualify an interaction as linguistic.

Linguistic dimensions of behavior include verbal as well as non-verbal morphologies. The behavior of the speaker, gesturer or writer becomes linguistic in a functional sense, only when it allows for a particular kind of mediation among the individuals and events interacting in a given situation. I shall define as linguistic not the isolated actions of an individual but the particular forms of organization of interactive episodes between the individual, other individuals, and objects and events in the environment.

This position may be summarized as follows:

1) The human environment is conventional, and this is possible only because of the interactive and practice-reproductive character of language;

2) Both environmental events and individual actions may have a linguistic character even when they display non-verbal morphologies;

3) Linguistic dimensions may be identified only in reference to interaction among individuals and events. Thus, it is not possible to describe as linguistic any behavior isolated from the interactive episode, even if the action is verbal according to morphological criteria.

The acquisition of conventional reactional systems[3] must be distinguished from the acquisition of the **aptitude** to engage in linguistic interactions, although, as it will be seen below, the former may be a necessary condition for the latter to develop.

There are three basic issues in the acquisition of conventional reactional systems: 1) the acquisition of "listening", "reading" or "observing" responses, which include integrated sensory or perceptual reactions to linguistic stimuli and events; 2) the acquisition of response units adjusted to linguistic morphology; and, 3) the acquisition of response styles or modes matching interactive patterning in the linguistic environment.

Although the analysis of the acquisition of conventional responding may be undertaken through the identification of "cumulative" expansion of the morphology and extension of response unit availability, this endeavor becomes meaningless unless it is related to the functional circumstances and relations under which responses are acquired and performed. The process of acquiring response morphologies is in fact a process of continuous differentiation and expansion of sensory, phonetic and graphic-producing responses. Stimulus discrimination, stimulus generalization, imitation, response shaping, and other known techniques are the procedural devices informally used in this process. Because there is a vast literature on this topic (Bijou and Baer, 1961; Staats and Staats, 1964; Sloane and MacAuley, 1968) I shall not review it once more.

Language and Functional Detachment of Responses

I previously remarked that although language as behavior consists in conventional responding, the availability of conventional reactional systems is not sufficient. Conventional responses as different from strictly biological or ecological responses have a wider range of detachment in regard to the physico-chemical properties of situational events. Non-conventional behavior consists in the individual responding to events according to their physico-chemical properties. The morphology and function of such responses are adjusted to the morphology and physico-chemical conditions of objects and events interacted with. In order to turn a knob there are few ways of handling it that are successful. The form, weight, resistance and texture of the knob restrict the range of possible morphologies. The same can be said about any other type of movement or sensory response. In short, the physico-chemical conditions of events shape the morphological features of responding and, therefore, the functional range of the behavior involved.

On the contrary, conventional responses are arbitrary in form, and hence, they do not sustain any necessary biological relation with the morphology of physico-chemical events interacted with. The particular morphology of an action related to events depends upon the contingency defined by social convention, although the convention itself is always to be identified on the basis of parameters related to the physico-chemical properties or to effects of the events involved. Conventional responses are not only arbitrary responses in regard to their morphology, but also in regard to their morphological correspondence with physico-chemical properties of objects and events. The arbitrariness of the relation between conventional responses and the morphologies of objects and situational contingencies in which they are performed, are the dimensions the **allow for** detaching the functions of such responses from biological restrictions relevant to physico-chemical environmental conditions. To detach the function of a response means several things. It means that:

a) Several conventional responses may be performed to the very same object or stimulus condition;

b) The same response may be performed to objects differing in physico-chemical properties;

c) Usual responding does not occur with respect to the physico-chemical dimensions of present objects or stimuli;

d) Responding may be performed to an object or event not present, but as responding according to its previous or probable occurrences;

e) Responding may be performed to an object or event taking place in a different environment;

f) Responding consists in acting with regard to objects and events properties that are not perceptually apparent, eg., beauty, radioactivity, etc.; and;

g) Responding may be performed in situations in which events and objects relate under varying moment-to-moment contingencies.

The first three forms of detachment of conventional responses are shared with non-conventional responses, but the last four are exclusive of conventional actions. The arbitrary character of conventional responses makes it possible to respond to past or probable events, events taking place in a different setting, acting events not apparent to sensory responding, or events under changing contingency relations.

It might be anticipated that even in the three former cases, conventional responses will be easier to detach than situationally-bound responses. This means that if we compare human and non-human subjects in their performance under situations involving the three former cases of functional detachment, as would be a conditional discrimination task for example, we might predict that human subjects, when matched in behavioral development with non-human subjects, would show faster acquisition and higher asymptotic levels (e.g., Sidman and Tailby, 1982).

Nevertheless, this is not an automatic process. Conventionality per se, although necessary, is not a sufficient condition for functional detachment to occur. Since the human environment is conventional from the very beginning for any individual, conventional responses are acquired "as if they were natural" forms of behavior to "natural conditions and events." Linguistic responses and other events become related in particular situations as if the contingencies relating them were universal. That is why young children respond to linguistic events as if they were specific to the situation where they were initially presented or performed. This happens also with retarded children, chronic psychotic patients, or sometimes with illiterate people. Linguistic actions are performed as situationally-bound responses, that is, as the only and necessary form of responding to a particular event relation. For functional detachment to occur a history of interactions promoting substitutional contingencies mediated by the individual conventional responding is required.[4]

Language Behavior as Substitutional Contingency Interaction

If language as behavior is to be defined in order to distinguish it from linguistic morphologies that share functional properties with non-conventional forms of responding, we might say that language is contingency-substitutional behavior.

Contingency-substitutional behavior as a form of interaction has two defining functional characteristics. First, to the extent that the interaction involves at least two distinctive **conventional** responses, individuals participating in such a relation respond to each other and to the events interacted with in terms that are not restricted to current contingencies as represented by the physico-chemical situational dependencies. The current interaction is expanded by way of contingencies introduced by conventional responding, which are not only added to situational circumstances but intruded as transforming substitutional *relations*. Second, these substitutional relations may consist of relations regarding a particular event or object, but detached from the temporal, spatial and apparent properties of such an event. When this is the case, we may call such relations *referential substitution*. Alternatively, substitutional relations may consist of relations regarding conventional response-produced events, without attachment to any particular physico-chemical event. These we may call *non-referential substitution*. In both cases, interactions are regulated by contingencies dependent upon the conventional responses involved in the relation.

Non-substitutional contingencies, on the other hand, refer to reciprocal dependencies among events and the individuals' behavior established by the **now-here-apparent** properties of the situation. The individual interacts with events in terms of present and observable functional dimensions. The kind of interaction, even when performed relative to linguistic morphologies both in stimuli and responses, remains prelinguistic in regard to the level of organization of behavior. This is tantamount to saying that, although involving verbal or linguistic morphologies, the interaction is attached to the current dimension of situational contingencies. Conventional behavior functions **as if** it were biological, situationally-bound behavior. It is important to point out that substitutional contingencies do not refer to a process of stimulus or response substitution, but to a process of contingency transformation regarding original and current events.

Contrast with Traditional Behavioral Views

In order to exemplify the difference between conventional interactions under substitutional and non-substitutional contingencies, let me examine some of the verbal operants proposed by Skinner (1957) in his analysis of language. I shall discuss only two of them, which seem basic to his taxonomy: the mand and the tact.

In the mand relation, a speaker utters a verbal response (or performs a gesture or indication) that is followed by the response of a listener (normally a non-verbal response) reinforcing the speaker according to the motivational state and reinforcer specified by the utterance. The mand is a pure instance of the non-discriminated operant; there is no available discriminative stimulus (although the listener as audience is sometimes a sort of "generalized" discriminative stimulus); there is a response emitted under particular motivational conditions (the lack or presence of some stimulus or object with **potential** positive or negative reinforcing properties); and there is a listener (which works as a surrogate for a mechanical device) providing the reinforcer specified by the mand. Asking for a glass of water or demanding a loud noise to be shut-off are classical examples of the mand relation.

The tact relation deals with the "epistemic" or "semantic" aspects of language. In the tact, there is an antecedent non-verbal stimulus (since verbal stimuli can not be tacted), whose physical properties develop stimulus control over the verbal response which is reinforced by generalized or educational reinforcement when occurring in their presence. The tact consists in a discriminated operant, where a non-verbal, physical stimulus is the discriminative stimulus controlling a verbal operant, the tact, which is followed by generalized reinforcement provided by the listener. Description, naming, identification, narration of events, and similar behavior exemplify the tact relation.

I shall not go into a discussion of some conceptual problems present in these categories. I shall limit myself to showing that both the mand and the tact relations describe situationally-bound interactions, and that in consequence, there is no need for an analysis different from that made of "non-verbal" operants. The inclusion of conventional responses (so-called verbal) on the side of the speaker does not modify the basic interactions that hold in animal behavior, where no conventional responses intervene.[5]

In both cases, the individual is responding not in such a way as to transform contingencies prescribed by the situational events, but under the particular contingencies that those events establish, for example, the deprivation conditions, the physical properties of prior stimulus events, the history of reinforcement for verbal responding in the presence of a particular listener, and so on. On the side of the **speaker** there does not seem to be any functional difference between asking for water, or physically forcing a "listener" to hand him a glass of water. The difference lies only in the effort exerted and the morphology of the emitted response.

There are differences, nevertheless, on the side of the **listener.** The listener's response in handing a glass of water to the speaker is linguistic to the extent that the relation between the petition and the behavior of looking for, serving and passing a glass of water, does not sustain any biologically or physically necessary relation with the speaker's behavior. Animal behaviors of pressing a lever when food-deprived and pulling a chain when water-deprived in order to be reinforced by a previously programmed equipment, are not different from uttering "food" or "water" by an individual "asking" for such stimulus consequences. The linguistic behavior is displayed by the experimenter who programmed the equipment in such a way that the animals get differential reinforcement for each type of response, in the same way that in the human mand relation, truly linguistic behavior is displayed by the listener. The tact relation shows similar problems to those discussed above, but centered on the response to the antecedent stimulus. The treatment given to the tact (as well as to the echoic or textual relations) does not allow for distinguishing human verbal behavior from animal non-verbal behavior, even when conventional stimuli or responses are involved.

Functional Stages in the Development of Conventional Behavior as Language Behavior

In this section, I shall introduce several concepts useful for the understanding of the development of conventional behavior as language behavior.

If our interest is not in behavior as mere action but in behavior conceived as interaction, any account of language as behavior must consider not only the bahavior of individuals as an event in sequential relation with other events in time and space, but also the particular form in which behavior participates in the organization of the interaction field. Individual behavior is not merely an effect to be looked for. It is a functional component intervening in the organization of contingencies in any situation. The function performed by the behavior of the individual will change in quality depending on how critical or relevant it becomes in the configuration of the ongoing contingencies. This qualitative character of behavior in shaping up contingencies, shall be called *functional aptitude.* A functional aptitude, then, is a concept describing the quality of the organization of behavioral interactions in contingency fields. Therefore, I assume that behavioral interactions may be classified along a qualitative continuum, in which the taxonomic criterion is based on the role performed by behavior in the organization of contingency fields. By the same token, the recognition of different functional aptitudes imposes the need to analyze language behavior processes in developmental terms.

The development of functional aptitudes regarding language behavior is conceived as a continuously **inclusive** process, in which each aptitude becomes the necessary condition to achieve the next developmental stage. The new aptitude level achieved, nonetheless, does not exclude previous ones. These are incorporated as components of the new form in which the individual's behavior enters into the organization of contingencies. But since "functional aptitudes" refers to a general disposition about modes of interaction, the achievement of a particular developmental stage does not preclude the subsequent occurrence of less complex forms of interaction regarding particular sets of responses and situational events.[6] Because of this, we must distinguish between functional aptitudes and functional competencies. The latter consist of sets of response morphologies which are functional in regard to certain conditions in the environment, conditions involving particular sets of objects, events and relations, or particular arrangements of contingencies, under a criterion of **effectiveness**. Competencies may be performed in the various levels of functional aptitude which I shall proceed to examine.

I propose five general stages of functional development, even though each aptitude level itself may comprise relatively differentiated modes of interaction.[7] The general stages are the following:

1) Behavior does not change contingencies in the environment. Contingencies among events act on the individual and the behavior evolves as differential reactivity to these contingencies. In the case of human behavior, it consists not only in orienting and motor displacement responses which allow for a differential effect of contingencies, but on the development of conventional morphologies integrated with those actions. This stage has to do, among other things, with the modulation of phonetic, sensory and motor behaviors, the recognition of stimuli, its patterning and "meaning" relations with objects and actions, the functional orientation to events in terms of the linguistic stimuli which form them, the emergence of imitative verbal and non-verbal behavior as regulated by verbal stimuli, and so on. Since the individual is reactive only to contingencies that depend upon proximal and spatial relations, this functional stage of development may be considered a **contextual** mode of interaction;

2) To the extent that particular forms of conventional behavior are modulated by the environment contingencies, the individual develops dispositions or tendencies to respond in such a way even in the absence of particular conditions in which such behavior is relevant. The occurrence of conventional behavior under circumstances consisting in partially ongoing contingencies is followed by the completion of those contingencies when the behavior takes place within the temporal and spatial boundaries in which events relate to each other and when other individuals may mediate them through their behavior (linguistic or not) according to standard social practices. This being the case, the individual's behavior performs a new role. Behavior is not limited to a reactive process, but becomes functional in the production of contextual relations. Behavior acts on the environment affecting contingencies to which the individual is already differentially reactive. Effective "manding" and "intraverbal" behavior develops in this stage.[8] Since the individual alters the occurrence of contextual contingencies acting on and changing the temporal and spatial conditions in which they take place, this functional stage of development may be considered as a **supplementary** mode of interaction.

3) As development proceeds according to social conventions and standards, contingencies become increasingly complex. Individuals must learn to interact with situations consisting in contingencies conditional to multiple and relational factors. These relational contingencies

require that individuals, instead of interacting with fixed particular properties of contextual and supplementary fields, become responsive to **classes of functional events** established according to relational properties of events. In human behavior, the events which regulate functional properties of varying physico-chemical dimensions of actions and events are linguistic. Most of the concrete operations stage behaviors described by Piaget and Inhelder (1978) are characteristic of this stage, as well as many apparently non-linguistic actions which are the "content" of moral and social development (Bijou, 1976). These interactions are still bound to the situational restrictions of contingencies, in such a way that they are not detachable from the temporal, spatial and apparent properties of the involved events. The individual is still interacting with events which are functionally independent of linguistic conventions. These act as *selector* factors over situational contingencies and behavior;

4) Conventional contingencies take over the regulation of interactions only when the individual is able to condition the behavior of other individuals to events in terms his or her linguistic interactions with both. The individual is not mediated by linguistic conventions but *mediates* through linguistic conventions the behavior of others in regard to behavioral and physical events. These other individuals have introduced new contingencies into the situation based on the conventional properties of the action as response and as stimuli that substitute for those prevailing in terms of the physico-chemical properties of events framed by in current situational conditions. In order to introduce or transform new contingencies into a situation which does not depend on current physico-chemical dimensions, the individual must respond to and generate stimuli which are detached from such dimensions. The new functional contingencies thus introduced are identifiable in physico-chemical terms, but are functional only to the extent that an individual responds to them in different temporal, spatial and perceptual dimensions.

This is only possible because conventional behavior (both by the referor and the referee)[9] does not sustain any necessary biological relation with contingencies framing the substitutional interaction. Talking about past events, describing abstracted properties of things, or reacting to events taking place in a different situation, are examples of new contingencies mediated by the conventional responding of an individual as the stimulus condition under which another individual responds to the mediated events. This stage may be described in terms of the process of *referential substitution.*

5) When the individuals are able to produce and respond to conventional stimuli with conventional behavior, contingencies no longer affect the interaction of another individual with substituted events. Contingencies as interdependent relations among events and behavior become restricted to conventional relations between conventional events. In this stage, conventional behaviors become the relevant stimuli, consisting of the contingencies in the functional and structural relationships among them.

To the extent that mediation takes place within conventional actions and their products, this stage may be characterized by a process of *non-referential substitution.* Examples of this level of interaction are conceptual problem solving, musical and literary composition, mathematical and logic behavior, and similar linguistic interactions involving symbolic actions.

Language Development as an Interactional Process

Since the acquisition of conventional morphologies and functions may be characterized as a developmental process, it may be analyzed in terms of the continuous transition of behavioral competencies taking place in a social interactive situation. In early stages, this situation is normally centered in the mother-child relation, although in the natural conditions in which development takes place linguistic interactions build up as complex relations including more than two individuals.

The interactive nature of language may only be dealt with through the analysis of at least diadic relations (Moerk, 1980). Nevertheless, in spite of the fact that language development must be conceived as a process dealing with necessary interactions between the individual and the significant members of the social environment, most approaches have focused on development as a one-sided process looking only for changes in the vocal behavior of the speaker. Taking language as an interactive process which develops in time according to progressively more complex social standards, requires of a methodology stressing longitudinal changes in both basic elements of the diadic unit. Hence, the analysis of language acquisition and development has to be dealt with in terms of reciprocal changes in mother and child behaviors in initial stages, and with structured exchanges with significant social individuals. The use of a longitudinal approach to language acquisition and development does not exclude experimental or comparative strategies. In fact, they become necessary to the extent that controlled replication of longitudinal observations are essential for an empirical validation of developmental concepts.

Because of this, the analysis of language development must be based on three methodological strategies, which may be combined in order to provide for stronger empirical foundations upon which to construct a theory of language as behavior:

a) Longitudinal studies looking at changes in the classes of interactions between the mother and the child in initial stages, as well as other diadic relations along the course of development, with an analysis of quantitative and qualitative changes in the separate behaviors of the child and the other person comprising such interactions;

b) Experimental studies synthesizing classes of interactions and competencies through the manipulation of situational and reactional variables; and

c) Comparative studies looking for similarities and differences in developmental stages between diads according to processes being identified both in longitudinal and experimental studies.

This multiple strategy assures the need for a common conceptual frame describing language processes as situational interactions and as developmental transitions. Observational categories, therefore, although descriptive of reactional dimensions of behavior, must be relevant to interactional processes taking place between the child, significant others and environment events. Being so, they may allow for reconstructing such processes under experimentally contrived conditions, both as terminal or as transitional stages. Additionally, they may provide for the necessary cues to select or sample stages in development in order to carry over to comparative observations among individuals with different developmental histories or individuals under different contextual variables.[10]

Concluding Remarks

I have pointed to the distinction between morphological and functional linguistic behaviors. Although both share their conventional character, the later consist in contingency substitutional behavior.

Contingency substitutional behavior always involves conventional responses, but under a form of interaction in which the speaker (or reader, or gesturer, or writer) introduces functional dimensions not present in the situation, which change the way a second individual (or the speaker himself under special conditions) interacts with the speaker and the events which the speaker is mediating through his conventional response. Both the behaviors of the listener and the speaker are linguistic since both participate in a contingency which substitutes those prevailing as a function of the physico-chemical conditions of situational events.

Substitutional contingencies operate only when the behavior of individuals becomes functionally detached from present physico-chemical based contingencies. Examples of linguistic behavior under substitutional contingencies are those describing how the speaker sets up differential reactions of a listener to events not present or not apparent according to what he says about them or about his behavior with respect to them. Rumor, prejudice, persuasion, planning, and similar social phenomena illustrate the effect of substitutional contingencies. Although issues related to communication and thinking are central to contingency substitutional behavior, there may also be similar phenomena including prelinguistic and paralinguistic communication and thinking (Epstein, Lanza and Skinner, 1980) which are non-substitutional. The arbitrary character of behavior, or its occurrence as an interactive episode between two organisms, does not seem to be a sufficient condition in order to consider it as linguistic behavior. Its function in substitution for contingencies seems to fulfill such a criterion.

References

Bijou, S. W. and Baer, D. M. (1961). *Child development,* Vol. I. N.Y.: Appleton Century Crofts.

Bijou, S. W. (1976). *Child development: The basic stage of early childhood.* N.Y.: Appleton Century Crofts.

Kantor, J. R. (1924-1926). *Principles of psychology.* Vol 1 and 2. N.Y.: Alfred Knopf.

Kantor, J. R. (1936). *An objective psychology of grammar.* Bloomington: Indiana University Publications.

Kantor, J. R. (1977). *Psychological linguistics.* Chicago: Principia Press.

Moerk, E. L. (1980). Relationships between parental input frequencies and children's language acquisition: a reanalysis of Brown's data. *Journal of Child Language, 7,* 105-118.

Piaget, J. (1947). *La psicologia de la inteligencia.* Buenos Aires: Psique.

Piaget, J. and Inhelder, B. (1978). *Psicología del ni¨o.* Madrid: Morata.

Ribes, E. (1982). *El conductismo: Reflexiones críticas.* Barcelona: Fontanella.

Ribes, E. (1985). Human behavior as operant behavior: An empirical or conceptual issue? In C. F. Lowe, M. Richelle, D. Blackman and C. Bradshaw (Eds.), *Behaviour analysis and contemporary psychology* (pp. 117-133). Hillsdale: Erlbaum.

Ribes, E. (1986). Language as behavior: Functional mediation vs. morphological description. In H. W. Reese and L. J. Parrott (Eds.), *Behavior science: Philosophical, methodological and empirical advances.* Hillsdale: Erlbaum.

Ribes, E. and López, F. (1985). *Teoría de la conducta; un análisis de campo y paramétrico.* México: Trillas.

Ryle, G. (1949). *The concept of mind.* London: Hutchinson.

Sidman, M. and Tailby, W. (1982). Conditional discrimination vs. matching-to-sample: An expansion of the testing paradigm. *Journal of the Experimental Analysis of Behavior, 37,* 5-22.

Sloane, H. and MacAuley, B. (1968). *Operant procedures in language training and remedial speech.* Boston: Houghton and Mifflin.

Skinner, B.F. (1957). *Verbal behavior.* N.Y.: Appleton-Century-Crofts.

Staats, A. and Staats, C. (1964). *Complex human behavior.* N.Y.: Holt, Rinehart and Winston.

Wittgenstein, L. (1953). *Philosophical investigations.* Oxford: Basil Blackwell.

Footnotes

1. The limitations of conditioning as a paradigm and its influence in Skinner's *Verbal Behavior* has been previously examined in Ribes (1982), Ribes (1985), and Ribes and Lopez (1985).
2. This argument is close to Wittgenstein's (1953) conception of language as a game.

3. I prefer to use Kantor's (1924-1926) term instead of that of response class, which has some conceptual weakness intrinsic to assumptions based on the reflex paradigm.

4. The taxonomy of verbal behavior proposed by Skinner (1957) is exemplary of the case of linguistic morphology that enters into functional relations identical to those involving non-conventional responses, eg., the discriminated and the non-discriminated operant.

5. When logically extended, Skinner's definition of verbal behavior (1957, pp. 224-225) considers the behavior of any experimental animal as a special case of manding or tacting (p. 108).

6. This process is similar to Piaget's (1947) concept of *decalage*.

7. These differentiated modes have been described as developmental *momentos* in Ribes (1986) and in Ribes and López (1985).

8. These terms are used only as examples because of their standard use in the field.

9. I prefer to use Kantor's (1977) conception of a bi-stimulational relation among referent, referor and referee, than the more restricted and ambiguous description in terms of a speaker and a listener.

10. The analysis of diadic linguistic relations have always a double interpretation. Since the goal is to identify the mediating role of one of the individuals, any episode may be analyzed from the perspective of both of the individuals in order to identify the mediating role performed by each of them in the contingency relations involved in the linguistic interaction. Therefore, the categories based on the kind of functional aptitudes previously described do not apply to the episode as such, but rather to the mediating role of each of the individuals interacting in the episode. Hence, each episode always will describe, at least, two kinds of contingency mediation, one corresponding to each of the participants.

A Discussion of Chapter 3

Problems of Drawing Distinctions Along Continua

Linda J. Hayes
University of Nevada, Reno
Simon M. H. Starbuck
Saint Mary's University

Ribes argues that when conventional behavior alters the natural contingencies operating in a situation, such that the interactions of persons with objects and other persons in that situation are regulated by the substituted contingencies, the behavior of the persons involved may be considered linguistic. While this statement may seem simple enough, it contains several technical terms, implies still others, and is the product of a complicated logic. The argument is worthy of the effort required for its understanding, though, and we will try to clarify certain features of the argument in this discussion. In the course of doing so, we will offer some suggestions for its further development.

Conventionality and Linguistic Acts

Let us look first at the issue of conventionality of action. Conventionality means that the morphological and functional properties of action do not depend on the biological conditions of responding organisms nor on the physico-chemical properties of stimulating things and events. Their formal and functional properties are, rather, matters of convention or social agreement. According to Ribes, linguistic acts on the parts of both speakers and listeners are conventional in character.

Conventionality does not imply that linguistic acts always have verbal morphologies nor that verbal morphologies always imply linguistic acts, though. According to Ribes, a linguistic act cannot be identified by its formal properties. A linguistic act can be identified only by the role it plays in an interactive episode; namely, by its substitution of contingencies.

But we are getting ahead of ourselves with the mention of contingency substitution and would do better to clarify certain other aspects of the present analysis before dealing with this issue. Specifically, what does it mean to say that a linguistic act has a conventional but not necessarily a verbal morphology? What does "verbal" mean in this context?

Presumably verbal forms are those making up the vocabulary of a given language community -- the forms we call "words." This being so, conventional gestures such as pointing or shaking the head fall into Ribes' linguistic category despite their nonverbal morphologies. This analysis indicates a primacy of function over form in defining operations, and is compatible with other functional perspectives on language, including that of B. F. Skinner.

Ribes' analysis departs from Skinner's in the opposite case, however, where acts may be denied linguistic status **despite** their verbal morphologies. From Skinner's perspective, verbal forms occurring as conditioned operants, irrespective of other defining criteria, are always regarded as instances of verbal behavior. Only in highly contrived circumstances (and possibly in the case of forms occurring in the early stages of language acquisition) would a verbal form produced by a human being not constitute a linguistic act from Skinner's perspective. For example, on an isolated occasion, a human might cry out in response to painful stimulation, the form of the response accidentally resembling a word. Skinner would not regard this response as verbal despite its verbal form because it is occurring as an unconditioned respondent. It is not just this sort of unlikely occurrence that Ribes is excluding from the linguistic domain. Many of Skinner's verbal operants, including the mand and the tact, fail to satisfy Ribes' more demanding functional criterion.

In summary, then, from Ribes' perspective a linguistic act cannot be identified on the basis of its morphology. Linguistic acts can be identified only on functional criteria: **Any** act, regardless of its morphology, may be a linguistic act provided that it operates in a particular way in an interactive episode. We should say, any **conventional** act, as it is only conventional acts that can so operate. The special operation of linguistic acts is made possible by what Ribes calls "functional detachment", a concept derived from Kantor's (1924) interpretation of implicit fields.

Functional Detachment

A stimulus function is the way a stimulus object acts; it is the stimulating of an object with respect to responding. Functional detachment, as the name implies, is the detaching of the way a thing acts from the thing; the detaching of the stimulating from the object. Stimulating is not "set free" by the process of detachment, however. Detachment of function always implies a complimentary process of attachment. In short, stimulating retains a relation to a source object under conditions of functional detachment; it is just a different source. Further, because stimulating and responding are aspects of the same event from Ribes' perspective, functional detachment may be described by reference to the response as well as the stimulus phase of this event. As such, functional detachment may be described as responding originally acquired with respect to one source of stimulation now occurring with respect to another source.

Conventionality and Ineffectuality

Ribes argues that functional detachment occurs readily when action has two properties: conventionality and ineffectuality. For example, consider the vocal response "chair," originally occurring with respect to the object chair. The form of this response, being independent of the physico-chemical properties of the object, is conventional. In addition, the execution of this response produces no change in the original source of stimulation for this act; that is, the chair is not effected in any way by the vocal response "chair." Consequently one may emit this response in the absence of the original source object -- one may **say** chair in the absence of a chair.

On the contrary, one cannot **sit** on a chair in the absence of a chair. The latter act is nonconventional. Its form is **not** arbitrary. It is dependent on the physico-chemical properties of the source object. Sitting, further, is an **effectual** act, producing a change in the source object. Consequently the act of sitting on a chair, in depending on the source object for its form, and in having the character of effecting a change in that source, cannot occur in the absence of a chair. To put it another way, nonconventional, effectual acts do not participate in situations involving functional detachment -- or so it would seem.

The significance of functional detachment is described by Ribes in a list of seven response possibilities enabled by this process. This list raises a number of questions. First, three of these possibilities (i.e., several responses performed to the same object; the same response performed to different objects; and no response performed to the physico-chemical properties of present objects) are said to pertain as well to nonconventional as to conventional acts, making it clear that functional detachment is not restricted to conventional responses. Further, since Ribes makes no claim to the contrary, we may assume that functional detachment is also not restricted to ineffectual responses. Both conventionality and ineffectuality, it would seem, are merely facilitating conditions.

This analysis is problematic in that it is not obvious how functional detachment involving a nonconventional, effectual response can occur. By definition, the form of such a response depends on the physico-chemical properties of the original source object and its execution produces a change in that object. It would seem that at least one of these response properties -- conventionality or ineffectuality -- must be present for functional detachment to take place.

The problem here seems to be the inclusion of several responses performed to the same object and the same response performed to different objects among the response possibilities enabled by functional detachment. If we assume that a given object has multiple properties, it is not clear how functional detachment is involved in these cases. For example, several different responses could be performed with respect to different physico-chemical properties of the same object. Likewise, the same response could be performed with respect to shared physico-chemical properties in otherwise different objects.

Ribes has characterized these events as products of functional detachment, however; and this implies morphologies not determined by the physico-chemical properties of objects -- that is, conventional acts. Alternatively, it implies morphologies determined by physico-chemical properties (nonconventional acts) but not dependent on them for their subsequent occurrences, namely, ineffectual acts. As examples of the latter, we may include affective acts and other sorts of activities involving the autonomic nervous system, among others. The problem with this suggestion is that it offers no means by which to distinguish the operations of conventional, ineffectual acts from acts not sharing these properties.

A second issue raised by Ribes' list of response possibilities produced by the process of functional detachment, already eluded to, is the implication that mutually exclusive or at least usefully distinguished categories of possibilities are contained in the list. This does not seem to be the case, however. For example, the possibility of responses being performed to objects not present makes up two separate categories differing only in whether the object is absent by virtue of space or time, the problem being that these two parameters amount to the same thing.

Moreover, these two categories may also overlap with that in which responding is performed to objects differing in physico-chemical properties, since this is implied in all cases of functional detachment and may be just another way of saying that the original source objects are absent by virtue of space-time. In this case, a response possibility common to both conventional and nonconventional responses overlaps with two possibilities assumed to prevail only in the case of conventional acts.

This kind and degree of overlap draws into question the utility of Ribes' list. Bear in mind that Ribes' ultimate goal is to identity linguistic events in terms of their operations in interactive episodes, and the discussion of functional detachment was introduced as a means of achieving this goal. Given this motivation, it would have been useful to devise categories of response possibilities pertaining either to conventional or to nonconventional acts, but not to both. In not making this distinction, it is unclear as to how Ribes' categories may be used to facilitate the identification of that which is distinctly linguistic in nature.

An attempt is made to distinguish linguistic from nonlinguistic acts in accordance with this list of response possibilities nonetheless. Linguistic acts are said to involve not mere substitution of functions, as is enabled by generic cases of functional detachment, but substitution of contingencies, to which we may now turn.

Contingency Substitution

To begin, it is important to point out that Ribes' use of the term contingency is at odds with that implied by "operant contingency." It has nothing to do with operant behavior, nothing to do with the reinforcement. It has to do with "if-then" relations of a more general sort involving the actions of both speaker and listener. Roughly speaking, a contingency involves a state of affairs -- the "if" condition -- and actions with respect to that state of affairs -- the "then" condition. Contingency **substitution** involves the substitution of a new state of affairs for that present in the situation by way of a speaker's linguistic act; and a listener's action with respect to the new state of affairs. The listener's action is also regarded as linguistic in such cases. Further, the acts of both speaker and listener involved in contingency substitutional situations are said to be conventional in kind and to depend on the process of functional detachment.

Referential Substitution

Two types of contingency substitution are identified: referential and nonreferential. In the former case, the new state of affairs -- the "if" condition -- pertains to a particular event but detached from the temporal, spatial or apparent properties of this event since it is not actually present; and the listener's action occurs with respect to these properties. The listener's action in such cases may be conventional, but is more likely to be nonconventional -- as when a listener sees a rose upon its mere mention. In more familiar terms, referential substitution from the speaker's perspective amounts to talking about things in their absence; from the listener's, responding to such things.

This analysis is somewhat disturbing in that it appears to restrict linguistic events of the referential sort to actions occurring with respect to **absent** events exclusively. For example, Ribes criticizes Skinner's mand and tact categories as situationally-bound interactions. This argument implies that speaking about something immediately present, along with a listener's actions with respect to that thing, are not properly considered linguistic acts.The utility of this analysis and the difficulty of its unambiguous application, draw it into question.

Nonreferential Substitution

Nonreferential substitution involves the introduction of an "if" condition by way of the products of conventional responding, and it is with respect to these products that the listener responds. In this case, the listener is not being referred to some thing in its absence. Rather, the listener is acting with respect to conventional stimuli in conventional ways. Reading, where conventional auditory responses are made to conventional, response-produced visual symbols, may serve as an example of nonreferential substitution.

It appears to be Ribes' intention to stress **relations** among events as the defining characteristic of contingency substitution: contingency substitution, which is to say, a linguistic event, involves an alteration of a relation among events. Alternatively, simple substitution of function, common to nonlinguistic events, is nonrelational. It is not obvious what sorts of relations Ribes is referring to, however, which makes it difficult to distinguish linguistic events from nonlinguistic events. This is, of course, a problem, as the concept of contingency substitution was introduced as a means of identifying linguistic events.

Conclusion

In summary, while Ribes' analysis overcomes many of the problems of Skinner's, namely the merely nominal functionalism of the latter, it lacks clarity on a number of critical issues. More specifically, the possibility of substitution appears to depend on the process of functional detachment. Contingency substitution, while not identical with simple substitution, may be assumed to come about by the same means. Functional detachment, in turn, would appear to require conventionality of response form and ineffectuality of function. Given these provisions, a definition of linguistic events could be constructed by reference to specific (i.e., relational) operations of detached functions.

Unfortunately, this is not how Ribes proceeds. In the first place, functional detachment is not restricted to responses showing conventionality of form and ineffectuality of function. Consequently, the conditions allowing for the process of functional detachment to take place remain unspecified, rendering the process itself somewhat unclear. At first glance, the list of response possibilities enabled by this process looks like a means of clarifying the difference between cases of functional detachment dependent upon conventionality and ineffectuality and those not so dependent. These possibilities do not represent mutually exclusive categories, though.

In the end, the distinction between linguistic and nonlinguistic events amounts to a distinction between substitution and contingency substitution, about which we know only that the later is relational, the former nonrelational.The implication of relation in this context does seem to be important (see S. C. Hayes, this volume; Hayes & Hayes, 1989); however, without further elaboration as to the nature of the relation involved, it does not suffice as a criterion by which to distinguish that which is linguistic from that which is not.

In short, Ribes touches on a number of important issues in the identification of linguistic events and grappling with these issues may eventuate in a workable definition of such events. But we are not there yet.

References

Hayes, S. C. & Hayes, L. J. (1989). The verbal action of the listener as a basis for rule governance. In S. C. Hayes (Ed.), *Rule-governed behavior: Cognition, contingencies, and instructional control* (pp. 153-190). New York: Plenum.

Kantor, J. R. (1924). *Principles of psychology.* Chicago: The Principia Press.

Part 2

Empirical Methods

An Analysis of Self-Editing:
Method and Preliminary Findings

Cloyd Hyten and Philip N. Chase

University of North Texas and West Virginia University

Our paper is about an experimental analysis of the verbal behavior called self-editing. Self-editing is the process of modifying one's own verbal responses, or the products thereof, to make them more appropriate to the social context or more effective in controlling the behavior of the listening audience. Self-editing is characteristic of all normal adult speech and writing to some degree. It is an essential professional skill for writers, and a desirable social skill for all who engage in the fine art of conversation. As such, it is an aspect of the production of speech and writing that deserves analysis.

Unfortunately, the topic has not received much attention in the laboratory. We could find no adequate experimental paradigms that permit observation and recording of the editing responses. Therefore, we have spent the last several years developing such a methodology. The conceptual analysis of self-editing that forms the framework for this research was stimulated by Skinner's extensive discussion of the topic in *Verbal Behavior* (1957). We have finished the first year of data collection and it would be premature to pass final judgment on the adequacy of Skinner's conceptual analysis or to propose a new one. We have produced, however, a promising method for the experimental analysis of self-editing, some interesting data, and some speculations about the variables that influence this behavior. The purpose of this paper is to describe our exploratory analysis in sufficient detail to stimulate discussion of self-editing and suggestions for future research. We will begin by explaining Skinner's conceptual analysis of self-editing, and then we will describe the methodology and discuss the data it has produced so far.

Skinner's Conceptual Analysis of Self-Editing

Skinner's (1957) analysis of self-editing is the only extensive behavioral treatment of this phenomenon to our knowledge. In *Verbal Behavior*, Skinner devoted two chapters to self-editing, which he defined as the speaker's examination and alteration of already-produced verbal behavior (p. 369). For editing to occur, the speaker must produce some verbal response, and then react to it in much the same way as a listener would. In this capacity, the speaker may then reject or modify the verbal response before allowing another person who is serving as the listener to respond to it. Thus, the self-editing sequence consists of the production of a verbal response, a review, rejection and/or modification of the verbal response, and "release" of the edited form to the listener.

Self-editing may take many forms, depending on the form of the verbal response itself. For example, editing a written response may consist of re-reading what has been written, and crossing it out or adding qualifying remarks. The behavior can not be consequated until it makes contact with the listener, and this is usually delayed quite a bit in written response interactions. The written responses and the edit responses in this example are overt or have overt records.

However, not all editing takes place at the overt level. In the course of speaking or writing there may be covert as well as overt verbal behavior produced. This covert behavior often serves as the "raw" verbal behavior which is edited and subsequently released overtly to the listener. For instance, a participant in an unpleasant conversation may covertly compose a rude reply as the first speaker completes a sentence, and then reject it in favor of a more polite remark before it is spoken. In Skinner's analysis, verbal behavior is operant behavior; it is maintained by reinforcement of one kind or another, usually provided by a listener. However, listeners do not always reinforce what is said; in fact many verbal responses are punished in some form by listeners for various reasons (as when we detect lying). Punishment has many effects on verbal behavior. According to Azrin and Holz (1966), a punishment procedure is defined by its suppressive effects on the rate of the operant response. Thus, in a punishing speaker-listener relation, we may expect that the rate of the speaker's punished verbal responses will decrease. Skinner (1957, p. 371) points out that punishment is also likely to generate or strengthen "incompatible" forms of behavior, that is, responses that are unlikely to be punished. These forms take on the characteristics of escape or avoidance behavior because they are maintained by reductions in aversive stimulation. In Skinner's view, then, punishment by the listener is likely to suppress some speaker responses while facilitating others.

One form of escape or avoidance behavior in verbal interactions is covert emission. If overt vocal responses are released to a listener and punished, the speaker may emit them subvocally or in a form not accessible to the listener and avoid punishment. This assumes that the motivating conditions for the behavior to be emitted are fairly strong also; were they not, verbal behavior would cease entirely or the speaker would simply stop interacting with the punishing listener. But, there is a Catch-22 here. While the speaker may successfully avoid punishers by behaving covertly, he or she will never be able to contact any reinforcers available from the listener as long as he or she emits only covert responses. Any additional behavior that alters the form of the response from a punished form to a reinforceable form will itself be indirectly reinforced by the reduction in punishment or subsequent increase in reinforcement when the altered form is released to the listener.

According to Skinner, these editing responses are more directly reinforced by the decrease in conditioned aversive stimulation generated by response forms which have been punished by a listener. The verbal responses or the private conditions which surround their emission acquire punishing properties via their pairing with listener punishment in the same way that a neutral CS becomes a CS- in a conditioned suppression procedure (cf. Estes and Skinner, 1941; Hake and Azrin, 1965). Successful editing eliminates these punishers. Thus, self-editing behavior can be acquired as a function of listener punishment, and maintained by reductions in punishment or additional reinforcement when edited responses are produced and released.

In sum, the critical elements of Skinner's analysis of self-editing are that under conditions of listener punishment, the verbal behavior of the speaker is particularly likely to recede to the covert level, and self-editing is likely to develop. To date, these elements have not been examined empirically in any adequate form. The single largest obstacle to the study of self-editing is the inaccessibility of this behavior. Self-editing can never be analyzed experimentally unless it, or some part of it, can be made observable. In order to carry out a strategy of making covert behavior accessible to measurement, we need to re-examine what is meant by "covert."

The term "covert" has several meanings in the analysis of verbal behavior. Most often when we analyze covert behavior we are dealing with acts of thinking or feeling. This behavior is considered covert because its form makes it inaccessible to all other observers. However, the critical feature of covert behavior is not that it is internal and unobservable; it is that it is immune from contact with others. In a given speaker-listener interaction, a response may be considered covert if it is not available to the listener. Covert, in this sense, means hidden from a particular listener, not hidden from all other observers. Thus, covert behavior in a speaker-listener relation may be of a form that is normally considered overt behavior. For instance, when the release of intimate details of one's life is likely to be punished by listeners, the speaker may write them instead in a diary. Writing words on paper is usually an overt activity, but writing them in a secret diary makes the behavior and its products functionally covert. The term "covert", then, can refer to both subvocal private events (e.g., thinking) as well as events of overt form which are functionally covert with respect to a particular listener or group of listeners.

Our strategy in analyzing self-editing was to study a functionally covert form of that activity. We arranged an experimental environment for the subject that encouraged composition and editing in a form that could be surreptitiously observed and recorded. The goal was to make as much of the behavior observable as possible while insuring that the behavior retained any characteristics imparted to it by a covert status. Although this functionally covert behavior was not identical in form to subvocal covert behavior, it was assumed to be analogous in terms of its controlling variables and the functions it served for the speaker.

The Experimental Method

We faced several problems in developing a methodology to study self-editing. We had to design an experimental social interaction between a speaker (the subject) and a consequating listener (the experimenter) that would allow both parties to communicate as in a conversation. A vocal format was ruled out because the speaker's self-editing would remain inaccessible to observation. Having subjects interact with the experimenter via written responses could provide the necessary records of self-editing as long as there was some way to detect erased or rejected text. The speed of a written interaction would have to be increased so that the experimenter could comment on the subject's writing and observe the effects on the subject's production and editing.

The solution was to design a procedure in which subject and experimenter interacted via computers. Communicating via computers retains characteristics of both talking and writing. It is like talking in that two people can instantly transmit their comments to each other. Like writing, composing text on a computer produces a visual and semi-permanent product that can be reviewed by the speaker. These products can be automatically recorded by the computer so that all aspects of on-screen production and editing are directly accessible to the experimenter. Using interactive microcomputers, we created an experimental interaction in which the subject repeatedly produced and released text to the experimenter who reinforced or punished the releases. The apparatus and procedure are described more fully below.

The subject's computer was connected to the experimenter's computer located out of auditory and visual range in an adjacent room. The monitor screen of the subject's computer was partitioned into three sectors (see Figure 1). The upper one-third of the screen was called the Experimenter Response Zone (ERZ), and was reserved for questions and comments from the experimenter to the subject. A narrow Boundary Line, highlighted in inverse video, separated the Experimenter Response Zone from the Subject Response Zone directly beneath it. The Subject Response Zone (SRZ) occupied approximately one-third of the screen, and it displayed any text the subject produced on the keyboard. All of the alphanumeric characters on the keyboard were available for display in this sector. The bottom one-third of the screen was highlighted in inverse video and contained the Point Counter Box, which displayed the cumulative number of points the subject had earned.

Two types of editing were available to the subject: backspacing and rejection. Backspace editing was accomplished by moving the cursor backwards within the line to the desired location and entering new text. Characters were deleted as the backspace cursor passed over them. In a world of sophisticated word processing software, this is a crude form of text editing. Equipment constraints did not allow us to program a text editor that permitted the cursor to move freely around the screen without deleting characters. Subjects could also edit by clearing the SRZ completely with one keystroke and starting over. This was called a "rejection".

All text that the subject produced was simultaneously displayed on the experimenter's monitor. In addition, a printer located in the experimenter's room produced a hardcopy transcript of the subject's production and editing responses as they occurred, and printed out trial and session summary data recorded by the subject's computer. Subjects were unaware that their behavior of composing and editing in the SRZ was being observed and recorded. As part of the instructions, subjects were told that the experimenter had to wait for the subject to release his/her answer by pressing a key marked "send" before he could read it. This deception was essential in order to establish the SRZ as being a functionally covert environment. From the subject's point of view, production and editing were covert, yet we were able to record all of their on-screen activity.

The Experimental Procedure

The principal question we addressed in this research was whether we could reliably affect self-editing through manipulation of listener consequences. Thus, we established an experimenter-subject interaction that stressed the role of the experimenter as a listener, and manipulated whether experimenter comments approved or disapproved what the subject wrote. The form of the experimenter-subject interaction was a teacher- student scenario in which the experimenter asked the subject a question, the subject composed and transmitted an answer, and the experimenter delivered a consequence indicating that the answer was either correct or incorrect. The consequences, however, were delivered independent of answer content. The

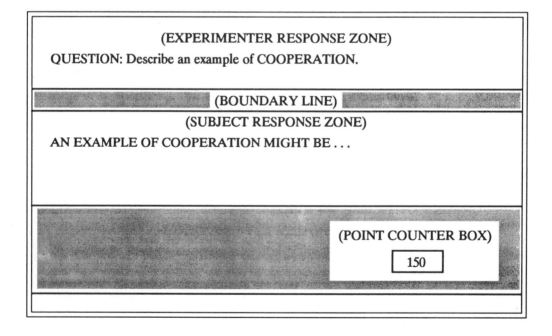

Figure 1. Subject's monitor display

distribution of answers deemed correct and incorrect by the experimenter was determined by the experimental phase. Although subjects were given deceptive instructions telling them that the experimenter had criteria by which to judge their answers, it was easier to control their exposure to the consequences by delivering them independent of content than to construct and apply such criteria. We counted on the deceptive instructions to keep subjects from detecting the arbitrary nature of the consequences.

Subjects completed eight trials per session. At the start of a trial, the experimenter transmitted a question to the ERZ on the subject's monitor asking the subject to define or exemplify a common, but often vaguely-defined concept (e.g., truth, beauty, character). The use of vague concepts was designed to afford the experimenter the freedom to consequate the subject's answer according to the experimental phase without appearing arbitrary to the subject. It would be easier for the subject to believe that a given answer was justifiably consequated because there are so many ways to define and exemplify such concepts. The subject answered by producing and editing text in the SRZ, and releasing the text to the experimenter. The experimenter terminated a trial by consequating the subject's release according to the experimental condition.

Two experimental conditions were manipulated in the study. During the first phase (Releases Approved), the subject was exposed to a baseline condition in which positive comments (e.g., "That's correct.", "Yes, that's acceptable.") and incrementing point values (+50 points) were transmitted to the subject's computer according to a schedule that randomly selected 5 out of the 8 trials per session, on the average, to be reinforcement trials. The remaining three trials terminated with the experimenter sending a neutral comment ("OK") which neither incremented nor decremented the point total. The purpose of this baseline phase was to provide a non-punishing environment for the subject in which editing would not be necessary.

The second phase of the experiment (Releases Disapproved) involved replacing the neutral consequences and some of the approval consequences with putatively punishing consequences. The punishing consequence consisted of a negative comment (e.g., "That's not a good definition.") followed by a decrement in the point total. Two subjects lost points in 150-point decrements, and three subjects lost points in 50-point decrements. Some subjects received disapproving consequences on 3/8 trials (on the average), while others received higher densities of disapproval. A third phase comprised a return to the Releases Approved condition. Points were equivalent to cents, and the subjects were paid for the cumulative number of points they had earned at the end of the experiment. They also earned $1.00 for each session attended.

The decision to consequate the subject's release as a unit within a discrete trials format was intended to address one of the major problems confronting verbal behavior research: the question of how to designate functional units of a speaker's verbal behavior. Units should not be defined solely in terms of structural properties such as words and sentences, but rather on the functional relation between a response of some form and its controlling variables (Skinner, 1957, p.20). In this procedure, consequences were contingent upon releases without any restrictions on the size or style of the released text; releases containing a few words as well as those that filled up the SRZ were treated as complete answers. The subject chose when to release the answer to the experimenter. The use of the "send" key to release the answer functioned as an electronic analog to a "turn-taking" utterance in a conversation, as when a speaker elicits listener comment by saying, "Do you know what I mean?" The form of the response was determined by the subject and his or her interaction with the contingencies, not imposed by the experimenter on structural grounds. Thus, answer size and style remained dependent variables.

Preliminary Findings

Seven measures of production, editing, and pausing were recorded in order to analyze the effects of listener approval and disapproval on the subjects' behavior. Production was measured in terms of the volume and rate of character production. Editing was measured by counts of the number of characters deleted by backspacing and screen rejections. Three categories were used to record pausing before, during, and after composition of the answer.

Self-editing decreased across the baseline Releases Approved phase (RA) for most of the subjects. Exposure to the Releases Disapproved phase (RD) elevated editing somewhat over that obtained in the RA phases for 3 of the subjects; the other two subjects showed no substantial change in the level of editing. Most of the subjects showed a decrease in the production rate at some point during the RD phase. Production rate measured how fast characters were produced while the subject was composing the answer prior to its release. An unexpected finding was that the volume of text released increased in the RD phase. That is, most subjects wrote more during the first few sessions of exposure to the disapproval consequences. Exposure to the second RA condition (RA2) led to a decrease in editing for most subjects, although it was common for high levels of editing to reappear for one or two sessions.

Some illustrative data will show how individual subjects reacted to the experimental conditions. Subjects 8 and 9 received disapproval consequences with a 150-point decrement on an average of three out of eight trials per session during RD. Figure 2 shows the number of characters released for Subject 8. Her on-screen editing showed little change in level, yet she wrote longer answers during the RD phase. This increase in production volume should not be confused with production rate, which decreased in RD relative to baseline and the last RA phase.

Figure 3 shows Subject 9's decreasing level of self-editing during baseline, a trend of increasing editing during RD, and a return to low levels in RA2. The "edit/release ratio" shown in the graph is the ratio of edited characters (backspaces and number of characters rejected) to the number of characters released. This proportional measure was used instead of raw counts of edited characters because the total number of edited characters could fluctuate with changing volumes of text. If a constant proportion of characters were edited (as might be expected if the subject were simply correcting typographical errors or making minor grammatical adjustments), a count of edited characters would increase when the subject wrote longer answers and decrease with shorter answers. A measure of editing relative to production volume ensured that observed changes in editing represented meaningful deviations from the constant proportion of minor "error correcting" editing. Subject 9 wrote longer answers in RD, so the increase in relative editing shown in Figure 3 resulted from the deletion of a greater proportion of produced text in that phase.

The effect shown in Figure 3 is not robust, yet it is consistent across every kind of data we recorded. Table 1 presents the means of the last few sessions in each phase of a number of measures of production, editing, and pausing. The subject released much more text during RD than in either RA condition. Despite the fact that the subject produced more text per release, production rate (characters produced / trial duration; row 2) decreased in the second phase. It appears that the lower production rate was due to longer pauses, not to a general decrease in typing rates. Latencies to respond to the prompt changed little across phases. However, there was a substantial increase in post-production pausing during the second phase (row 3 in Table 1). A post-production pause was the interval between the last keystroke and the release of the answer to the experimenter. The increase in pausing during the disapproval phase may have occurred for several reasons. The subject may have spent more time reviewing her answer, trying to see if there were any features likely to "cause" disapproval. She may also have been delaying the emission of a response (releasing the text) that had a relatively high probability of punishment in this phase.

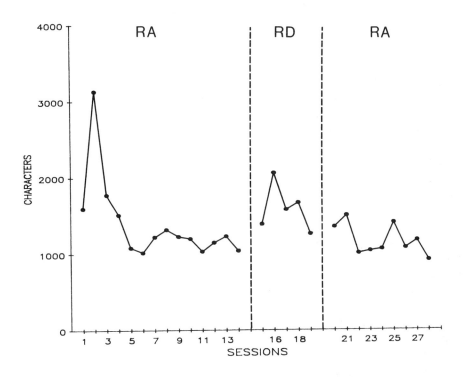

Figure 2. Volume of released text for Subject 8 across approval and disapproval phases.

Table 1 also reveals that increased rejecting (row 4) accounted for a large portion of the increased editing in the Releases Disapproved condition for Subject 9. This subject rejected (cleared her screen and re-composed her answer) ten times in the last four sessions of RD, compared to two rejections seen in the last four sessions of each of the RA phases. Rejections are quite dramatic forms of editing; the effort involved in re-composing the answer from scratch is substantial if several lines of text have already been produced. Subject 9's sessions stretched from 40 minutes in length to over an hour in the last few RD sessions when she was rejecting text frequently. Rejections were often easy to predict as we watched her compose an answer (remember that the experimenter's monitor echoed hers). When her answer seemed to be getting long and going nowhere she would pause for longer than usual, presumably re-reading the whole answer, before clearing her screen. Curiously, this subject often re-composed her long answer with only minor changes after rejection.

We were able to record interkeystroke intervals (IKIs) as a measure of the length of pauses while subjects composed their answers. Latencies to begin production and post-production pausing were excluded from IKI recording. Thus, IKIs measured "run pauses", i.e., those intervals between keystrokes that constituted pauses between letters, words, and sentences. Run pauses were important to measure because subjects may have been composing and editing

Table 1

Summary of Production and Editing Data of Subject 9

Phase:	RA	RD	RA
1. CHARACTERS RELEASED/SESSION: 4889		5502	4604
2. PRODUCTION RATE:	165 cpm[a]	152 cpm	166 cpm
3. POST-PRODUCTION PAUSE:	16.9 s	75.2 s	44.1 s
4. TOTAL REJECTS:	2(460 ch[b])	10(1120 ch)	2(118 ch)
5. INTERKEYSTROKE INTERVALS:			
a. Bin 1: 0.00-1.85 s	98.13%	98.09%	98.43%
b. Bin 2: 1.85-8.45 s	1.71%	1.64%	1.42%
c. Bin 3: > 8.45 s	.15%	.26%	.15%

[a] characters per minute
[b] characters

Note. Phase RA is Releases Approved condition; phase RD is Releases Disapproved condition. Rows 1-3 present means of the last 4 sessions in each phase. Post-Production Pause data are the means of the total post-production pause time per session. Row 4 (Total Rejects) shows the total number of rejects followed by the sum of the characters rejected for the last 4 sessions in each phase. Interkeystroke Interval data shown in rows 5a,b,c are the percentages of the total keystrokes that fell in each IKI bin. Percentages are based on bin counts summed across the last 6 sessions in each phase.

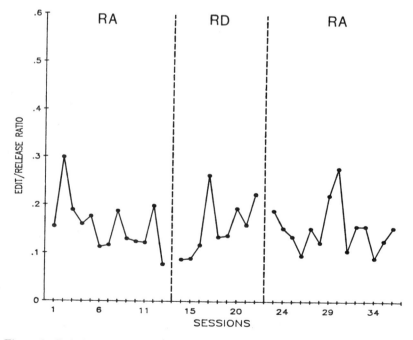

Figure 3. Relative editing of Subject 9 across approval and disapproval phases.

to themselves during these pauses before entering text on the keyboard. It is safe to say that subjects engaged in some form of covert activity during run pauses. The nature of such truly covert behavior remained unknown, but IKIs provided a rough indicator of fluctuations in the amount of this behavior. IKIs were recorded in much the same manner as IRTs are collected: pauses were timed and assigned to a bin in an array according to the duration of the pause.

IKI measures revealed that the number of long pauses during production runs increased in the second phase relative to baseline levels (see row 5c of Table 1). These data require some elaboration. The percent of responses that fell in each bin is shown rather than the number of keystrokes because the total number of keystrokes changed across the experimental phases. Across all three phases, over 98% of the keystrokes fell within 1.85 s of each other. Keystrokes with IKIs greater than several seconds were a small proportion of the total number of keystrokes per session, yet they reflect run pauses of significant length. The .26% shown in Bin 3 of the RD column represents 112 keystrokes separated by at least eight and one-half seconds, out of a total of over 42,000 keystrokes in the last six sessions of the phase. This percentage is a 73% increase over the percentage of long IKIs in the first RA phase. These data suggest that the subject spent more time thinking before entering text in the disapproval condition than in the approval conditions. Such results are consistent with Skinner's hypothesis that verbal behavior recedes to the covert level when exposed to listener punishment.

Subjects 10 and 12 showed a remarkably similar pattern of self-editing during RD, despite the fact that Subject 10 lost points on all eight trials and Subject 12 lost points on five out of eight trials per session during RD. Figures 4 and 5 show that both subjects' editing decreased during baseline, followed by a one-session increase in editing on the third session of RD. Production rates for these high-edit sessions were substantially below those obtained on other sessions. For Subject 12, increased editing was accompanied by a large increase in the volume of text produced. These effects vanished for the rest of the RD phase. Subject 10 was exposed to a second Disapproval phase at a lower density of disapproval. On-screen editing changed little, but production rates dropped and latencies to respond to the prompt increased relative to the previous RA phase. A third subject run under conditions similar to those experienced by Subject 12 showed unusual effects. During RD, her editing decreased slightly and her production rate increased.

In the next to last session of RD, we noticed that Subject 10 produced longer and what appeared to be better answers. The transcripts revealed a different style of answer than had been seen during previous RD sessions. Specifically, she wrote more integrative examples; she referred to an aspect of her definition of the concept from the previous trial in her example. This style change reappeared and persisited during the following RA condition. These were informal observations; we did not try to develop a coding scheme nor did we obtain measures of interobserver agreement. At this stage the experimenter was merely using his experience as a verbal organism to detect any differences in the structure of the subject's answers according to experimental condition. She also wrote multiple definitions of the concept on more of the definition trials in RA2 than she had during the RD phase. The volume of text produced during this RA phase was nearly double previous levels. It appeared that this style change was induced by the RD phase, but adventitiously reinforced by the second RA phase.

Sources of Variability

Although subjects showed changes in the various measures of production and editing behavior across the experimental conditions, these effects were sometimes weak and often transitory compared to the effects of consequence manipulations on other kinds of human and non-human behavior. This kind of behavior has not been analyzed experimentally before, so it

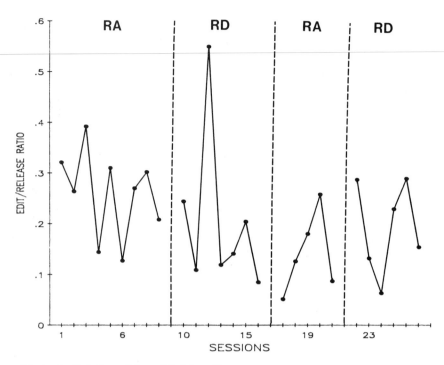

Figure 4. Relative editing of Subject 10 across approval and disapproval phases.

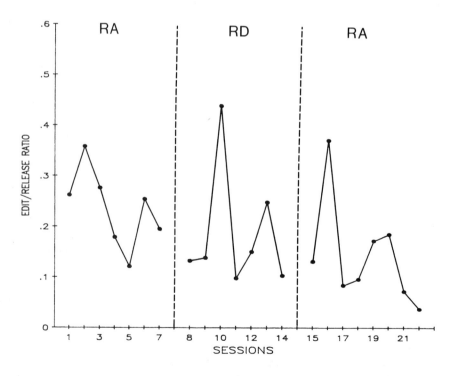

Figure 5. Relative editing of Subject 12 across approval and disapproval phases.

is difficult to tell what good data look like in this area. It may be that these data are the best records obtainable of this behavior. It is far too early in the development of this research, however, to conclude that self-editing is more elusive than other forms of verbal or nonverbal behavior. Therefore,we continue to operate under the assumption that we can obtain better control over the subject matter with procedural modifications. The focus of these modifications will be on: 1) reducing variability, and 2) enhancing the persistence of editing. Gaining experimental control over the subject matter necessarily requires further conceptual analysis and speculation about self-editing and its controlling variables.

There are several primary sources of variability that can affect self-editing. The subject's history of verbal interactions is a significant factor. The subject brings to the experiment various production and editing skills that have been shaped by previous vocal and written interchanges. These skills interact with the experimental contingencies, resulting in the particular pattern of responses emitted by each subject. For example, the fluency of the speaker (in terms of having several verbal subrepertoires) may influence how he or she reacts to a disapproving audience. It is possible that a highly fluent speaker might not edit at all, but will emit verbal responses from an alternative subrepertoire. An experienced teacher, for example, might be able to alternate readily between an advanced subrepertoire of descriptions of a topic for sophisticated students and a lower level subrepertoire for students who have difficulty understanding the topic. The speaker who has limited experience with multiple subrepertoires may edit the most because of the difficulty in generating alternative responses. The speaker who has no other subrepertoires available may simply emit more of the same responses.

These skills are the products of histories that are complex and idiosyncratic. As an experimenter, it is imperative to gain control over these skills during the baseline phase, and yet the relations produced during baseline represent only a tiny fraction of the long and diverse history of the adult subject. No matter how uniformly we control baseline responding across all subjects, we may still expect to see individual variation when subjects encounter an experimental contingency which is similar to those they have experienced frequently in their lives.

Although we cannot exert much control over subject history, we can try to assess it in better ways. The assessment of important historical factors has traditionally been the domain of personality psychologies. The analysis of personality does not have much precedent within the experimental analysis of behavior (Harzem, 1984), but it will be increasingly important to our understanding of behavior as complex as verbal behavior. We are at a loss to recommend specific assessment devices for analyzing those aspects of a subject's history that are relevant to self-editing. Perhaps the necessary information could be gathered via structured interviews, or through accessible records of relevant experiences (e.g., scores on achievement tests). Ideally, the assessment device should provide measures of at least two factors that appear to be important in accounting for individual differences in self-editing: composition skills in speaking and writing, and sensitivity to social consequences for these activities.

Of equal importance is the monitoring of the subjects' extra-experimental activities that might influence behavior within the experiment. This is perhaps more important with verbal behavior studies than with studies of nonverbal behavior because of the frequency with which the subject emits the same or similar behavior outside of the sessions. Subject 9's two sessions of high editing in the second RA phase might well have been influenced by outside activities that stimulated self-editing. On one day she came directly from a job interview and the other day she came directly from a long essay test.

A source of variability that can be controlled is the format of the experimental task. Using vague concepts as stimuli for definitional and exemplification tasks is advantageous for generating large quantities of the subject's verbal behavior, but they have the drawback that subjects find some of the concept questions easier to answer than others. That is, subjects edit more on some concepts than others, contributing to the variability. The variable responding is a problem likely to occur in many experimental situations in which adults interact with verbal stimuli from everyday language. One way to reduce the variability is to have subjects either define the concepts, or exemplify them, but not both within the same experiment. The style of the answers and the degree of editing seems to vary too much across these two types of tasks. Most subjects edit more on definitions and write more on examples. We plan to use only definition prompts in subsequent experiments.

Is it possible to modify the procedure to produce stronger and more persistent editing? There are several variables that may have accounted for the weak or transitory editing seen with several subjects. First, it must be remembered that all of our data on editing were measures of *on-screen editing* -- the functionally covert behavior. Surely subjects also composed and edited verbal responses "in their heads" while working at the computer. Thus, we were capturing only some proportion of the subjects' total editing. It is impossible to estimate what that proportion was; measures of pausing give a rough indication of relative levels of covert behavior, but they do not provide accurate measures of specific quantities of covert behavior, nor do they enable the experimenter to distinguish covert production from covert editing. It is possible that the contingencies had substantial effects on this truly covert behavior and we couldn't detect it with our measurement system. If this is true, then it is remarkable that we detected any changes in editing at all. We tried to insure that subjects maximized the amount of on-screen activity by using only those people who were fast typists, and by making it relatively easy for them to edit. We will continue to search for ways to encourage subjects to respond on the computer. Nevertheless, it is always easier to think than it is to type, so it is likely that subjects will retreat to this form of verbal behavior when they find it difficult to produce an answer.

Second, it is possible that subjects would have edited more if more effective consequences were manipulated. We have several parameters of the contingencies to adjust in future research, such as the intensity and frequency of the punishing consequences. Beyond the simple parametric manipulations lies another possibility. The nature of the consequence package (verbal remarks and monetary gain or loss) may not exert the proper kind of control over this behavior. Money is not the most effective consequence for all subjects. Furthermore, it appears that subjects often react to amounts of earned money as more or less important at different times throughout the experiment. It is upon this tenuous base that we stacked additional consequences such as points and standardized remarks hoping that they acquired powerful conditioned consequence functions.

Consequences other than money may be more effective in manipulating self-editing. An important factor in evoking self-editing in non-laboratory interactions seems to be the social relation between the interacting people. Specifically, it appears that we edit to a greater extent when interacting with listeners whom we respect, admire, desire, or find otherwise important. It is these people whose disapproval functions effectively as a punisher. This effectiveness probably stems from the ability of these people to control other aspects of the speaker's behavior, such as grades in a classroom, advancement in a job, and so on. In a laboratory procedure such as ours, there is no extra-experimental social relation between the experimenter and the subjects. In fact, such relations are typically prohibited by ethical protocols, and yet they might be vital to the control of self-editing. If we could find some other way of establishing the experimenter as a "prestigious audience" for the subjects we might magnify the effects of disapproval.

The transitory effects observed in the behavior of Subjects 10 and 12 could be due to several variables. Subjects may not have continued to edit during RD because, despite the deceptive instructions, they detected the fact that consequences were independent of the content of their answer. Thus, they gave up trying to write good answers because the feedback seemed arbitrary, especially after a baseline in which everything they said was fine. Subject 12 reported during debriefing that at some point during RD he thought consequences were arbitrary, although he reported that he did not continue to think this after he started earning money again in RA2. The instructions will be altered for new subjects so that they are told that the "criteria" for acceptable answers may change at different points in the experiment and that they must adapt to these changes. Perhaps this will make the disapproval consequences appear less arbitrary to them. Ultimately, we will refine the procedure so that listener consequences are dependent on answer style or content. Although this makes it more difficult for the experimenter to control the distribution of approval and disapproval consequences within an experimental phase, it should permit more precise control over the subject's behavior.

The lack of persistent editing in RD may also be accounted for by the process of extinction. In Skinner's analysis, self-editing is maintained because it is effective in terminating or avoiding forms of punishment from the listener. Subjects were unable to terminate the disapproval consequences in RD despite their attempts to alter their answers. Editing may have extinguished because it was not effective. The high degree of editing by Subjects 10 and 12 in the third session of the disapproval phase can be interpreted as an extinction burst. The extinction may have been hastened by the relatively high density of disapproval consequences these subjects received. Subject 10 received disapproval consequences on all eight trials per session for most of the disapproval phase. Subject 12 lost points on five out of the eight trials per session in RD. Remember that Subject 9 lost points on only three trials per session, and she engaged in more persistent editing. Additional subjects will have to be run under the different parameters before any conclusions can be reached about the conditions under which self- editing extinguishes.

There is a possibility that we may not obtain anything but transitory self-editing with many subjects because of the nature of the self-editing they engage in outside of the laboratory. Most of the subjects we use (young undergraduates) do not have extensive experience in producing and editing manuscripts. They have far more experience editing their vocal behavior. We suspect that editing in vocal interactions is likely to occur more quickly, and be more quickly extinguished if it is not effective, than editing in written interactions. There are several reasons why this might be true. The speed of the interchanges between participants in normal conversation is such that the long pauses and repeated attempts at saying something that characterize extensive self-editing in writing would be inappropriate. Sluggish self-editing on the part of the speaker may be aversive to the listener, resulting in the termination of the conversation or reduction in the frequency of subsequent conversations. The embarrassment of struggling for words is often felt by both speaker and listener. These contingencies would shape a rapid style of editing in vocal interactions. It may also be the case that editing is successful in terminating or avoiding listener punishment relatively immediately in informal vocal interactions, or the speaker simply disengages contact with the difficult listener. Given a choice, few of us remain in conversations with listeners who are consistently negative toward our remarks. This would make it likely that people who have histories of editing predominately in informal vocal interactions do not have histories of persistent editing. Perhaps we should select subjects for this research who have extensive experience in written compositions, such as senior journalism students or professional writers, or prolific experimental scientists who get their manuscripts frequently rejected.

Concluding Comments

Some tentative conclusions about self-editing might help to direct further investigations. It appears that Skinner's analysis of self-editing is a useful way to approach the topic, both conceptually and experimentally. Although Skinner did not suggest a method for studying human editing, his analysis fits well into our present-day methodology of interfaced microcomputers. It is clear that much more work needs to be done to clarify the controlling variables in this area, but the data obtained so far suggest that subjects respond to listener disapproval (punishment seems too narrow a term here) with many of the reactions Skinner hypothesized. Disapproval suppresses the rate of production while facilitating the covert behavior of self-editing.

An additional effect not described by Skinner is that subjects frequently reacted to disapproval by increasing the volume of released text. This seemingly contradictory effect makes sense when we look at it in terms of its function for the speaker. It is possible that many people have a history of successfully coping with a difficult audience not by editing but by dazzling them with verbosity! The listener then finds something acceptable in the speaker's barrage, and the speaker continues on his merry way. To the extent this behavior has been successful it may become the speaker's first reaction to disapproval, with substantial self-editing occurring only as a secondary reaction if verbosity fails.

In closing let us comment on our research paradigm. The methodology used in this research is important for several reasons. It has enabled us to manipulate contingencies that affect the relation between a type of covert verbal behavior and its final overt form, and we have been able to record that covert behavior. The use of interactive microcomputers offers other advantages for the analysis of verbal behavior. A listener can almost instantly respond to the released response of the speaker; this social dynamic is an essential element in the study of complex verbal interactions. By using interactive computers, speaker and audience are separated and extraneous social stimuli are readily controlled. In addition, audience variables (such as having two or more listeners) can be manipulated easily through programming without requiring the presence of additional confederates. Without such a methodology, self-editing would remain virtually inaccessible to experimental observation.

The methodology needs refinement for further research on self-editing. The data collected so far have been measures of quantity and rate. In subsequent research, we plan to devise a coding system so that changes in answer style and content can also be analyzed. It is apparent from a review of session transcripts that the form of the answers given by subjects changed with exposure to both approval and disapproval consequences. Style changes appear to be associated with high levels of self-editing sometimes, but on other occasions answer style changed with little on-screen editing. The relation between editing and answer style needs to be examined more closely. When more is known about how response form varies under the contingencies of the present procedure, the procedure can be re-designed so that releases are consequated depending on their style or content. This will permit a more direct examination of the complex relations between response form, self-editing, and listener consequences.

The study of verbal behavior has been a field in search of a methodology. We think that the use of interactive computer systems may open a new arena for the investigation of a variety of issues relating to self-editing in particular and social interactions between verbal organisms in general. It has been nearly 30 years since the publication of Skinner's book. As Michael (1984) and others have noted, it has generated little research up to this time. Perhaps *Verbal Behavior* was only awaiting the computer age.

References

Azrin, N. & Holz, W. (1966). Punishment. In W. K. Honig (Ed.), *Operant behavior: Areas of research and application* (pp. 380-447). Englewood Cliffs, New Jersey: Prentice-Hall.

Estes, W. & Skinner, B. F. (1941). Some quantitative properties of anxiety. *Journal of Experimental Psychology, 29,* 390-400.

Hake, D., & Azrin, N. (1965). Conditioned punishment. *Journal of the Experimental Analysis of Behavior, 8,* 279-293.

Harzem, P. (1984). Experimental analysis of individual differences and personality. *Journal of the Experimental Analysis of Behavior, 42,* 385-395.

Michael, J. (1984). Verbal behavior. *Journal of the Experimental Analysis of Behavior, 42,* 363-376.

Skinner, B. F. (1957). *Verbal behavior.* New York: Appleton-Century-Crofts.

A Discussion of Chapter 4

Toward a Methodology for Studying Verbal Behavior

Margaret E. Vaughan
Salem State College

The work that Cloyd Hyten and Philip Chase present is testimony to the wide application of microcomputers awaiting the experimental analysis of verbal behavior. With the clever use of a computer, they have designed a technique that allows one to study and potentially manipulate the variables of which self-editing are purportedly a function. The computer provides the experimenter with direct observation of a verbally behaving organism interacting with a verbal environment - a simulated conversation that is recorded instantaneously.

But any new approach to a subject matter has a way of generating a flurry of experimentation that can set the course for all future research with respect to that subject matter. It comes as no surprise then, that the experimental community is a bit cautious when it comes to innovation. Not only is special attention given to the particulars of such research, philosophical questions arise pertaining to the nature of the endeavor (e.g., what is its overall basic mission?) It was within this spirit that Hyten and Chase's research was discussed.

Hyten collected data on seven features of self-editing: volume and rate of production, number of characters deleted by backspacing or total rejections, and length of pauses before, during and after composition. Following up on Skinner's analysis of punishment and its effects on self-editing, Hyten and Chase recorded the various changes in the dependent variables during three experimental conditions: Releases Approved, a baseline condition where five out of eight releases were randomly awarded 50-point increments; Releases Disapproved, where at least three out of eight releases were randomly followed by either a 50 or 150-point decrement; and finally, a return to the Releases Approved Condition.

Despite some variability across subjects, Hyten and Chase found that in general most subjects showed a decrease in self-editing during the Releases Approved Phases and an increase in self-editing during the Releases Disapproved Phase. Interestingly, in the Releases Disapproved Phase, they not only found a decrease in the rate of production but a corresponding increase in the amount of text released.

Although it is important to know that self-editing is a class of behavior affected by consequences, Steven Hayes stressed that such experimentation should be more than demonstration research: one needs to do more than show support for Skinner's analysis. Self-editing is a class of behavior distinct from other classes because of its unique features. But what are these features and of what are they a function? Kurt Salzinger suggested that Hyten and Chase begin by pulling apart the various functional response classes characterizing self-editing.

Linda Hayes and Richard Malott raised another issue. An analysis of self-editing in terms of punishment seemed inadequate. While it was true that there was a suppression in the rate of production during the Releases Disapproved Phase, there was also an increase in the volume of released text and changes in style that could not be characterized as increasing or decreasing. Malott suggested that perhaps one should view the situation as involving negative reinforcement, in that the behavior which reduced the conditioned aversive properties of the situation was strengthened. That is, the subjects were attempting to avoid the conditions that led to point reduction. Hyten readily agreed, pointing out that their interpretation of the data was in fact based on an analysis of negative reinforcement.

Steven Hayes voiced another concern: how effective were the deceptive instructions? Subjects were told that they would receive or lose points based upon their answers. But in fact, consequences were delivered independent of the subject's answer. If the obtained results are to be meaningful, then the integrity of their deceptive instructions must be validated: it is not enough to ask subjects what they thought, one must experimentally show that subjects were deceived. That is, one must demonstrate that the subject's behavior is insensitive to manipulations of variables that would otherwise show behavior change if the deceptive instructions had not been given. Although an important point, there were no suggestions made as to how Hyten and Chase might actually modify their procedure to resolve the issue.

The various points raised during the discussion all seemed to hang ultimately on one aspect of self-editing the authors acknowledged as the most difficult to control and one aspect not directly manipulated in the study: changes in content. It was Hayne Reese who pointed out that the subjects could never make accurate predictions regarding the effect their verbal behavior would have on the listener since the punishing consequences were randomly administered. Although subjects were told that their responses where being evaluated by the experimenter, the criteria used to evaluate each released bit of text were not specified. As a result, subjects were forced into guessing what kind of an answer would result in point increment and point decrement. Given the fact that the consequences were random, one could not be too surprised to find variation in amount and type of self-editing. Obviously, establishing the variables of which particular changes in content and style are a function may be one of the most difficult subject matters put to an experimental analysis but it is extremely important if we are to fully understand the process of self-editing. Phil Hineline suggested tapping into already established writing programs where students are learning how to write on a computer. An analysis of such data might provide the kinds of information for which Hyten and Chase's research has whetted our appetites.

One final point is worth noting. This research emphasizes self-editing where the speaker and listener are different people. One might refer to self-editing under these conditions as a process of developing more effective verbal behavior. Undoubtedly, most people engage in self-editing so as to reduce the probability of punishment from the listener. But it seems as if there is another function of self-editing: discovering what one has to say. That is, a distinction can be made between those cases where another individual serves as the audience and those cases where the speaker serves as his or her own audience. The difference lies in the source of reinforcement. When one serves as his or her own listener, verbal behavior that is automatically reinforced is behavior which, for example, clarifies some issue for the speaker or comes very close to saying concisely what the speaker wants to say (see Vaughan & Michael, 1982, for an analysis of automatic reinforcement). The reaction of others is not the issue, describing something accurately is. The skillful behavior of poets, artists and photographers seems to exemplify this kind of self-editing. Poets, for example, often seem to be interested in describing a set of circumstances so as to elicit the same emotions now or previously experienced. They are their own audience. That poets have seldom been a powerful force in any culture may be because they are not writing to alter the human condition; they are writing to recreate the human condition via the written word. It has been said that Dylan Thomas spent hours attempting to find the "right" word. Effective verbal behavior, on the other hand, seems more related to influencing the behavior of someone else. Political leaders, religious leaders, educators and therapists perhaps exemplify this type of self-editing. Their job is to influence voters, souls, students and patients, respectively; their success depends upon the behavior of others. The contingencies seem quite different in these two cases: in the first, reinforcement seems dependent upon a correspondence between what one says and what is; in the second, reinforcement seems dependent upon a correspondence between what one says and what others want to hear. Obviously, both sources of reinforcement are important and undoubtedly much of our behavior is multiply controlled. But to fully understand these processes it seems necessary to begin to tease apart these two separate sources of reinforcement. In the present research subjects were to believe another individual was reacting to what they said. It is also important that we examine the conditions under which one serves as his or her own listener.

In sum, there was genuine agreement over the value of this research. The methodology is still evolving but the ultimate results of such a research project are fascinating to consider. For such a methodology may be the start of an experimental analysis of scientific behavior. Not only would we be able to articulate the ways in which people become more effective speakers, we may learn about the intricacies of discovering what we have to say. This area of investigation could be one very important step in the evolution of the experimental analysis of behavior.

Reference

Vaughan, M., & Michael, J. (1982). Automatic reinforcement: An important but ignored concept. *Behaviorism, 10,* 217-227.

Chapter 5

Conversation Analysis and the Analysis of Verbal Behavior

Ullin T. Place
University of Leeds [1]

The Analysis of Verbal Behavior as the Link Between Biology and the Humanities

In the aftermath of Noam Chomsky's (1959) review of Skinner's (1957) book Verbal Behavior, behavior analysis in general and the analysis of verbal behavior in particular have, as I put it in a recent paper, "been consigned to a kind of academic ghetto - cut off by mutual suspicion and incomprehension, not only from other approaches within psychology, but from virtually every other adjacent discipline from philosophy, linguistics and sociology on the one hand and ethology and the neuro-sciences on the other" (Place, 1985a, p. 38). Yet, as I also remarked in the same paper, "the analysis of verbal behavior should provide the essential link between the biological sciences on the one hand and the social sciences and humanities on the other," a role which "cognitive psychology, in my view, is totally disqualified from playing . . . because it rides roughshod over the vital distinction drawn by Skinner (1969) . . . between contingency-shaped and rule-governed behavior" (Place, 1985a, p. 38).

The Concept of the Sentence in Pragmatics, Semantics and Syntactics

As I see the matter, in order to rectify this situation and restore the analysis of verbal behavior to its rightful place in the scientific scheme of things, two things are necessary. In the first place we need to find some way of meeting the valid criticisms made by Chomsky of Skinners's book. In particular, we need to find a way of answering the criticism that Skinner's account of language contains:

(1) no proper concept of the sentence as the effective unit of linguistic communication,

(2) no recognition that the kind of sentence which performs this communicatory function is seldom repeated word for word, but is constructed anew on each occasion of utterance,

(3) no recognition that the ability to construct sentences that the speaker has never before uttered and which the listener has never before encountered enables the speaker to construct sentences which will evoke from the listener behavior which he or she has never before emitted or communicate information about contingencies which the listener has never before encountered.

If the analysis of verbal behavior can be extended so as to accommodate these features, it should be possible to close the theoretical gap which separates it from other approaches to language and take the second of the two steps which are needed in my view, namely the establishment of links between the analysis of verbal behavior from the behavior analytic standpoint and other traditions of empirical research into the phenomenon of linguistic communication.

In order to incorporate the concept of the sentence, its structure and the control it exercises over the behavior of the listener within the behavior analytic approach to language we need to make use of the distinction, first formulated by the behaviorist philosopher Charles Morris (1938, 1946) between the three divisions of semiotic or the general theory of signs of which verbal or linguistic signs are a special case, pragmatics which deals with the function of the sign within the behavior of both speaker and listener, semantics which deals with the relation or pseudo-relation[2] between the sign and what it "signifies", "means" or "refers to" and syntactics which deals with the relations between one sign or word and another which give form or structure to the sentence and thereby determine the functions it performs within the context of utterance. In terms of this distinction the behavior analytic concept of the sentence differs from that of the grammarian, linguist or philosopher in that it is defined, not in terms of a particular syntactic structure, but in pragmatic or functional terms. In other words the sentence is defined in the first instance in terms of the control which it is capable of exercising over the behavior of any listener who is a competent member of the verbal community within which that string of phonemes is recognised as an intelligible sentence. Given that initial definition, we can account for the phenomenon whereby the speaker can construct novel sentences which act for the listener as discriminative stimuli with respect both to behavior which he or she has never previously emitted and to contingencies which he or she has never previously encountered in terms of the principle which I have referred to elsewhere (Place, 1983) as "behavioral contingency semantics."

Behavioral Contingency Semantics and its Interdisciplinary Affiliations

Behavioral contingency semantics is the principle according to which a sentence acts as a discriminative stimulus which, to use Kantor's term, "orientates" the behavior of the listener towards a particular contingency or type of contingency by virtue of a correspondence between the form and content of the sentence on the one hand and the form and content of the contingency or contingency term or "leg", as I prefer to say, which it thereby "specifies" on the other.

As I see it, this principle fills a number of important gaps in the behavior analytic approach to language as developed by Skinner in *Verbal Behavior*. Besides offering an account of how novel sentences can generate novel behavior and supply new information, it offers an explanation of the meaning of the verb to "specify" which plays a key role both in *Verbal Behavior* and in Chapter 6 of *Contingencies of Reinforcement,* but is nowhere defined in Skinner's writings. But it also has the virtue of opening up much needed links between the analysis of verbal behavior and a number of other traditions within general linguistics, philosophical logic and the philosophy of language. Thus, in developing an account of the sentence in these terms in a previous paper (Place, 1983), use was made both of Chomsky's (1958) generative and transformational grammar and of Frege's (1879, 1891) "function and argument" analysis of the sentence.

In suggesting that we can think of the sentence as a kind of map or plan of a part or sometimes the whole of the contingency for which it thereby acts as a discriminative stimulus, I have consciously modelled my account on the so-called "picture theory" of the meaning of sentences as developed originally by Russell (1918-1919) in his theory of Logical Atomism and refined and extended by Wittgenstein (1922) in his *Tractatus Logico-Philosophicus*. Again, in analysing the elements and structure of the contingency that correspond to the elements and structure of the sentence, I have relied heavily on ideas derived from Aristotle's *Metaphysics,* and in so doing I have given an account of the internal structure of the events and states of affairs which constitute the terms or legs of a contingency which, I have since discovered, is virtually identical with that given by Barwise and Perry (1983) of "a situation" in developing what has become known as "situation semantics" in their book *Situations and Attitudes.*

For Barwise and Perry, sentences map onto situations. Situations are either events which involve change at or over time or states of affairs which remain the same over a period of time. On my account, simple or "atomic" sentences, like "The baby is crying," "Give the baby a bottle" or "The baby will go back to sleep," map onto a single contingency term or leg. In the case of "The baby is crying," the sentence specifies behavior on the part of the baby, but an antecedent condition which calls for behavior on the part of the baby sitter. Similarly, "Give the baby a bottle" specifies a consequence of the behavior emitted by the baby and the behavior to be performed on the part of the baby sitter, while "The baby will go back to sleep" specifies further behavior on the part of the baby and the anticipated consequence of the behavior to be emitted by the baby sitter. Moreover, each of these sentences specifies a discrete event which stands in a causal relation either as effect with respect to the event which precedes it and/or as cause with respect to the one which follows, and as such it qualifies as "a situation" in the Barwise and Perry sense.

The Failure of Verbal Behavior to Generate a Program of Empirical Research and the Reasons for It

While it is of particular satisfaction to me as a philosopher to be able to establish links of this kind between a behavior analytic approach to language and some of the more traditional, as well as some more recent thinking in linguistics and philosophy, my training as a psychologist makes me equally sensitive to the need to establish links of a more practical and empirical kind between the analysis of verbal behavior on the one hand and empirical studies of language and communication within other research traditions and other disciplines on the other.

In this connnection I have long been impressed by the fact that what concerns the experimental behavior analyst who values Skinner's contribution in other areas of research for its robust no-nonsense empiricism is not so much Chomsky's criticisms as the fact that in *Verbal Behavior* Skinner relies exclusively on the traditional literary device of artificially constructed examples, interspersed with the occasional anecdote, without any systematically collected empirical data to support the conclusions reached. The book contains no suggestions for a program of empirical research which might develop out of it. Nor has any significant program of such research been generated over the quarter of a century since the book was first published. The citations of *Verbal Behavior* recently surveyed by McPherson, Bonem, Green and Osborne (1984) represent little more than a drop in the ocean when compared with the enormous proliferation of both theoretical and empirical studies of language formulated in terms of other conceptual frameworks over the same period.

There are three factors, in my judgment, which can be invoked to explain this failure of *Verbal Behavior* to generate an effective program of empirical research. In the first place there are the conceptual deficiencies of Skinner's analysis with respect to the concept of the sentence and the stimulus control exercised by novel sentences over the behavior of the listener. Related to these conceptual deficiencies is the lack of a satisfactory and coherent taxonomy for the classification of verbal operants. I have discussed the inadequacy of and confusions within Skinner's existing taxonomy based on the concepts of mand, tact, autoclitic, intraverbal, echoic and textual response in a number of recent articles (Place, 1985a, 1985b, 1985c) and I shall not repeat those arguments here. I propose, instead, to concentrate on the third of the three factors which in my view explain the failure of *Verbal Behavior* to generate an effective on-going program of empirical research. This third factor is the exclusive commitment of behavior analysis to an experimental methodology which, in my view, has only a very limited application to the study of verbal behavior.

The basis for this judgment is the observation that at the level of tactical execution the verbal behavior of a linguistically competent human adult is a skilled performance which, like other forms of skilled performance such as playing tennis or driving a car, is shaped to the contingencies governing such behavior by repeated practical experience of the immediate consequences of behaving in one way rather than another. In terms of the distinction drawn by Skinner in Chapter 6 of *Contingencies of Reinforcement,* verbal behavior at the level of tactical execution is "contingency-shaped" rather than "rule- governed". What this means is that, instead of planning what she or he is about to say in terms of a verbal specification of the behavior to be emitted and the predicted consequences of emitting behavior of that kind in the prevailing context of utterance, verbal behavior is shaped by repeated exposure to the consequences of emitting behavior belonging to the same response classes[3] on relevantly similar occasions in the past. Moreover, the effect of these past consequences on the subsequent emission of verbal behavior by the speaker is not mediated, as it is in the case of most rule-governed behavior, by the formulation of a verbal specification of the behavior-consequence relation.

One of the striking features of verbal behavior is its dependence for reinforcement on the response of the listener. In a person-to-person verbal interaction, the maintenance of ongoing verbal behavior by the speaker requires the constant emission by the listener of a stream of verbal reinforcers, known to conversation analysts as "continuers" (Jefferson, 1980c). These include expressions of agreement like "Right," "Mmhmm," nodding the head, etc. which are used to reinforce opinion-stating behavior, expressions of comprehension like "Yes," "No," "I see," etc. which are used to reinforce instruction-giving behavior, expressions of surprise like "Really?," "Well I never did!," "You don't say!," etc. which are used to reinforce news-telling (Jefferson, 1981), expressions of concern and sympathy like "Oh dear!," "I'm so sorry!," "You poor thing," etc. which are used to reinforce what Jefferson (1980a, 1980b,) has called "troubles talk", and the laughter which reinforces joke-telling behavior (Jefferson, 1979).

Evidence that verbal behavior is directly shaped by these verbal reinforcers/continuers, rather than being subject to control by a verbal formula or "rule" specifying the behavior-consequence relation, comes from the fact that, in terms of the verbal reports they are able to give, both speakers and listeners are almost totally oblivious, in the case of speakers, both of the occurrence of the continuers and of the effect they are having and, in the case of listeners, of their behavior in supplying them.

The phenomenon whereby spontaneous verbal behavior on the part of the speaker is maintained, with minimal awareness by either party, through verbal reinforcers/continuers supplied by the listener is one which does not easily lend itself to reproduction in the experimental laboratory. The reason for this is that if you attempt to reinforce verbal behavior which is under the control of artificial instructions such as the instruction to "say all the words you can think of" (Greenspoon, 1955) or the instruction to complete an incomplete sentence presented on a stimulus card (Taffel, 1955), particularly if, as in many studies of this type, a conspicuous expression of approval like "Good!" is used as the reinforcer, the effect is to create just the kind of problem situation which Skinner describes in Chapter 6 of *Contingencies of Reinforcement* in which the subject attempts to solve the problem of how to satisfy the demands of the experimenter by generating "a rule", i.e., a verbal formula which serves to "specify" the relevant contingency. As a result, the behavior exhibited in the experimental situation acquires a conscious premeditated "rule- governed" character quite different from the "contingency-shaped" character of verbal behavior in its natural setting.

It is true that in his survey of experimental studies of the operant reinforcement of verbal behavior Krasner (1958) concluded (a) that most subjects in these studies were "unaware" of the contingency involved, and (b) that the effect of reinforcement in strengthening and of disinforcement in weakening the propensity to emit responses of the relevant class did not depend on the subject's ability to provide a correct verbal specification of the contingency in question. However, Spielberger and Levin (1962) reviewed the same literature in the light of further studies carried out in the intervening period and concluded that the results obtained in the studies reviewed by Krasner were an artifact of the procedure whereby subjects were only questioned about the contingency involved in the experiment after their earlier hypotheses had been undermined by the extinction phase required by the ABA experimental design. Spielberger and Levin claim that, if subjects are questioned about the contingency at the end of the acquisition phase of the experiment, (a) most subjects are able to supply a correct verbal specification of the contingency, and (b) those that cannot specify the contingency show no learning effect. If this is correct, it shows that the behavior observed in these studies is in fact rule-governed rather than contingency-shaped and is to that extent unrepresentative of verbal behavior as it occurs in its natural setting.

The only experimental study I know of that escapes criticism on these grounds is that of Verplanck (1955) who showed that when an experimenter engages a subject in normal conversation in a natural setting, the number of opinions expressed by the subject during a 10-minute experimental session can be significantly increased, if every expression of opinion is reinforced by an expression of agreement, such as Yes, you're right, That's so etc., or by nodding the head or "smiling affirmation." It was also shown that opinion-stating behavior returned to its pre-experimental baseline level during a subsequent 10-minute extinction session during which opinion-stating behavior was no longer reinforced. The contingency-shaped character of this effect is demonstrated by the fact that none of the subjects in this experiment were aware that their behavior was being modified in this way, except that "during extinction some Ss got angry at E and commented on his disagreeableness, or noted his 'lack of interest.'" (Verplanck, 1955, p. 671)

Systematic Field Observation of Naturally Occurring Verbal Interactions

While there is no doubt a limited scope for further experimental investigations along the lines pioneered by Verplanck, it is evident in my view that the methodology of choice in studying the verbal behavior of older children and adults has to be the systematic field observation of naturally occurring verbal interactions. This is not an altogether novel suggestion as far as the analysis of verbal behavior from a behavior analytic standpoint is concerned. There have been isolated studies of this kind which have attempted to make use the taxonomy of verbal operants proposed by Skinner in *Verbal Behavior*. Horner and Gussow (1972), for example, used the concepts of the "mand" and the "tact" in their study of the verbal interactions of urban blacks in the family setting. McLeish and Martin (1975) were more ambitious. They tried to use the complete taxonomy of *Verbal Behavior* in their study of verbal interactions in a psychotherapeutic setting. But in neither of these cases are the results obtained particularly encouraging. Nor have their authors been sufficiently reinforced by the consequences to attempt further studies along these lines.

But whereas the attempt to analyse naturally occurring verbal interactions between linguistically competent human adults and children in terms of the taxonomy of verbal operants proposed by Skinner in *Verbal Behavior* seems to have petered out, the last decade has seen a remarkable escalation of observational studies of naturally occurring verbal interactions (cf., van Dijk, 1985) inspired by what at first sight appear to be quite different and, in some cases (e.g., Grice, 1975; Brown & Levinson, 1978) quite alien conceptual schemes. Those who have participated in this development come from a variety of disciplines and subdivisions within those disciplines. There are linguists with a variety of interests from phonetics through syntax to what is variously known as "pragmatics" or "sociolinguistics." There are psychologists, mainly of a "cognitive" persuasion, drawn from the developmental, clinical and social areas, and there are sociologists interested in what is known as "conversation analysis" (Heritage, 1985). It is this latter research tradition which, in my view, bears the closest affinities with behavior analysis and it is with the links between these two research traditions that I shall be dealing in what follows.

Conversation Analysis and its Affinities with Behavior Analysis

Conversation analysis emerged as a branch of sociological enquiry in the United States towards the end of the 1960's under the leadership of the late Harvey Sacks and his two principal collaborators, Emmanuel Schegloff and Gail Jefferson. It was and to some extent remains an outgrowth of the ethnomethodological movement within sociology, founded in the 1960's by Harold Garfinkel (1967). Nevertheless, in its single minded pursuit of scientific accuracy in the transcription and analysis of naturally occurring verbal interactions unconstrained by any theoretical preconceptions of whatever kind and from whatever source, conversation analysis offers the nearest thing to a body of uncontaminated empirical data on the way language is actually used in everyday life. As such it presents a challenge to the interpretative skills of anyone interested in the phenomenon of human language, be he or she a linguist, a phonetician, a philosopher, a psychologist, whether of the behaviorist or of the cognitive persuasion, a social psychologist or, like the conversation analysts themselves, a sociologist.

Although there have never been any formal links or active interaction between the two research traditions, there are a number of respects in which there is a remarkable affinity between conversation analysis and behavior analysis:

(1) Conversation analysis and behavior analysis share a common commitment to the kind of *radical empiricism* which refuses to accept phenomena whose existence cannot be demonstrated in the available empirical data. Curiously enough, as I pointed out recently (Place 1985/6), it is this commitment to radical empiricism which leads the conversation analyst to question the reality of what I have called the "extra-episodic" or from-trial-to-trial effects of utterances like "Thank you!" in reinforcing the previous speaker's propensity to emit behavior similar to that which he or she has just emitted on relevantly similar occasions in the future. Conversation analysts are familiar with the "intra-episodic" or within-trial effects of verbal reinforcers or "continuers", as they call them, in maintaining ongoing verbal behavior on the part of the current speaker. But because their data contain no record of the behavior of the individuals concerned on subsequent occasions, the extra-episodic reinforcement effects of an utterance like "Thank you!" belongs as far as they are concerned to the realms of speculative fantasy. All they can see is the intra-episodic effect of "Thank you!" in bringing the interchange to an appropriate close.

(2) Like the behavior analyst, the conversation analyst insists that behavior can only be properly understood in relation to its context, what precedes it, its antecedents, and what follows, its consequences.

(3) Like the behavior analyst, the conversation analyst is suspicious of statistics, particularly statistical tables which report frequencies of occurrence for certain types of behavior within a given body of data. They regard such information as useless, since it fails to distinguish between two kinds of behavior which may have the same net frequency of occurrence, where one has a high natural probability of emission which is partially suppressed by the disinforcing effects of social disapproval, while the other has a relatively low natural probability of emission which has been increased by social reinforcement.

(4) Like the behavior analyst, the conversation analyst tends to regard with suspicion introspective protocols of the kind that are assiduously collected from the participants in a verbal interaction by social psychologists in the cognitive tradition after the interaction has been recorded. Conversation analysts regard such protocols as massively irrelevant. The controlling variables, as the behavior analyst would put it, are all there, to the discerning eye, in the objectively observed data of behavior and its context.

(5) Finally the attitude of conversation analysts to questions of theory is remarkably reminiscent of that expressed by Skinner (1950) in his paper "Are theories of learning necessary?" Just as Skinner professes not to have a theory of learning in the sense that, say, Hull and Tolman proposed such theories, so the conversation analysts are inclined to deny that their work depends on any kind of preconceived theory. Of course, like Skinner, conversation analysts do have their own system of theoretical concepts. Without those concepts, no analysis of the data would be possible. But like Skinner, they insist that this conceptual scheme is entirely data-driven. It does not and should not reflect any extraneous theoretical preconceptions.

Apart from superficial differences of terminology whereby the conversation analyst uses, for example, the word "action" where the behavior analyst speaks of an "operant", the only major difference between these two research traditions is a difference of methodology. Whereas behavior analysis belongs to the tradition of experimental psychology in which the method of controlled laboratory experiment tends to be treated as if it were the only legitimate way of generating empirical data, conversation analysis is equally firmly committed to the methodology of the systematic field observation of behavioral phenomena in their natural setting without any form of experimental manipulation and with a minimum of interference from whatever audio or video equipment is used to record the data.

This difference in preferred methodology between the two research traditions contributes, as we have seen, to a difference of view with respect to the extra-episodic reinforcement effect of an utterance like "Thank you." But it is not sufficient in my view to constitute a major obstacle to mutual understanding. It is in this belief that I have been attempting over the past two years to increase my understanding of conversation analysis with a view both to persuading behavior analysts that conversation analysis provides us with the missing body of empirical research that should have been generated by *Verbal Behavior,* but never was, and to persuading conversation analysts that the concepts of behavior analysis, particularly that of the three term or three legged contingency, provide a more satisfactory basis for a more adequate taxonomy of "verbal operants", alias "speech acts", alias "actions" than anything else that is currently available to them. To this end during the winter of 1985-86 I attended a course on the principles of conversation analysis given by Drs. Paul Drew and Tony Wootton in the Department of Sociology at the University of York. As my final course assessment I prepared the exercise to which the remainder of this paper is devoted.

The exercise begins with a transcript of a verbal interaction recorded in the main Departmental Office of the Leeds University Department of Philosophy in October 1985 between Mrs Penny Ewens, a mature student in her second undergraduate year and one of the Senior Departmental Secretaries Mrs Rose Purdy. I am indebted to Mrs Ewens and Mrs Purdy for their permission to publish this data. The transcript has been substantially emended, vetted and finally approved as an accurate record by Dr. Paul Drew of the Department of Sociology, University of York, to whom I am likewise deeply indebted. The phonetic conventions used in the transcript are to be found in Appendix I.

92

Transcript of the Verbal Transaction - First Year Party 10/85

Penny: ((Enters and approaches))

Rose: |^he<u>ll</u>o Penny.   ['sawrigh(t)
                           [
Penny: (so[rry)

Penny: =can I inter<u>ru</u>pt y[er a <u>mom</u>ent. I'm <u>sorry</u> ex<u>cuse me</u>,=
                            [
Rose: [yes do:

Penny: it's <u>just</u> this bus'ness uv (.) th'<u>pah</u>tee   [fer the=
                                        [
Rose: [ye:h(s)
                                   ((Knock))

Penny: =<u>first</u> y:e:ahrs. <u>I</u> won't (.) be <u>i</u>:n temorro mo:rning.
Rose: yes   no=

Penny: =I've <u>left</u> a <u>no</u>tice on the <u>bawd</u>.
Rose: yeah.=

Penny: =an ther's a <u>note</u> fer th'm %uv the <u>money</u>.=

Rose: =<u>who</u> wants te pick it up?
Penny: we:ll (.) th<u>e:</u>'re on that=

Penny: =<u>li:</u> [st.
          [
Rose: [oh the're %aw- on that <u>list</u>. (.) and any-any uv these=
Rose: =people [can <u>have</u> i˜t, (.) can they.
           [
Penny: [yes:: (.)   ah <u>do</u>:: know John's girl=

Penny: =friend <u>knows</u> about it. bu(t) <u>she:</u>'s not <u>free</u> at the same time=

Penny: =as <u>them</u> tomorro. so:th- <u>lots</u> uv people <u>know</u> about it,=

Rose: =anan <u>the:</u>'re goin te <u>get</u> the shoppin(g) ou [t uv it. (.)
                                           [
Penny: [yes (.)

Rose: I see   [(   )
             [
Penny: [yes ah've put a list uv what I=

Penny: =suggest [they get
             [
Rose: [yeah (.) okay   [(then)
                      [
Penny: [an I've got all the rest uv the=

Penny: =shopping.
Rose: oh you've got all the rest. an they know that.=

Rose: =but anybody c'n: t-take this money that's in heah.=

Penny: =wul- (.) th(u) people o [n that list (.) yeh] are the people=
                        [   ]
Rose: [on that list yes]

Penny: =who said they wud help with it=

Rose: = [o: k a y   P e n n y] thanks then=
        [   ]
Penny: = [thank you very much]

Rose: =very much ye:s u:m (.) so down to "persuaded me."

Pragmatic Analysis I - List of Adjacency Pairs

Having transcribed this "sequence", as such things are called in conversation analysis, the next step is to generate the first Pragmatic Analysis consisting of a list of "adjacency pairs." As it is used in conversation analysis an *adjacency pair* (Schegloff, 1968, Schegloff & Sacks, 1973), may be defined in terms of the concepts of behavior analysis as a pair of consecutive actions/operants emitted by two different speakers of which the first is a verbal operant or effective sentence utterance which acts as an antecedent "establishing condition" (Michael, 1982) which "calls for" and is thus reinforced by the emission of the second member of the pair by the listener/second speaker. The second member of the pair may be either verbal, as in answering a question, or non-verbal, as in complying with a request to shut the door. Examples of Adjacency Pairs given by Levinson (1983) include Question-Answer, Greeting-Greeting, Offer-Acceptance and Apology-Minimalisation.

However, in adapting the concept of Adjacency Pair (AP) for use as a basic analytical tool in the pragmatic analysis of naturally occurring verbal interactions, it seemed desirable to broaden the concept so as to include any pair of consecutive actions/operants emitted by two separate speakers/agents in which the first member of the pair is a verbal operant and the second is a verbal or non-verbal response under the control of the first in its capacity as stimulus. The effect of broadening the concept in this way is that it allows us to use the concept to describe the actual consequences of emitting a particular verbal operant, instead of restricting it to the reinforcing consequences which are "called for" by verbal operants of that type. In other words a question followed by an apology for speaker's inabilty to answer counts as an adjacency pair on this usage, just as much as a question followed by an answer that is both correct and genuinely informative.

In analysing the transcript as a sequence of "adjacency pairs" defined in this way, we begin by breaking it down into a sequence of "turns" and "turn segments." In conversation analysis, a verbal interaction involving two or more participants is conceived as a *sequence* of alternating *turns* in each of which one of the participants speaks or otherwise "holds the floor" without being interrupted and without pausing for longer than, say, 0.5 seconds.

Turns in this sense are classified for the purposes of the present analysis as either "bivalent" or "univalent." A *bivalent turn* (C/A) consists of a gesture, token, sentence or sequence of sentences emitted by one speaker which acts both as a consequence (C) with respect to an immediately preceding turn emitted by another speaker and as an antecedent (A) with respect to another speaker's immediately succeeding turn. In other words, a bivalent turn is a turn which forms part of two consecutive adjacency pairs, contributing the second member to the first of the two pairs and the first member to the second pair.

Bivalent turns, according to this classification, are of two kinds - "single" and "double." A *single bivalent turn* (SB) is one which consists of a single gesture token or sentence which "looks" in both directions, both back towards the preceding turn and forward towards the next turn to be emitted by another speaker. A *double bivalent turn* (DB) consists of two distinct parts, either two sentences or a sentence followed by a sequence of sentences, the first of which acts as a consequence with respect to an immediately preceding turn emitted by another speaker, while the second acts as an antecedent with respect to another speaker's immediately succeeding turn.

A *univalent turn* is one which "looks" in only one direction, either forward as an antecedent with respect to an immediately succeeding turn to be emitted by another speaker without acting as consequence with respect to a preceding turn of that speaker, as in the case of the *opening turn* (OT) of a sequence, or backward as a consequence with respect to the immediately preceding turn of the other participant without acting as an antecedent with respect to a succeeding turn. The *closing turn* (CT) of a sequence is one case of such a backward-looking univalent turn. Another is the case of the verbal reinforcers or *continuers,* already mentioned, which overlap with and sustain without interrupting the other speaker's turn. A turn consisting of two or more sentences, punctuated and sustained by continuers supplied by the listener, constitutes what is known, for the purposes of the present analysis, as an *extended turn* (ET).

In breaking down the transcript into a sequence of Adjacency Pairs for the first Pragmatic Analysis, these extended turns emitted by a single speaker are analysed as a succession of *turn segments* the divisions between which are marked by the onset of an overlapping continuer emitted by the listener. In this way an extended turn is analysed as a succession of adjacency pairs each of which, except in the case of the final segment, consists of a turn segment followed by a continuer emitted by the listener.

In this way each successive utterance in the transcript is represented alternately as the first or as the second member of an adjacency pair, the only exception being the case of a single bivalent term which appears twice, once as the second member of the preceding adjacency pair and once as the first member of the following pair. Having analysed the sequence as a succession of adjacency pairs in this way, each pair is given a number and a description is assigned to the two members of the pair which reflects the relation between them.

By assigning these descriptions in accordance with the principle whereby a particular kind of verbal operant calls for a particular kind of reply or response which provides the reinforcing consequence for its emission, it is hoped to derive an empirically based taxonomy of speech acts/verbal operants which can be applied to the analysis of all kinds of verbal interaction. A provisional attempt to draft such a taxonomy is presented in Table 1.

Table 1 is divided vertically between the Antecedents or first members of the Adjacency Pairs on the left and the corresponding Consequences or second members on the right.

Horizontally, there is a division on the Antecedent side between First or primary antecedents and Second(ary) antecedents which consist in Pursuits, Confirmations, Corrections of and Repairs to First or primary antecedents. First or primary antecedents are sub-divided into Mands and Tacts, while there is a corresponding division on the Consequence side between Replies which pair with Mands and Responses, a category which includes most continuers, pairing with Tacts. Mands are finally subdivided into Instructions, Invitations, Applications, Offers and several varieties of (inter)Rogative. Tacts are similarly subdivided into those which are Informative, Evaluative, Narrative and Troubles-telling. There is corresponding complexity on the Consequence side in the subdivisions of Replies and Responses. As it stands, the table includes only the **reinforcing** consequences called for by the types of antecedent listed. It also includes only those adjacency pairs found in the so-called "Main Sequence" and excludes those peculiar to the so-called "Pre-sequence" and "Post-sequence."

Table 1. - Draft Taxonomy of Speech Acts/Verbal Operants

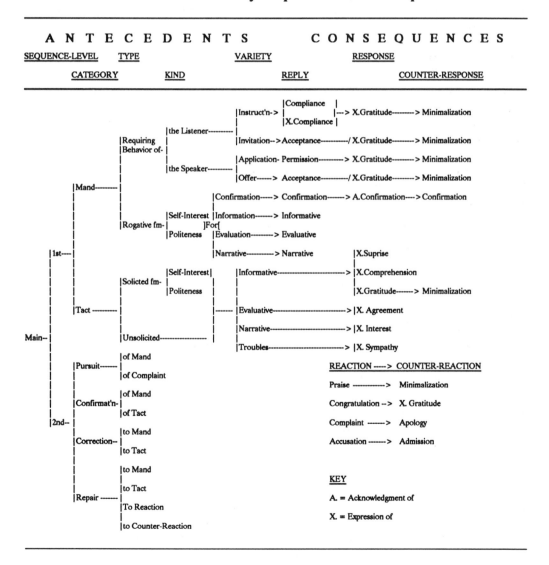

First Year Party 10/85 - Pragmatic Analysis I : List of Adjacency Pairs

Language Game: Leaving Instructions with a Peer

AP01 : ATTENTION-BID - GREETING/A.RECOGNITION
P01 : ((Enters and approaches))   A
                                                                      AP01
R01 : |ˆhe<u>llo</u> Penny.   C/A

AP02 : GREETING/A.RECOGNITION - APOLOGY
R01 : |ˆhe<u>llo</u> Penny.   C/A
                                                                      AP02
P02 :   (so[rry)   C/A

AP03 : APOLOGY - ACCEPTANCE/?APOLOGY TO THIRD PARTY
P02 : (so[rry)   C/A
                                                                      AP03
R02 :   ['sawrigh(t)   C/A

AP04: INVITATION TO OPEN M.S.-APOLOGY/INTERRUPTION-APPLICATION
R02 :   ['sawrigh(t)   C/A
                                                                      AP04
P03 :   can I inter<u>rupt</u>   C/A

AP05 : APOLOGY/INTERRUPTION-APPLICATION -
                        ACCEPTANCE/PERMISSION
P03 : can I inter<u>rupt</u> y[er a <u>moment</u>.   C/A
                          [AP05
R03 :   [yes do: C/A

AP06 : APOLOGY ACCEPTANCE/PERMISSION - APOLOGY
R03 : [yes do: C/A
                                                                      AP06
P04.1:   I'm <u>sorry</u> ex<u>cuse me,</u>   C

AP07 : UNSOLICITED INFORMATIVE - X.COMPREHENSION/CONTINUER
            (OPENING M.S.)
P04.2: it's <u>just</u> this bus'ness uv (.) th'<u>pahtee</u>[A
                                                                      AP07
R04 :   [ye:h(s)   C
AP08 : UNSOLICITED INFORMATIVE - X.COMPREHENSION/CONTINUER
P05 : [fer the <u>first</u> y:e:ahrs.   A
                                                                      AP08
R05 :   yes   C

AP09 : UNSOLICITED INFORMATIVE - X.COMPREHENSION/CONTINUER
  (INSTRUCTION)   (X.COMPLIANCE)

P06 : I̲ wᴏn't (.) be i̲:n temorro mo:rning.   A
                   AP09
R06 :   no   C

AP10 : UNSOLICITED INFORMATIVE - X.COMPREHENSION/CONTINUER

P07 : I've le̲ft a no̲tice on the ba̲wd.   A
                   AP10
R07 :   yeah.   C

AP11 : UNSOLICITED INFORMATIVE - INFORMATION-ROGATIVE
  (INSTRUCTION)   (X.COMPLIANCE)

P08 : an ther's a no̲te fer th'm %uv the mo̲ney.   A
                   AP11
R08 : who̲ wants te pick it up?   C/A

AP12 : INFORMATION-ROGATIVE - SOLICITED INFORMATIVE
       (SIGNALLING REDUNDANCY)

R08 : who̲ wants te pick it up?   C/A
                   AP12
P09 :   we:ll (.) the̲:'re on that li̲:[st. C/A

AP13 : SOLICITED INFORMATIVE - X.SURPRISE/X.COMPREHENSION
  (SIGNALLING REDUNDANCY)   (ECHOIC)

P09 : we:ll (.) the̲:'re on that li̲:[st.   C/A
            [AP13
R09.1:   [oh the're %aw- on that li̲st. C

AP14 : X.COMPREHENSION/CONFIRMATION-ROGATIVE - CONFIRMATION
  (EXTRAPOLATION)

R09.2: (.) and any-any uv these people [can ha̲ve i˜t, (.) can they. C/A
            [AP14
P10.1:   [yes:: (.)   C

S-D : SELF-DIRECTED INFERENCE
P10.2: ah do̲:: know John's girl friend kno̲ws about it. S-D
P10.3: bu(t) she̲:'s not fr̲ee at the same time as the̲m temorro S-D
P10.4: so:th- lo̲ts uv people kno̲:w about it,   A

AP15 : UNSOLICITED INFORMATIVE - X.COMPREHENSION/
           CONFIRMATION-ROGATIVE
           (EXTRAPOLATION)

P10.4: so:th- lo̲ts uv people kno̲:w about it,   A
                   AP15
R10 : anan the̲:'re goin te ge̲t the shoppin(g)   C/A

AP16 : CONFIRMATION-ROGATIVE - CONFIRMATION
    (EXTRAPOLATION)

```
R10  : anan the:'re goin te get the shoppin(g) out    [              C/A
                                                      [              AP16
P11  :                                          [yes                C
```

AP17 : A.CONFIRMATION - CONFIRMATION

```
R11  : ou[t uv it. (.) I see  [(    )                               C/A
             [                                                      AP17
P12.1:       [yes                                                   C
```

AP18 : UNSOLICITED INFORMATIVE - X.COMPREHENSION/CONTINUER

```
P12.2: ah've put a list uv what I suggest                           C/A
                                                                   AP18
R12  :                        [yeah                                 C
```

AP19 : UNSOLICITED INFORMATIVE - X.COMPLIANCE/CLOSURE
    (INSTRUCTION)   (WEAK-OVERRIDDEN)

```
P13  : [they get                                                    A
                                                                   AP19
R13  :        okay. [(then)                                         C
```

AP20 : UNSOLICITED INFORMATIVE - X.SURPRISE/X.COMPREHENSION
    (ECHOIC)

```
P14  : [an I've got all the rest uv the shopping.                   A
                                                                   AP20
R14.1: oh you've got all the rest. an they know that                C
```

AP21 : X.COMPREHENSION/   CONFIRMATION/CORRECTION
    CONFIRMATION-ROGATIVE
    (EXTRAPOLATION)

```
R14.3: =but anybody c'n: t-take this money that's in heah.=         C/A
                                                                   AP21
P15  : =wul (.) th(u) people o[n that list (.) yeh]                 C/A
```

AP22 : UNSOLICITED INFORMATIVE - X.COMPREHENSION/CONTINUER
    (SHADOWING)

```
P15  : wul (.) th(u) people o[n that list (.) yeh ]                 C/A
                             [                   ]                 AP22
R15  :                       [on  that  list  yes ]                 C/A
```

AP23 : X.COMPREHENSION - UNSOLICITED INFORMATIVE
    (SHADOWING)   (INSTRUCTION)

```
R15  : [on that list yes]=                                          C/A
                                                                   AP23
P16  : are the people who said they wud help with it=               C/A
```

AP24 : UNSOLICITED INFORMATIVE - X.COMPLIANCE/CLOSURE
        (INSTRUCTION)

P16 : are the people who said they wud help with it =	C/A
	AP24
R16 : =[o: k a y P e n n y]	C/A

AP25 : X.COMPLIANCE - X.GRATITUDE
                (OVERLAPPING)

R16 : [o: k a y P e n n y]	C/A
[ ]	AP25
P17 : [thank you very much]	C/A

AP26 : X.GRATITUDE - X.GRATITUDE

P17 : [thank you very much]	C/A
	AP26
R17.1: thanks then very much	C

See Appendix II for a key to symbols and conventions used in this analysis that are not explained in the text or in Appendix I.

Pragmatic Analysis II - List of Single Bivalent, Double Bivalent and Extended Turns

The second pragmatic analysis below is derived from the first by removing the numbers of the adjacency pairs, the duplications of the single bivalent turns and the continuers which divide up the extended turns into their constituent turn segments. The effect of this is to reveal a sequence of single bivalent, double bivalent and double bivalent/extended turns alternating between the different participants in such a way that each turn so defined acts as a consequence with respect to the immediately preceding turn emitted by another speaker and as antecedent with respect to another speaker's immediately succeeding turn. This pattern is emphasised by classifying and numbering each turn in a list of single bivalent (SB), double bivalent (DB) and extended turns (ET).

Finally the sequence is subdivided into its three phases. The first of these is the Pre-sequence in which self-identification is solicited and/or offered, recognition is acknowledged, enquiries about each other's health and welfare and observations about the weather, etc. are exchanged, and the opening of the subsequent Main Sequence is negotiated. The Main Sequence which follows contains the business transaction, information transfer, evaluation exchange, etc. for which the sequence was initiated in the first place. This is followed by the Post-sequence which contains expressions of gratitude, wishes for the successful outcome to the other's pre-occupying uncompleted contingencies, arrangements for subsequent interaction and final leave taking.

First Year Party 10/85 - Pragmatic Analysis II: List of Single Bivalent, Double Bivalent, and Extended Turns

Language Game - Leaving Instructions with a Peer

PRE-SEQUENCE BEGINS

OT-P	: ATTENTION-BID	
P01	: ((Enters and approaches))	A
SB1-R	: GREETING/A.RECOGNITION-ACKNOWLEDGEMENT	
R01	: |ˆhe<u>ll</u>o Penny.	C/A
SB1-P	: APOLOGY	
P02	: (so[rry)	C/A
SB2-R	: ACCEPTANCE/INVITATION TO OPEN M.S.	
R02	: ['sawrigh(t)	C/A
SB2-P	: APOLOGY/INTERRUPTION-APPLICATION	
P03	: can I interr<u>u</u>pt y[er a <u>mom</u>ent.	C/A
SB3-R	: ACCEPTANCE/PERMISSION	
R03	: [yes do:	C/A
DB1/ET1-P		
	: APOLOGY	
P04.1	: I'm <u>sorry</u> ex<u>cuse me,</u>	C

MAIN SEQUENCE BEGINS

	: UNSOLICITED INFORMATIVE	
P04.2	: it's <u>just</u> this bus'ness uv (.) th'<u>pah</u>tee [	A
	: UNSOLICITED INFORMATIVE	
P05	: [fer the <u>first</u> y:e:ahrs.	A
	: UNSOLICITED INFORMATIVE (INSTRUCTION)	
P06	: <u>I</u> won't (.) be i̱:n temorro mo:rning.	A
	: UNSOLICITED INFORMATIVE	
P07	: I've <u>left</u> a <u>no</u>tice on the <u>bawd.</u>	A
	: UNSOLICITED INFORMATIVE (INSTRUCTION)	
P08	: an ther's a <u>note</u> fer th'm %uv the <u>money.</u>	A
SB4-R	: INFORMATION-ROGATIVE	
R08	: who wants te pick it up?	C/A

SB3-P : SOLICITED INFORMATIVE (SIGNALLING REDUNDANCY)
P09   : we:ll (.) the:'re on that li:[st.   C/A

DB1-R:
        : X.SURPRISE/X.COMPREHENSION (ECHOIC)
R09.1 : [oh the're %aw- on that list.   C

        : X.COMPREHENSION (EXTRAPOLATION)/
                   CONFIRMATION-ROGATIVE
R09.2 : (.) and any-any uv these people [can have i˜t, (.) can they.   C/A
DB2/ET2-P
        : CONFIRMATION
P10.1 : [yes:: (.)   C

        : SELF-DIRECTED PREMISE
P10.2 : ah do:: know John's girl friend knows about it.   S-D

        : SELF-DIRECTED PREMISE
P10.3 : bu(t) she:'s not free at the same time as them temorro   S-D

        : SELF-DIRECTED CONCLUSION/UNSOLICITED INFORMATIVE
P10.4 : so:th- lots uv people kno:w about it,   A

DB2-R
        : X.COMPREHENSION (EXTRAPOLATION)/
                   CONFIRMATION-ROGATIVE
R10   : anan the:'re goin te get the shoppin(g) ou[t uv it. (.)   C/A

        : CONFIRMATION
R11   : I see [(   )   C/A

DB3-P
        : CONFIRMATION/UNSOLICITED INFORMATIVE
P12   : [yes ah've put a list uv what I suggest [they get   C/A

        : UNSOLICITED INFORMATIVE
Pl4   : [an I've got all the rest uv the shopping.   A

DB3/ET1-R
        : X.SURPRISE/X.COMPREHENSION (ECHOIC)
R14.1 : oh you've got all the rest.   C

        : CONFIRMATION ROGATIVE
R14.2 : an they know that.   C

        : X.COMPREHENSION (EXTRAPOLATION)/CONFIRMATION-ROGATIVE
R14.3 : but anybody c'n: t-take this money that's in heah.   C/A

DB4-P

	: CONFIRMATION/CORRECTION	
P15	: wul (.) th(u) <u>peo</u>ple o[n that list (.) yeh]	C/A
	: UNSOLICITED INFORMATIVE (INSTRUCTION)	
P16	: are the <u>peo</u>ple who <u>said</u> they wud <u>help</u> with it	C/A

POST-SEQUENCE BEGINS

SB5-R	: X.COMPLIANCE/CLOSURE	
R16	: [<u>o:</u> k a y P e n n y]	C/A

SB4-P	: X.GRATITUDE	
P17	: [thank you very much]	C/A

CT/DB4-R

	: X.GRATITUDE	
R17.1	: <u>thanks</u> then very much ye:s u:m (.)	C

SEQUENCE ENDS - INTERRUPTED MAIN SEQUENCE RESUMES

R17.3	: so <u>down</u> to "per<u>sua</u>ded me."	A

Semantic Analysis - Contingencies of the Three Agents Arranged in Chronological Order

The semantic analysis is derived from the List of Single Bivalent, Double Bivalent and Extended Turns in three stages. In the first stage the pragmatic descriptions and notation of the individual turns and turn segments are removed. At the same time Pre-and Post- sequences are dropped on the grounds that the stereotyped sentences of which they consist have a purely pragmatic function and are of no semantic significance. The remaining sentences are then given a semantic classification based on the principle of Behavioral Contingency Semantics. On this principle, each sentence in the sequence is classified, regardless of who is the current speaker, in terms of the particular contingency term or leg (A for "antecedent", B for "behavior" and C for "consequence") which it specifies relative to the behavior of the speaker (S), the listener (L) and some other person or persons mentioned in the sequence (O).

The second stage in the semantic analysis is to split up the sequence into three separate lists of semantically significant sentences for each of the three agents whose contingencies are specified in it, the two participants and the other person or persons mentioned in the dialogue. In the case of the two participants, sentences uttered by that participant as speaker (S:) are included along with those uttered by the other participant to which that agent responds as listener (L:). A serial number is then assigned to the contingency specified by the sentence in question according to its position on a list of contingencies defined in relation to the behavior of the particular agent in the chronological order of the occurrence of that behavior. Finally, the relationship of the event or state of affairs represented in each sentence to the "now" of utterance is indicated by means of the symbol " < " for past " < > " for present and " > " for future. This prepares the way for the third and final stage in which the sentences which specify the legs of the contingencies of the three agents are re-arranged in the chronological order of occurrence of the behavior relative to which the contingency in question is defined in the time scale represented in the dialogue. This permits all the sentences which specify parts of a particular contingency to be grouped together under a heading which describes the contingency by reference to its defining behavior.

First Year Party 10/85 - Semantic Analysis

I. Penny's Contingencies in Chronological Order

CONTINGENCY 1. - DOING THE SHOPPING
P14 : [an I've got all the rest uv the shopping.   S:B1C1<

CONTINGENCY 2. - TELLING THE HELPERS ABOUT THE ARRANGEMENTS
P07 : I've left a notice on the bawd.   S:B2C2<
P10.2: ah do:: know John's girl friend knows about it.   S:C2.1<
P10.4: so:th- lots uv people kno:w about it,   S:C2.1<
P10.3: bu(t) she:'s not free at the same time as them temorro   S:C2.3>

CONTINGENCY 3. - MAKING A LIST OF WHO IS TO HAVE THE MONEY
P08 : an ther's a note fer th'm %uv the money.   S:B3C3<
P09 : we:ll (.) the:'re on that li:[st.   S:C3<
R09.2: (.) and any-any uv these people [can have i˜t, (.) can they.   L:C3.1>?
R14.3: but anybody c'n: t-take this money that's in heah.   L:C3.1>?
P15 :wul- (.) th(u) people o[n that list (.) yeh]
P16 : are the people who said they wud help with it   S:C3.2>

CONTINGENCY 4. - MAKING THE SHOPPING LIST
P12.2: ah've put a list uv what I suggest [they get   S:A4<>B4C4<
R10 : anan the:'re goin te get the shoppin(g) ou[t uv it.   L:C4.1>?

CONTINGENCY 5. - HANDING OVER THE MONEY AND LISTS TO ROSE
P03 : can I interrupt y[er a moment.   S:B5<>
P08 : an ther's a note fer th'm %uv the money.   S:B5.1<>
P04.2: it's just this bus'ness uv (.) th'pahtee
P05 : [fer the first y:e:ahrs.   S:C5>
CONTINGENCY 6. - NOT COMING IN TOMORROW
P06 : I won't (.) be i:n temorro mo:rning.   S:B6

II. Rose's Contingencies in Chronological Order

CONTINGENCY 1. - LISTENING TO PENNY
P03 : can I interrupt y[er a moment.   L:A1<>
CONTINGENCY 2. - TAKING CHARGE OF THE MONEY AND THE LISTS
P08 : an ther's a note fer th'm %uv the money.   L:A2<>/

CONTINGENCY 3. - NO NEED TO TELL THE HELPERS ABOUT
                              THE ARRANGEMENTS
P07 : I've left a notice on the bawd.   L:A3<
P10.2: ah do:: know John's girl friend knows about it.   L:A3.1<
P10.4: so:th- lots uv people kno:w about it,   L:A3.2<
P06 : I won't (.) be i:n temorro mo:rning.   L:A3.3>

P10.3: bu(t) <u>she:'s</u> not <u>free</u> at the same time as <u>them</u> temorro   L:A3.4>

CONTINGENCY 4. - CHECKING WHETHER AN APPLICANT CAN HAVE THE MONEY AND GIVING IT TO THEM

P15 : wul- (.) th(u) <u>peop</u>le o[n that list (.) yeh]
P16 : are the <u>peop</u>le who <u>said</u> they wud <u>help</u> with it   L:A4<
P08 : an ther's a <u>note</u> fer th'm %uv the <u>money</u>.   L:A4.1< >
R08 : who wants te pick it up?   S:A4>?
P09 : we:ll (.) th<u>e:</u>'re on that <u>li:</u>[st.   L:A4.1< >
R09.2: (.) and any-any uv these people [can <u>have</u> i^t, (.) can they.   S:B4>?
R14.3: but <u>any</u>body c'n: t-<u>take</u> this <u>money</u> that's in heah.   S:B4>?

CONTINGENCY 5. - NO NEED TO TELL THEM WHAT TO GET

P14 : [an <u>I've</u> got all the <u>rest</u> uv the shopping.   L:A5<
P12.2: ah've put a list uv what I <u>suggest</u> [they <u>get</u>   L:A5.1>
R10 : anan <u>the:</u>'re goin te <u>get</u> the shoppin(g) <u>ou</u>[t uv it.   S:C5>?
P04.2: it's <u>just</u> this bus'ness uv (.) th'<u>pahtee</u>
P05 : [fer the <u>first</u> y:e:ahrs.   L:C5>

III. Contingencies of the Others in Chronological Order

CONTINGENCY 1. - RESPONDING TO PENNY'S COMMUNICATION

P15 : wul- (.) th(u) <u>peop</u>le o[n that list (.) yeh]
P16 : are the <u>peop</u>le who <u>said</u> they wud <u>help</u> with it   O:B1<
P10.2: ah <u>do</u>:: know John's girl friend <u>knows</u> about it.   O:C1<
P10.4: so:th- <u>lots</u> uv people <u>kno:w</u> about it,   O:C1<

CONTINGENCY 2. - APPLYING TO ROSE FOR THE MONEY

P15 :wul- (.) th(u) <u>peop</u>le o[n that list (.) yeh]
P16 : are the <u>peop</u>le who <u>said</u> they would <u>help</u> with it   O:A2<
R08 : wh<u>o</u> wants te pick it up?   O:B2>?
P09 : we:ll (.) th<u>e:</u>'re on that <u>li:</u>[st.   O:B2>
R14.3: but <u>any</u>body c'n: t-<u>take</u> this <u>money</u> that's in heah.   O:B2>?
R09.2: (.) and any-any uv these people [can <u>have</u> i˜t, (.) can they.   O:C2>?

CONTINGENCY 3. DOING THE REST OF THE SHOPPING

P14 : [an <u>I've</u> got all the <u>rest</u> uv the shopping.   O;A3<
P08 : an ther's a <u>note</u> fer th'm %uv the <u>money</u>.   O:A3.1< >
P12.2: ah've put a list uv what I <u>suggest</u> [they <u>get</u>   O:A3.2< >
R10 : anan <u>the:</u>'re goin te <u>get</u> the shoppin(g) <u>ou</u>[t uv it.   O:B3>?
P04.2: it's <u>just</u> this bus'ness uv (.) th'<u>pahtee</u>
P05 : [fer the <u>first</u> y:e:ahrs.   O:C3>

References

Barwise, J. and Perry, J. (1983). *Situations and attitudes.* Cambridge, MA: M.I.T. Press.

Brentano, F. (1911). Appendix to the classification of mental phenomena. In O. Kraus (Ed.). *Psychology from an empirical standpoint.* English translation L. L. McAlister (Ed.). London: Routledge & Kegan Paul, 1973.

Brown, P. & Levinson, S. C. (1978). Universals in language usage: Politeness phenomena. In E. Goody (Ed.). *Questions and politeness: Strategies in social interaction.* Cambridge: C.U.P.

Chomsky, N. (1958). *Syntactic structures.* The Hague: Mouton.

Chomsky, N. (1959). Review of B. F. Skinner's *Verbal Behavior. Language, 35,* 26-58.

van Dijk, T. A. (Ed.). (1985). *Handbook of discourse analysis.* New York: Academic Press.

Frege, G. (1879). Begriffschrift. English translation P. T. Geach. In P. T. Geach & M. Black (Eds.). *Translations from the philosophical writings of Gottlob Frege.* 2nd. Ed. Oxford: Blackwell, 1960.

Frege, G. (1891). Function and concept. Jenaischer gesellschaft fuer medicin und naturwissenschaft. English translation P. T. Geach. In P. T. Geach & M. Black (Eds.). *Translations from the philosophical writings of Gottlob Frege.* 2nd. Ed. Oxford: Blackwell, 1960.

Garfinkel, H. (1967). *Studies in ethnomethodology.* New York: Prentice-Hall.

Greenspoon, J. (1955). The reinforcing effect of two spoken sounds on the frequency of two responses. *American Journal of Psychology, 68,* 409-416.

Grice, H. P. (1975). Logic and conversation. In P. Cole & J. L. Morgan (Eds.). *Syntax and semantics 3: Speech acts.* New York: Academic Press.

Heritage, J. C. (1985). Recent developments in conversation analysis. *Sociolinguistics, 15,* 1-19.

Horner, V. M. & Gussow, J. D. (1972). John and Mary: A pilot study in linguistic ecology. In C. B. Cazden, V. P. John, & D. Hymes (Eds.). *Functions of language in the classroom.* New York: Teachers' College Press.

Jefferson, G. (1979). A technique for inviting laughter and its subsequent acceptance/ declination. In G. Psathas (Ed.). *Everyday language: Studies in ethnomethodology.* New York: Irvington Press.

Jefferson, G. (1980a). Final Report to the British Social Science Research Council on the Analysis of Conversations in which "Troubles" and "Anxieties" are Expressed.

Jefferson, G. (1980b). On "trouble-premonitory" response to inquiry. *Sociological Inquiry, 50,* 153-185.

Jefferson, G. (1980c). The abominable Ne?. Dialogforschung: Jahrbuch 1980 des Instituts fuer deutsche Sprache, *Sprache der Gegenwart, 54,* 53-88 (Shortened version).

Jefferson, G. (1981). *The abominable Ne?.* University of Manchester, Department of Sociology, Occasional Paper No. 6. (Complete version), Manchester, England.

Krasner, L. (1958). Studies of the conditioning of verbal behavior. *PsychologicalBulletin, 55,* 148-170.

Levinson, S. C.(1983). *Pragmatics.* Cambridge: C.U.P.

McLeish, J. & Martin, J. (1975). Verbal behavior: A review and experimental analysis. *The Journal of General Psychology, 93,* 3-66.

McPherson, A., Bonem, M., Green, G., & Osborne, J. G. (1984). A citation analysis of the influence on research of Skinner's *Verbal Behavior. The Behavior Analyst , 7,* 157-168.

Michael, J. (1982). Distinguishing between discriminative and motivational functions of stimuli. *Journal of the Experimental Analysis of Behavior, 37,* 149-155.

Morris, C. W. (1938). Foundations of the theory of signs. In the *International Encyclopedia of*

Unified Science, Vol. 1, No. 2. Chicago: University of Chicago Press.

Morris, C. W. (1946). *Signs, language and behavior.* New York: Prentice-Hall.

Place, U. T. (1983). Skinner's *Verbal Behavior* IV - How to improve Part IV, Skinner's account of syntax. *Behaviorism, 11,* 163-186.

Place, U. T. (1985a). A response to Sundberg and Michael. *The Analysis of Verbal Behavior, 3,* 38-45.

Place, U. T. (1985b). Three senses of the word "tact". *Behaviorism, 13,* 63-73.

Place, U. T. (1985c). Three senses of the word "tact" - a reply to Professor Skinner. *Behaviorism, 13,* 155-156.

Place, U. T. (1986). *The invisibility of extra-episodic reinforcement as a problem in presenting behavior analysis to conversation analysts.* Paper presented at the Annual Conference of the Experimental Analysis of Behaviour Group, St. Andrew's, Scotland, April 1986.

Russell, B. (1918/1919). The philosophy of Logical Atomism. *The Monist, 28,* 495-527, 29:32-63, 190-222, 345-380. Reprinted in B. Russell, *Logic and knowledge: Essays 1901-1950.* R. C. Marshall (Ed.). London: Allen & Unwin, 1956.

Schegloff, E. A. (1968). Sequencing in conversational openings. *American Anthropologist, 70,* 1075-1095. Reprinted in J. J. Gumperz & D. Hymes (Eds). *Directions in sociolinguistics.* New York: Holt, Rinehart & Winston, 1972.

Schegloff, E. A. & Sachs, H. (1974). Opening up closings. *Semiotica* 289-372. Reprinted in R. Turner (Ed.). *Ethnomethodology.* Harmondsworth, Middlesex: Penguin Books.

Skinner, B. F. (1950). Are theories of learning necessary? *Psychological Review, 57,* 193-216.

Skinner, B. F. (1957). *Verbal behavior.* New York: Appleton-Century-Crofts.

Skinner, B. F. (1969). *Contingencies of reinforcement.* New York: Appleton-Century- Crofts.

Spielberger, C. D. & Levin, S. M. (1962). What is learned in verbal conditioning? *Journal of Verbal Learning and Verbal Behavior, 1,* 125- 132.

Taffel, C. (1955). Anxiety and the conditioning of verbal behavior. *Journal of Abnormal and Social Psychology, 51,* 496-501.

Verplanck, W. S. (1955). The control of the content of conversation: Reinforcement of statements of opinion. *Journal of Abnormal and Social Psychology, 51,* 668-676.

Wittgenstein, L. (1922). *Tractatus logico-philosophicus.* English translation by C. K. Ogden & I. A. Richards. London: Kegan Paul.

Footnotes

1. Now at the University College of North Wales, Bangor.
2. As Brentano (1911) points out, the objects, events and states of affairs to which words and sentences intentionally refer do not exist and you cannot have a relation one of whose terms is non-existent.
3. The construction of novel sentences requires that any such sentence be a member of a number of response classes.

APPENDIX I - Phonetic Conventions

(adapted from those used in conversation analysis more particularly in transcripts made by Dr. Gail Jefferson)

1. superimposed square brackets either: [a......z]

          [   ]

          [a......z] as in:

```
P15 :wul- (.) th(u) people o[n that list (.) yeh]
                            [                    ]
R15 :                       [on  that  list  yes ]
```

```
      or [a.....z
         [
         [a.....z   as in:
```

```
R03 :  [yes do:
       [
P04.1: y[er a moment. I'm sorry excuse me,
```

indicate overlapping.

2. Equals symbol =a.....z= as in:

Penny: =who said they would help with it=

indicates no discernible gap between the preceding or following utterances, whether of the same or of different speakers.

3. A full stop within curved brackets, (.) as in:

P06 : I won't (.) be i:n temorro mo:rning.

indicates a micropause between utterances.

4. A comma ....z, at the end of a phrase or sentence as in:

P10.4: so:th- lots uv people kno:w about it,

indicates an upward intonation at the end of the word it follows.

5. A question mark ....z? at the end of a sentence as in:

RO8: who wants te pick it up?

indicates an upward intonation on the whole word that precedes it.

6. A **full stop** ....z. at the end of a sentence as in:

P07 : I've l<u>ef</u>t a <u>no</u>tice on the <u>bawd</u>.

indicates a downward intonation, either over the course of the word that precedes it or at the end of the word.

7. **Colons** a::...z: as in:
P10.2: ah <u>do</u>:: know John's girl friend <u>knows</u> about it.

indicate prolonging or stretching of the sound of the preceding letter or syllable, the more colons the more the stretching.

8. **Underlining** <u>a</u>....z as in:

P03 : can I interr<u>upt</u>

indicates stress either by pitch or by volume.

9. A **percent symbol** %a....z as in:

P08 : an ther's a <u>no</u>te fer th'm %uv the <u>mo</u>ney.

indicates a very soft tone or low volume.

10. An **upward line and carrot** |ˆa....z as in:

R01 : |ˆhe<u>llo</u> Penny.

indicates a sharp upward intonation in the syllable following the line and carrot.
11. A **dash** ....z- as in:

P09 : we:ll (.) th<u>e:</u>'re on that l<u>i:</u>[st.
                                    [
R09.1:   [oh the're %aw- on that <u>list</u>.

indicates a cut-off of the preceding sound or word.

12. A **tilde** ....˜z as in:

R09.2: (.) and any-any uv these people [can <u>have</u> iˉt, (.) can they.
                                        [
P10.1:   [yes:: (.)

indicates an accentuation of a final consonant.

13. **Empty brackets ( )** as in:

P11 : [yes
    [

R11 : <u>ou</u>[t of it. (.) <u>I see</u> [(   )
                    [

P12.1:   [yes

indicate that the speaker made some sound or utterance which could not be heard sufficiently to be transcribed.

14. **Words or letters in curved brackets (a....z)** as in:

P02: (so [rry)
        [

R02 : ['sawrigh(t)

indicate that the transcriber is in some doubt about the word or sound actually emitted or whether any sound was actually made in this position.

15. **Words in double curved brackets ((A....z))** as in:

Penny: it's <u>just</u> this bus'ness uv (.) th' <u>pah</u>tee [fer the=
                                        [

Rose: [ye:h(s)
                              ((Knock))

indicate sounds on the tape other than the speakers' verbalizations.

APPENDIX II - Conventions Used in the List of Adjacency Pairs and Not Explained Elsewhere in the Text

S-D   = A self-directed turn in which a speaker is "thinking aloud" in such a way that no response is called for from the listener.

A...Z - A..   = The boundary between the descriptions of the two members of an adjacency pair.

A...Z/A...   = The boundary between the descriptions of the consequence and antecedent functions of a single bivalent (C/A) turn.

A.   = "Acknowledgment of"

M.S.   = The main sequence

(A....Z)   = An additional function performed by the utterance in question or a description of the way in which the function of the utterance in question is performed.

X.   = "Expression of"

(ECHOIC)   = An utterance in which the speaker repeats part of the previous speaker's utterance word for word.

(SHADOWING) = An utterance in which the concluding word or words of the speaker's sentence are uttered simultaneously by the listener.

A Discussion of Chapter 5

Place's Conversation Analysis

Hayne W. Reese
West Virginia University

The discussion of Place's presentation at the Institute centered on five issues: (1) the role of rule-governance in verbal behavior, (2) the nature of rules in verbal behavior, (3) the goals of conversation analysis, (4) correspondence between verbal behavior and the world, and (5) context effects on verbal behavior. Each of these issues is discussed in turn in this commentary.

The Role of Rule-Governance in Verbal Behavior

Place commented that cognitive psychology "rides roughshod" over Skinner's distinction between rule-governance and contingency-shaping. Although he did not elaborate on the point, it is accurate with respect to both computer-simulation cognitive psychology and psycholinguistics, as shown in the rest of this section.

Computer simulation. In the computer-simulation approach to cognitive development the developmental mechanisms have been imposed by the keyboard operator, who thereby functions as a deus ex machina, and are not intrinsic to the computerized part of the simulation. That is, the keyboard operator inserts a set of already-formed rules, which perforce "govern" the behavior/output of the computer; but the presumed acquisition of these rules in real life is not included in the simulation. Cognitive psychologists do not believe that a god inserts various full-blown sets of rules into the minds of children at various ages; but they have so far not been able to write a program that successfully simulates the development of these sets of rules. Thus, they emphasize rule-governance and not the acquisition of rules, which according to the consensus of behavior analysts is a matter primarily of contingency-shaping.

The participants at the Institute concurred that much verbal behavior is contingency-shaped rather than rule-governed; as Salzinger commented, for example, verbal responses are often too fast to be rule-governed. However, as Salzinger also noted, rules can come into play, as in experiments in which the subject must think about what to do. He commented that he has done a number of studies involving awareness of rules.

Psycholinguistics. Chomsky (1959) and many other psycholinguists (e.g., Deese, 1970; Slobin, 1974) criticize behavioral approaches to language -- often citing only Skinner's (1957) *Verbal Behavior* and almost never citing any of the relevant behavioral research. A recurrent criticism is that reinforcement cannot account for language acquisition because the child acquires so much in so little time with so little input. Further, if language acquisition is not a product of reinforcement, it must be innate. Putnam (1975) commented: "What this 'argument' reduces to is 'Wow! How complicated a skill every normal adult learns. What else could it be but **innate**'" (p. 115).

In Chomsky's system, language acquisition is attributed to innate language concepts and an innate language acquisition device. Putnam pointed out that no actual acquisition device or mechanism is specified (but he also said "the evidence is today slim that **any** learning requires reinforcement 'in any interesting sense'" -- p. 114). However, success in science is an empirical matter and not a matter of logic or philosophy, which are nonscientific branches of knowledge and have nonscientific methods of inquiry and nonscientific ways of determining truth. Thus, Chomsky (1988) agreed that the analysis of language and language acquisition could be done in other ways than his and that his way could be wrong, but he argued that the philosophical points can be ignored and that psycholinguists should get on with the analysis and construct the best theories they can.

Chomsky's answer to Putnam's criticism is reasonable, and its essence works equally well for the behavior analytic approach to language: Granted that behavior analysts have not yet successfully analyzed some of the complexities such as paraphrase and generativity, let them get on with it and construct the best conceptual and experimental analyses they can.

The Nature of Rules in Verbal Behavior

Discussion of the nature of rules in verbal behavior centered around whether they are descriptive or causal, and involved some terminological dispute. Place commented that verbal behavior is contingency-shaped rather than rule-governed, and that consequently nobody can generate rules that will be of much use for the understanding of verbal behavior. A suggestion was made that the rules generated would only **identify** regularities, and would therefore be descriptive rather than controlling. Malott suggested that they might be called laws rather than rules. Salzinger objected to calling them laws, on the argument that laws are about the control of behavior and that the rules referring to verbal behavior are not about the control of this behavior. I commented that psycholinguists are interested in the rules as descriptions and have been much less concerned with the control of verbal behavior; they are interested almost exclusively in language competence rather than language performance, or verbal behavior. Place pointed out that disobeying such rules can have social consequences; however, although the rules would then be entered into a law of the sort Salzinger referred to, they would still not be causal in themselves.

I have discussed these issues in detail elsewhere (Reese, 1988, 1989) and will not pursue the discussion further here, other than to offer the following summary statement: The rules of verbal behavior that are offered by psycholinguists and by behavior analysts are descriptive; they refer to linguistic regularities but do not account for these regularities. Current theory and evidence indicate that the social environment accounts for the regularities.

The Goals of Conversation Analysis

S. Hayes asked two fundamental questions about conversation analysis: What do we want to know about a conversation and why do we want to know it? Place replied that an immediate aim is to demonstrate the applicability of behavior analysis to language, and a longer-term aim is to develop a taxonomy that will allow the computer to do language analyses. He pointed out that at present, field observation rather than experimental analysis is the method of choice, and that studies are yielding rules about the many ways verbal behavior proceeds, but that these are "rules" only in a descriptive sense -- they do not **account for** the behavior. This point is considered further later.

Place noted that interest in a phenomenon generates questions, and the questions generate research. He pointed out that preliminary research in conversation analysis has generated a taxonomy of rules, which needs to be studied in further research. Hayes commented that the further research might require changing the taxonomy. Place replied that the present aim is to develop a data base to test theory about how verbal behavior works. As noted earlier, his position was that verbal behavior is contingency-shaped rather than rule-governed and that the rules as such will therefore be of little use for understanding verbal behavior. This point is also considered further later.

Place's position is that conversation analysts and behavior analysts agree on (a) rejection of levels other than the level observed and (b) to some extent, the need to consider context; but (c) they disagree to some extent on methods.

(a) Both kinds of analyst reject the attribution of behavior to rules and other entities for which the only evidence of existence is the behavior that the rules are intended to explain.

(b) Both kinds of analyst recognize the need to consider context. However, in my opinion the extent to which this recognition influences their actual conceptual work is open to question. For example, according to Place a sentence functions as a discriminative stimulus, orienting the listener to a particular contingency by virtue of a correspondence between the content of the sentence and the content of the contingency it specifies. Sentences map onto events or states, that is, "situations." Thus, "The baby is crying" and "Give the baby the bottle" are related implicitly to the same situation and implicitly to the same contingency. However, an objection to this analysis is that although these sentences are often related implicitly to the same situation, each also occurs in different situations in which it implies a different contingency. For example, in some situations "The baby is crying" is not related implicitly to the same contingency as "Give the baby the bottle" but rather is related implicitly to "Change the baby's diaper." In short, one must often know the situation--the context--in which sentences are uttered in order to know what contingencies they imply. In these cases, the manifest content of the sentences is interpretable only if the context is known.

Cognitive psychologists will probably object to the emphasis on context, given that they see language development as a progressive freeing of language (and cognition) from context. For example, according to Luria (1982) language progresses from being "sympractical" to being "synsemantic": *Sympractical speech* consists of words with diffuse meanings, which become understandable and specific only in the context of the behavior the words accompany and the situation in which the behavior and the words occur. *Synsemantic speech* is independent of this kind of context; it develops ontogenetically as words "gradually become separated from action to become independent signs which designate objects, actions and properties (and later, also relationships)" (Luria, 1982, p. 34).

Synsemantic speech is illustrated by Place's conveying his meanings to us at the Institute independently of the contexts in which his observations were made. However, none of the sentences he uttered was entirely context-independent, in that the sentences as a group constituted a context that influenced the meaning of each specific sentence. After the Institute, Chase commented that Place's presentation probably had different effects on different members of the audience because the context was not the same for all of them. Chase added that this is a problem with all such "highly" developed speech. Another problem is that many utterances by even mature speakers such as Place are not grammatical sentences, especially in informal conversation. Many of these utterances are likely to be sympractical speech, that is, uninterpretable without knowledge of its context.

(c) The first step in conversation analysis is to develop a taxonomy based on field observations. In contrast, the preferred method for behavior analysis is the laboratory experiment. However, although conversation analysis is done in the natural setting initially, it can later be taken into the laboratory; and although behavior analysis is largely experimental-manipulative, it is by no means entirely so. Thus, this difference between conversation analysis and behavior analysis is not as great as it initially seems to be.

However, another question that aroused discussion at the Institute was why so little behavior analytic work has been done on verbal behavior. One possibility that was suggested is that Skinner's *Verbal Behavior* is conceptually deficient; another was that mature verbal behavior is not easily subject to experimental-manipulative research. Verbal behavior in its natural setting is shaped by immediate consequences. In laboratory research, verbal behavior is rule-governed, or at least very much of it is rule-governed, and therefore the verbal behavior observed in laboratory research is not necessarily observable in natural settings.

The problem, I think, is to analyze the **development** of verbal behavior, which is believed by most behavior analysts to be contingency-shaped for the most part. At the mature level, which occurs fairly early in childhood, verbal behavior is so regular that it appears rule-governed. However, as Bugelski (1956, p. 401) said with respect to one-trial learning that follows discrimination learning-set training, the key to explaining the final level of performance is to explain the errors that occur during the training. Or as Baer (1982) said in answer to the question of how persons extract square roots with paper and pencil, they were taught. That is, the acquisition history of any behavior--learning set, arithmetic algorithm, or language--is the analysis of that behavior, the explanation of how it occurs.

The next question, then, is whether conversation analysis is relevant to development, that is, does analysis of conversations between mature speakers reveal anything about development? Place felt that it might, but noted that for the study of development maybe an experimental approach is more appropriate. Work is needed, because behavior analysts have done very little on language development.

Correspondence

The problem of correspondence is implicated in Johnson-Laird, Herrmann, and Chaffin's (1984) pointing out that network theories of meaning deal with relations among words but not with relations between words and their referents. The issues of reference and correspondence were discussed at the Institute, but without reaching a consensus. Linda Hayes asked for clarification of Place's concept of correspondence between the form of a sentence and the contingency it specifies. Place gave as an example, "If the baby cries, give it the bottle, and it will go back to sleep." He pointed out that this sentence consists of three atomic sentences tied together by if-then connections. As I understood his position, the noun phrases within each atomic sentence are related in some way, and the correspondence is between the relations in the atomic sentences that are tied together by if-then connections. That is, given two atomic sentences with an if-then connection, the relation within one atomic sentence corresponds to the relation within the other atomic sentence. Thus, the behavior of the giver with something given corresponds to the behavior of the givee in response to the giving. Correspondence gives a sentence its function as a discriminative stimulus.

Marr commented that we can talk about unicorns, the square root of 2, democracy, etc., which obviate correspondence because they do not have concrete referents; and when the pigeon pecks green and not red, no one brings up reference and correspondence. Similarly, if the sentence is functioning as a discriminative stimulus, then again correspondence--and reference--are pseudo-issues.

Place agreed that correspondence is probably ultimately intelligible in terms of discrimination learning. However, he pointed out that the problem it is related to is how a novel sentence induces behavior the listener has never done before. The instructions yield the behavior, but why? Correspondence and reference. The issues of correspondence and reference are obviously complex, and although the discussion continued along philosophical lines, the issues were understandably not resolved.

Context Effects on Verbal Behavior

As an example of the kind of utterance that needs to be dealt with, Place quoted the sentence, "There are no black scorpions on this table," which led Skinner to develop *Verbal Behavior.* However, I consider the first step needed in analyzing this sentence, or any other sentence, is to identify the context in which it occurred. Disembodied from a context, either physical as in sympractical speech or semantic as in synsemantic speech, no utterance is interpretable. For example, in the context of a table with black scorpions on it, the utterance would be an untrue tact; and in many contexts it would be a mand in tact form if uttered with a certain intonation pattern.

Intonation pattern, which includes pitch, stress, length, and pause (Key, 1975, p. 51), is one aspect of "paralanguage," which together with "kinesics" constitutes a class of contextual aspects that are ignored in much of the research on language and language development, including psycholinguistic, behavior analytic, and, apparently, conversation analytic research. Key (1975) described paralanguage and kinesics as follows:

> *Paralanguage* is some kind of articulation of the vocal apparatus, or significant lack of it, i.e. hesitation, between segments of vocal articulation. This includes all noises and sounds which are extra-speech sounds, such as hissing, shushing, whistling, and imitation sounds, as well as a large variety of speech modifications, such as quality of voice (sepulchral, whiney, giggling), extra high-pitched utterances, or hesitations and speed in talking. Ostwald calls these "nonverbal acoustic signs." *Kinesics* is articulation of the body, or movements resulting from muscular and skeletal shift. This includes all actions, physical or physiological, automatic reflexes, posture, facial expressions, gestures, and other body movements. (p. 10)

The written language conveys meanings with words and their sequence, with word choice, punctuation, and other symbols to represent paralinguistic and kinesic aspects. The following examples illustrate paralinguistic effects on meaning. The intonation pattern of interrogation is symbolized by the question mark at the end of the following two sentences (from Key, 1975, p. 51), and the comma in the first sentence symbolizes a pause that indicates a difference in the meanings of the two sentences:

"Would you like tea, or lemonade?" (Choose one of the two.)

"Would you like tea or lemonade?" (Would you like something to drink?)

An excellent example of the role of kinesics is in *The Virginian* (the book, not the television series) where Trampas says to the Virginian, in a poker game, "Your bet, you son-of-a-_____ " and the Virginian draws his pistol and says gently, "When you call me that, **smile**" (Wister, 1902, p. 29; blank and emphasis in original). Another example is the increasing degree of displeasure communicated by a moue, pout, grimace, and rictus. Still other examples are gestures (Smith & Williamson, 1977, Chap. 7) and spacing between persons (Chap. 8).

Given the effects of paralanguage and kinesics on word meanings, and the ways these aspects are indicated in the written language, the emphasis of psycholinguists on grammar is understandable. In informal, spontaneous speech, paralanguage and kinesics are even more important than in written language, because much of real speech is telegraphic or otherwise ungrammatical and many meanings are conveyed without conventional words.

Despite the known importance of paralanguage and kinesics in real speech, much of the research on language **development** has been based on verbatim transcriptions of spontaneous speech with no coding of the paralinguistic and kinesic aspects. Admittedly, coding these aspects is likely to be enormously complicated (although I suspect that it need not be as complicated as in Birdwhistell's [1970] system, which included 61 symbols for just the face, for example.) However, unless these aspects are coded, the transcriptions provide an incomplete basis for interpreting both the meaning and the grammatical structure of the utterances.

An approach is limited when it omits important aspects of a domain, as conversation analysis seems to do with respect to paralanguage, kinesics, and other contextual aspects. However, this limitation is not inherent in conversation analysis as a general approach, nor in the method of transcription analysis. It can be overcome by including the currently omitted aspects in the transcription--no easy task, to be sure, but I think a necessary one.

References

Baer, D. M. (1982). Applied behavior analysis. In G. T. Wilson & C. M. Franks (Eds.), *Contemporary behavior therapy* (pp. 277-309). New York: Guilford.

Birdwhistell, R. L. (1970). *Kinesics and context: Essays on body motion communication.* Philadelphia: University of Pennsylvania Press.

Bugelski, B. R. (1956). *The psychology of learning.* New York: Holt.

Chomsky, N. (1959). Review of *Verbal behavior.* By B. F. Skinner. *Language, 35,* 26-58.

Chomsky, N. (1988, February). *Language and its use: A rule-free perspective.* Advertised title of lecture at the Center for Philosophy of Science, University of Pittsburgh, February 24, 1988.

Deese, J. (1970). *Psycholinguistics.* Boston: Allyn & Bacon.

Johnson-Laird, P. N., Herrmann, D. J., & Chaffin, R. (1984). Only connections: A critique of semantic networks. *Psychological Bulletin, 96,* 292-315.

Key, M. R. (1975). *Paralanguage and kinesics (nonverbal communication).* Metuchen, NJ: Scarecrow Press.

Luria, A. R. (1982). *Language and cognition* (J. V. Wertsch, Ed.). New York: Wiley.

Putnam, H. (1975). The "innateness hypothesis" and explanatory models in linguistics. In H. Putnam, *Mind, language and reality: Philosophical papers, Volume 2* (pp. 107-116). Cambridge: Cambridge University Press.

Reese, H. W. (1988). Rules as nonverbal entities. Paper presented at the Second International Institute on Verbal Relations, Tequesquitengo, Mexico, June 1987.

Reese, H. W. (1989). Rules and rule-governance: Cognitive and behavioristic approaches. In S. C. Hayes (Ed.), *Rule-governed behavior: Cognition, contingencies, and instructional control* (pp. 3-84). New York: Plenum.

Skinner, B. F. (1957). *Verbal behavior.* New York: Appleton-Century-Crofts.

Slobin, D. I. (1974). *Psycholinguistics.* Glenview, IL: Scott, Foresman.

Smith, D. R., & Williamson, L. K. (1977). *Interpersonal communication: Roles, rules, strategies, and games.* Dubuque, IA: Brown.

Wister, O. (1902). *The Virginian: A horseman of the plains.* New York: Macmillan.

Author Note

The audiotape recordings of the discussion of Dr. Place's paper at the Institute turned out not to be transcribable. Therefore, this summary of the discussion is based on written notes taken at the time -- mine and those of Linda J. Parrott. I am grateful to Dr. Parrott (now Dr. Linda J. Hayes) for making her notes available, and I apologize to her and the participants for any errors I may have made in interpreting her and my notes.

Part 3

Alternative Traditions

Chapter 6

The Selectionist Approach to Verbal Behavior: Potential Contributions of Neuropsychology and Connectionism

John W. Donahoe
University of Massachusetts

Radical behaviorism is an instance of selectionism, a general class of approaches to understanding complexity in which higher-level organization is the by-product of the action of lower-level processes. The theoretically most advanced example of selectionism is the Darwinian account of the evolution of organic complexity through natural selection. Radical behaviorism is the application of a selectionist approach to the development of behavioral complexity, and its chief proponent is B. F. Skinner.

In this chapter, I begin by describing two of the major selectionist principles derived from experimental analyses conducted within the conceptual framework of radical behaviorism. After exposing these principles, some of their implications for understanding complex behavior -- especially verbal behavior -- are explored. Although neuropsychological data and the results of computer simulations have received relatively little attention within radical behaviorism, findings from these fields will be emphasized here. The argument is made that there can be a productive interchange between radical behaviorism, neuropsychology, and computer simulations informed by the theoretical approach known as connectionism (Feldman & Ballard, 1982).

The Selectionist Approach to Complexity

Before identifying specific selectionist principles arising from the experimental analysis of behavior, it is useful to outline some of the major features of selectionism generally.

All historical sciences -- whether concerned with the development of the universe, of species, or of the individual -- face a common problem: They are confronted with a set of complex, yet highly organized, phenomena whose developmental course is only partially accessible to observation. This is true whether considering the evolution of the solar system, of the feathers on a peacock's tail, or of the utterance of a grammatical sentence. Faced with organized complexity and an incomplete knowledge of its origins, layperson and scientist alike have often been tempted by philosophical idealism, or essentialism. Essentialism endows the object of observation -- whether it be a planet, a peacock, or a person -- with the very characteristic that an experimental analysis seeks to explain. The characteristic is viewed as the reflection of an inherent property, or essence, of the phenomenon. From an essentialist view, the planets follow their regular orbits because it is in their nature to move in the perfect form of a circle, peacocks have ornate tails because all living organisms express a part of some grand design for nature, and humans speak because they possess within themselves a language-specific capacity.

One-by-one, modern science has replaced these essentialist accounts of natural phenomena with selectionist accounts. A defining feature of selectionism is that complexity is not viewed as the expression of inherent processes acting at the level of the observed organization, but as the by-product of external processes acting at more molecular levels. Organized complexity is the unintended outcome of these more molecular processes, and not their "purpose". Thus planetary motion is the outcome of the action of gravitational processes described by Newtonian principles and the peacock's tail is the outcome of natural-selection processes described by Darwinian principles. (For a more general discussion of selectionism in science, see Campbell, 1974).

It is only in the account of complex behavior, particularly complex human behavior, that essentialist ideas have maintained their dominant position. And, even in this last bastion of essentialism, the essentialist core of the account is often disguised. For example, it is rare that any serious person now says that man acts wisely because he is endowed with reason (although the economist's notion of rational man comes close to this view) or that man is affected by his experience because he has memory. Modern essentialism is more subtle. Thus, we are said to remember because we have hierarchically organized semantic networks (e.g., Collins & Quillian, 1969) or to speak because we have an innately given, language acquisition device as an organ of the mind (Chomsky, 1980). Even animal research using operant conditioning procedures has not wholly escaped essentialist influences, as when the distribution of responses among several alternatives is attributed to a molar principle such as matching (Herrnstein, 1970). (The great insight of the matching formulation -- that the frequency of one response is dependent in part on the consequences of other responses as well as its own consequences -- endures as a separate point that is logically independent of the attribution of interdependence to the matching principle.)

In contrast to essentialism, selectionism seeks to find more molecular processes that are sufficient to produce molar order. Three steps are recognized in the selectionist account of the sequence of events leading to the development of organized complexity. These steps are: variation, selection, and retention. A selectionist account begins with variation in the characteristics that are to undergo selection. A selection mechanism then favors a subset of those characteristics over others. Finally, the favored characteristics are maintained through the action of some retention mechanism. This three-step process, when repeatedly applied, has been widely accepted as an adequate account of the emergence of complexity in the physical and biological realms. Radical behaviorism seeks to extend the selectionist approach to the behavioral realm. (See Campbell, 1974 for a discussion of selectionism as a general model for the development of knowledge. Within philosophy, this field is known as evolutionary epistemology. In biology, its clearest modern statement is contained in the work of Ernst Mayr, 1982.)

Variation

The evolution of species begins with the variation that exists among different individuals in their genes. This variation provides the building blocks from which are constructed the complexity and diversity of existing species. Similarly, radical behaviorism holds that the complexity and diversity that we see in the behavioral repertoires of experienced individuals arise from initial variations in the individual organism's response to differing environments.

The ultimate source of behavioral variation is, of course, the interplay of genetic and environmental variation. It is important to realize that behavioral variation occurs independently of the characteristics that are subject to subsequent selection. Variation itself is undirected. In the first instance, simple behaviors do not vary in order to produce more complex behaviors any more than genes vary in order to produce more complex proteins. However, it should also be stressed that the characteristics contributing to present variation are the product of selections retained from earlier environments. The behaviors that have been acquired in these earlier environments then provide the substrate upon which subsequent selection acts. Thus two pigeons with varying reinforcement histories for keypecking may differ in their subsequent behavior after exposure to a common schedule of reinforcement, and two persons with differing verbal repertoires may differ in their behavior after exposure to the same verbal community.

Selection

Once variability exists, the second step toward complexity may be taken: A selection mechanism favors some characteristic over others. For example, in biological evolution the genes of more successfully reproducing individuals become relatively more numerous in subsequent generations than the genes of those which less successfully reproduce. Thus the selected genes, and the proteins and structures that are built under their guidance, come to predominate. The principle of natural selection summarizes the selection principle in this instance, and more diverse and complex organisms are the product of its action. By extension, to understand the emergence of complex behavior what is required is a mechanism that selects from among varying behaviors. In radical behaviorism, the principle describing this function is called the reinforcement principle.

Because of the committment of radical behaviorism to a selectionist approach to complexity, a major goal of empirical and theoretical research has been the formulation of a reinforcement principle. For radical behaviorism, an adequately formulated principle of reinforcement should illuminate the study of individual development as brilliantly and broadly as does the principle of natural selection the study of species development.

In a later section of this chapter, I shall briefly describe my best understanding of the reinforcement principle. For now, it will be useful to note one general property of selection mechanisms: Although selection imposes a direction on otherwise undirected variation, there is no enduring or ultimate destination toward which selection is headed. The absence of a final goal for selection stems from the fact that selection is always based upon the conditions that prevail at the moment of selection. If future selecting environments are similar to previous selecting environments, then the outcome of past selections serves the organism well. A major contribution to continuity in the selection of human behavior is made by the social environment. Society -- or, more precisely, the contingencies specified through its laws and customs -- spans the generations encouraging stability and permitting a sensitivity to deferred consequences (see Campbell, 1975; Skinner, 1974). Because similar selections are apt to be made by similar environments and because many aspects of the environment change rather slowly, belief in the "rationality" and "foresight" of our species is fostered. However, when the selecting environment changes abruptly, such beliefs are revealed to be comforting illusions at best.

Retention

Once a favored variation has been selected, the characteristic must endure to be acted upon by subsequent selections if increased complexity is to arise. Thus a third step -- retention -- must follow variation and selection.

We now know comparatively little about the biological mechanisms responsible for the retention of selected behaviors. In this respect, our position is similar to Darwin's at the time he proposed the principle of natural selection. (It will be recalled that Mendel's work on genetics was not generally known until some eighteen years after Darwin's death and modern gene theory lay still further in the future.)While the events underlying retention surely reside in the nervous system, more particularly in the neurochemistry that mediates communication between and within neurons, information about these neurochemical events is only now becoming available (e.g., Farley and Alkon, 1985; Klein and Kandel, 1980). However, if the parallels with Darwinian evolution hold, we may be optimistic that considerable progress can be achieved in understanding behavioral complexity without precise knowledge of the neurochemistry responsible for retention. Darwin made giant strides toward understanding biological complexity in spite of his ignorance of population genetics and molecular biology.

Similarly, behaviorism has made substantial progress in understanding the retention of behavior without knowledge of the neural changes underlying retention (see, for example, Palmer in this volume). Progress in the behavioral analysis of retention is largely logically independent of knowledge of the neurochemistry of retention just as progress in the Darwinian analysis of evolution was largely independent of knowledge of the genetics of retention. Nevertheless, it must be recognized that lack of knowledge of genetics continually plagued Darwin, as in his disputes with the Scottish engineer Fleeming Jenkins, and hindered the acceptance by the scientific community of natural selection as the source of evolution. General acceptance of natural selection did not occur until evolutionary theory had been integrated with population genetics -- some eighty years after Darwin's original proposal! If the parallel with natural selection holds, the acceptance of reinforcement as the source of behavioral complexity may await the identification of the neurochemical events underlying retention. Although analyses at the behavioral and neurochemical levels comprise largely independent disciplines, the historical dependence of the acceptance of natural selection on knowledge of genetic mechanisms may provide good reason for radical behaviorists to wish their neuroscientist bretheren well.

Selectionist Principles of Behavior

In this section, I briefly describe two central principles that have emerged from basic behavioral research with nonhuman animals. (A brief justification, within the framework of radical behaviorism, for basing an understanding of complex human behavior on research with simpler organisms will be given toward the end of this section.) The two principles concern the selection mechanism itself -- reinforcement -- and the environmental guidance of behavior that is the outcome of selection -- stimulus control. (For a more complete discussion of the reinforcement principle, see Donahoe, Crowley, Millard, & Stickney, 1982; for a more complete discussion of stimulus control, see Donahoe & Wessells, 1980).

Reinforcement

Living organisms find themselves continuously immersed in a flow of environmental events in whose presence they are continuously behaving. Technically, environmental events are termed stimuli and behavioral events are termed responses. In order to identify the conditions under which a response is selected to come under the control of a stimulus, experimenters have inserted into this flow of events another stimulus having the property that it reliably elicits a measurable response. This stimulus is called an eliciting stimulus and the response that it evokes is called an elicited response. The eliciting stimulus together with the response that it evokes is called an elicitation process. An example of an elicitation process would be the evocation of salivation by the introduction of food into the mouth. Figure 1 illustrates the intrusion of an elicitation process into an ongoing series of environmental and behavioral events.

The experimenter typically inserts an elicitation process into the stream of stimuli and responses according to either of two procedures. In one procedure -- the Pavlovian, or respondent, procedure -- the elicitation process is inserted after a specified stimulus. For example, food (and the salivation that it evokes) might be presented after the sound of a tone.

In the second procedure -- the Thorndikean, or operant, procedure -- the elicitation process is inserted after a specified response. For example, food might be presented after a lever has been pressed. As the figure indicates, however, whether the experimenter inserts the elicitation process after a stimulus or after a response, the elicitation process necessarily follows events of both types: The environment is always present and the organism is always behaving. Thus, while the respondent and operant procedures may appear quite different from the experimenter's perspective, they are fundamentally similar from the organism's perspective -- and it is the organism's perspective upon which selection must be based.

ENVIRONMENTAL EVENTS (STIMULI)

$$S_1, S_2, S_3, S_4, \ldots, \quad S_i, \ldots, \quad S_m$$

$$S_{eliciting} \quad ---- \quad R_{elicited}$$

$$R_1, R_2, R_3, R_4, \ldots, \quad R_j, \ldots, \quad R_n$$

BEHAVIORAL EVENTS (RESPONSES)

Figure 1. The introduction of an elicitation process ($S_{eliciting}$ - $R_{elicited}$) into an ongoing stream of environmental and behavioral events. The elicitation process must necessarily occur after both an environmental stimulus (S_i) and a behavioral response (R_j). The S_i - $S_{eliciting}$ relation defines respondent conditioning; the R_j - $S_{eliciting}$ relation defines operant conditioning.

Since both environmental and behavioral events necessarily precede every elicitation process, the respondent and operant procedures are best viewed -- not as two types of conditioning -- but as simply two laboratory techniques that differ with respect to which relationship with the elicitation process is manipulated by the experimenter and which is left relatively free to vary. In the respondent procedure, the experimenter manipulates the environment-elicitor relation and leaves the behavior-elicitor relation unconstrained. In the operant procedure, it is the behavior-elicitor relation that is manipulated and the environment-elicitor relation that is unconstrained. The most salient feature that the two procedures have in common is that the elicitation process, no matter when it is inserted, causes the organism to behave differently than it otherwise would have behaved in that environment.

The principle of reinforcement that has emerged from experimental analyses of findings obtained with the respondent and operant procedures may be summarized as follows: Whenever the insertion of an elicitation process creates a difference, or discrepancy, between ongoing behavior and the behavior evoked by the eliciting stimulus, whatever stimuli are present prior to the insertion of the eliciting stimulus acquire control over whatever responses are present. In the respondent case, these responses include notably the elicited response itself -- as when a tone precedes food and the tone thereby acquires control over food-elicited salivation. In the operant case, these responses include the operant as well as the elicited response -- as when leverpressing precedes food and the sight of the lever thereby acquires control of leverpressing as well as salivation. This account of the reinforcement principle is equally descriptive of eliciting stimuli that result from natural selection by the ancestral environment (unconditioned reinforcement) and those that result from selection by reinforcement in the individual's prior environment (conditioned reinforcement) (Donahoe et al, 1982).

When the introduction of an elicitation process brings about a change in the stimulus control of behavior, the eliciting stimulus is said to function as a reinforcer. Laboratory research with both respondent and operant procedures has shown that an eliciting stimulus will function as a reinforcer if and only if the specific response that it evokes would not have otherwise occurred at that moment. (Although differently interpreted than here, the crucial experiments leading to this formulation were conducted by Kamin, 1968 and Rescorla & Wagner, 1970; see also Stickney & Donahoe, 1983 and vom Saal & Jenkins, 1970.) If the organism already engages in the elicited response in that environment, then contiguous environmental stimuli do not acquire control over behavior. In such circumstances, acquisition of stimulus control is said to be blocked by the effects of prior selection by reinforcement.

One effect of the selection process described by the reinforcement principle is to bring the learner's behavior into correspondence with the behaviors evoked by the various eliciting stimuli present in that environment. Prior to selection, there is a discrepancy between the learner's customary behavior and the behaviors that are evoked by newly introduced eliciting stimuli. Subsequent to selection, the learner enters the environment already engaging in the behaviors evoked by the eliciting stimuli found in that environment. A second, and perhaps the most important effect of the selection process, is that responses (i.e., operants) that reliably precede eliciting stimuli also come under the control of the environment. Since responses that reliably precede eliciting stimuli often do so because they produce the eliciting stimuli, a major effect of selection is a causal analysis of environment-behavior-elicitor relations.

Stimulus control

Strictly speaking, selection by reinforcement should not be viewed as simply changing the strength of particular responses. More comprehensively, selection by reinforcement changes the probability that particular responses will occur in the presence of particular stimuli. The outcome of reinforcement is always a change in the environmental control of behavior and not merely a change in the strength of behavior. In Skinner's terms, selection reflects a three-term contingency involving a stimulus, a response, and a reinforcer.

The result of selection by reinforcement is that only the stimuli present immediately prior to the occurrence of the elicitor acquire control over behavior. What, then, occurs when the organism encounters an environment that differs in some respects from the ones in which selection has previously taken place? The implication of the reinforcement principle is that the changed environment evokes only those responses the control of which has previously been acquired by the stimuli present in that environment. Given this view, it is not the organism that is the source of creative responding in new environments. Rather, creativity originates from the new environment itself, which acts upon an organism that has been changed by prior selections. New combinations of stimuli call forth new combinations of old behaviors.

A clearer sense of the foregoing analysis of stimulus control is provided by findings from several experiments conducted in this laboratory. In the first study (Collins, 1974; cited in Donahoe and Wessells, 1980, p. 195), keypecking in pigeons was reinforced with food during either of two wavelengths transilluminating a disk mounted on the wall of the test chamber. During one wavelength (S1 of 554 nm), pecks occasionally produced food for rapid responding (less than 1 sec between successive pecks). During the other wavelength (S2 of 569 nm), food was occasionally produced for slow responding (more than 3 sec between successive pecks). The upper portion of Figure 2 shows that the average rate of pecking was greatest during S1 and declined to lower rates when other wavelengths were presented that differed from the wavelengths present during training. However, the most important result for present purposes concerns the moment-to-moment pattern of responding during the various stimuli. As shown

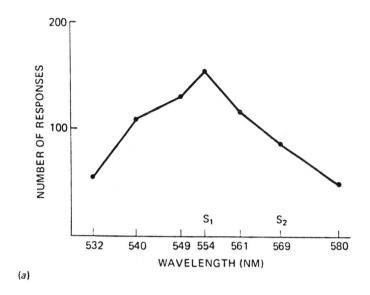

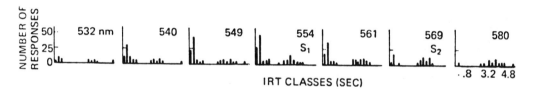

Figure 2. Keypecking by pigeons after discrimination training on the wavelength dimension. During S1, successive keypecks of less than 1 sec occasionally produced food; during S2, successive keypecks of more than 3 sec occasionally produced food. The upper portion of the figure shows the overall frequency of keypecking during a generalization test. The lower portion contains the distributions of interresponse-times (IRTs) between successive keypecks for each of the stimuli presented during testing. (Collins, 1974, from Donahoe & Wessells, 1980).

in the lower portion of Figure 2, the times between successive pecks (the interresponse times, or IRTs) during all stimuli corresponded to those times that had been selected by reinforcement during training. Thus new environments (wavelengths) did not call forth new behaviors, but new mixtures of old behaviors. This conclusion is supported by the fact that the behaviors occurring in the new environments were the same duration as the behaviors previously selected in training.

A second study indicates the generality of the first result. The same basic finding was obtained with a different nonhuman species, a differently defined response, and a different stimulus dimension (Crowley, 1979). Rats received occasional food for holding a lever down for either a short (less than 1 sec) or a long (more than 5 sec) time in the presence of either of two light intensities. Following this training, the animals were presented with other light intensities. As shown in Figure 3, the changed environments called forth only response durations that had been selected by reinforcement during training. (See Donahoe & Wessells, 1980 and Bickel and Etzel, 1985 for summaries of experiments on this issue.)

We have conducted a similar study using three human subjects and have obtained comparable results (Donahoe, Millard, and Cardello, 1982, described in Donahoe, Palmer, and Carlson, in press). Pressing a telegraph key at different rates was differentially reinforced with money during either of two light intensities. When tested with occasional presentations of either of three intermediate light intensities, only the two patterns of keypressing that had been established during training were observed. A provocative supplemental finding was that, when asked after the experiment how many light intensities they had seen, the subjects all replied that they had seen only two different intensities. These reports occurred in spite of the fact that, in a subsequent psychophysical study with these same subjects, all light intensities were discriminated from one another without error. Thus, the verbal behavior of the subjects, as well as their keypressing behavior, corresponded to the number of response classes that had been selected by reinforcement.

The conclusion to be drawn from this brief summary of experimental work on reinforcement and stimulus control may be summarized as follows: Elicitation processes, when functioning as reinforcers, select specific behaviors to come under the control of specific stimuli. Environments that differ from those present during selection call forth mixtures of the behaviors that are under the control of the various stimulus components that comprise these changed environments.

Infrahuman Research and the Understanding of Complex Human Behavior

Before moving to a consideration of how principles derived from experimental-analytic work with animals may aid the interpretation of verbal behavior, some justification should be given for undertaking the effort at all. Many nonselectionists believe that there is little of central importance in common between the factors that affect human behavior -- especially verbal behavior -- and those that affect the behavior of nonhumans. For such nonselectionists, using experimental-analytic principles to try to understand verbal behavior is a bit like attacking a dragon with a toothpick -- while the effort may display courage, it is even more indicative of foolhardiness.

Radical behaviorism, as an instance of a selectionist approach to complexity, takes a very strong position on the relevance of nonhuman research to the understanding of human behavior. As has been noted earlier, selectionists view organized complexity as the product of the repeated action of more molecular processes. If the molecular processes are sufficient to generate organized complexity, then those molecular processes are accepted as adequate interpretations of the more molar observations. Such interpretations are preferred to accounts based on molar principles because, if the molecular processes are sufficient, then the organism is insulated from the effects of selection at the more molar level -- whether by the ancestral environment or by the individual environment.

Selection is an inherently conservative method of change. Speaking metaphorically, the environment teaches the organism only what it needs to know at that moment, not what it might be well for the organism to know at some unspecified time in the future. To repeat, if molecular selection processes are sufficient to generate the complexity that is observed, then there is no need to look elsewhere for other processes. There is certainly no need to endow the organism demonstrating the complex behavior with special faculties, or other essentialist notions, to "explain" the behavior. If molecular selectionist principles derived from experimental-analytic research are sufficient to account for behavioral complexity, then the burden of proof for those who would propose alternative molar principles rests solely upon those who would propose them.

The following study illustrates the distinction between selectionist and essentialist approaches to complexity, and also indicates that at least some complex human behavior is not

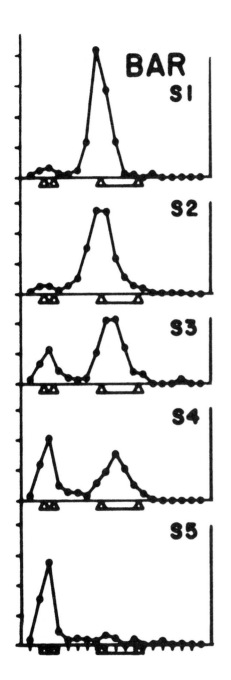

beyond the reach of basic selectionist principles.

It is well known from research with "judgment" tasks -- such as diagnosing a disease from a symptom -- that judgment responses often display a particular bias: There is a strong tendency to over-estimate the validity of a characteristic, such as a symptom, as a predictor of an individual's membership in a group, such as a diagnostic category, when the size of that group is small (Tversky & Kahneman, 1982). If a person shares a characteristic with other members of a small group, then the person is often judged to be a member of that group even when the same characteristic is also often present in members of a much larger group. For example, if 90% of those having a rare disease display a symptom such as a rash, then an undiagnosed individual displaying the rash is thought to have the rare disease even when the same rash occasionally occurs in people having a much more common disease. This judgement is "unreasonable" since, even though the rash is infrequent with the more common disease, there are so many more people afflicted with the common disease that it is more likely that the person has the common disease than the rare disease.

The tendency to weigh heavily the similarity of an individual to members of a group and to neglect information about the size of the other groups to which the person might belong has been attributed to an inherent bias in human judgement to employ what is called a representativeness heuristic (Tversky and Kahneman, 1982). (A heuristic is a "rule of thumb" used for making inferences.) If a characteristic is representative of a group, then the individual is assigned to that group irrespective of the size of the group and the occurrence of the characteristic in larger groups. The appeal to a "rule of thumb" for the interpretation of this apparent judgement bias smacks of essentialism since it

Figure 3. Leverholding by rats after discrimination training on the visual intensity dimension. During S1, leverholding durations of greater than 5 sec occasionally produced food; during S5, leverholding durations of less than 1 sec occasionally produced food. The panels depict the distributions of leverholding durations obtained for each of the five stimuli presented during testing. The Y axis indicates the percent of total testing time allocated to the various durations of leverholding, where each tic = 5 %. The X axis indicates the duration of leverpressing, where each tic = 0.5 sec. and the two criterion durations are shown by brackets. (From Crowley, 1979)

gives the appearance of "explaining" the behavior by postulating a molar principle -- a representative heuristic. Selectionism, on the other hand, would attempt to understand "judgment" just as it would other instances of behavior, i.e., as the result of the basic processes governing stimulus control. Returning to our example, the selectionist would explore the conditions under which a stimulus (the symptom) would acquire stronger control of the response (the diagnosis) of the rare disease than of the common disease. In terms of stimulus control, why should control of the diagnosis of the common disease by the symptom be blocked?

To evaluate whether observations leading to the conjecture of a representative heuristic are within reach of selectionist principles, subjects were given a series of trials on a contrived diagnostic task. Patients having any of four symptoms were to be assigned to one of two disease groups -- Group A or Group B (Gluck & Bower, 1988). Whether the judgment was correct or incorrect was indicated after each trial. The task was constructed such that only 25% of the patients were members of Group A and all symptoms were equally or less strongly predictive of membership in Group A. Subjects were exposed to enough trials to acquaint them with the distribution of symptoms and the relative frequency of the two diseases. Then, they were asked to state the likelihood of a disease given each of the four symptoms.

The characteristics of the task and the results of the experiment are summarized in Figure 4. The left panel depicts the true probability of a disease for each symptom as derived from probability theory. The middle panel shows the actual probability of diagnosis for each symptom based upon the diagnostic judgments of the subjects. In agreement with previous work, a stimulus (Symptom 1, for example) more strongly controlled the judgment response of membership in the smaller group than in the larger group (middle panel) when compared with the true probabilities (left panel). The rightmost panel shows the strengths with which each symptom was expected to control the judgment of each disease according to a selectionist reinforcement principle. (These predicted strengths are based upon a quantitative statement of the same reinforcement principle that was qualitatively described earlier in this chapter. Other quantitative formulations of the reinforcement principle are contained in Rescorla &

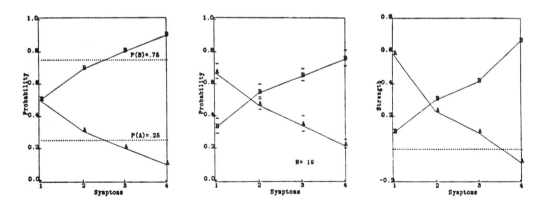

Figure 4. The relative strengths of each of four symptoms for the judgment of membership in either diagnostic group A or B. The left panel shows the true strengths from probability theory (the inverse probability of group membership given the symptom). The middle panel shows the obtained strengths based upon the actual judgments of the subjects. The left panel shows the predicted strengths based upon the reinforcement principle. (From Gluck & Bower, 1988).

Wagner, 1970; Rummelhart & McClelland, 1986; and Sutton & Barto, 1981 among others.) As is clear, a selectionist principle accounts for the pattern of results without recourse to a molar principle such as the representativeness heuristic. A symptom, such as symptom 1, is relatively less often accompanied by the other symptoms in the rarer disease and, hence, control of the diagnostic judgement by symptom 1 is less blocked in Group A than Group B.

The interpretation of the foregoing experiment on human judgement using reinforcement and stimulus control principles derived from infrahuman research advances the selectionist agenda. Two further examples -- both taken from the area of verbal behavior -- are now described, and the outcomes are similarly encouraging.

Stimulus control studies with infrahuman organisms show that when responses have one consequence during one set of stimuli and a different consequence during a neighboring set of stimuli, the change in response strength becomes magnified at the boundary between the two sets of stimuli. This abrupt change in responding is called an edge effect (e.g., Blough, 1975). Edge effects occur, according to the reinforcement principle, because -- in the region of the boundary -- the discrepancy is greatest between the behavior of the organism and the behavior elicited by the reinforcer. The following example gives a sense of how edge effects come about according to this analysis. Suppose that a reinforcer is highly probable in the presence of one stimulus but that the stimulus is highly similar to a neighboring stimulus in which the reinforcer is much less probable. Because of generalization from the second stimulus, it is initially unlikely that the organism will make the reinforcer-elicited response during the first stimulus. Thus, when the reinforcer does in fact occur during the first stimulus, there will be a large discrepancy between the ongoing behavior of the organism and the behavior elicited by the reinforcer. Since a large discrepancy fosters strong stimulus control, the first stimulus should acquire strong control of whatever responses occur during that stimulus. If, however, a stimulus is similar to another stimulus -- but the reinforcer is equally probable during both stimuli -- an analysis of the same type would predict a smaller discrepancy and, therefore, weaker stimulus control. Thus, paradoxically, the greatest difference in the strength of stimulus control should occur for stimuli in the near vicinity but on opposite sides of the boundary.

This abrupt shift in responding when a boundary is crossed is exactly what is observed in the response to speech sounds (phonemes). As the acoustic stimulus is gradually changed from one phoneme to a neighboring phoneme, human subjects do not report hearing a gradual change in sound but an abrupt transition from one phoneme, e.g., /b/ to the neighboring phoneme, e.g., /d/ (Liberman, Harris, Hoffman, & Griffith, 1957). This result, which is called categorical perception in the psycholinguistic literature, has been taken to support the claim that speech perception involves unique, speech-specific processes. Basic experimental-analytic research with infrahumans indicates that the phenomenon is a general outcome of stimulus control produced by selection by reinforcement and is not restricted to either humans or speech stimuli. Subsequent research has borne out this expectation, with nonhumans also displaying categorical perception of phonemes (e.g., Kuhl & Miller, 1975).

The second example of the relevance of selection by reinforcement to verbal behavior illustrates that verbal responses, just as other responses, may be controlled by a variety of stimuli. There is not necessarily a special relation between speech sounds and speech perception (cf., Liberman, 1982). Adult subjects were shown, via a television monitor, a picture of a person making mouth movements as if repeatedly uttering a speech sound, e.g., /ba/, /ba/, /ba/,.... However, the loudspeaker accompanying the monitor could present either an acoustic stimulus that corresponded to the visual stimulus, e.g., /ba/, /ba/, /ba/,..., or one that did not, e.g., /da/, /da/, /da/, ... Note that, in the latter case, the acoustic stimulus could not be produced by the mouth movements shown on the video monitor. The lips must momentarily close to produce /ba/, but must remain open to produce /da/ (MacDonald & McGurk, 1978).

The results of the study showed that, when the visual and auditory stimuli were in conflict, the subjects reported hearing the speech sound that corresponded to the mouth position and not to the acoustic stimulus! Other research indicated that the effect was less often present in young children, and that it grew stronger with age (McGurk & MacDonald, 1976).

From a radical behavioral perspective, the disassociation between a verbal response and its "natural" controlling stimulus is not problematic if it can be shown that, under conditions in which the visual and acoustic stimuli are in conflict, it is the visual stimulus that is the more valid predictor of the speech sound. Under such conditions, the more valid visual stimulus would block control by the acoustic stimulus. And, just those circumstances obtain in noisy environments -- environments to which the listener is increasingly exposed with age. In a noisy environment, lip position reliably distinguishes /ba/ from /da/ since the latter phoneme cannot be uttered with the lips touching. Thus, when the acoustic stimulus conflicts with the visual stimulus provided by the speaker, it is the latter that controls the listener's response. Given this interpretation, the effect should become even more apparent if the experiments were repeated under the noisy conditions that exist in such situations as a cocktail party.

Having presented several specific examples of the use of selectionist principles in the interpretation of complex human behavior, I move now to two general areas of the application of these principles -- neuropsychology and computer simulations guided by connectionism. These areas were chosen in part because non-behaviorists, and even some radical behaviorists, may erroneously regard work employing physiological and computer-simulation methods as irrelevant to or even inconsistent with a radical behavioral agenda.

Selectionism and Neuropsychology

The subject matter of neuropsychology is the behavior of persons who have suffered damage to their nervous systems, particularly the brain. Since the damage is not experimentally induced, but is typically the result of events such as strokes or accidents, the precise nature of the damage varies considerably from person to person and sometimes cannot be well described until after death. While such uncertainties complicate the task of those seeking to correlate neuroanatomy with function, the behavioral changes produced by brain damage are informative to the radical behaviorist even without such knowledge.

For the radical behaviorist, complex behaviors are the result of prolonged selection by complex environments. The history of these selections is, at best, only partially known since we cannot follow even one person throughout life. The radical behaviorist trying to interpret the behavior of an adult human is in much the same position as the paleontologist trying to interpret the evolutionary history of an existing species. While neither paleontologists nor radical behaviorists can directly observe the selection histories of their subject matters, traces of the past endure that provide glimpses of that history. For the paleontologist, these traces reside in the fossil and genetic records of the species. For the radical behaviorist, they reside in the nervous system of the individual and the behavior controlled by that nervous system. When the nervous system is damaged, some of the prior selections are undone, possibly revealing evidence of still other prior selections whose behavioral effects would otherwise be inaccessible to observation. Although insufficiently exploited by radical behaviorists, neuropsychological observations offer a potentially rich source of information about the history of selection that leads to complex behavior. Skinner recognized this clearly in his intermittent use of neuro-psychology in discussions of aphasia in *Verbal Behavior* (1957).

The present discussion of the interrelation between radical behavioral and neuro-psychological research will focus on three main issues: (a) the role of individual differences in selection histories on the effects of brain damage on verbal behavior, (b) neuropsychological and experimental-analytic conceptions of the functional unit in verbal behavior, and (c) the implications of neuropsychological data for the view that there are brain systems with verbal-specific properties.

Individual Differences

If interconnections in the brain reflect selection by reinforcement as well as by natural selection and if selection by reinforcement affects verbal behavior, then the verbal behavior of individuals with different reinforcement histories should be differently affected by what appear to be highly similar brain lesions. Wernicke, one of the founders of the neuropsychology of verbal behavior, reached this conclusion early on. From his work, it was known that damage to certain brain areas involved in hearing adversely affected the ability of persons to read. Wernicke thought that this was because most people learn to read by "sounding out" words. He speculated that, when a deaf person learned to read, damage to these same areas should not affect reading (described in Geschwind, 1972). Subsequent research has shown Wernicke's hunch to be correct. As an example, damage to Wernicke's area affects the spelling of hearing persons, but not of the deaf (Luria, 1970). Moreover, if the deaf person is a lip reader, then the effects on reading are more similar to those observed with hearing persons (Cameron, Currier, & Haerer, 1971).

In Indo-European languages generally, there is a one-to-one correspondence between the visual stimuli produced by writing and the acoustic stimuli produced by speaking. However, this correspondence is not always present in Chinese and Japanese. Consistent with this difference, comparable brain lesions do not have the same effect on reading in these populations. Chinese speakers, for whom there is little correspondence between visual and acoustic stimuli, can read after sustaining a lesion that abolishes reading in speakers of Indo-European languages (Luria, 1970). However, both Chinese and Indo-European speakers can no longer respond appropriately to speech sounds after these same lesions. In Japanese speakers, some visual stimuli in the written language have acoustic correspondences (kana characters) and others do not (kanji characters). A brain lesion that abolishes reading in Indo-European speakers affects the reading of kana but not of kanji characters in Japanese speakers (Sasunama, 1975).

Units of Verbal Behavior

The radical-behavioral perspective anticipates that there will be profound differences in the effect of brain lesions as a function of the language community in which the verbal behavior was acquired. The evidence reviewed above, and much other besides, supports this expectation. Radical behaviorism also anticipates that there will be equally profound differences as a result of the particular circumstances that obtained within a single language community when verbal behavior was acquired.

Even within a single verbal community, the specific stimuli present when a particular verbal response is acquired will differ somewhat from one individual to the next. Since selection by reinforcement brings a response under the control of only immediately preceding stimuli, then two individuals may emit verbal responses of the same form, or topography, (i.e., the same "words") but the controlling stimuli for the responses may be different. As previously noted, it is incomplete to describe the outcome of selection as simply the acquisition of a response -- a response always comes under the control of a stimulus. For this reason, response topography alone cannot provide an adequate basis for the analysis of verbal behavior -- or any other behavior for that matter. For this same reason, two responses that have the same topography, may be differently affected by the same brain lesion.

Consider the following hypothetical example. Suppose that the verbal response, "spoon", had come under the control of both the visual stimuli provided by looking at a spoon and the tactile stimuli provided by touching a spoon. Suppose further that a brain lesion had subsequently interrupted pathways leading from the visual to the speech production areas but had left intact pathways from the tactile area. A person suffering such brain damage would be able to say "spoon" when he touched a spoon, but would no longer be able to say "spoon" when he looked at it! With an intact brain, the same utterance -- "spoon" in the present example -- is controlled by many stimuli. The control of most verbal responses by multiple stimuli, encourages such essentialist notions as "having a concept", e.g., the concept of spoon. Because a particular verbal response is often controlled by many stimuli, the observer is given the erroneous impression that the response is independent of particular features of the environment -- i.e., that the response reflects a "concept".

In some instances of brain damage, pathways are selectively interrupted and the specificity of the stimulus control of verbal responses is revealed. This specificity is difficult to observe with an intact brain that has been changed by a prolonged history of selection by reinforcement, thereby bringing verbal responses under the control of complex arrangements of many stimuli. The neuropsychological literature is replete with examples of such specific losses. Here are several examples of loss of control of verbal responses by stimuli from one modality while control by stimuli from another modality persists.

Control by tactile stimuli with loss of control by visual stimuli: A patient was shown a hammer and asked to name it. After failing to do so, the patient picked it up and then said it was a hammer. When shown a picture of a pistol, the patient was unable to name it. However, as he continued to look at the picture, his "trigger finger" began to move and the patient raised his arm thrusting it forward as if firing a pistol. He then said, "Oh! It's a gun...a pistol" (Margolin & Carlson, 1984).

Control by auditory stimuli with loss of control by visual stimuli: A sighted patient was confronted by a person well known to him, but the patient could not recall his friend's name upon seeing his face. However, when he heard his friend's voice, the patient immediately spoke the correct name (Kolb & Whishaw, 1985). There are also examples in which brain damage has selectively impaired the control of some verbal responses by stimuli within a modality, but has spared the control of other responses by stimuli within that same modality.

Control of spelling responses, but not textual (reading) responses, by visual stimuli: A patient was able to correct spelling errors in words that she could not read. She was also unable to name pictures of objects that corresponded to the unreadable words. In spite of being unable to read the words or to name the corresponding pictures, she correctly matched the words with the pictures (Margolin and Carlson, 1982).

Control of a verbal response by an auditorily presented verbal stimulus, but the failure of a verbal response of the same topography to be controlled by other auditory stimuli: A patient hearing the first lines of a simple poem, "Roses are red, violets are blue", could continue the poem flawlessly, but could not emit any of these response topographies when presented with other stimuli that ordinarily control their emission. For example, if asked to name a sweet-tasting substance whose name began with the letter "s", she could not do so (Geschwind, Quadfasel, & Segarra, 1968). There are other examples that demonstrate that response topography does not provide an appropriate functional unit for verbal behavior, but in which the precise nature of the controlling stimulus is less clear than in the preceding cases. Many such examples involve contrasts between the literal use of a word and its metaphorical use. As an illustration, a patient was able to use the verbal responses "down" and "up" to describe the mood of herself and others correctly, but was not able to correctly use these same response topographies to indicate whether the floor and ceiling were "down" or "up" (Carlson, 1984). Here, the metaphorical senses of "up" and "down" remained whereas the spatial senses had been lost.

Although behavioral observations of brain-damaged persons are frequently provocative, the unit of analysis in neuropsychology is too often defined by response topography with insufficient analysis of the stimuli controlling the topography. For example, a former salesman relating the story of Little Red Riding Hood made an error when stating what the wolf thought when the wolf realized that the woodcutters would prevent him from making a meal of the girl. The salesman said, "Alors, il se dit qu'il va manquer la commande." (Then he says to himself that he is going to miss the sale.) (Nespoulous & Lecours, 1984). While this error was interpreted by the authors of the paper as an intrusion of an irrelevant schema into the narrative -- an interpretation that suggests a very complexly determined response -- the error may simply be an intraverbal. That is, the salesman had almost certainly more often said that he "missed the sale" than that he missed the chance to gobble up Little Red Riding Hood. In the effort to understand verbal behavior, both neuropsychology and radical behaviorism have much to learn from one another.

Specialization of the Brain for Verbal Behavior

For the selectionist, verbal behavior should demonstrate considerable continuity with other behaviors in the processes that influence it. This belief stems from the basically conservative nature of selectionism. Because every behavioral domain -- verbal or otherwise -- is subject to a partially unique type and sequence of selections, every domain is in a sense special. However, the resulting "specialness" is not interpreted as the consequence of domain-specific principles, but as the consequence of the repeated action of common processes operating on domain-specific stimuli and behaviors occurring in domain-specific sequences. For the essentialist, on the other hand, verbal behavior tends to be seen as fundamentally different from other behaviors -- to require a set of language-specific principles that differentiate it from other behaviors. The clearest statement of an essentialist approach to language is contained in the work of some linguists (e.g. Chomsky, 1980; see Palmer, 1986 for a detailed critique of this view).

Within the brain, the fact that neurons active during related functions tend to be found in close proximity to one another is not evidence for specialization. Localization of function in the brain may be understood quite readily as the outcome of more molecular principles. For example, assume that it is important for an organism's reproductive success that adjacent parts of the visual environment be differentiated from one another. In order for the visual environment to be differentiated, the neural response to adjacent parts of the environment must be different. If such neural differentiation requires different neurons to be active, then those neurons must communicate with one another. If the neurons must communicate, then the closer together they occur within the brain, the shorter are the connections and the faster the communications between them. Thus, localization of function can occur for reasons -- the minimization of proteins required to construct the interconnections and the maximization of speed of communication along the interconnections -- that have nothing to do with specialization. Localization of function has no clear-cut implications for the existence of domain-specific principles.

Consider the well-known specialization of the left hemisphere of the human brain for speech reception and production. Although speculative -- as must be all interpretations of incompletely known histories of selection -- if there is specialization of the left hemisphere of the brain, the specialization appears to be for the discrimination and differentiation of sequences of many events, and not merely of those involved in speech reception and production.

Efficient control of movement of the mouth, which is essential for the ingestion of nutrients, may have furnished the early source of selection pressure for the lateralization of sequential neural networks. The mouth is the only unpaired effector system, so the usual crossed relation between effector and brain would have required many long interhemispheric connections to generate co-ordinated mouth movements. Lateralization of the control of jaw, tongue, lip, and throat movements would have enhanced co-ordination by reducing the length of interconnections.

With the subsequent freeing of the forelimbs of our hominid ancestors from the demands of locomotion, the neural networks controlling the hands could then be subject to further selection pressure for sequentially co-ordinated movements. Since the brain areas important for control of the mouth are immediately adjacent to those controlling the hand, the types of neural connections required for co-ordinated mouth movements may have spread to the adjacent hand area and provided the impetus for hand preference. In turn, continued selection for co-ordination of movements in the preferred hand would have shaped the neural networks controlling hand movements still further, and these could then have spread back to the nearby brain areas controlling mouth movements. This interplay between the mouth and the preferred hand in the development of the types of neural networks required to control ever-finer sequences of movements, when coupled with the changes in head and neck anatomy accompanying an upright posture, could have yielded the exquisite motor control required for speech. Indeed, it has been suggested that spoken language had its origins in an earlier gestural communication system (Kimura, 1976).

Selectionism and Computer Simulation

Other historical sciences, such as those that deal with the evolution of the solar system or of species, face the same question that radical behaviorism must answer: How is complexity to be understood when that complexity is the product of a long history of selection only a portion of which is open to observation? One of the techniques that these other sciences have used is computer simulation of the selection process. That is, a computer program is written that embodies the principles uncovered by experimental work, and these principles are then allowed to operate repeatedly upon conditions that are likely to have existed prior to the appearance of the complexity. If the simulation generates the complexity, then the simulation demonstrates that the principles are sufficient to interpret the phenomena that define the science. Radical behaviorism has been wary of computer simulations, and of mathematical techniques generally, as aids to genuine understanding of complexity. These reservations have arisen from the way that quantitative procedures have often been used in psychology -- as refuges from the data (Skinner, 1950) -- rather than from formal objections to quantitative theorizing as such. Too often, quantitative theories have simply implemented the intuitions and hunches of the theorist rather than well established principles each of which has been separately verified in prior experimental work. This practice stands in marked contrast to the use of computer simulations in other sciences. For example, simulations of the development of the solar system are guided by Newtonian principles and simulations of the origin of species are guided by Darwinian principles.

In the final section of this chapter, I shall describe the results of several computer simulations that are informed by a selection principle, the principle of reinforcement. In these simulations, the principle is applied not only to responses that directly contact the environment -- and, hence, are observed -- but also to covert responses that are one or more steps removed from the environment. Some justification must be given for the application to covert responses of a principle derived from the study of overt responses.

The capacity for the selection of overt responses by reinforcement is itself the result of natural selection, of course. As is ever the case, natural selection occurs only for those behavioral characteristics that are expressed, not those that are "latent". Thus, for behavior as for the structures that permit behavior, selection occurs for the phenotype and not the genotype. In Huxley's words, "The great end of life is not knowledge, but action". Great minds unaccompanied by great deeds are not favored by selection.

In primitive organisms -- but those complex enough to have nerve cells -- all neurons were in direct contact with the selecting effect of the environment. Thus, whatever the properties of neurons that permitted them to be modified within the lifetime of the organism, that capacity would have been quite general. As nervous systems became more complex -- and interneurons occurred that were not in direct contact with the environment -- the same capacity for change would be retained. If natural selection favored (or, at a minimum, did not disfavor) organisms having modifiable interneurons -- so-called "hidden elements" -- then the same selection principle would apply throughout the nervous system. Evolutionary speculations of the foregoing sort encourage the working hypothesis that a reinforcement principle based upon behavioral work with infrahuman organisms under laboratory conditions may be widely applicable. Consistent with this assumption, the behavior of presentday organisms having relatively simple nervous systems, such as those of invertebrates, is describable by the same reinforcement principle uncovered through work with vertebrates (e.g. Sahley, Rudy, & Gelperin, 1981). (This could -- of course -- be the result of convergent evolution, and not of common ancestry.)

Distributed Networks

In the computer simulations that follow, a number of units -- which may be thought of as neurons or functional clusters of neurons -- are interconnected to form a network. Knowledge of the actual interconnections among neurons in the brain requires detailed neuroanatomical data that are currently available for only very simple nervous systems or for portions of more complex nervous systems. Accordingly, the present concern is to determine whether networks having certain general properties that are known to exist in the real nervous system are sufficient, in principle, to accommodate behavioral phenomena when those networks are modified by environmental selection by reinforcement.

As an example of such a network, Figure 5 shows three input units sensing the environment, six internal -- or hidden -- units, and three output units. Different environmental events are represented as different patterns of activity of the input units. For example, if only the upper input unit were active that might represent one environmental event. If only the middle input unit or only the upper two input units were active these patterns of activity might represent still other environmental events. Different responses are represented as different patterns of activity of the output units. The network is called a recurrent network because it is possible to follow connections from some of the later units in the network back to earlier units. In this way, later units in the network may influence the subsequent activity of earlier units. Recurrent networks are necessary if an input to the network is to produce a sequence of behaviors as the output (Jordan, 1986).

In a computer simulation using a network of this general type, Jordan identified the pattern of activity of the output units as eight distinctive features involved in speech production (e.g., voicing, place of articulation, and so forth). (With three output units, each either active or inactive, there are 23 unique output patterns. With intermediate levels of activity of the units, different strengths of the eight unique patterns are possible.) The computer simulation adjusted the strength of the connections between units according to the discrepancy between the activity

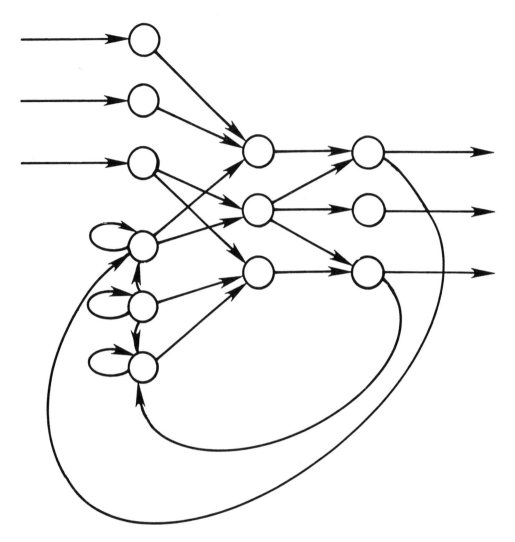

Figure 5. An example of a recursive network of functional units showing stimulus (input), internal (hidden), and response (output) units with interconnections among the various units. (From Jordan, 1986).

of the unit on that trial and the activity required to produce the activity pattern in the output units corresponding to the distinctive features appropriate for the German phrase "sinistre structure". After the network had been repeatedly exposed to the selection process, the following sequence of articulatory responses was produced by the network (see Figure 6). Only that portion of the record corresponding to the middle speech sounds, /istrstry/, of the phrase is show

The sequence of articulatory responses produced by the network corresponds closely to the sequence of responses observed in human speech when the phrase, "sinistre structure", is uttered. The close correspondence indicates that selection on the basis of the discrepancy

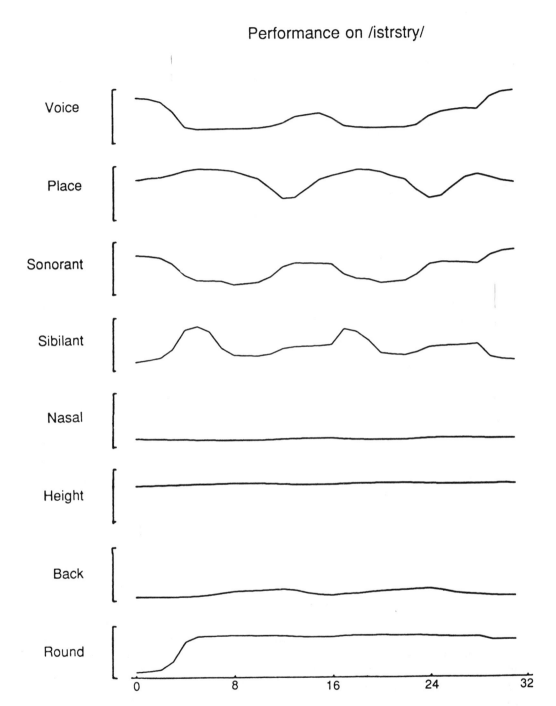

Figure 6. After selection within a recursive network of units, the final strengths of various distinctive features of articulatory movements during the utterance of /istrstry/, a part of the German phrase "sinistre structure". (From Jordan, 1986).

between the emitted and the required sequence of articulatory responses is sufficient to change appropriately the strength of the connections within the recurrent network.

Moreover, the sequence of articulatory responses displays another characteristic of human speech -- parallel transmission. Note that rounding of the mouth, which is necessary in order to produce the /y/ phoneme, occurs much earlier in the sequence than required by the "u" in "structure". This anticipatory rounding of the mouth did not occur in another simulation in which the target phrase was "sinistre stricture". Since the mouth is not rounded to produce the /i/ in "stricture", no rounding occurred. The other responses occurred much as before, however -- e.g., the sibilant movement for /s/. As with human speech, the simulated articulatory movements -- and, hence, the acoustic stimulus emitted for different phonemes -- varied with the context in which the phoneme occurred. This phenomenon is known as context-conditioned variation (see Donahoe & Wessells, 1980).

Network Functioning

The foregoing computer simulation indicates that recursive networks of units subjected to selection are sufficient to model a number of characteristics of one complex human behavior: aspects of speech production. Networks of this general type have been shown to capture other characteristics that replicate additional features of complex human behavior. In order to provide a better sense of some of these features, the output of the networks in the figures that follow is represented pictorially. That is, a given pattern of activity of the output units corresponds to a given pictorial representation. As various characteristics of the stimuli impinging on the network are changed, the corresponding changes produced in the output units are shown by means of a picture. (The various simulations differed from one another in a number of ways, but the features displayed in the pictures are general characteristics of networks exposed to selection. For a survey of network models, see Hinton & Anderson, 1981; Jordan, 1986; McClelland & Rummelhart, 1986.)

Effect of noise (variable stimulation) on responding. Living organisms are able to respond appropriately even when the stimulus departs appreciably from the stimuli present during original learning. A friend's face is recognized in dim light; a word heard at a noisy party is correctly recognized. As Figure 7 shows, the output of the network remains relatively invariant as noise is gradually added to the stimulus input. Thus, the behavioral output of the network is robust with a noisy input. In fact, selection is improved when the input is variable since variability makes it less likely that the strength of the connections between units will remain in a locally adequate, but generally non-optimal final state of strength (Anderson, 1984).

Effect of repeated presentations of similar stimuli. When many specific instances of environment-behavior pairs are reinforced similarly, it is sometimes said that the organism has "formed a concept". This is especially the case when new, but similar, stimuli are responded to in the same way. Thus, after the verbal response,"dog", has been strengthened in the presence of many specific dogs, the child is apt to emit "dog" when novel instances appear. To illustrate that networks may display this characteristic, a network was exposed to several presentations of similar stimuli, here various photographs of Freud's face. As shown in Figure 8, the final response of the network was greatest to stimuli that shared features in common with the separate presentations. Thus, from many separate experiences, it is as if a "prototype" had been constructed (Eich, 1985). This characteristic of distributed networks is reminiscent of the finding that a test sentence never previously read may seem more familiar than an actually experienced sentence (e.g., Bransford & Franks, 1971). Such a phenomenon should occur if the test sentence contains many stimuli in common with sentences that have been previously presented.

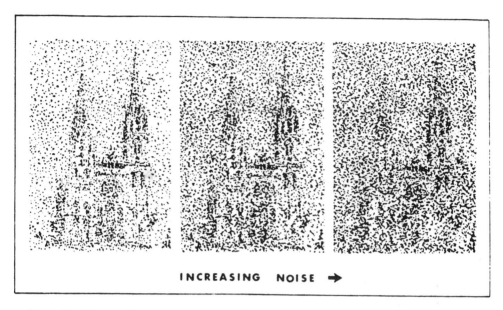

Figure 7. Effects of increasing amounts of random noise upon the output of a distributed memory when the input was a clear image of a cathedral. (From Eich, 1985. With the permission of the American Psychological Association).

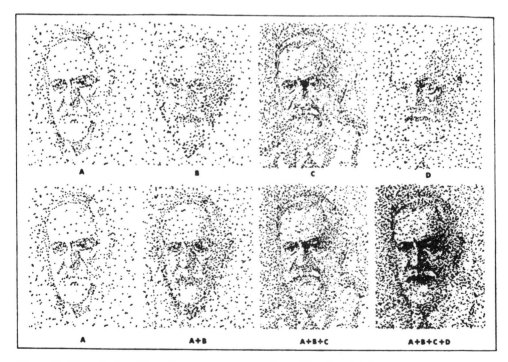

Figure 8. Cumulative effect of exposure to several specific stimuli (pictures A, B, C, and D of Sigmund Freud) on the output of a distributed memory. (From Eich, 1985. With the permission of the American Psychological Association).

Effect of presentation of a stimulus in an environment in which a similar stimulus has already acquired control of behavior. In earlier work with infrahuman organisms, we saw that the behavior occurring in an environment that differed from the one present during training consisted of a mixture of the responses previously conditioned to the stimuli contained in the new environment. A simplified illustration of this phenomenon is shown in the next simulation (Jordan, 1986). A recursive network was shaped by selection to produce a series of movements that, when represented pictorially, described a rectangle. During training, the initial stimulus input corresponded to a movement that began at one of the corners of the rectangle. From that initial position, connections in the network were strengthened that led to a rectangular path of movements. To test the behavior of the network when a new stimulus was presented, the initial stimulus input was moved to a point corresponding to a position outside the rectangle. As shown by the spiraling curve in Figure 9, the network reacted to this new input with an output that ever more closely approximated the sequence of movements that had been conditioned to the original input used in training. The tendency of networks of this type to respond to new inputs with previously acquired outputs is quite general, and is known in the simulation literature as attractor dynamics.

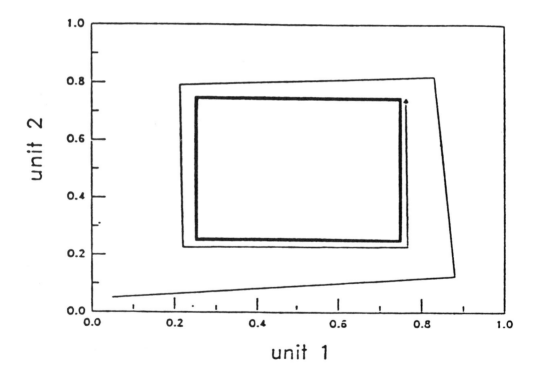

Figure 9. Effect of a new stimulus on the output of a network whose two output units had previously been trained to give the series of movements depicted by the heavy rectangular path. The new output path was produced when a test input differed from the training input causing the movement to begin outside the rectangle. The new movement path is shown by the spiral that increasingly approximates the originally trained rectangular path. (From Jordan, 1986).

Effect of presentation of only a portion of the stimuli present during original selection. If we see only a portion of a friend's face or hear only a portion of a conventionally phrased utterance, we often recognize the friend or understand the utterance. How do networks react to such degraded stimulus inputs? The left pair of faces in Figure 10 illustrates the effect of randomly eliminating some of the stimuli present during learning. The leftmost face of the pair is the degraded stimulus; the face to the right is the response of the network. As can be seen, the network's response is relatively unchanged. The right pair of faces illustrates the effect of degrading the stimulus input in another way, this time by eliminating entirely one portion of the normal input while leaving the remainder unchanged. This might correspond to seeing a friend's face partially occluded by an intervening object or missing some of the words in a sentence that is conventional in a given environment. As the rightmost face of the pair shows, a stimulus degraded in this way also leaves the response of the network largely unchanged (Kohonen, 1977).

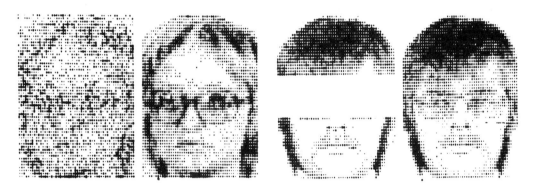

Figure 10. Effects of degraded stimuli on the output of a network. In the left pair of faces (a), the left picture is the stimulus degraded by random noise and the other member of the pair is the output of the network. In the right pair of faces (b), the left picture is the stimulus degraded by omission of a part of the normal input and the other member of the pair is the output of the network. (From Kohonen, 1977).

Effect of the degree of connectivity of the network. A final characteristic of human behavior is that it is often quite resistant to the effects of diffuse brain damage. While the complete interruption of specific pathways has effects of the type previously discussed, diffuse and incomplete losses in specific connections may have relatively little effect. Figure 11 shows what happens to the output of a network when a stimulus is input to a network in which some of the interconnections between units have been eliminated after training. The left picture represents the response of the network when all connections present during training are intact. The right picture represents the response when, after training, a substantial number of the interconnections have been randomly eliminated. It is clear that the response of the network remains quite good even when connectivity is reduced substantially (Kohonen, 1977).

Systematic studies of loss of connectivity in distributed networks confirm the impression given by Figure 11: Adaptive networks are quite resistant to diffuse loss (Anderson, 1984). Further studies in which networks were given periods of training interspersed between successive episodes of loss of connectivity revealed that the deficits were reduced still further (Wood, 1983). This finding corresponds to the common experimental finding that successive

142

brain lesions in animals are often less disabling than loss of the same tissue in a single operation.

Two final points should be made before leaving this presentation of connectionistic simulations of complex behavior using networks that are modified by selection. First, a given output of a network may occur in many different ways, and these differences in process reflect the specific selection history of the network. Thus, in agreement with radical behaviorism and neuropsychology, the proper object of study is the individual organism, because it is the individual organism that is the locus of selection (Marin & Gordon, 1979) Another consequence of the fact that different selection histories produce different patterns of the strengths of connections within a network -- but patterns which may lead to indistinguishable response outputs -- is that response topography alone does not provide an appropriate basis for a functional analysis of behavior. Once again, radical behaviorism, neuropsychology, and connectionism converge to the same conclusion.

A second point, is that the outcome of selection in networks is not some local representation of experience. Memories are not stored as discrete entities as if they were papers in a file drawer; concepts are not nodes in a semantic network with their features somehow attached to them. Selection simply operates to change the functional connectivity of the network. The view that experience changes the organism so that subsequent inputs of the same stimuli produce different outputs is, of course, the view held by radical behaviorism (Skinner, 1974, p. 109; 1977).

Concluding Comments

As an historical science committed to a selectionist approach, radical behaviorism attempts to identify principles that are sufficient to generate complex behavior when those principles are repeatedly applied to the environmental-behavioral relations that are the legacy of natural selection. The close correspondence between the implications of reinforcement and stimulus control

Figure 11. Effects of reduced connectivity on the output of a network. The upper picture represents an output from the network when all interconnections between units remained intact after training. The lower picture represents the output when fifty percent of the interconnections were randomly eliminated after training, which simulates the effect of "lesions" on the performance of the network. (From Kohonen, 1977).

principles and the outcome of neuropsychological and connectionist simulation studies encourages the belief that we are proceeding on the right track. Moreover, there are many suggestions that an integration of knowledge from these superficially unrelated fields may be both possible and fruitful. For example, it is conceivable that verbal behavior does not involve language-specific capabilities, but that the left hemisphere is specialized for the processing of sequential events generally. That is, neurons in the left hemisphere may be interconnected in ways characteristic of recursive, distributed networks. Detailed neuroanatomical work -- particularly of long, intermodal association fibers -- is required to evaluate this conjecture (cf. Geschwind, 1972).

Earlier in this chapter, I remarked that if selectionist principles are sufficient to account for behavioral complexity, then the burden of proof for those who would propose otherwise rests squarely on their own shoulders. The provocative relationships among radical behaviorism, neuropsychology, and connectionism indicate that the burden is growing ever heavier.

References

Anderson, J. A. (1984) Neural models and a little about language. In D. Caplan, A. R. Lecours, and A. Smith (Eds.), *Biological perspectives on language.* Cambridge, MA: MIT Press.

Bickel, W. K. & Etzel, B. C. (1985). The quantal nature of controlling stimulus-response relations as measured in tests of stimulus generalization. *Journal of the Experimental Analysis of Behavior, 44,* 245-270.

Blough, D. S. (1975). Steady state data and a quantitative model of operant generalization and discrimination. *Journal of Experimental Psychology: Animal Behavior Processes, 1,* 3-21.

Bransford, J. D. & Franks, J. J. (1971). The abstraction of linguistic ideas. *Cognitive Psychology, 12,* 331-350.

Cameron, R. F., Currier, R. D., & Haerer, A. F. (1971). Aphasia and literacy. *British Journal of Disorders of Communication, 6,* 161-163.

Campbell, D. T. (1974). Evolutionary epistemology. In P. A. Schlip(Ed.), *The philosophy of Karl Popper.* (Vol. 14, pp. 413-463). LaSalle, IL: Open Court Publishing.

Campbell, D. T. (1975). On the conflicts between biological and social evolution and between psychology and moral tradition. *American Psychologist, 30,* 1103-1126.

Carlson, N. R. (1984). *Psychology: The science of behavior.* Boston, MA: Allyn & Bacon.

Chomsky, N. (1980). *Rules and representations.* New York: Columbia University Press.

Collins, A. M. & Quillian, M. R. (1969). Retrieval time from semantic memory. *Journal of Verbal Learning and Verbal Behavior, 8,* 240-247.

Collins, J. P. (1974). *Generalization and decision theory.* Unpublished doctoral dissertation. University of Massachusetts.

Crowley, M. A. (1979). The allocation of time to temporally defined behaviors: Responding during stimulus generalization. *Journal of the Experimental Analysis of Behavior, 32,* 191-198.

Donahoe, J. W. & Wessells, M. G. (1980). *Learning, language, and memory.* New York: Harper and Row.

Donahoe, J. W., Crowley, M. A., Millard, W. J., & Stickney, K. A. (1982). A unified principle of reinforcement. In M. L. Commons, R. J. Herrnstein, & H. Rachlin (Eds.), *Quantitative analyses of behavior (Vol. 2): Matching and maximizing accounts* (pp. 493-521). Cambridge, MA: Balinger.

Donahoe, J. W., Palmer, D. C., & Carlson, N. R. (in press). *Complex human behavior: A biobehavioral approach to cognition.* Boston: Allyn & Bacon.

Eich, J. M. (1985). Levels of processing, encoding specificity, elaboration, and CHARM.

Psychological Review, 92, 1-38.

Farley, J. & Alkon, D. L. (1985). Cellular mechanisms of learning, memory, and information storage. *Annual Review of Psychology, 36.*

Feldman, J. A. & Ballard, D. H. (1982). Connectionist models and their properties. *Cognitive Science, 6,* 205-254.

Geschwind, N. (1972). Language and the brain. *Scientific American, 226,* 340-348.

Geschwind, N., Quadfasel, F. A., & Segarra, J. M. (1968). Isolation of the speech area. *Neuropsychologica, 6,* 327-340.

Gluck, M. A. & Bower, G. H. (1988). From conditioning to category learning: An adaptive network model. *Journal of Experimental Psychology: General, 117,* 227-247.

Herrnstein, R. J. (1970). On the law of effect. *Journal of the Experimental Analysis of Behavior, 13,* 243-266.

Hinton, G. & Anderson, J. A. (Eds.) (1981). *Parallel models of associative memory.* Hillsdale, NJ: Erlbaum.

Jordan, M. I. (1986). *Serial order: A parallel distributed processing approach.* Institute for Cognitive Science Technical Report No. 8604, University of California, San Diego, CA.

Kamin, L. J. (1968). Attention-like processes in classical conditioning. In M.R. Jones (Ed.), *Miami symposium on the prediction of behavior: Aversive stimulation.* Miami, FL: University of Miami Press.

Kimura, D. (1976). The neural basis of language and gesture.In H. Avakina-Whitaker & H. A. Whitaker (Eds.), *Studies in neurolinguistics.* New York: Academic Press.

Kimura, D. & Archibald, Y. (1974). Motor functions of the left hemisphere. *Brain, 97,* 337-350.

Klein, M. & Kandel, E. R. (1980). Mechanism of calcium current modulation underlying pre-synaptic facilitation and behavioral sensitization in Aplysia. *Proceedings of the National Academy of Science, 77,* 6912-6916.

Kohonen, T. (1977). *Associative memory.* New York: Springer- Verlag.

Kolb, B. & Whishaw, I. Q. (1985). *Fundamentals of human neuropsychology (second edition).* New York: Freeman.

Kuhl, P. K. & Miller, J. D. (1975). Speech perception by the chinchilla: Voiced-voiceless distinction in alveolar plosive consonants. *Science, 190,* 69-72.

Liberman, A. M. (1982). On finding that speech is special. *American Psychologist, 37,* 148-167.

Liberman, A. M., Harris, K. S., Hoffman, H. S., & Griffith, B. C. (1957). The discrimination of speech sounds within and across phoneme boundaries. *Journal of Experimental Psychology, 54,* 358-368.

Luria, A. R. (1970). The functional organization of the brain. *Scientific American, 222,* 66-79.

Margolin, D. I. & Carlson, N. R. (1982). *Common mechanisms in anomia and alexia.* Paper presented at the annual meeting of the Academy of Aphasia, Lake Mohonk, NY.

Marin, O. S. & Gordon, B. (1979). Neuropsychological aspects of aphasia. In Tyler, Richard, & Dawson (Eds.), *Current neurology* (vol. 2). New York: Houghton-Mifflin.

MacDonald, J. & McGurk, H. (1978). Visual influences on speech perception processes. *Perception and Psychophysics, 24,* 253- 257.

Mayr, E. (1982). *The growth of biological thought: Diversity, evolution , and inheritance.* Cambridge, MA: Cambridge University Press.

McClelland, D. E. & Rumelhart, J. L. (Eds.) (1986). *Parallel distributed processing.* Cambridge, MA: MIT Press.

McGurk, H. & MacDonald, J. (1976). Hearing lips and seeing voices. *Nature, 264,* 746-748.

Nespoulous, J-L & Lecours, A. R. (1984). Clinical description of aphasia: Linguistic aspects. In D. Caplan, A. R. Lecours, & A. Smith (Eds.),*Biological perspectives on language.* Cambridge, MA: MIT Press.

Palmer, D. C. (1986). Chomsky's nativism: A critical review. In P. N. Chase & L. J. Parrott (Eds.), *Psychological aspects of language* (pp. 44-60). Springfield, IL: Charles C. Thomas.

Petersen, M. R., Beecher, S. R., Zoloth, D. B., Moody, D. B., & Stebbins, W. C. (1978). Neural lateralization: Evidence from studies of the perception of species-specific vocalizations by Japanese macques (*Macada puscata*). *Science, 202,* 324-326.

Rescorla, R. A. & Wagner, A. R. (1970). A theory of Pavlovian conditioning: Variations in the effectiveness of reinforcement and nonreinforcement. In A. H. Black & W. F. Prokasy (Eds.), *Classical conditioning II: Current research and theory* (pp. 64-99). Englewood Cliffs, NJ: Prentice-Hall.

Sasunama, S. (1975). Kana and kanji processing in Japanese aphasics. *Brain and Language, 2,* 369-383.

Skinner, B. F. (1950). Are theories of learning necessary? *Psychological Review, 57,* 193-216.

Skinner, B. F. (1957). *Verbal behavior.* New York: Appleton-Century-Crofts.

Skinner, B. F. (1974). *About behaviorism.* New York: Knopf.

Skinner, B. F. (1977). Why I am not a cognitive psychologist. *Behaviorism, 5,* 1-10.

Stickney, K. J. & Donahoe, J. W. (1983). Attenuation of blocking by a change in US locus. *Animal Learning and Behavior, 11,* 60-66.

Sutton, R. S. & Barto, A. G. (1981). Toward a modern theory of adaptive networks: Expectation and prediction. *Psychological Review, 88,* 135-171.

Tversky, A. & Kahneman, D. (1982). Judgements of and by representativeness. In D. Kahneman, P. Slovic, & A. Tversky (Eds.), *Judgments under uncertainty: Heuristics and biases.* Cambridge, UK: Cambridge University Press.

vom Saal, W. & Jenkins, H. M. (1970). Blocking the development of stimulus control. *Learning and Motivation, 1,* 52-64.

Wood, C. (1983). Implications of simulated lesion experiments for the interpretation of lesions in real nervous systems. In M. A. Arbib (Ed.), *Neural models of language processes.* New York: Academic Press.

Footnote

Preparation of this paper was supported in part by a grant from the National Science Foundation, BNS-8409948, and by a grant from the University of Massachusetts Faculty Research Fund.

A Discussion of Chapter 6

A Selectionist Approach to Verbal Behavior: Sources of Variation

T.V. Joe Layng
The University of Chicago

Parsimony has always been an important characteristic of the experimental analysis of behavior. We consider as suspect complex explanatory mechanisms and often suggest that they indicate something fundamental is being overlooked. Even so, the temptation to explain observed events (rather than describe them) in terms of some overriding external molar process (matching, maximizing, etc.), or some unobserved internal molecular process (i.e., two-factor theory), is difficult to resist.

John Donahoe in this volume is arguing for an approach to understanding the basis of human verbal behavior that is at once simple and powerful. Donahoe argues that a selectionist approach will produce the same benefits for understanding behavioral complexity as it has for understanding biological complexity. He further suggests that a selection mechanism is at work in each case. For behavioral complexity, it is selection by reinforcement contingencies; for biological complexity, it is selection by survival contingencies.

Donahoe makes his case by first distinguishing between essentialist explanations of behavior, the most noteworthy for verbal behavior are biologically built-in grammatical knowledge or rule systems (see Palmer, 1986), and selectionist explanations of behavior. To perhaps oversimplify, essentialist positions assume an essential directing force or property. Essentialist explanations have accompanied the development of science throughout history, and are with us today as evidenced by the claims of "creation science" in the study of biology and "cognitive science" in the study of behavior. Selectionist accounts, however, look to the organism's relation to its environment. This relation requires three components--variation, selection, and retention.

Once described, Donahoe uses the selectionist framework to suggest that data provided by neuropsychology and computer science may be of use in the analysis of verbal behavior. Whereas verbal behavior data from brain damaged humans has interested radical behaviorists for sometime (see, for example, Goldiamond, 1976; Sidman, Stoddard & Leicester, 1971), computer science has been left to cognitive scientists. Donahoe provides evidence that computer simulation, long thought to be exclusively an essentialist or cognitive domain, is showing that reinforcement contingencies are quite capable of establishing complex behavior. Work with "adaptive networks" is demonstrating that powerful programs can be designed that behave much the same way humans would behave in a similar situation (see Rumelhart & McClelland, 1986; McClelland & Rumelhart, 1986). Such behavior is produced not by recourse to thousands of preprogramed rules, but through consequential arrangements. It should be noted, however, that most of the investigators in this area do not consider themselves radical behaviorists. Many take great pains to deny any commonality with behaviorists (e.g., Rumelhart & McClelland, 1986). Unfortunately, most of these network-based learning systems are quite primitive, based on old learning theories, and a variety of algorithms not informed by current research from the experimental analysis of behavior (but, see Barto 1985; Williams, 1986). Still, the results are impressive, making it imperative that radical behaviorists become increasingly more involved in this research.

A complete commentary on the many intriguing points raised by Donahoe would necessitate many more pages than the current effort allows. Additionally, these points are so well articulated that such a commentary might in the end be superfluous. Instead, I will use this opportunity to take a closer look, occasioned by Donahoe's chapter, at the possible sources of behavioral variation that are available for selection by reinforcement.

For selection by reinforcement contingencies to work, the pattern selected must first occur. Accordingly, the behavior, or pattern of behavior, must originate from a source other than the contingencies that shape and maintain it. An overview of some of these sources will be presented and their implications for the study of verbal behavior noted. Additionally, I will attempt to demonstrate that the selectionist account offered by Donahoe also brings us into useful contact with some of the observations of Ethologists and Comparative psychologists.

Morphology-Environment Relations as Sources of Variation

From its inception, modern evolutionary theory has assigned a primary role to morphological variation in natural selection. The classic example is that of giraffes, some with longer necks than their relatives, living to reproduce other long neck giraffes. Their shorter neck cousins, not able to reach enough food in a changing environment, do not live to reproduce. What has not been so readily acknowledged is the role morphology plays in providing behaviors for possible selection by reinforcement contingencies.

The physical make-up or morphology of an organism is going to limit or restrict the ways it can respond to its world. Confronted with the same physical environment, two animals may bring to it behaviors that let it come into contact with that environment in different ways. A pointed nosed dog with upright ears and thin legs will respond to the same physical environment differently than will a rounded nosed, floppy-eared, thick legged dog. A dog with a particular morphology may simply not be able to physically produce certain behaviors that would be reinforced. Indeed, developmental biologists have used just such an approach to account for the behavioral differences in different breeds of sheep dogs (Coppinger & Coppinger, 1982). Although tempted to describe these differences in terms of an essentialist account they instead traced them to an interaction between the running, bounding, barking, etc. behaviors of the dogs and the response of sheep and predators to these behaviors. Stated differently, morphological characteristics, together with current environmental events, may serve to make certain classes of behavior highly probable, thereby providing a source of behavior for selection by reinforcement. These relations may be considered as yet another category of establishing events (after Michael, 1982). In addition to making an event effective as a reinforcer, these establishing relations make other elements of the three term contingency effective, as well.

Looking at similar relations Liberman (1984) has proposed that the there are key morphological differences in ape and human morphology that might account for the evolution of language and its development during the early years of the human lifespan. Holland (1987) is extending and refining this approach within the specific context of selection by reinforcement contingencies, and is providing a strong basis for a selectionist account of verbal behavior development in children.

Species-Specific Sources of Variation
Phylogenetic Establishing Events

Certain behavior patterns sometimes called innate, instinctive, or species-specific have been observed by ethologists in a wide variety of animal species. A species-specific pattern such as pulling grass for nest building may be observed to occur in the place of other species-specific behavior such as fighting. Such "displacement" is often explained in terms of an instinctive energy spill-over when the primary pattern is blocked, and certain reproductive advantages displacement might provide the organism (Lorenz, 1957). Stated differently, the phylogenetic establishing events, releasers, hormones, etc., that make fighting highly likely still occur, however, another species-specific pattern that does not have such damaging survival consequences, but has similar behavioral consequences, occurs in its place, and is selected. A species-specific pattern established under one condition, may be recruited if it occurs on a different condition as a result of the reproductive advantage it provides. Overlooked is that certain species-specific patterns may provide the basis for selection by reinforcement.

Ontogenetic Establishing Events

In a classic study, Schiller (1957) was able to demonstrate that Kohler's famous insight and problem solving studies could be explained by the recruitment by reinforcement contingencies of chimpanzee species-specific play patterns. When reaching for a banana with a bare hand was not successful chimps were observed to engage in previously observed species-specific play behavior that involved the carrying of sticks etc. The chimps, eventually used sticks to reach the banana. These "displaced behaviors" came readily under reinforcement control. Schiller observed that several historical species-specific patterns may be recruited into a single behavioral solution. Certain untrained early sounds and crying responses may likewise provide the basis for more complex verbal operants.

Operant Sources of Variation

Phylogenetic Establishing Events

Skinner (1969) has made the case that operant behavior may serve as an early evolutionary source for later species-specific behavior. More recently Tierney (1986), a developmental biologist, has made a similar argument. However, certain other interactions between operant and species-specific patterns may be of more interest to those studying verbal behavior. A recent study by Andronis (1983) showed that when an untrained physical attack response by pigeons is prevented, an operant response involving manipulating house lights correlated with high work requirements can be recruited to occur in its place. Among the obvious questions raised is how verbal attack of various kinds may serve to replace (or displace) physical attack, and how this may have in turn influenced the evolution of human verbal behavior.

Ontogenetic Establishing Events

Another, and recently more studied, source of behavior available for selection is behavior established by reinforcement. Using a framework similar to Schiller's, Epstein and his colleagues (1983, 1984, 1985) have shown that previously trained operant behavior may recur on subsequent occasions when other behavior, currently maintained under those occasions, is prevented from occurring. And upon such recurrence the behavior may be recruited by current reinforcement contingencies. Additionally, they, as did Schiller (1957), also observed that several historical patterns may be recruited into a single behavioral solution.

Unit of Selection

Consideration of the unit of selection, or unit of analysis for the study of verbal behavior, is of some importance to the contributors of this volume. Donahoe in his discussion of the reinforcement principle, and later when describing the contributions of neuropsychology, made an important distinction between behavior and behavior under stimulus control. Ray and Sidman (1971), Stoddard and Sidman (1971), and Sidman (1978) have argued that what is reinforced is not simply behavior, nor behavior in the presence of a stimulus, but an occasion-behavior relation, or stimulus-response topography.

If the unit of selection is an occasion-behavior relation, then it becomes important to determine the conditions under which certain of these relations become more or less probable when other current relations are and are not being reinforced. For these relations will provide the foundation for yet other patterns. Moreover, the original controlling relation may not be as revealing as subsequent relations, much the same as a metaphorical extension can not be so classified after its first occurrence (e.g., Layng & Andronis, 1984).

If the primary unit of selection is the occasion-behavior relation and not simply behavior this may have an effect on how we might investigate occasion-behavior relations established by rules (see Chase & Danforth, and Andronis in this volume). If rules restrict variability by limiting the likelihood of alternative relations this would also limit the opportunity for their selection; if rules increase variability we should see an increased opportunity for other occasion-behavior relations to arise.

For example, when human button pressing is shaped the occasion for hand movement toward the button is continually changing and may involve such features as the position of the hand prior to the last movement and the temporal relation between a movement and consequence delivery. Conversely, when button pressing is instructed, say through a brief demonstration of button pressing at a particular rate, such features may be absent. A history of response variability combined with variable reinforcement delay is omitted in the second case. Two different occasion-behavior relations may be established even though the behaviors and consequences in each case may end up being topographically in the same class. Accordingly, changes in reinforcement schedules may affect the variability of the occasion-behavior relation in the case of the shaped behavior, and have little affect on the separate occasion-behavior relation in the case of the instructed behavior. Greater variability should allow new patterns to come into contact with changed contingencies and therefore be candidates for selection by the new reinforcement contingencies. Early data provided by Chase and Danforth (this volume) offer support for this point of view.

Taken together we can see that there are wide sources of behavior, both trained and untrained, species-specific and operant, that can serve as candidates for selection by reinforcement. A "unit of selection" therefore, need not be a single simple response, but may be an entire repertoire (Chase, 1986). In the case of verbal behavior the unit could range form a simple gesture or a grunt to a soliloquy. Given such rich sources it should come as no surprise that complex human behavior, including verbal behavior, can be the outcome of selection by reinforcement as argued by Donahoe.

References

Andronis, P. T. (1983). *Symbolic aggression by pigeons: Contingency coadduction.* Ph.D. dissertation. The University of Chicago.

Barto, A. G. (1985). *Learning by statistical cooperation of self-interested neuron-like computing elements.* COINS Technical Report 85-11. Department of Computer and Information Science, University of Massachusetts, Amherst, MA.

Chase, P. N. (1986). An alternative to the sentence as a basic verbal unit. In P. N. Chase and L. J. Parrott (Eds.), *Psychological aspects of language* (pp. 61-65). Springfield, Illinois: Charles C. Thomas.

Coppinger, L. & Coppinger, R. (1982). Dog in sheep clothing guarding flocks. *Smithsonian, 13,* 64-73.

Epstein, R. (1985). The spontaneous interconnection of three repertoires. *The Psychological Record, 35,* 131-143.

Epstein, R., Kirshnit, R., Lanza, R., & Rubin, R. (1984). "Insight" in the pigeon: Antecedents and determinants of an intelligent performance. *Nature, 308,* 61-62.

Epstein, R. & Medali, S. (1983). The spontaneous use of a tool by a pigeon. *Behavior Analysis Letters, 3,* 241-247.

Goldiamond, I. (1976). Coping and adaptive behavior in the disabled. In G. L Albrecht (Ed.), *The sociology of physical disability and rehabilitation* (pp. 97-138). Pittsburgh: University of Pittsburgh Press.

Holland, J. G. (May 1987). *Behavioral interpretations of language acquisition data.* Association for Behavior Analysis, Nashville, TN.

Layng, T. V. J. & Andronis, P. T. (1984). Toward a functional analysis of delusional speech and hallucinatory behavior. *The Behavior Analyst, 7,* 139-156.

Liberman, P. (1984). *The biology and evolution of language.* Cambridge, MA.: Harvard University Press.

Lorenz, K. (1957). The past twelve years in the comparative study of behavior. In C. H. Schiller (Ed.). *Instinctive behavior* (pp. 288-310). New York: International Universities Press.

McClelland, J. L. & Rumelhart, D. E. (1986). *Parallel distributed processing: Explorations into the microstructure of cognition: Vol. 2. Psychological and Biological Models.* Cambridge, MA: Bradford Books/MIT Press.

Michael, J. L. (1982). Distinguishing between discriminative and motivational functions of stimuli. *Journal of the Experimental Analysis of Behavior, 37,* 149-155.

Palmer, D. (1986). Chomsky's nativism: A critical review. In P. N. Chase and L. J. Parrott (Eds.). *Psychological aspects of language* (pp. 44-60). Springfield, Illinois: Charles C. Thomas.

Ray, B. & Sidman, M. (1971). Reinforcement schedules and stimulus control. In W.N. Schoenfeld (Ed.) *The theory of reinforcement schedules* (pp. 187-214). New York: Appleton-Century-Crofts.

Rumelhart, D. E. & McClelland, J. L. (1986). *Parallel distributed processing: Explorations into the microstructure of cognition: Vol. 1. Foundations.* Cambridge, MA: Bradford Books/MIT Press.

Rumelhart, D. E. & McClelland, J. L. (1986). PDP models and general issues in cognitive science. In D. E. Rumelhart & J. L. McClelland (Eds.). *Parallel distributed processing: Explorations into the microstructure of cognition: Vol. 1. Foundations.* Cambridge, MA: Bradford Books/MIT Press.

Schiller, P. H. (1957). Innate motor action as a basis of learning. In C.H. Schiller (Ed.), *Instinctive behavior* (pp. 264-287). New York: International Universities Press.

Sidman, M., Stoddard, L. T. & Leicester, J. (1971). Behavioral studies of aphasia: Methods of investigation and analysis. *Neuropsychologia, 9,* 119-140.

Sidman, M. (1978) Remarks. *Behaviorism, 6,* 265-268.

Skinner, B. F. (1969). The phylogeny and ontongeny of behavior. In B. F. Skinner, *Contingencies of reinforcement: A theoretical analysis* (pp. 172-220). Englewood Cliffs, NJ.: Prentice-Hall.

Stoddard, L. T. & Sidman, M. (1971). The removal and restoration of stimulus control. *Journal of the Experimental Analysis of Behavior, 16,* 143-154.

Tierney, A. J. (1986). The evolution of learned and innate behavior: Contributions from genetics and neurobiology to a theory of behavioral evolution. *Animal Learning and Behavior, 14,* 339-348.

Williams, R. J. (1986). *Reinforcement learning in connectionist networks: A mathematical analysis.* ICS Report 8605. Institute for Cognitive Science. University of California at San Diego, La Jolla, CA.

Chapter 7

Mentalistic Approaches to Verbal Behavior

Hayne W. Reese
West Virginia University

One purpose of this paper is to summarize and criticize mentalistic approaches to verbal behavior, including network theories, psycholinguistics, and the Soviet theory of the origins of thinking in social speech. The approaches are summarized by selected topics rather than by theories, because the scope of the paper would otherwise be too broad to be manageable. A second purpose is to argue that cognitivists and behavior analysts are interested in different phenomena, but that each group could profitably borrow (through translation) certain concepts from the other group. The paper begins with an explication of what is meant by mentalism and by verbal behavior, then proceeds to the summary of the approaches, and ends with a brief summary and concluding remarks.

Explication of Terms

Mentalism

In *Webster's Third New International Dictionary of the English Language* (1971, p. 1411)), "mentalism" is given three basic definitions. The first definition has two versions:

Definition (1a): "a doctrine that mind is the fundamental reality." This definition is philosophical and although it is relevant here, it can be ignored for present purposes because the mentalistic theories to be considered give material reality a role in language acquisition. That is, even though language competence, or knowledge about language, is the domain of interest in these theories, the development of language competence or knowledge is assumed to have a basis in experience.

Definition (1b): "a doctrine that distinguishes mental processes fundamentally from the accompanying brain activity." This definition is not relevant at all. It refers to a mind-body dualism that ignores any possible relation between mind and brain.

Definition (2): "a view that conscious processes as revealed by introspection are the proper data of psychology -- opposed to **behaviorism**." This definition is too confused to be useful. The phrase "as revealed by introspection" is unnecessary because it refers to method rather than goal; and the term "data" is appropriate only if the classical interpretation of the introspective method is accepted. If the introspective method is not interpreted as yielding factual, observational information about mental processes, then the appropriate term is "inferences" instead of "data."

Definition (3): "a hypothesis that special factors of mind must be assumed to analyze, classify, or explain some or all phenomena of language." If "of language" is changed to "of behavior," this definition is the most relevant one for the purpose of this paper: A theory is mentalistic if it includes mental processes as basic concepts in the analysis, description, or explanation of behavior.

Definition (3) can be contrasted with the behavior analytic definition of mentalism. According to Skinner (1969, pp. 237-238), an approach is mentalistic if its descriptions or explanations refer to a level that is different from the level observed. "Level" in the intended sense refers to what might better be called a domain of knowledge. ("Domain" seems a better label because "level" may imply a hierarchy and a hierarchy may imply that reductionism is warranted. Skinner rejected reductionism [e.g., 1974, pp. 240-241], as did the interbehaviorist J. R. Kantor [e.g., 1942, pp. 176-177].) The domains of knowledge include many scientific domains, such as biological and psychological, but these domains are parallel rather than hierarchical. Being parallel does not mean that all domains of knowledge are equal in completeness or persuasiveness; it means that each is an enterprise in itself, and it means that no domain is reducible to another. That is, no one domain is closer than any other to some hypothetical basis or fundamental science. Even if the laws of psychology turned out some day to be completely explained by the laws of biology, the laws of psychology would still be laws of psychology, even though within biology they would be applications of the laws of biology.

By Skinner's definition, his (1945) approach to mental or "private" events is mentalistic because the domain under observation is verbal behavior that is assumed to tact events that are not in the same observational domain. A person who is observed to say, "I have a toothache," is assumed to have tacted an event "observed" by the person; but this event is from a different observational domain from the verbal behavior.

I personally do not care that Skinner is a mentalist in his own sense of this term, but the term as he used it has so wide a scope of meaning that it is applicable to cognitivists, reductionists, and behaviorists--it covers Chomsky, Piaget, Hull, the Kendlers, Skinner, Skinnerians, etc. Therefore, I will use the relevant version of the dictionary definition: A theory is mentalistic if it includes mental processes as basic concepts in the analysis, description, or explanation of behavior.

By this definition, behavior analysts and behaviorists in the stimulus-response learning theory tradition are not mentalistic because in both of these approaches the unobserved phenomena the theories refer to are conceptualized as either physiological processes or covert behaviors. However, cognitivists are mentalistic by this definition because their theories refer to cognitive operations or strategies, semantic networks, and so on, that are conceptualized as mental phenomena. (Many cognitivists [e.g., Brown, 1975] use the euphemism "in the head" instead of "in the mind," but as a way to disguise their mentalism rather than to avoid mentalism.)

Verbal Behavior

I will not give a technical definition of "verbal behavior," mainly because it is not a technical term. "Verbal behavior" is useful as the name of a chapter or book, but Skinner's (1957) book and criticisms of it demonstrate that it does not need a precise definition. It is a loosely defined generic label, but even if it were a precisely defined generic label it would still refer to an abstraction. No one can show me a verbal behavior, but almost anyone can show me an instance of this rough class of behaviors. The problem of psychological interest is not to explain how the class or class name develops but how instances of the class develop.

Verbal behavior is not a thing that can be acquired. The phrase "verbal behavior as such" does not mean anything, because verbal behavior is not an "as such." However, verbal behavior includes a number of "as such's," such as specific sentences classified as declarative, interrogatory, passive, etc., and specific parts of sentences classified as subjects and predicates, or as agents (i.e., actors), instruments (means, actions), and patients (recipients of actions), or as other classes. I can show you instances of these classes, and in this sense they are things that can be acquired.

Let me emphasize what I mean. If verbal behavior is a class of behaviors, it is so general a class that the question of how it develops is relevant perhaps to the domain of the formation of abstract concepts, but it is not relevant in any other sense to the domain of how a child learns to communicate verbally. The latter domain deals with how a child learns to emit understandable statements, questions, etc., which includes stringing words together in certain standard ways--and in certain acceptable nonstandard ways.

Cognitive Approaches to Selected Topics

The cognitive approaches to language and speech, concepts and concept formation, and the origin of thinking are summarized in the next three sections. These topics do not exhaust the domain of cognitive approaches, but they are very good illustrations of these approaches and they provide nice contrasts with the behavior analytic approach.

Language and Speech

Kaplan (1964, p. 8) distinguished between "logic in use" and "reconstructed logic." Logic in use, in science, consists of the procedures scientists use to justify conclusions and interpretations; reconstructed logic is a philosophical analysis or formalization of logic, referring not so much to logic in use as to logic in idealized form. A similar distinction is made between speech and language. Speech is a means of actual communication, or attempted communication; language is an idealized form of this means of communication. That is, speech is how persons talk about things, and language is speech in its ideal form. Psycholinguists and other language scientists try to infer the structural properties and transformational rules of this ideal form. In contrast, behavior analysts try to discover the conditions that affect actual communication.

The study of language is divided into pragmatics, syntactics, and semantics, but only the last two pertain to language proper. Pragmatics pertains to speech rather than language. Pragmatics is also called sociolinguistics, and deals with communicative competence, or knowing how to make requests, to tell a joke, to adjust comments to the listener's perspective, and so on (paraphrased from Rice, 1982, p. 255). Ullin Place covers this domain in the present volume, and I will not discuss it herein, other than to point out that its being functional and related to speech rather than language might make it highly relevant for behavior analysis of verbal behavior. However, it might also not be highly relevant in that the unit of analysis may be several successive comments rather than a sentence or a word--standard pragmatics may be too holistic for behaviorists' tastes.

Syntactics

Syntactics deals with the structure or form of language. Among the problems dealt with are syntactical ambiguity, complexity, and synonymity and substitutability.

Ambiguous sentences. Psycholinguists interested in syntax seem to be fond of bizarre sentences such as "They were entertaining speakers" and "The missionaries were ready to eat," which are ambiguous because "they" in the first sentence could be the speakers or the speakers' hosts and "ready to eat" in the second sentence could mean "ready to dine" or "ready to be dined upon." Such sentences are ambiguous because they contain words or phrases that have more than one syntactic interpretation, or deep syntactic structure. However, they are bizarre as examples of ambiguous sentences because adults to whom they are presented seldom find them ambiguous until the ambiguities are pointed out.

Embedded sentences. Psycholinguists are also interested in another kind of bizarre sentences--sentences that are hard to understand because of the complexity of their syntactic structure. Gleitman and Wanner (1984) cited the following example from the letters section in the *TV Guide:*

How Ann Salisbury can suggest that Pam Daubner's anger at not receiving her fair
share of acclaim for *Mork and Mindy's* success derives from a fragile ego escapes me.
(p. 215)

This is an example of embedded sentences. Embedded sentences are bizarre in that the
likelihood that they can be understood when uttered is much more remote than that they can
be understood when written, with leisurely analysis permitted. Such sentences can be
understood much more easily if they are spoken or written as a series of simple declarative
sentences. The example from the *TV Guide* can be rewritten:

Pam Daubner did not receive her fair share of acclaim for *Mork and Mindy's* success.
She was angry. Ann Salisbury suggested that Pam Daubner's being angry reflected a
fragile ego. The basis of Ann Salisbury's suggestion escapes the letter-writer.

A second example is from a textbook by Wingfield (1979) on learning and memory:

The race that the car that the people that the man sold, won, was held last summer. (p.
249)

A third example--the last one I will present--is from an introductory book by Deese (1970) on
psycholinguistics:

The book that the box that the dog that the boy that you chased belonged to dug up
contained was a first edition. (p. 13)

Evidently, these sentences are too complex to be easily processed even at leisure: In the
second example, "that the people" has no verb; and in the third example "belonged to" should
be "owned." A corrected version of the second example is:

The race that the car that the people that the man sold, saw, won, was held last summer.

It can be rewritten:

The man sold a car. The people saw the car. The car won a race. The race was held
last summer.

A corrected version of the third example is:

The book that the box that the dog that the boy that you chased owned dug up contained
was a first edition.

It can be rewritten:

You chased a boy. The boy owned a dog. The dog dug up a box. The box contained
a book. The book was a first edition.

I will return to the issue of embedded sentences later (in "A proposed matrix of sentences").

Synonymity and substitutability. Psycholinguists are also interested in limits on synonymity and substitutability. For example, according to Gleitman and Wanner (1984):

English babies learn to say "I won't put up with that" but not "I won't tolerate with
that," and "I painted the wall blue" but not "I painted the wall beautiful." (p. 231)

I must be missing some technical point, because I do not see the problem. In the first instance
the verb is "put up with," not "put up," and therefore "I won't put up with that" is synonymous
with "I won't tolerate that." I am implicitly supposing that "put up with" is functionally one word
for English babies, generalizing from the fact that "all gone" is one word, "allgone," for very
young children (e.g., Palermo, 1970). If so, then they would have no reason to insert "with"
following "tolerate." In the second instance, "blue" and "beautiful" are admittedly not
substitutable in the sentence frame given, but they are substitutable in "I made the wall ____."
Furthermore, although "blue" and "beautiful" are from the same grammatical class--adjec-
tives--they are from different subclasses in that "blue" refers to a concrete property of objects
and "beautiful" refers to an interpretation of objects.

A proposed matrix of sentences. Actually, of course, no babies-- English or other--say any
of the sentences mentioned by Gleitman and Wanner. They are fictions created by psycholin-

guists to make certain points about language, not about speech. Psycholinguists often fail to distinguish among sentences that can be separated into four classes in a two-by-two matrix: (a) sentences that are actually produced versus sentences that conceivably could be produced and (b) uttered sentences versus written sentences.

All the examples cited were sentences actually produced, in that somebody wrote them, but in the matrix I mean "actually produced" in the real world for a purpose other than demonstration of a theoretical point. "Conceivably could be produced" means that the sentence is not from the corpus of "actually produced" sentences, but rather is from the corpus of sentences that psycholinguists conceive. The embedded sentence quoted by Gleitman and Wanner from the *TV Guide* can be taken as evidence that some embedded sentences are "actually written"; but this example--and perhaps the whole corpus of such sentences--is much simpler than the examples conceived by Wingfield and by Deese.

Psycholinguists acknowledge that much of what is actually uttered is ungrammatical. I would add that much of what is actually written is ungrammatical, or at least poorly grammatical, and psycholinguists' failure to make the second distinction has resulted in their being concerned, for example, with why "thunder" is both a noun and a verb while "lightning" is only a noun. I submit that anyone who believes that "lightning" is only a noun has been reading too much or listening too little, because one hears such statements as "It thundered and lightninged last night." (But a point that might interest psycholinguists is that one does not hear "It thunders" or "It lightnings.")

Ambiguity and set. A final point is that none of the objections raised in this section on syntactics undermines the structural analysis of syntax as an aspect of language (as contrasted with speech). Syntactical ambiguity exists in language even if nobody recognizes it in speech: The fact that adults generally fail to notice any ambiguity when they hear "The shooting of the hunters was dreadful," for example, is a fact in the speech domain, not the language domain. It is reminiscent of findings on perceptual and cognitive set, showing that situations that are ambiguous in objective conceptual analysis are often unambiguous in actual subjective perception. I will illustrate this point with two anecdotal examples and one research example: (a) On Monday morning at the Institute we had scrambled eggs for breakfast, and they were too dry for my tastes. However, on Wednesday Kurt Salzinger pointed out that they were actually an omelette rather than scrambled eggs, and my liking was reversed because I prefer omelettes dry. (b) On my airflight coming to the Institute the dessert served with dinner was a tart, and one bite showed me that it was almost inedible. The crust was doughy rather than crusty and it had an off-taste. However, the aftertaste was of cheese, and I decided that the tart was actually a cheesecake. As a cheesecake, it was pretty good. (c) Figure 1 is almost always seen as a rat if it is shown after a series of drawings of animals, and almost always as a bald-headed man wearing glasses if it is shown after a series of human faces. (Brief summaries of this research were given by Reese, 1970, pp. 263-268, and 1976, chap. 7.)

Language Acquisition

Psycholinguists believe that language is too complex to have been learned without the aid of innate mechanisms, such as Chomsky's (1965) "language-acquisition device" (e.g., p. 32). In fact, they often seem to believe that anything complex must have an innate basis. Gleitman and Wanner (1984) referred to "an infinite variety of things that must, and therefore cannot, be learned" (p. 231). They asserted that if child language is taught by mothers, then the mothers must be endowed with innate language tutorial skills (instead of the children being endowed with innate language acquisition skills). But who said complex skills cannot be learned? Psycholinguists look at the utterances of mothers to their children and ask how can you get from

Figure 1. An ambiguous figure. (After Bugelski & Alampay, 1961, Fig. 1, p. 206. Copyright [1961], Canadian Psychological Association. Used by permission.)

these utterances to mature language (not speech, but language)? The answer they seem to have overlooked is, "very gradually."

Chomsky (1959) offered the speculation--which he clearly identified as a speculation--"that the brain has evolved to the point where, given an input of observed Chinese sentences, it produces (by an 'induction' of apparently fantastic complexity and suddenness) the 'rules' of Chinese grammar . . .; or that given an observed application of a term to certain instances it automatically predicts the extension to a class of complexly related instances. If clearly recognized as such, this speculation is neither unreasonable nor fantastic; nor, for that matter, is it beyond the bounds of possible study" (p. 44). It is perhaps neither unreasonable nor fantastic, but it is certainly circular and therefore beyond the bounds of possible independent study. However, if the untestable speculative mechanisms are ignored, then the phenomena Chomsky was describing are respectively interpretable as complex, perhaps higher-order versions of "relational frames" (Hayes, this volume) and of stimulus equivalence.

Motherese. "Motherese" is the generic name given to the way mothers, fathers, other adults, and older children talk to infants and young children. Motherese consists of "short, simple sentences; restricted selection of vocabulary, frequent repetitions, slow rate, with pauses to mark phrases and psycholinguistic units; and models of dialogue interchanges" (Rice, 1982, p. 263). It also "contains many questions, many imperatives, few past tenses, little coordination or subordination, and few disfluencies" (Molfese, Molfese, & Carrell, 1982, p. 309); and it matches well with what the child is likely to do, in that it contains many action directives and the young child is likely to act in response to even partially understood speech (Gleitman & Wanner, 1984, footnote 4, pp. 198- 199).

According to Molfese et al., the initial reason for the research on motherese "was to refute the strong nativist view of language acquisition" (p. 308) that had gripped this field. It was successful only in part, they said, because although the simplified speech could be interpreted as providing models easy to imitate, it was seldom a reaction to the child's grammar--that is, it was seldom intended as a language lesson (Gleitman & Wanner, 1984; Rice, 1982). But so what? The implicit assumption that learning results only from lessons is wrong, as shown, for example, by research by Goetz and Baer (1973) on children's creativity in block- building. Creativity includes, among other aspects, fluency and originality (e.g., Reese & Parnes, 1970). Goetz and Baer reinforced the fluency of children's block-building, that is, variation in constructions, and found that the children's block-building also became more original. In other words, Goetz and Baer's research showed that lessons about fluency influenced not only fluency but also originality. Whatever the intentions of the speaker of motherese in talking to an infant, the possible spin-offs cannot be convincingly limited by a theory--they can be limited only by evidence. Another consideration is that the extent of children's imitation of speech models is underestimated, according to some definitions, if the only criterion is topographical similarity of the observer's and model's behavior. Many behaviorists believe that similarity of function is sufficient for many purposes (Reese, 1980).

Implications of the motherese research. Molfese et al. argued that the motherese research did not support a conclusion that language acquisition has no innate component. They said, "It is absurd to argue that any complex behavior is entirely innate or entirely learned; innate and environmental factors always interact in the development of complex skills. However it is not absurd to ask how large or how small a role is played by innate versus environmental factors" (p. 309). Actually, the question about "how much" is absurd; it is like asking whether hydrogen or oxygen has the more powerful role in composing water -- hydrogen because water consists of twice as many atoms of hydrogen as of oxygen, or oxygen because only half as much is needed? When an outcome depends on an interaction of antecedents, the role of both antecedents is essential and any attempt to quantify the importance of either role is absurd.

The meaningful question, as Anastasi (1958) pointed out long ago, in what turned out to be a futile argument, is not "How much?" but "How?" What roles do innate and environmental variables play? Or better, what does the role-playing metaphor mean concretely with respect to stimuli, behaviors, and other variables indexed by the general labels "innate variables" and "environmental variables"? Instead of the absurd quest for quantification of the roles, the task should be to identify the variables and describe the nature of their interaction with respect to the outcomes of interest.

Chomsky argued that motherese cannot aid language acquisition, because--as Gleitman and Wanner (1984) put the argument--"narrowing the learner's data base, although it might do no harm, certainly cannot do good if the outcome of learning is to be a grammar covering the full range of the language. The narrower the range of data, the more hypotheses can describe them. In fact, the difficulty of proving the learnability of language formally would be considerably reduced if it were plausible to suppose that the learner received and could analyze complex input data . . . because the trans-clausal relations within sentences . . . are revealed only in complex sentences" (p. 229). The argument is not altogether convincing because research has shown that learning simple behaviors can yield complex behaviors, as in shaping, learning-set training, and acquiring rules in a piecemeal way (e.g., Levinson & Reese, 1967).

Mechanisms of acquisition. The problem may be that psycholinguists are basically not developmentalists. They look at simple speech inputs from the environment and simple speech outputs by the infant and then in perplexity ask how the complexities of mature language can possibly emerge from these simple beginnings. Chomsky hinted at an answer, which he thereafter has overlooked, in his 1959 review of Skinner's *Verbal Behavior:* "A young child of immigrant parents may learn a second language in the streets, from other children, with amazing rapidity . . . while the subleties that become second nature to the child may elude the parents despite high motivation and continued practice" (p. 42). Is this not the difference between contingency-shaped and rule-governed behavior? In a footnote to the last paragraph of his review of Skinner's *Verbal Behavior,* Chomsky admitted that language acquisition could be based on learning such as that exhibited in learning sets (footnote 48, p. 57).

In short, although the child's acquisitions in syntax (and, as will be seen later, in vocabulary) are amazing, attributing them to learning is at least as plausible as and no more fantastic than attributing them to innate mechanisms that have no other role than language acquisition and that have no other evidence for their existence than the fact that language is normally acquired by children.

The key to understanding mature behavior is not to look at the mature behavior but to look at its genesis. How can one-trial learning be explained? The answers cognitivists have usually given refer to "hypotheses," strategies, and other mental processes (for reviews, see Reese, 1963, 1964). However, they paid too little attention to the acquisition data: I reviewed the literature on the development of discrimination learning set in rhesus monkeys and found that every variable that affects acquisition in a single discrimination-learning task affects acquisition of the discrimination learning set in the same way. Unfortunately, the primary reviewer of the manuscript did not see the point of recapitulating information about acquisition of a single discrimination and asked me to give the argument in a summary way. I acquiesced and the point was therefore less salient in the published version (Reese, 1964) than I wanted it to be.

In referring to an "infinite" variety of things that must be learned, Gleitman and Wanner (1984) may have given an overestimate; but even if the child must actually acquire an infinite variety of things, an innate mechanism need not be assumed. For example, research on stimulus equivalence clearly shows that training some relations among items yields relations among the other items without explicit training. Classes of classes learned in the same way would enormously increase the amount of acquisition with relatively little increase in the amount of training.

Chomsky gave the basic principle of cognitive approaches to language in the last paragraph of his review of Skinner's *Verbal Behavior.* The principle is an instantiation of what Overton and Newman (1982) referred to as the "Kantian question": "What must one **necessarily** assume about the nature of the organism in order for it to have the behaviors which it does exhibit?" (pp. 218-219). The question refers to "the problem of determining what the built-in structure of an information-processing (hypothesis-forming) system must be to enable it to arrive at the grammar of a language from the available data in the available time" (Chomsky, 1959, p. 58).

Nature of the grammar. According to a relatively early (1960's) theory of syntactic development, the young child uses a "pivot grammar" in which the lexicon is divided into two grammatical classes--a "pivot" class and an "open" class (for a brief review, see Palermo, 1970). The details are of no concern here because the theory has been abandoned in favor of a "case" grammar in which semantic classes are invoked. For example, a young child's utterance, "Mommy sock," could refer to the mother's sock or the mother's putting a sock on the child's foot (Rice, 1982). Pivot grammar does not distinguish between these two meanings grammatically; but in a case grammar the meanings can be represented as possessor/object versus agent/object, both meanings conveyed with the same words (Rice, 1982).

Gleitman and Wanner (1984) argued that in the utterance "Mail come," "mail" cannot be the agent because an agent is defined as an animate instigator of an action. The flaw in their argument is that this is the adult definition of an agent, and the child may have a definition that makes "mail" in "mail come" an "agent." I have seen hundreds of sentences like the following, all written not merely by adults but by adults with a doctorate in psychology:

This study intended to examine the effects of . . . .

Their article concluded that the effects . . . .

Studies and articles are not animate instigators of any actions, and adults seem often not to use the psycholinguistic definition of an agent. That the child may have a different definition is not at all surprising.

If young children speak in a case grammar, they will talk agent, instrument, patient (actor, means, recipient); but Gleitman and Wanner argued that such a grammar cannot account for children's speech because the children would still need to map from the cases to grammatical notions such as "subject" and "object." However, this argument is not persuasive because if the child speaks case grammar the so-called grammatical notions such as subject do not exist as far as the child is concerned, leaving nothing to be mapped to. (Incidentally, the theoretical literature on language and speech is crowded with references to "mappings" of various sorts, usually with no apparent awareness that this word is being used metaphorically and no attempt to specify a concrete mechanism.)

Semantics

Semantics deals with the content of language, as contrasted to its structure or form, which is the domain of syntactics. The two major opposing theories of semantics in the mentalistic approach are compositional or componential theories, on the one hand, and holistic theories on the other hand. The componential theorists include John Locke, Wittgenstein, and much more recently, Eleanor Rosch. Jerry Fodor is an outstanding example of a modern holistic theorist.

According to componential theories, a concept is a list or network of components or features. For example, the concept of a cat consists of the features whiskers, fur, four legs, a tail, purring, etc. According to holistic theories, the concept of a cat refers to a collection of features taken as a whole, such that the whole is catness. Gleitman and Wanner (1984) objected that holistic theories require assuming innate, internal processes sufficient to represent the whole and to recognize instances of it. Just why the processes have to be innate, or even internal, is not clear. I would have thought that prototypical meanings could be induced from instances through some sort of averaging process, rather than the matching of instances to some genetically given idea of the prototype. In fact, the idea of a genetically given prototype seems totally unnecessary, as shown by studies demonstrating the induction of prototypes for nonsense shapes (e.g., Brown & Evans, 1969; Reed, 1976).

Semantic Development

According to Carey (1978), the average 6-year-old has a vocabulary of 14,000 words, which Rice (1982) said "works out to an average of about nine new words a day, or almost one word per waking hour" (p. 255). Must we therefore assume that the child has an innate word acquisition device different from other learning mechanisms? At least three considerations lead to a negative answer.

First, even 2- and 3-month-old infants have been shown to form memories quickly. According to Rovee-Collier and Hayne (1987), after only 18 minutes of experience in controlling the movement of a mobile hanging above their crib, infants at that age remember how to control the movement for at least a month.

Second, infants may actually receive vast exposure to speech. On the average, young infants urinate about 19 times a day and defecate about 5 times a day (Halverson, 1940). On a demand feeding schedule they eat about 6 to 8 times a day. Even with overlaps, these activities could easily provide more than a dozen periods each day during which a caregiver talks to the infant. Instances of soothing and other forms of caregiving and instances of playing with the infant could provide many more daily exposures to speech. Thus, a hundred learning periods per week is a plausible estimate for young infants. For older children, the number of learning periods cannot be estimated, because older children interact verbally with many more individuals and because, according to Kuczaj (1982), children play with aspects of the language system they are currently acquiring, thus providing learning opportunities that could replace those lost from caregiving interactions.

Finally, the estimate Carey gave may well be an overestimate. For one thing, she pointed out in a footnote that the 14,000 words included inflected and derived words, and that "For root words only, the estimate falls to around 8,000, or roughly five new root words a day" (footnote 1, p. 264). The estimates she gave were from a study by Templin (1957), who used a multiple-choice vocabulary recognition test in which each word correctly recognized earned credit for knowing 505 words. Templin's estimate for the median number of root words recognized at age 6 years was 7,800 and for total words, 13,000 (these estimates were corrected for guessing). Even for the estimate of 14,000 words cited by Rice, the mean is not Rice's "about nine new words a day," but only 6.4 words per day--and furthermore this is not "new" words per day. The mean number of new words per day is about 3.6, or about .4 new word per waking hour. This is still an amazing feat, but it is not overwhelmingly so, especially because as Miller (1977) pointed out, the child can be working on many more than one word at a time.

Two final points need to be mentioned: First, the generalization of trained relations in stimulus equivalence to untrained relations could have an innate basis, supporting at least in part the argument of the mentalists. Nonhuman animals do not exhibit this kind of stimulus equivalence (D'Amato, Salmon, Loukas, & Tomie, 1985; Sidman, Rauzin, Lazar, Cunningham, Tailby, & Carrigan, 1982). However, the kind of innate mechanism that would need to be assumed is much less specific than Chomsky's language acquisition device, and would offer little support to the mentalistic position. Second, although the infant and child are normally exposed to speech in a vast number of periods, mere exposure is not enough according to the behavioral perspective--reinforcement is required. The occurrence of reinforcement, or at least corrective feedback, has been documented (Rondal, 1985), but experimental research with manipulation of the contingency is needed.

Concepts and Concept Formation

I am devoting a separate section to semantic development--concept formation--because I believe that the developmental approach is the most efficient and effective path to understanding of a domain. This approach has been widely recommended and used, for example by cognitivists such as Piaget (1947/1963, pp. 48-49), Soviet psychologists such as Vygotsky (1978, chap. 5; Wertsch, 1981), and behaviorists such as Watson (1926) and Baer (1982).

The word *concept* has several meanings, but I will use it to refer to a known fact or truth that has some degree of generality. I am not using "known" and "generality" as technical words; but at the risk of belaboring the obvious, let me explain what I mean.

Saying that an individual *knows* a fact or truth means that the fact or truth was learned by the individual or that it is an a priori, innate idea. For example, a child who has been frightened by a dog may have learned the "fact" that this dog is fearsome and may exhibit this knowledge by cringing whenever the dog appears. This is an example of a learned concept; examples of a priori, innate concepts are causality, according to Kant (Prosch, 1964, chap. 5), and certain perceptual equivalences, according to Bornstein (1978).

A fact or truth has *generality* if it is generalized to instances not previously associated with the fact or truth. For example, the child who has been frightened by a dog may have learned not merely that this dog is fearsome but that dogs are fearsome. If so, the child may exhibit this knowledge by cringing whenever any dog appears, even one that the child has never seen before. A generalized concept can also be called a category, and the formation of generalized concepts can be called category learning, or learning to categorize phenomena and events of particular kinds.

Two Kinds of Concepts

As John Donahoe mentions in Chapter 6 of the present volume, cognitivists distinguish between "knowing that" and "knowing how." "Knowing that" is also called "declarative knowledge"; it includes concepts in the sense of information, that is, categories into which things and events are divided. "Knowing how" is "procedural knowledge"; it refers to concepts as behaviors. The behaviors may be physical, as in driving a golf ball, or mental, as in memorizing a poem. (For further discussion, see Reese, 1989.)

A person who accurately describes the required chain of behaviors involved in driving a golf ball has declarative knowledge about this behavior. A person who successfully drives a golf ball has procedural knowledge about this behavior. However, these can be different persons: The person who has declarative knowledge about a domain does not necessarily have procedural knowledge about it, and vice versa. For example, I have only declarative knowledge about driving a golf ball, and almost everyone has only procedural knowledge about transforming sentences from the active voice to the passive voice (Slobin, 1979, p. 5).

Declarative knowledge can be divided into verbal and nonverbal concepts. Sokolov (1972) pointed out that a concept is not the same as a noun because a single noun can symbolize more than one concept (p. 13). (Sokolov cited Aristotle's *Categories,* but without a specific locus. The relevant material is in Chapter 1 of *Categories.*) A verbal concept is the name given to a purported phenomenon. I say "purported" because the phenomenon may or may not actually exist. "Ghost" is an example of names given to phenomena that do not actually exist. Verbal declarative knowledge can be tested by asking a person to define the word in question or to supply the word when the phenomenon is shown or described.

Nonverbal declarative knowledge refers to the phenomenon as such, a regularity in nature that a person responds to and generalizes from but has not learned to name. This kind of knowledge is perhaps exhibited most clearly by young children. For example, they can learn to respond to a size relation such as middlesizedness without being able to name this relation (Reese, 1968).

Behavioral Theories of Concept Formation

Behavior analysis. In behavior analysis, concept formation consists of the learning of stimulus classes and response classes. The interest is in (a) how classes are learned, with current emphasis on the stimulus equivalence paradigm in the case of stimulus classes, and (b) how they function, with current emphasis on concepts as rules or precurrent behaviors in problem-solving chains.

Stimulus-response learning theory. In stimulus-response learning theory, concept formation consists of the learning of cue-producing responses. The learning is assumed to consist of conditioning a selected response to a selected set of stimuli. The set of stimuli is selected because all its members share at least one common property, which could be natural or entirely arbitrary. The response is selected as a name for that property or set of properties.

A concept may function as a "mediator," as in the acquired equivalence of cues or in the acquired distinctiveness of cues, in which, respectively, the concept facilitates or inhibits generalization. However, a concept may lack this function early in development (Reese, 1962).

Cognitive Approaches to Concepts

Soviet psychologists appear to have been concerned more with the functions of concepts than with the nature of concept formation. Luria (1981) included a chapter on concept formation (chap. 4) in his book *Language and Cognition*, but it dealt much more with methods than with findings. The emphasis in the Soviet position is on speech, rather than language, consistently with the Marxist emphasis on practice as opposed to theory.

American cognitive psychologists have been much less concerned with how concepts develop and what functions they serve than with their structural properties. By structural properties, I refer to meaning or content and mode or format. Farah and Kosslyn (1982) summarized several cognitive theories of these structural properties, and some of the relevant research. The account that follows is based on their summary.

Content. The content of a concept is the information it consists of, that is, the meaning of the concept. Cognitivists have been less interested in the specific meanings of concepts than in the way meanings are represented, or encoded. According to Farah and Kosslyn, the three major classes of theories represent the information in a concept by rules of application, by individual exemplars of the concept, or by a summary of exemplars. According to rule-based representations, a concept consists of the necessary and sufficient attributes for category membership. For example, a large amount of laboratory research on concept formation, or rule learning, as it was also called, dealt with learning to categorize multidimensional stimuli. The concept or rule to be learned might be a conjunctive rule such as "positive instances (i.e., members of the category) are red and large," or a disjunctive rule such as "positive instances are red and/or large." Another example of a concept as defined in this approach is the representation of "dog" as "four-legged, hairy, barking animal" (p. 130).

A major problem for this approach was how to deal with natural language concepts, most of which are not defined by a set of necessary and sufficient conditions but rather are defined by family resemblance. That is, all exemplars of a concept share similarities, but no one similarity is shared by all exemplars and no one similarity excludes all nonexemplars. What is necessary and sufficient is not a set of attributes, but family resemblance with respect to specified similarities.

For example, according to Webster's (1971) dictionary, "furniture" means (among other things) "articles of convenience or decoration used to furnish living quarters, offices, public and private buildings--usu. used of movable articles (as tables and chairs) as distinguished from such permanent installations as bathroom fixtures" (p. 924). Vacuum cleaners and toasters are articles of convenience found in living quarters and they are moveable, but they are not furniture. They are appliances--"a household or office utensil, apparatus, instrument, or machine that utilizes a power supply, esp. electric current (as a vacuum cleaner, a refrigerator, a toaster, an air conditioner)" (*Webster's,* 1971, p. 105). However, although refrigerators and stoves are appliances by this definition, they may also be considered furniture. Evidently, refrigerators and stoves have similarities to some other items called furniture, but the similarities refrigerators and stoves have to vacuum cleaners and toasters are not shared with items of furniture.

Prototype and cue set representations. Farah and Kosslyn summarized two kinds of summary representations--prototype and cue set representations. A prototype is a single representation that is most similar to all the exemplars in the category. In one version of prototype theory, the knower constructs the prototype by some sort of averaging of the properties of the exemplars. The networking computer programs described by Donahoe in this volume can do averaging of this sort, as shown by his example of the development of Freud's prototypical face. This kind of prototype is therefore maximally similar to all exemplars that had been experienced and included in the averaging. In another version of prototype theory, the prototype is itself an exemplar, specifically whichever one is most similar to the other exemplars. For example, for the set of all possible triangles with the same base and height, the prototypical triangle is an equilateral triangle. (If height is free to vary, the prototype will be an isosceles triangle of indefinite height.)

A cue set representation is the set of properties of the exemplars. In some versions the properties are weighted by the frequency of their occurrence in the exemplars.

Finally, in some theories the representation is assumed to include a representation of each exemplar, with no summarizing but perhaps with some selectivity. (This assumption is reminiscent of an assertion by James Mill that the idea [image] of "everything" must consist of the image of every thing [1869, p. 116].) Farah and Kosslyn suggested, "it is reasonable to suppose that the learner becomes selective as the number of stored exemplars grows, so that only exemplars that differ significantly from those already stored are added to the set of stored representations" (p. 144). Although this suggestion is reasonable, it also makes the representation partly rule-based.

Format. The mode or format of a concept is the nature of the stored symbols that represent it. For example, concepts can be represented mentally not only as verbal symbols but also as motoric images and as visual, auditory, and other sensory images, or in Bruner's (1964) terms, the representation can be symbolic, enactive, or iconic. (According to Bruner, the sequence of emergence in ontogeny is enactive-iconic-symbolic, but all three modes remain available throughout life.)

Many cognitive theorists avoid the issue of the modality of storage by assuming that the stored symbols are amodal. Such theorists distinguish between the lexicon, in which a person's vocabulary is stored, and semantic memory, in which a person's concepts are stored. Storage in the lexicon is verbal, but storage in semantic memory is amodal (Paivio, 1975a, 1975b).

Network Representations of Concepts

The general features of semantic network representations can be explicated by reference to a concrete example. Figure 2 shows part of a semantic network representation of animal concepts. Details of this kind of representation are discussed in the following paragraphs (more extensive overviews and critiques can be found in, for example, Anderson, 1990, chap. 5; Howard, 1983, chap. 6; Smith, 1978).

Propositions. The ovals represent *propositions,* which Anderson (1990) defined as follows: "A proposition is the smallest unit of knowledge that can stand as a separate assertion; that is, the smallest unit about which it makes sense to make the judgment true or false" (p. 123). Anderson gave as an example the statement "Nixon gave a beautiful Cadillac to Brezhnev, who was the leader of the USSR." This statement contains three propositions:

Nixon gave a Cadillac to Brezhnev.

The Cadillac was beautiful.

Brezhnev was the leader of the USSR. (p. 123)

Although these propositions are expressed verbally here, they need not be expressed verbally in the mind--they can be nonverbal *concepts.*

Nodes. A proposition consists of a relation and relata (the concepts that are related). The proposition, relation, and relata are called *nodes* in the semantic network.

Links. The nodes in a semantic network are connected by arrows called *links.* The links shown in Figure 2 are "Subject," "Relation," "Object," and "Isa" connections. The "Isa" connection links nodes to their superordinate class ("is a"), not their superordinate class *name* but their superordinate concept node.

164

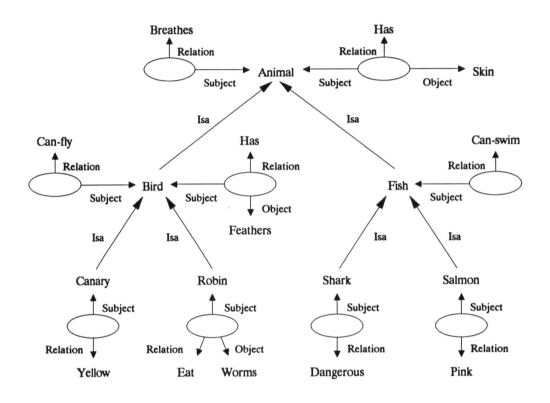

Figure 2. Part of a semantic network representation of animal concepts.
(From *COGNITIVE PSYCHOLOGY AND ITS IMPLICATIONS,* Third Edition, by John
R. Anderson. Copyright © 1980, 1985, 1990 W. H. Freeman and Company.
Fig. 5-9 , p. 132. Used by permission.)

Cognitive economy. The figure shows that nodes representing specific birds are linked to
the Can-fly and Feathers nodes indirectly, through the Bird node. The principle is that nodes
are linked directly only at the most general applicable level. This principle, called the principle
of "cognitive economy" (e.g., Collins & Loftus, 1975; Kail & Bisanz, 1982), greatly reduces the
number of links that would be required if each instance of a class were linked directly to all the
properties of the class. The principle is now known to have many exceptions, but it holds in a
general way. Another aspect of cognitive economy is indicated by the fact that although Can-
fly is actually not a property of all birds, it is a property of so many birds that cognitive "space"
is preserved by linking Cannot-fly directly to the exceptions.

Activation. When a node is "activated," for example by presentation of a stimulus word,
the activation spreads to linked nodes. The spread of activation is assumed to take place in real
time, and therefore activation should take less time to spread from the Canary node to the Bird
node than from the Canary node to the Animal node. Research has confirmed this prediction,
in that research participants verify propositions such as "A canary is a bird" more rapidly than
"A canary is an animal," and "A canary can fly" more rapidly than "A canary has skin."
However, they verify "A chicken is a bird" more slowly than "A canary is a bird," leading
network theorists to develop the concept of *typicality* of instances. That is, a canary is more
typical of the concept of birds than is a chicken (perhaps because chicken is a "food"). In a

semantic network, typicality is represented by the length of the arrow symbolizing the link, and longer links are assumed to require more time for the spread of activation.

Another aspect of semantic network theory that is noteworthy here is the Isnota link. Research showed that propositions such as "A canary is a fish" required less processing time than was predicted by the number of intervening nodes, leading to the assumption of direct links of exclusion ("is not a") as well as inclusion ("is a"). In general terms, the network of knowledge about a concept can include information about what it does not mean as well as what it means. Both kinds of information are important; they can facilitate knowing what to avoid and what to approach (Cross & Vaughter, 1966, attributing the suggestion to D'Amato & Jagoda, 1961, who had noted that for animals under appetitive drive the major problem is to learn avoidance because the approach response is already strong).

Strength. Typicality is one source of variations in the *strength* of a link. Figure 3 shows a developmental change in the strengths of links: The categories are more perceptual than conceptual for the younger child and vice versa for the older child. In network terminology, "the important developmental change is that category relations (*isa ...*) become stronger relative to property links (*is, has*)" (Kail & Bisanz, 1982, p. 60).

The assumptions about typicality and strength can also be used to explain a phenomenon that David Palmer describes in this volume: A person objects to being called a "nerd" even after hearing it defined as "highly intelligent and well-coordinated." Semantic network theory can explain this phenomenon on the assumption that the old definition is linked more closely (i.e., strongly) to the node representing Nerd than is the new definition, and therefore activation spreads more quickly to the node representing the old definition, and from there spreads to a negative emotional reaction.

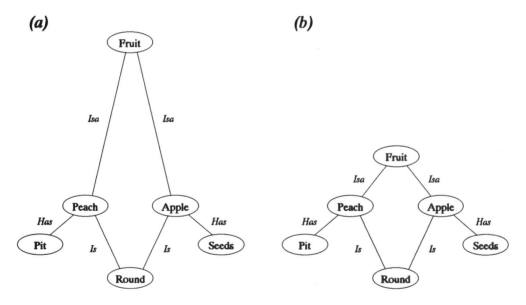

Figure 3. Portions of the knowledge base concerning fruits. (a) The knowledge of a 5-year-old, for whom peaches and apples are alike primarily because they are both round. (b) The knowledge of an 8-year-old, for whom peaches and apples are similar primarily because they are both fruits. (Figure and caption from Kail & Bisanz, 1982, Fig. 5, p. 60. Used by permission.)

166

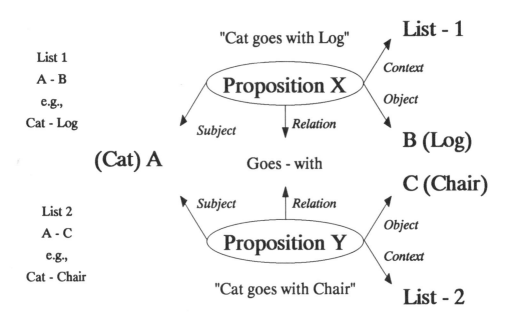

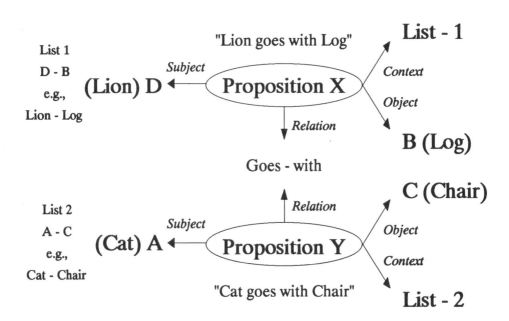

Figure 4. A semantic network representation of the classical associative interference paired-associates design (top) and the classical control condition (bottom). Two lists of pairs are presented, with the same stimuli in both lists in the interference condition (symbolized A-B, A-C) and with different stimuli in the lists in the control condition (symbolized D-B, A-C). The representation shows a sample set of pairs for each condition.

Applications of Network Theory

Semantic networks can be used to model many kinds of associations. Two examples are considered in the following subsections.

Associative Interference

The upper part of Figure 4 shows a semantic network interpretation of the classical associative interference design in paired-associates learning. Interference should occur in List 2 unless the contexts are distinctively different because in List 2, Proposition Y is activated from two nodes ("A" and "List 2") and Proposition X is also activated from one of these nodes ("A"). (Proposition X is also activated through the Relation node, but this activation should be negligibly weak because the same relation occurs in all the propositions in the list. If activation from this source were strong, such lists would be harder to learn than they in fact are, because of massive within-list interference. Therefore, this source must have a weak effect.)

The lower part of Figure 4 shows the classical control condition used in this design. Interference should not occur in List 2 because the only link between Propositions X and Y is through the Relation node.

Kurt Salzinger mentions in his paper in this volume a study in which proactive interference did not build up across lists when the lists were presented in different contexts. Semantic network theory can explain this phenomenon in the same way it explains classical associative interference.

Stimulus Equivalence

Sokolov (1972) and Luria (1981, pp. 76-82) summarized evidence from Soviet research that is relevant to network theory. An example is a study by A. Ya. Fedorov (Sokolov, 1972):

In a child 12 years of age repetition was used to establish a firm association between six words: "pigeon," "turkey," "hawk," "owl," "chicken," and "swallow." One of these words ("pigeon") was then reinforced several times with a food stimulus (cranberry with sugar). All the words of this complex were found to have turned into conditional stimuli, each one evoking intense secretory (salivary) conditioned reflexes. However, all other words designating, for instance, animals, trees, and fruits did not evoke this response. Nor was the response evoked by the names of other birds not belonging to the original complex, but the general name "bird" produced an intense response. (p. 60)

A network interpretation. A possible semantic network interpretation of this study is shown in Figure 5. In the model, the X node represents the superordinate category of having been associated in the preliminary training, the Turkey node is used to represent the nodes of all the words except "pigeon" that were associated in the preliminary training (turkey, hawk, owl, chicken, swallow), and the Robin node is used to represent the nodes of all the birds that were not in this set but were named in the test. After conditioning has occurred, presentation of the word "pigeon" should activate the Pigeon node, and the activation should spread through the Proposition node (the oval in the model) to the Sweet-taste node and thence to the Salivary-response node. Presentation of any word in the associated set should spread activation through the X node (and the Bird node) to the Pigeon node and eventually to the Salivary-response node. Presentation of the word "bird" should also spread activation eventually to the Salivary-response node.

A problem is that the model implies that activation should also spread from the Robin node to the Bird node and therefore eventually to the Salivary-response node. The finding that "robin" did not lead to the salivary response is therefore inconsistent with the model. However,

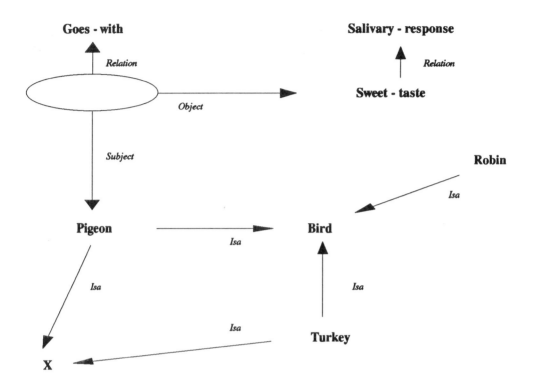

Figure 5. A semantic network representation of the situation assessed by Fedorov. The node labeled X represents the set of words associated in preliminary training (i.e., pigeon, turkey, hawk, owl, chicken, swallow); the node labeled Turkey represents the nodes of each of these words individually, except pigeon; and the node labeled Robin represents the nodes of all birds not associated in preliminary training but used in the test for generalization.

if the laboratory training established an Isnota link between the Robin node and the X node (and the other non-X bird nodes and the X node), this finding can be easily explained. (In an earlier draft of this paper, I proposed a more complex model; the present model is based on an idea suggested by Dr. Philip N. Chase, personal communication, August 1987.) According to the model:

(a) For the word "pigeon," activation spreads directly from the Pigeon node to the Proposition node through the *Subject* link, and salivation occurs. (Activation might also spread from the Pigeon node through the Bird and X nodes and eventually back to the Pigeon node, but by then the Proposition node would have already been activated. Similar long paths of activation can be found for the other stimulus words, but they can also be ignored for the same reason.)

(b) For "turkey" (and analogously all birds other than pigeon in the pretraining set), activation of the Turkey node spreads to the Pigeon node through the X node and through the Bird node, thence to the Proposition node, and salivation eventually occurs.

(c) For the stimulus "bird," activation spreads from the Bird node to the Pigeon node both directly through the Isa link and indirectly via the Turkey-X link, and therefore activation spreads to the Proposition node and salivation occurs.

(d) For the stimulus "robin," activation spreads indirectly to the Pigeon node through the Isa links of Robin to Bird and Bird to Pigeon and through the Isnota link of Robin to X and X to Pigeon. Thus, Robin has both an inclusion (Isa) link and an exclusion (Isnota) link to Pigeon; consequently, activation does not spread to the Proposition node and salivation does not occur. In effect, "robin" does not activate the salivary response because although a robin is a bird, it is not a pigeon, turkey, hawk, owl, chicken, or swallow and therefore does not have the new-found property of these birds--the association with a sweet taste.

A behavior analytic interpretation. The results of the Fedorov study can also be explained on the basis of stimulus classes and stimulus equivalence as studied in behavior analysis. A stimulus class is defined as a set of stimuli such that if a response is conditioned to any member of the set, the response is associated with all members of the set without further training. The preliminary training in the Fedorov study established the words used as a stimulus class, as demonstrated by the fact that associating the salivary response with "pigeon" associated it with the other words without further training. If the stimulus class is symbolized as X and the salivary response as R, then this effect can be diagrammed as:

X--R.

Because of prior learning, all members of the class X were already associated with "bird":

X--"bird."

As a result of stimulus equivalence, "bird" therefore had the same stimulus function as X:

"bird"--R.

The question raised by this interpretation is why other bird-names that might have the same stimulus function as X because of prior association with "bird" do not have an association with the salivary response. For example,

"robin"--"bird"

should yield

"robin"--R.

As noted by Philip N. Chase (personal communication, August 1987), under some conditions "robin" might be part of such an equivalence class, but under the conditions given it would not be because it was not included in the initial stimulus class (X). In effect, a relation like the Isnota link was learned in the preliminary training. Such a relation is learned in "exclusion" (Dixon, 1977), in which learning a word-to-object Isa link can simultaneously establish an Isnota link of

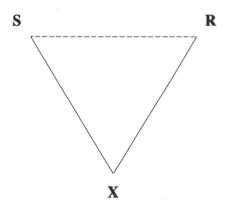

Figure 6. Vygotsky's concept of "mediation." See text for explanation. (From Vygotsky, 1978, Fig. 1, p. 40. Used by permission.)

other words to the trained object. It can also be learned in matching-to-sample and oddity types of tasks because nonmembers of the stimulus class are explicitly excluded through extinction or punishment procedures. The preliminary training in the Fedorov study may have implicitly had the same effect (Philip N. Chase, personal communication, August 1987; Abdulrazaq A. Imam, personal communication, November 17, 1987).

Soviet interpretation. The question raised for the behavior analytic interpretation can be raised for the Soviet theory. Figure 6 shows Vygotsky's (1978) diagram of the relation between the environment and behavior. The diagram could be used to represent the establishment of stimulus equivalence: Train S--X and X--R and get S--R. It could also be used to represent mediation as interpreted in stimulus-response learning theory (e.g., Goss, 1961): The relation between S and R is mediated by associations of S and R to X. Vygotsky called the phenomenon represented in his diagram "mediation," but he meant that the link between S and R is illusory-- it is mediated by a mental process that transforms S, and the transformed S evokes R.

The difference between the stimulus-response learning theory interpretation and Vygotsky's interpretation is diagrammed in Figure 7 with traditional symbols from stimulus-response learning theory. Model A represents a conditioned (respondent) response; Model B represents the classic view of mediation; and Models C through F represent various cognitive views of

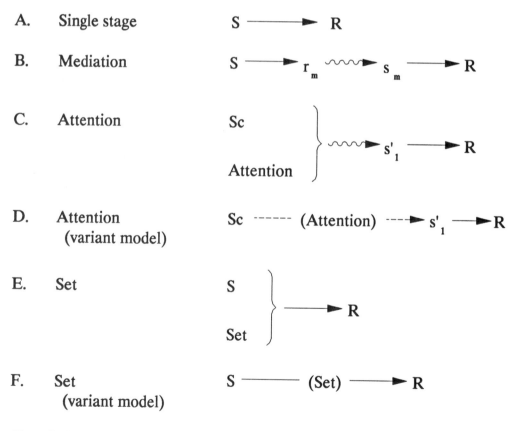

Figure 7. Models of conditioned (A) and mediated (B - F) responding. Models A and B are consistent with stimulus-response learning theory. Models C - F are consistent with cognitive theories. (From Reese, 1971, Fig. 1, p. 19. Used by permission.)

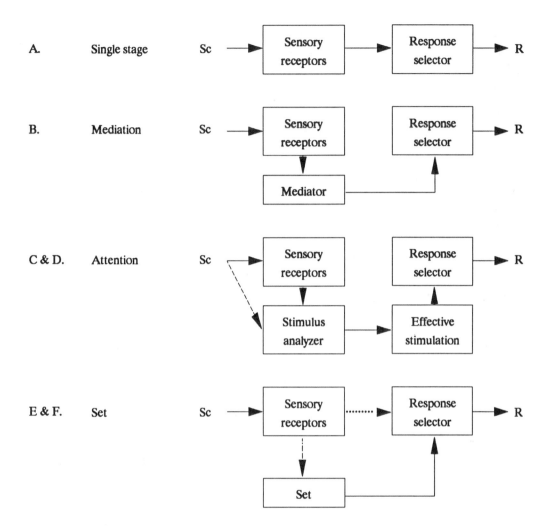

Figure 8. Flow charts of the models shown in Figure 7. The Attention model with the dashed line included is Model C in Figure 7; without the dashed line it is Model D. The Set model with the dashed line excluded is Model E in Figure 7; with the dashed line included and the dotted line excluded it is Model F in Figure 7. (Adapted from Reese, 1971, Fig. 2, p. 21. Adapted by permission.)

mediation. The common theme in the cognitive views (except Model E) is that some mental process--attention or set in the figuremodifies the stimulus and the modified stimulus elicits the response. Vygotsky's theory is best represented by Model D, but with "Thinking" substituted for "Attention" to emphasize the difference from Model B.

The models shown in Figure 7 are represented in Figure 8 with symbols from information-processing theories, in order to show that these theories can deal with simple conditioning as well as mediated responding. (The diagrams of Models E and F in Figure 8 show that these models differ from the other cognitive models in assuming that the effect is on the response rather than on the effective stimulus.)

To return to the issue under consideration: Vygotsky's concept of mediation (Figure 6) provides no way to link the salivary response to "bird" without also linking it to "robin" (for example). The results pose the same problem for stimulus-response learning theory, for essentially the same reasons. Nevertheless, the Soviet theory is not compatible with stimulus-response learning theory--nor with behavior analysis. The relations among these approaches are analogous to Donahoe's comment about the resemblance of a production-system computer simulation and behavior analytic concepts. As I pointed out elsewhere (Reese, 1986b), a production explicitly consists of a condition and an action, and implicitly it includes an outcome; but the condition-action-outcome sequence is not the same as the S^D-R-S^R sequence: (a) The condition in computer simulation must be present in its entirety for the action to occur, but as a result of generalization the discriminative stimulus in behavior analysis can be partial; (b) the action in computer simulation is usually mental; the response in behavior analysis is usually overt; and (c) the outcome in computer simulation is usually a transformation of information in short-term memory; the reinforcing stimulus in behavior analysis is usually a material stimulus.

The Origin of Thinking in Speech

I have discussed elsewhere (Reese, 1986a) the relation between thinking and language (in a nontechnical sense) in Watsonian and Skinnerian behaviorism, as well as in Piagetian theory and the Soviet theory. I will, however, briefly summarize the Soviet theory here because it has a unique feature: Thinking originates in social speech, in that it is based on the internalization of social speech; but after it is internalized, its nature changes such that it is no longer under control of the social environment. On the contrary, "inner speech" frees the individual from social control, thereby permitting really independent activity.

Marx said, "Ideas have no existence apart from language" (quoted by Sokolov, 1972, p. 2, from *Archives of Marx and Engels,* Vol. 4, 1935, p. 99). However, unless he meant "language" in a special sense, current Soviet theory disagrees. Thinking is inner speech, according to Soviet theory; but although inner speech is "verbal in its genesis, structure, and functioning" (Sokolov, 1972, p. 264), it is not speech (p. 262). Inner speech originates in external speech, but "external speech is functionally dependent on inner speech" (Sokolov, 1972, p. 65).

Vygotsky's account of the development of inner speech from social speech is very clear, in my opinion, and the further point that inner speech is not merely subvocal speech is also very clear. The basic unit of inner speech is not the same as that of semantics or of oral speech.

The basic unit of semantics is the word, and the basic unit of oral speech is the sentence, but with "sentence" defined as the unit that communicates a thought or an idea rather than as a particular syntactic structure (Luria, 1981, pp. 115-116). Communicating a particular thought or idea depends on particular content in a particular context. Sometimes the context may be conveyed grammatically in oral speech, as in the distinction between "The dog chased the cat" and "The dog was chased by the cat"; sometimes it can be conveyed by prosody (Smith & Williamson, 1977, p. 221) or by kinesics (Key, 1975), as when "The cat chased the dog" is said with an even (declarative) intonation versus a rising (interrogative) intonation or is said with an even intonation and with a neutral countenance versus a raised eyebrow; and sometimes the context is conveyed by other utterances--for example, in the utterance "John's killing bugs," "killing" may be a present participle ("What is John doing?" "John is killing bugs") or a gerund ("What were you laughing at?" "John's killing of the bugs") or a gerundive ("Whose bugs killed all the aphids?" "John's killing bugs").

However, inner speech is not analyzable into words or sentences. Inner speech is predicative, that is, it does not refer to the "theme" or subject of the action, which is "old information"; rather, it refers to the "rheme" or predicate, which is "new information" (Luria, 1981, pp. 107-108, 154-155). According to Vygotsky, a thought is initiated and is represented in inner speech, and may finally be expressed in oral speech (Luria, 1981, chap. 10).

Inner speech has a self-regulative function and, when expressed in oral speech, a social/ communicative function (Luria, 1981). The regulative function in the sense of planning may be lacking in young children; but even if so, Meacham (1979) has suggested that speech-for-self can have a regulative function in the sense of facilitating "remembering of the anticipated goals of motor actions, so that the outcomes of motor actions can be evaluated relative to the anticipated goals and compensatory or corrective actions can be engaged in if needed" (p. 257).

Summary and Conclusions

In his review of Skinner's *Verbal Behavior,* Chomsky (1959) asserted that "replacing 'X wants Y' by 'X is deprived of Y' adds no new objectivity to the description of behavior" (p. 47). Skinner wanted to remove the assumption of an inferred state (a want or need); but here Chomsky was saying not that the two sentences are necessarily equivalent, but rather that they are equivalent whenever the latter sentence is asserted without any evidence of deprivation independent of the behavior the deprivation is supposed to explain. That point was valid; but after all, Skinner was facing a voluminous lack of relevant data. Some of the other papers in this volume survey relevant data that have since been collected, as well as relevant new behavioral theories that have been developed in part to account for these data.

The various mentalistic approaches have generated a tremendous amount of information. However, much of this information is not relevant to the behavioral theories because the behaviorists have focused primarily on the pragmatic aspect of language--speech as communication--and the mentalists have focused primarily on the syntactic and semantic aspects--the structure of language. Speech as communication is reflected in language performance; the structure of language is reflected in language competence, that is, the knowledge of mature speakers about language. This knowledge is revealed by analyses of syntactical ambiguities of various sorts, among other analyses. The mentalists have also studied language development, but characteristically their primary interests have been in the structural aspects--syntactic and semantic development. Some behaviorists have denigrated mentalistic interests and methods, but these interests and methods are as legitimate and, on the ground rules of mentalistic world views, as scientific as the behavioral interests and methods.

In the mentalistic approach to concepts and concept formation, content or meaning is a major interest, but again the primary interest is in structure. For example, in network representations of concepts, meanings are represented by nodes in the network but the focus is on how the nodes are interlinked. Network representations have many applications, and can explain (that is, describe) such behavioral phenomena as associative interference and stimulus equivalence.

The Soviet approach differs from other mentalistic approaches in that it is materialistic, but because it is based on dialectical materialism it is not mechanistic. Thus, although the origin of thinking is in social speech, thinking becomes independent of speech during ontogeny and independent of the social environment. It becomes a means of transforming experience rather than remaining only a reflection of experience. (Being materialistic seems to contradict the definition of "mentalistic" given herein in the introductory section *Mentalism.* However, being dialectical resolves this apparent contradiction. For discussion, see Payne, 1968, pp. 17-29.)

In conclusion, I will hazard a few guesses as to how behaviorists might use the fruits of the mentalistic approaches to verbal behavior. From syntactics, the case grammars should be borrowed because they differentiate syntactical elements on functional rather than structural grounds and therefore already have an affinity to the behavioral approach. From semantics, models of network representation should be borrowed because they emphasize the links, which are readily translatable as behavioral chains. Finally, from the Soviet theory, the conception of the development of thinking might be useful. However, although the idea that thinking originates in social speech is clearly compatible with the behavioral approach, the idea that it is subsequently transformed such that it loses its speechlike form and content poses problems for the behavioral approach. I suggest that attempting to solve these problems may be a source of progress for the behavioral approach.

References

Anastasi, A. (1958). Heredity, environment, and the question "How?" *Psychological Review, 65,* 197-208.

Anderson, J. R. (1990). *Cognitive psychology and its implications* (3rd ed.). New York: Freeman.

Baer, D. M. (1982). Applied behavior analysis. In G. T. Wilson & C. M. Franks (Eds.), *Contemporary behavior therapy* (pp. 277-309). New York: Guilford.

Bornstein, M. H. (1978). Chromatic vision in infancy. In H. W. Reese & L. P. Lipsitt (Eds.), *Advances in child development and behavior* (Vol. 12, pp. 117-182). New York: Academic Press.

Brown, A. L. (1975). The development of memory: Knowing, knowing about knowing, and knowing how to know. In H. W. Reese, (Ed.) *Advances in child development and behavior* (Vol. 10, pp. 103-152). New York: Academic Press.

Brown, B. R., & Evans, S. H. (1969). Perceptual learning in pattern discrimination tasks with 2 schema categories. *Psychonomic Science, 15,* 101-103.

Bruner, J. S. (1964). The course of cognitive growth. *American Psychologist, 19,* 1-15.

Bugelski, B. R., & Alampay, D. A. (1961). The role of frequency in developing perceptual sets. *Canadian Journal of Psychology, 15,* 205- 211.

Carey, C. (1978). The child as word learner. In M. Halle, J. Bresnan, & G. A. Miller (Eds.), *Linguistic theory and psychological reality* (pp. 264-293). Cambridge, MA: MIT Press.

Chomsky, N. (1959). Review of *Verbal Behavior*. By B. F. Skinner. *Language, 35,* 26-58.

Chomsky, N. (1965). *Aspects of the theory of syntax.* Cambridge, MA: MIT Press.

Collins, A. M., & Loftus, E. F. (1975). A spreading-activation theory of semantic processing. *Psychological Review, 82,* 407-428.

Cross, H. A., & Vaughter, R. M. (1966). The Moss-Harlow effect in preschool children as a function of age. *Journal of Experimental Child Psychology, 4,* 280-284.

D'Amato, M. R., & Jagoda, H. (1961). Analysis of the role of overlearning in discrimination reversal. *Journal of Experimental Psychology, 61,* 45-50.

D'Amato, M. R., Salmon, D. P., Loukas, E., & Tomie, A. (1985). Symmetry and transitivity of conditional relations in monkeys (*Cebus apella*) and pigeons (*Columba livia*). *Journal of the Experimental Analysis of Behavior, 44,* 35-47.

Deese, J. (1970). *Psycholinguistics.* Boston: Allyn & Bacon.

Dixon, L. S. (1977). The nature of control by spoken words over visual stimulus selection. *Journal of the Experimental Analysis of Behavior, 27,* 433-442.

Farah, M. J., & Kosslyn, S. M. (1982). Concept development. In H. W. Reese & L. P. Lipsitt (Eds.), *Advances in child development and behavior* (Vol. 16, pp. 125-167). New York: Academic Press.

Gleitman, L. R., & Wanner, E. (1984). Current issues in language learning. In M. H. Bornstein & M. E. Lamb (Eds.), *Developmental psychology: An advanced textbook* (pp. 181-240). Hillsdale, NJ: Lawrence Erlbaum Associates.

Goetz, E. M., & Baer, D. M. (1973). Social control of form diversity and the emergence of new forms in children's blockbuilding. *Journal of Applied Behavior Analysis, 6,* 209-217.

Goss, A. E. (1961). Verbal mediating responses and concept formation. *Psychological Review, 68,* 248-274.

Halverson, H. M. (1940). Genital and sphincter behavior of the male infant. *Journal of Genetic Psychology, 56,* 95-136.

Howard, D. V. (1983). *Cognitive psychology: Memory, language, and thought.* New York: Macmillan.

Kail, R., & Bisanz, J. (1982). Information processing and cognitive development. In H. W. Reese (Ed.), *Advances in child development and behavior* (Vol. 17, pp. 45-81). New York: Academic Press.

Kantor, J. R. (1942). Preface to interbehavioral psychology. *Psychological Record, 5,* 173-193.

Kaplan, A. (1964). *The conduct of inquiry: Methodology for behavioral science.* San Francisco: Chandler.

Key, M. R. (1975). *Paralanguage and kinesics (nonverbal communication).* Metuchen, NJ: Scarecrow Press.

Kuczaj, S. A. II. (1982). Language play and language acquisition. In H. W. Reese (Ed.), *Advances in child development and behavior* (Vol. 17, pp. 197-232). New York: Academic Press.

Levinson, B., & Reese, H. W. (1967). Patterns of discrimination learning set in preschool children, fifth-graders, college freshmen, and the aged. *Monographs of the Society for Research in Child Development, 32(7,* Serial No. 115).

Luria, A. R. (1981). *Language and cognition* (J. V. Wertsch, Ed.). New York: Wiley.

Meacham, J. A. (1979). The role of verbal activity in remembering the goals of actions. In G. Zivin (Ed.), *The development of self-regulation through private speech* (pp. 237-263). New York: Wiley.

Mill, J. (1869). *Analysis of the phenomena of the human mind* (Vol. 1). London: Longmans Green Reader and Dyer.

Miller, G. A. (1977). *Spontaneous apprentices: Children and language.* New York: Seabury.

Molfese, D. L., Molfese, V. J., & Carrell, P. L. (1982). Early language development. In B. B. Wolman (Ed.), *Handbook of developmental psychology* (pp. 301-322). Englewood Cliffs, NJ: Prentice-Hall.

Overton, W. F., & Newman, J. L. (1982). Cognitive development: A competence-activation/utilization approach. In T. M. Field, A. Huston, H. C. Quay, L. Troll, & G. E. Finley (Eds.), *Review of human development* (pp. 217-241). New York: Wiley.

Paivio, A. (1975a). Coding distinctions and repetition effects in memory. In G. H. Bower (Ed.), *The psychology of learning and motivation: Advances in research and theory* (Vol. 9, pp. 179-214). New York: Academic Press.

Paivio, A. (1975b). Imagery in recall and recognition. In J. Brown (Ed.), *Recall and recognition* (pp. 103-129). New York: Wiley.

Palermo, D. S. (1970). Language acquisition. In H. W. Reese & L. P. Lipsitt (Eds.), *Experimental child psychology* (pp. 425-477). New York: Academic Press.

Payne, T. R. (1968). *S. L. Rubinstejn and the philosophical foundations of Soviet psychology.* Dordrecht, Holland: Reidel.

Piaget, J. (1963). *The psychology of intelligence* (M. Piercy & D. E. Berlyne, trans.). Paterson, NJ: Littlefield, Adams. (Original work published in 1947)

Prosch, H. (1964). *The genesis of twentieth century philosophy: The evolution of thought from Copernicus to the present.* Garden City, NY: Doubleday.

Reed, N. E. (1976). *A developmental study of abstraction with children.* Unpublished master's thesis. West Virginia University, Morgantown.

Reese, H. W. (1962). Verbal mediation as a function of age level. *Psychological Bulletin, 59,* 502-509.

Reese, H. W. (1963). Discrimination learning set in children. In L. P. Lipsitt & C. C. Spiker (Eds.), *Advances in child development and behavior* (Vol. 1, pp. 115-145). New York: Academic Press.

Reese, H. W. (1964). Discrimination learning set in rhesus monkeys. *Psychological Bulletin, 61,* 321-340.

Reese, H. W. (1968). *The perception of stimulus relations: Discrimination learning and transposition.* New York: Academic Press.

Reese, H. W. (1970). Set. In H. W. Reese & L. P. Lipsitt (Eds.), *Experimental child psychology* (pp. 263-278). New York: Academic Press.

Reese, H. W. (1971). The study of covert verbal and nonverbal mediation. In A. Jacobs & L. B. Sachs (Eds.), *The psychology of private events: Perspectives on covert response systems* (pp. 17-38). New York: Academic Press.

Reese, H. W. (1976). *Basic learning processes in childhood.* New York: Holt, Rinehart & Winston.

Reese, H. W. (1980). A learning theory critique of the operant approach to life span development. In W. J. Hoyer (Chair), Conceptions of learning and the study of life span development: A symposium (pp. 368-376). *Human Development, 23,* 361-399.

Reese, H. W. (1986a). Behavioral and dialectical psychologies. In L. P. Lipsitt & J. H. Cantor (Eds.), *Experimental child psychologist: Essays and experiments in honor of Charles C. Spiker* (pp. 157-195). Hillsdale, NJ: Lawrence Erlbaum Associates.

Reese, H. W. (1986b, May). *Computer simulation and behavior analysis: Similarities and differences.* Paper presented at the meeting of the Association for Behavior Analysis, Milwaukee WI.

Reese, H. W. (1989). Rules and rule-governance: Cognitive and behavioral views. In S. C. Hayes (Ed.), *Rule-governed behavior: Cognition, contingencies, and instructional control* (pp. 3-84). New York: Plenum.

Reese, H. W., & Parnes, S. J. (1970). Programming creative behavior. *Child Development, 41,* 413-423.

Rice, M. L. (1982). Child language: What children know and how. In T. M. Field, A. Huston, H. C. Quay, L. Troll, & G. E. Finley (Eds.), *Review of human development* (pp. 253-268). New York: Wiley.

Rondal, J. A. (1985). Social behaviorism and the interpersonal determinants of language acquisition. *International Newsletter of Social Behaviorism, 4,* 2-21.

Rovee-Collier, C. & Hayne, H. (1987). Reactivation of infant memory: Implications for cognitive development. In H. W. Reese (Ed.), *Advances in child development and behavior* (Vol. 20, pp. 185-238). New York: Academic Press.

Sidman, M., Rauzin, R., Lazar, R., Cunningham, S., Tailby, W., & Carrigan, P. (1982). A search for symmetry in the conditional discriminations of rhesus monkeys, baboons, and children. *Journal of the Experimental Analysis of Behavior, 37,* 23-44.

Skinner, B. F. (1945). The operational analysis of psychological terms. *Psychological Review, 52,* 270-277.

Skinner, B. F. (1957). *Verbal behavior.* New York: Appleton-Century-Crofts.

Skinner, B. F. (1969). *Contingencies of reinforcement: A theoretical analysis.* New York: Appleton-Century-Crofts.

Skinner, B. F. (1974). *About behaviorism.* New York: Knopf.

Slobin, D. I. (1979). *Psycholinguistics* (2nd ed.). Glenview, IL: Scott, Foresman.

Smith, D. R., & Williamson, L. K. (1977). *Interpersonal communication: Roles, rules, strategies, and games.* Dubuque, IA: Brown.

Smith, E. E. (1978). Theories of semantic memory. In W. K. Estes (Ed.), *Handbook of learning and cognitive processes. Vol. 6: Linguistic functions in cognitive theory* (pp. 1-56). Hillsdale, NJ: Lawrence Erlbaum Associates.

Sokolov, A. N. (1972). *Inner speech and thought* (G. T. Onischenko, trans.; D. B. Lindsley, Ed.). New York: Plenum.

Templin, M. C. (1957). *Certain language skills in children: Their development and interrelationships.* Minneapolis: University of Minnesota Press.

Vygotsky, L. S. (1978). *Mind in society: The development of higher psychological processes* (M. Cole, V. John-Steiner, S. Scribner, & E. Souberman, Eds.). Cambridge, MA: Harvard University Press.

Watson, J. B. (1926). What the nursery has to say about instincts. In M. Bentley, K. Dunlap, W. S. Hunter, K. Koffka, W. Kohler, W. McDougall, M. Prince, J. B. Watson, & R. S. Woodworth, *Psychologies of 1925: Powell Lectures in Psychological Theory* (pp. 1-35). Worcester, MA: Clark University Press.

Webster's third new international dictionary of the English language. (1971). Springfield, MA: Merriam.

Wertsch, J. V. (1981). Editor's introduction. In A. R. Luria, *Language and cognition* (J. V. Wertsch, Ed.; pp. 1-16). New York: Wiley.

Wingfield, A. (1979). *Human learning and memory: An introduction.* New York: Harper & Row.

A Discussion of Chapter 7

A Behavior Analysis of Themes in Cognitive Science: Comments on Mentalistic Approaches to Verbal Behavior

Philip N. Chase
West Virginia University

The purpose of the Summer Institute on Verbal Relations was to raise problems and questions that behavior analysts have had studying verbal relations, and to suggest some research programs that might address these issues. Reese's chapter raises a number of questions and problems, albeit from cognitive investigations and not behavior analytic. His chapter describes some of the critical topics that cognitive scientists have addressed, criticizes them and suggests some areas that are ripe for further exploration. Throughout, the chapter emphasizes the problems that mentalists have had with their own investigations, with occasional asides about the relevance of these problems to a behavior analytic audience.

For the most part, these asides stimulated the discussion by the participants at the Summer Institute. Participants asked questions about the definition of verbal behavior, the function of pivotal words in children's grammar, the distinctions between semantics, syntactics, pragmatics and sociolinguistics and a few categories of cognitive investigations that seem particularly susceptible to behavior analytic interpretation. The discussion was lively, productive and resulted in too many themes to adequately cover in this discussion. Therefore, the theme of this discussion will be to extend just a few of the topics discussed and to concentrate on a behavior analytic perspective on these themes. I believe the contrast between how Reese describes these problems and how I will discuss them will reveal how cognitive problems might be addressed from a behavior analytic view. Hopefully, this contrast will also reveal the value of comparing these positions.

Perceptual Set

One of the classic issues in cognitive science that Reese addresses is the problem of ambiguous sentences. It has been concluded that ambiguous sentences can be understood and be unambiguous if a particular perceptual set is established. Perceptual-set refers to a context. If a particular context has been established, then a particular sentence has a specific, unambiguous effect on the listener. If the context is not established, the effect on the listener may be harder to predict. A sentence taken out of context, like "They were entertaining speakers", may be ambiguous. Given a context provided by a conversation or a paragraph in a book, however, the sentence makes perfect sense to the listener or reader.

This type of verbal relation can easily be interpreted in terms of what we know about conditional discriminations (Sidman, 1986). Conditional discrimination, as described elsewhere in this book under the topic of stimulus equivalence, explicates the conditions that lead

A prototype, for example, would then define the family resemblance and would be derived from summaries of group responding.

Family resemblance is a useful concept from a behavior analytic perspective, therefore, when it is translated into statements about the relation among different individuals' learning history with respect to objects and events. If family resemblance refers to a summary statement of a group's responding to a set of objects or events, then we can refer to the family resemblance when we are trying to account for observations that indicate discrepancies among individuals and consistencies across individuals. Such accounts may be critical to understanding the complexities and ambiguities of verbal behavior that are learned from the interaction with people from diverse learning histories.

Summary

This discussion has attempted to address two of the points that Reese raised about cognitive science which can be addressed by behavior analytic interpretation and might be addressed by behavior analytic research. I hope I have shown that the issues that have led cognivists to an interpretation of perceptual set can also be interpreted as an example of conditional discrimination. Conditional discrimination refers to the conditions that lead to a stimulus having at least two effects on an observer. Thus, a stimulus may be responded to in one way under one set of conditions and in another way under a second set of conditions. As this appears to be the gist of perceptual set it might be fruitful for behavior analysts to isolate problems in the perceptual set literature that could be addressed with the methodologies and concepts of the conditional discrimination literature.

I also argued that family resemblance is consistent with behavior analytic theory when it is discussed in terms of the overlap among the critical features of the environment to which individuals respond when classifying examples of concepts. Given this interpretation of family resemblances, prototypes and cue sets are not features of the objects and events that comprise conceptual stimuli nor are they types of organization within the mind, but rather they are descriptions of behavior-environment relations that take into account individual differences in responding to environmental features.

As stated in the introduction there are a number of other topics that could also be addressed. For example, I believe that research on stimulus equivalence and other kinds of complex conditional relations[1] can account for the relations that Reese describes as isa links and isnota links. However, space limits the discussion to the two points described above. I would like to end, therefore, with a call for research. I believe that the issues raised by Reese are of interest to many people, and they are issues that have rarely been addressed from a behavior analytic perspective. I see the critical effect of Reese's chapter as isolating some significant research topics that might be investigated with behavior analytic methodologies and concepts.

References

Sidman, M. (1986). Functional analysis of emergent verbal classes. In T. Thompson & M. D. Zeiler (Eds.). *Analysis and integration of behavioral units* (pp. 213-245). Hillsdale, N.J.: Erlbaum.

Footnotes

1. In fact it might be better to drop the word equivalence because it connotes that the stimuli are equal or the same when in fact it is meant that they are related and the relation can probably be one of oddity, greater than, less than, not the same, etc.

Chapter 8

Cognitive Problems, Behavioral Solutions

Kurt Salzinger
Polytechnic University and the New York State Psychiatric Institute

It is only fitting that as students of verbal behavior, we realize the power of the word. Cognitive psychologists have been very much aware of this power in sequestering the word "cognitive" unto themselves. It is as if they said, with no apologies to Descartes, "I think, therefore I am a cognitive psychologist and therefore I study cognitive functioning." On the other hand, methodological behaviorists have said, "I study behavior, therefore thinking does not interest me." Perhaps if methodological behaviorists had read Skinner's (1945) important paper about private events, they would have realized that they need not reject what Cognitive psychologists have embraced, but that paper has unfortunately not received the attention it deserves. In any case, the first cognitive problem that radical behaviorists have to deal with is the confusion that Cognitive psychologists have sown by using the same term to describe both the theory they espouse and the subject matter they study.

Their theory is the Cognitive problem with the capital letter "C." Many behaviorists are now discussing it, for we are being pushed from without, and invaded from within, by the Cognitive psychologists' ways of thinking and other modes of verbal behavior (Salzinger, 1986). Cognitive psychology of the day has adopted the language of the computer, the latest metaphor to be employed by psychologists to gain an understanding of why people behave in certain ways. Not content with adopting that metaphor, practitioners of the art have decided that everybody must explain it in order to arrive at an explanation of behavior, particularly that of human beings. Thus they tell us we have to explain, to take but a sample of their verbal behavior, "encoding, short term memory, working memory, long term memory, storage, retrieval, hierarchical structuring," and so on. But these are not data to be explained; they are concepts that need explanation. The trouble is, Cognitive psychologists run so quickly to concepts that the data appear only tachistoscopically before us. They speak so little of responses and the contingent stimuli that affect them that all that is left to explain is their concepts. This problem has been discussed elsewhere (Skinner, 1977; Salzinger, 1986). I will therefore turn to the second type of problem.

This problem, and in the long run the more important one, is the cognitive problem with the lower case letter "c." Here I speak of the areas long discussed by psychologists under such headings as thinking, problem solving, memory, and language. In this area of research, many psychologists (and typically not enough radical behaviorists) inquire about children's ability to emit words under different conditions and at different ages. They study the effect of aging in older people and increasingly they investigate aphasia and dementia. They focus on discovering howpeople think and solve problems and otherwise emit verbal behavior. I know, when I say that not enough radical behaviorists do this kind of empirical research, that I am joined by an increasingly larger number of behavior analysts. I am going to present some examples of how both behavior analysts and Cognitive psychologists with a capital letter "C" can collect data on cognitive problems in a useful way.

Some Experiments

Allow me to examine some experiments, including one inspired by Cognitive theorizing, that nevertheless collected unambiguous data in the area of cognitive functioning. Given that as behavior analysts, we are always interested in unambiguous data, these experiments could be useful to us in doing our own work.

A Cognitive Experiment

Wiegel-Crump and Dennis (1986) described their study as an investigation of "word-finding." Although this description appears to be atheoretic, it actually fails to be so. The very term "word-finding" suggests a particular kind of activity which forms the basic metaphor, traces of which confront us later in the same article. The introduction thus talks of being able to compare "different forms of lexical access for the same set of words" (p. 3). It speaks of being concerned, not with the acquisition of vocabulary, but with "how children are able to access already existing lexical items . . . although present in the lexicon, the words are not equally available under all access conditions." (p. 18). Later on the authors say "the organizational basis of the children's lexicon seems to be semantic." (p. 19).

What is interesting about these descriptions is that no attempt is made to separate the theoretical characterization from the data. The authors simply assume that they are describing their results and their hypotheses objectively and meaningfully. Perhaps even more interesting, however, is the fact that their data are independent of the theory that generated the experiment and produce a significant set of results and conclusions for behavior analysts to consider.

Let me describe the procedures used. Although named in terms of cognitive theory, namely "lexical access," the conditions refer to different kinds of stimulus control. The subjects, consisting of children ranging in age from 6 to 14 years, are asked to guess the word that the

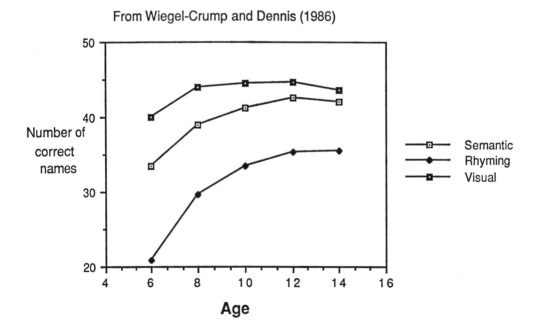

Fig. 1. Number of correct naming responses as a function of age. Based on Table 5 in Wiegel-Crump and Dennis (1986).

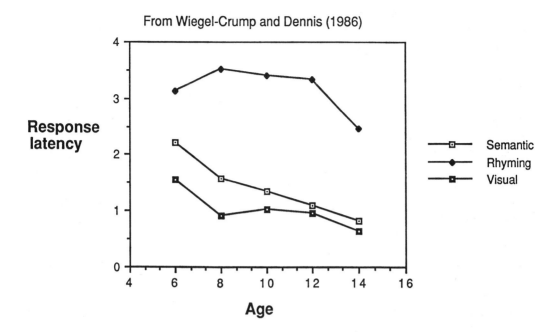

Fig. 2. Response latencies as a function of age.
Based on Table 6 in Wiegel-Crump and Dennis (1986).

experimenter "has in mind." The experimenter provides each subject with different kinds of "clues" for each condition. For the semantic condition, the experimenter begins by saying the category (animal, food, clothing, household, or action), followed by stating, in the case of the animal category, where it lives, how it moves, and two of its characteristic physical or functional features; for the category of food, the experimenter says the subcategory it belongs to, such as fruit, how it is produced or consumed, and two characteristic physical or functional characteristics. In other words, increasingly limiting clues are provided the subject. After all the clues have been presented, the subject is asked to emit the so-called target word.

For the rhyming condition, the subject is given the semantic category and a sound with which it rhymes. Thus the sound and the category form the discriminative stimuli for the verbal response in this condition. One should note here that this complex of clues, as in the case of the other conditions, can alternatively be envisioned in terms of conditional relations, such that the sound is viewed as an S^D, conditional on the semantic category supplied as another stimulus. The final condition is visual; here the subject is shown an outline drawing of a target and is asked to name it or the action it is performing. From the point of view of the experimental analysis of behavior, we have a situation in which the subject is provided a series of S^D's. In the semantic condition, the S^D's are all verbal; in the rhyming condition, the S^D's are first verbal (the category) and then sound; in the visual condition, the S^D's may be described as generalization stimuli to the actual objects or actions that they portray, or they may themselves constitute the stimuli to which the subjects had learned to respond.

The data were analyzed by age category vs. number of correct names out of a maximum of 45 (Fig. 1), and by age vs. latency of correct response (Fig. 2). These figures constructed on the basis of tables in Wiegel-Crump and Dennis (1986) show a gradual increase in the emission of the socially acceptable (socially conditioned) word with age. As further evidence of the strength of the response, we also find that its latency generally decreases with age. In addition, the experimenters find substantial differences among, what the authors call, the different lexical access conditions. Thus, the sound D (what the authors call the rhyming access condition) shows the lowest probability of evoking a "correct" response and the greatest increase over age, whereas the visual S^D shows the highest probability of appropriate response from early age on, with the smallest change over the age range tested. The semantic condition which, as you recall, consists of a series of verbal prompts falls in between the other two conditions both in terms of absolute emission probability and in change of that emission probability.

What can we say about these results? Despite the fact that the data are represented in the form of group averages, the figures show a respectable regularity. Analysts of behavior would prefer to track individual children as they grow older (presuming that the changes are related to learning) but there is little reason to believe that the general shape of the curves for individuals would be markedly different from the group averages presented. The conditions under which the responses were emitted are not badly described, although given the age of the younger children, one cannot help but wonder about the extent to which the lower emission probability of the words is to be ascribed to their general lack of training in doing such tasks as opposed to specific training of the words to the S^D's in question. Inspection of Figs. 1 and 2 makes it quite clear that all kinds of stimulus control increase with age. Secondly, although visual control increases with age, it is already close to maximum at age 6. Third, the rhyming condition is consistently least powerful in controlling the emission of the required response, showing the largest increase, but failing to catch up to the other forms of stimulus control. Findings about stimulus control ought be of interest to behavior analysts, of course.

Are the authors aware of learning? Probably. The difference between their view of learning and that of behavior analysts seems to lie in their appeal to changes in what they call organization rather than in emission probability. Indeed, they specifically say "the present study concerns not the acquisition of vocabulary, but how children access already existing lexical items" (p. 18). We would describe this change in terms of stimulus control. The words to be prompted were so selected as to be high frequency words in the English language (as reflected in tabulations of the frequency of occurrence of words in written materials) and therefore typically learned at an early age in our society. Recall that the authors state, "although present in the lexicon, the words are not equally available under all access conditions." (p. 18). They use the high frequency of emitting the correct word in the visual S^D condition as proof that the words are part of the vocabulary of even the youngest children.

What does it mean to say that the words are not available? The metaphor implied, although not explicitly stated, is clearly one of storage and retrieval. What does it mean to a behavior analyst? That some S^D's have more often been followed by appropriately reinforced verbal responses than others. To be sure that is an inference only; what it implies is that we should check on this inference by working with young children and specifically training them to emit these responses to various S^D's. The variable of age as used in this study can be viewed simply as an indicator of training. But here is another question to be pondered and that is, what are the implications of the finding that sound S^D's are less powerful in evoking words at all ages? Cognitive psychologists tentatively conclude that both children and adults do not have sound access to the words in their lexicon (wherever that may be). Yet we know that sometimes we misspeak ourselves in ways that we would attribute to generalization to similar sounding words. Referring to a study of slips of the tongue, they admitted that "words may sometimes be accessed through phonological channels." Again the metaphor in use speaks of events occurring within the person. Nevertheless, we can agree with the fact if not with the way in which the fact is described.

Let us look at still another characterization of the results of this study. The authors say: "The lack of correspondence between different access conditions for the same words implies that naming pictures and consulting a dictionary in reverse (the semantic condition) involve at least partially separate linguistic operations." As behavior analysts we are again tempted to translate this into a data statement: The strength of evoking the same word varies with different S^D's. Now we might be further tempted, as are the authors of this study, to say something about how this relates to speech in conversation or for that matter how this relates to writing behavior. The authors suggest that the semantic condition would be more effective in revealing to a clinical diagnostician the difficulty that a patient might have of emitting words in conversation than would the visual condition.

In sum then, what can we say about this (C)cognitive experiment? Should we as behavior analysts pay attention to it and other experiments like it? I believe the answer is "yes." As I said above, we may not like the form in which the data are analyzed, i.e., group rather than individual analysis, but it does supply findings that we can pursue to understand verbal behavior in general, and in terms of Skinner's system (1957) in particular, since the study deals with tacts and intraverbal relations. The experiment also raises two other issues, namely that of the appropriate response unit and that of the best situation in which verbal behavior can be examined. As you will see below, I believe that the optimal way of measuring difficulty in speech is to examine the speech itself rather than trying to use approximations to it. I will return to this issue later. Let us first consider the problem of response unit.

The Problem of Response Unit

What is involved in the emission of words and what is involved when the speaker says, "what's his name" or "what do you call it" or finishes by saying "that blond woman" because he cannot emit (recall) her name? I believe that we will eventually have to analyze -- in behavioral terms -- what happens when people say that a word is on the tip of their tongue. Clearly we are able to respond to the probability of emitting responses as well as to emit them. A mere nuisance for the normal speaker, "word finding," or perhaps more accurately "word losing," is a serious problem for aphasic patients and those suffering from dementias of various kinds and of course must be related to what we call their memory problems.

When we are engaged in the activity of trying to think of someone's name, we are somewhat like the bird that looks back and forth between two keys before hitting the one that will be followed by food. As in problem solving, our verbal behavior is reinforced by making possible other behavior (either verbal or nonverbal) and eventually some form of reinforcement. Presumably the analogue to the bird's headturning behavior which brings the different keys into view is the subvocal word emission to which the speaker responds either by speaking or by emitting words subvocally. It appears that the aphasic and the demented individuals are unable to emit the appropriate word in response to their own response-produced verbal stimuli. In continuous speech, these response-produced stimuli are to be found, at least in part, in the words that the speaker has just uttered. It is that assumption that has formed the basis for the research on Alzheimer's Disease that Portnoy and I (Salzinger & Portnoy, 1987) have recently embarked on.

Before we describe that approach to verbal behavior, we must review some other forays into the area because they are the context in which the study of speech arose. They consist of the study of the nonsense syllable, eventually supplanted by the sentence, operant conditioning experiments which made it possible to examine what constitutes a reasonable response unit, and finally the response-produced stimulus-control approach which brought us to the examination of speech as a whole.

First let us look at the nonsense syllable. A part of the cognitive revolution was undoubtedly provoked by the omnipresence of the almost obsessive investigation of the nonsense syllable, a study which has taught us more than we wanted to know about how human learners acquire and recall nonsense syllables of varying meaningfulness. The Cognitive psychologist's disdain for the god nonsense syllable, however, led ironically enough to the deification of the sentence. Chomsky and his students pointed to the sentence as a universal that all human beings are capable of uttering and understanding. They even went so far as to suggest that such a unit of response is built into a so-called language acquisition device housed somehow and somewhere in the brain of all children. It is my view that the sentence is certainly one kind of response unit that is worthwhile to study, but it is by no means the only response unit of which verbal behavior is composed.

Some years ago, I wrote a review (Salzinger, 1973) which showed that any number of different agglomerations of sounds, letters, syllables, phonemes, words, phrases, sentences, and much larger collections of verbal behavior can, under various conditions, act as units of response. To find out whether a potential response unit is in fact acting like one, it is necessary to determine whether counting its occurrence in case of a conditioning experiment, for example, shows the expected lawfulness that we have found when we examined well established response units. One difference between animal behavior units and human verbal behavior units is that only in the former can we set up arbitrary boundaries with relative ease and in most cases get the resulting responses to behave lawfully. By contrast, in verbal behavior, we are more limited in changing those units of response that the speakers already acquired without our aid because those responses are multiply determined and continue to be controlled in that way outside our experimental situation. This is not to say that we cannot modify such response units; indeed, it is the object of experiments such as those done to eliminate stuttering (Flanagan, Goldiamond & Azrin, 1958), but it is not easy to do so, given that the influence of society around our subjects must continue.

Using an operant approach to examination of verbal response units, we conducted a number of conditioning studies of verbal behavior. More sophisticated (with the aid of hindsight) than the original Greenspoon (1955) experiment in which subjects had to emit individual words as responses, our experiments used interviews and monologues as vehicles for evoking speech and thus did not have subjects spend all their time trying to figure out what was really going on. The subjects were schizophrenic patients (Salzinger & Pisoni, 1958; 1961; Salzinger & Portnoy, 1964; Salzinger, Portnoy & Feldman, 1964), normal patients, hospitalized for physical causes rather than psychological ones (Salzinger & Pisoni, 1960), and normal college students (Salzinger & Portnoy, Zlotogura, & Keisner, 1963). These studies showed that verbal behavior can be conditioned even though the subjects were under the impression that they were being interviewed or providing some information rather than undergoing an experiment. The studies showed that one could form response classes such as self-referred affect in which the subjects emitted responses such as "I love," "I hate," "I'm sad," "I can't stand it," "I feel terrific" and showed increases and decreases in these responses as a function of the delivery or withholding of reinforcement. It was also possible to demonstrate that the response classes that changed as a function of the reinforcement became gradually more specific and narrower, for example, from a response class of speech in general to a response class of self references, to a response class of self-referred affect.

It seemed to me, however, having demonstrated what seemed fairly obvious, namely that speech is conditionable, that the essence of verbal behavior required that we study response -

response control as well as external control. We (Salzinger & Eckerman, 1967) made use of Jabberwocky along with function words (e.g., prepositions, conjunctions, articles, and auxiliary verbs) and grammatical word endings, such as "ed" for verbs and "s" for nouns (bound morphemes) for the nonsense syllables that constituted the "lexical" words to form the sentences that the subjects had to learn. Lexical words are usually nouns, verbs, adjectives and adverbs. The function words are a subclass of what Skinner (1957) calls autoclitics. He describes them (p. 332): "They do not occur except when they accompany other verbal behavior -- they are 'meaningless' by themselves ..." In constructing sentences, we made use of the combination of what Skinner (1957) calls the autoclitic of assertion and the relational autoclitic. The idea here was to check on the importance of grammatical sequences and their basic nature in the emission of verbal behavior. Sentences were constructed of two different degrees of grammatical complexity. The first was the simple declarative sentence, the second was the passive negative question, and the third form of the sentence was the randomly ordered sequence of "words" as a control "sentence."

The results showed that both types of grammatically ordered sentences were more easily learned than were the randomly ordered sentences. However, our results suggested that the critical aspect of what was learned had to do with the frequency of the elements that made up the sequence, and the frequency of presentations of the particular sequences. Furthermore, the more complex sentence, namely the passive negative question was, after some minimal practice, as easy to learn as the simple declarative sentence. Thus the higher frequency of occurrence of the sequences (the simple declarative sentence occurs much more frequently in the English language than does the passive negative question) made for the difference in recall, not the complexity of the sentence structure that the Cognitive psychologists implicated. Furthermore, this experiment showed that the function words were more dependent on the contexts in which they were found than were the lexical words here represented by the nonsense syllables, such as, nouns, verbs, adjectives, and adverbs. The function words apparently did not stand alone; they could exist only in the presence of the other words to which they were connected.

This research showed that sentences can act as units of response, but it showed that a hierarchical transformation from one sentence type to another is unnecessary to explain how a listener understands complex sentences. The idea that varying unit lengths along with varying response classes contribute much to explaining how sentences are uttered and understood was verified. In addition, we already have an interesting schedule of reinforcement, namely the DRL schedule, as a model for a particular complex sentence structure, namely embedded sentences. You remember that schedule requires an animal to emit responses spaced by periods of no response in order for reinforcement to occur. Such a schedule is not very different from sentences containing embedded clauses, as in, "The Cognitive psychologist who is here today will be gone tomorrow." The clause "who is here today" in the sentence may be viewed as the pause that intervenes between the successive responses in the DRL schedule. In other words, one does not have to invoke the special mechanisms that some of the transformation linguists used to propose in order to explain complex behavior.

I would like to call your attention to some additional early experiments on normal verbal behavior. Schoenfeld and Cumming (1973, actually performed during the academic year 1952-1953) took a passage of verbal behavior and instructed normal subjects to divide it into "idea" units (similar to dividing the material into sentences). They also subjected the same passages to a serial guessing task in which subjects were given one word at a time and were then required to guess the next one on the basis of the earlier ones. The partitioning of the passages was then compared to the probability of guessing the words to determine what the relationship might be between the idea boundaries and the degree to which each word is controlled by the preceding ones. Although the probability of guessing the words did decrease at sentence boundaries, they also decreased at other points in the sentences. These results led to the direct examination of the sentence, as shown below.

The studies made use of the sentence as a response unit and studied its integrity by having subjects emit such sentences under different degrees of stimulus control. Schoenfeld and Cumming (1973) and Feldman (1973) presented subjects with words in particular sentence positions and studied the degree of stimulus control that they exerted over the responses the subjects emitted to produce sentences. S. Salzinger (1973) compared the responses that subjects emitted when filling in word chains constituted as sentences and when they were essentially lists of words (paradigmatic responses as found in word association tests). Information-theory derived measures quantified the amount of response-produced control exerted. Both sentence position and words presented in the sentence frames turned out to be important variables in predicting the amount of determination of the verbal responses.

Miller and Selfridge (1950), in a related experiment, studied response unit size by using statistical approximations to English. The greater the approximation to English, the larger the number of successive words that determine the next word. This finally brings me to discussion of a method of analyzing verbal behavior that I would like to commend to you. We took the passages of varying statistical approximation to English and subjected them to the "cloze" procedure (Salzinger, Portnoy & Feldman, 1962): Every fifth word was deleted and a space indicated by a line of constant length was substituted for it. Naive subjects were then asked to guess the missing words. The higher the approximation to English, the larger the number of correct guesses, showing that when words were determined by a larger number of other words, they formed a more cohesive unit for both speaker and "listener," in this case the person guessing the words that had been deleted. The point is that what constitutes a unit depends on the text that is emitted.

It is interesting to note that the original reason for the cloze procedure was to arrive at a measure of the comprehensibility of various texts. Taylor (1953) devised it and incidentally named it the cloze procedure. He took the writings of such authors as Gertrude Stein, Erskine Caldwell, and James Joyce and subjected them to the kind of mutilation described above. Taylor found, as you would expect, that Caldwell's texts were much easier to restore than those of Joyce or Stein. The latter two were difficult to predict for two different reasons, viz., Joyce because of vocabulary in addition to unexpected word sequences but Stein mostly because of the unexpected sequences of words that invest her writings and make it interesting. In other words, he was primarily interested in devising a measure of readability which went beyond the mere frequency of occurrence of words in the English language. I adopted this method for two reasons: first to study the relationship among verbal responses and second to employ it to learn something about schizophrenia.

To begin with the second reason, I might just point out that we (Salzinger, Portnoy & Feldman, 1964; 1966; Salzinger, Portnoy, Pisoni & Feldman, 1970) were first motivated by the notion that the malady of schizophrenia produced a lack of comprehensibility in their speech; later, we adopted the term communicability, which we felt described, at least in some way, the difficulties that schizophrenic patients have, as evidenced in their ostracism by others even early in their adolescent period and before the symptoms of schizophrenia appear in full bloom. Finally, most recently, I (Salzinger, 1985a) realized that I had been studying the reinforcement potential of the speech of schizophrenic patients. To the degree that a person's speech is understandable, as measured by the cloze procedure of guessing deleted words, to that extent is that speech reinforcing to the listener. The fact that the cloze procedure thus specifies the behavior of the listener should be of interest to L. (Parrott) Hayes (Parrott, 1984) who has been emphasizing the importance of the behavior of the listener.

I should also add here that when we applied the cloze procedure method to the speech of schizophrenic patients, we found that the number of words that cohered in a unit was smaller than that of normal speakers. That particular result gave rise to the Immediacy Hypothesis of schizophrenic behavior and states essentially that the behavior of schizophrenic patients is more likely to be controlled by stimuli closer to the time of the response than is the behavior of normal subjects. Because the response-produced stimuli control the verbal behavior in much the same way as do the external stimuli, the resultant response units are shorter in schizophrenic speech than in normal speech.

Let us now return to the first reason for my interest in the cloze procedure. It revolved around the question of a new way of studying verbal behavior, a way which was behavioral, that is, not mentalistic, but which was not limited by requiring that we study verbal behavior exclusively in terms of frequency of occurrence. Our first excursion into this approach (as already described) was through the study of the statistical approximations to English. Our success with the second application, namely the study of schizophrenic speech inspired us to apply the same technique to our third application, namely Alzheimer's Disease.

The Application of the Study of Verbal Chains to Alzheimer's Disease

As the population of the western world is aging, we are becoming aware of a new series of diseases. An affliction of frightening proportions, Alzheimer's Disease is commonly recognized as a memory disorder, although eventually the demented person becomes incapable of caring for him or herself entirely, with death following within a few years. In 1985, I presented a behavioral analysis of the memory problem in Alzheimer's Disease (Salzinger, 1985b) and therefore I won't rehearse it here. I would like to say, however, that it is possible to view memory in terms of stimulus control. Indeed, it is also possible to view all stimulus control as a kind of memory problem. When you are asked to read, you are, after all, recalling some verbal responses to the S^D's of the printed word. Furthermore, recall is always promoted by a stimulus, such as being asked for certain information, being shown a picture, or otherwise being presented an S^D that occasions the recall response. One also presents oneself with an S^D when uttering a sentence, sometimes vocally and sometimes subvocally. And occasionally all of us experience starting to say something which we seem unable to emit aloud.

It follows, then, that people who are having trouble remembering things also ought to have difficulties in their verbal behavior in general. Evidence somewhat akin to aphasia in Alzheimer's Disease patients has been reported (e.g., Bayles, 1982). Folstein and Breitner (1981;1982) concluded that only one type of Alzheimer's Disease is heritable. That type suffers from aphasia-like symptoms and is more likely to have relatives suffering from Alzheimer's as well. Thus the analysis of verbal behavior of Alzheimer's patients is of interest for a number of reasons. If it distinguishes between such patients and normals, it suggests the possibility of a diagnostic screening technique perhaps in the early stages of this dread disease, at which point drugs might arrest the deterioration of the brain associated with the disease. In addition, if it serves to mark the heritable type of Alzheimer's, then it may serve to point to a high risk population to which medical treatment might be applied even earlier in an attempt to prevent the disease.

As you can probably guess, I have been leading up to a study that I have been conducting. Stephanie Portnoy and I (Salzinger & Portnoy, 1987) have been collecting speech samples from patients in various, but usually early, stages of probable Alzheimer's Disease. These patients have included those who have just been diagnosed as well as those who received their diagnosis some months ago and who participated in a study on the effect of physostigmine (a drug being tested for its ability to improve the memory of Alzheimer's patients). Since it involves a double blind design and the code has not yet been broken, some of the patients we observed were under the influence of the drug, some had been given a placebo, and some had not been included in the drug study at all. Keeping in mind these limitations, it nevertheless is interesting to see what an analysis of intraverbal response control in Alzheimer's patients, as opposed to that of a control group of normal spouses, shows us.

The first question to be answered in this kind of study is that of the effect of external stimulus control. For that reason, we obtained speech samples in response to four different S^D's: In the first, the subject was instructed to speak about the most pleasant experience that he or she had recently undergone. The second one instructed the patient to speak about his or her memory problem, how it started, when it seems worse and when better; it instructed the normal person to describe her or his spouse's memory problem in similar detail.

The third condition used a visual S^D with instructions. This condition used the so-called "Cookie theft" picture from the Boston Diagnostic Aphasia Examination; it shows a mother absentmindedly drying dishes while her sink is overflowing causing a puddle of water to form right under her feet, and while her son is taking a cookie from a jar, apparently to give it to his sister who stands on the floor with an outstretched hand. The stool on which the boy is standing to reach the cookies is at such an angle that it is clear he will shortly come down with a crash. In response to the third S^D the subject was asked to describe the picture; to the fourth S^D, the subject was asked to make up a story about the picture. Clearly, we made an attempt to construct four different conditions under which the subjects would be emitting verbal behavior. The hope was that the "most pleasant experience" condition would evoke some verbal behavior which reinforces the speaker because the events to be described should have been positively reinforcing. As it turns out, subjects had more difficulty speaking in response to the "pleasant experience" instructions than speaking about their memory problem. The "memory" condition evoked speech both from the patients and the spouses. In some cases, the speech sample was quite short, but it was adequate despite the fact that we expected discussing the memory problem to be negatively reinforcing and therefore less productive of speech. Subjects were able to describe the picture (the third condition) but could not come up with any stories beyond repeated description.

We have started to look at the speech emitted in the memory problem condition. We took the first 54 words of speech emitted without the need for any prompts and typed them up for the cloze procedure to provide us with 10 deleted words for each speech sample. Every fifth word was deleted and a blank of standard length was substituted for it. The unpunctuated typescript was given to a group of ten native speakers of English and they were instructed to guess the missing words in each passage. Each passage was scored in terms of the proportion of words that matched exactly the words originally emitted by the speakers -- Alzheimer's patients or normal spouses. The resulting proportion of successful matches was approximately the same for both types of passages, that is, there was no statistically significant difference between patients and normal spouses.

We also examined the probability of guessing the correct words separately for two different word classes, namely the lexical and the function words mentioned earlier in the paper. Recall that the function words form a separate class because they perform differently in the chain of verbal responses than do the lexical words. Function words, such as conjunctions and prepositions, cannot be emitted alone except in a grammar lesson, whereas lexical words such as nouns can be emitted alone. When I say "can be emitted alone," I mean that these words are potentially reinforced by the listener.

What did we find? For the normal subjects (those not suffering from Alzheimer's Disease), function words have a higher probability of being guessed correctly than do the lexical words, whereas for the Alzheimer's patients, function words are as likely to be guessed as lexical words; indeed the lexical words are significantly more likely to be guessed for the Alzheimer's patients' speech than for the speech of the normal subjects. On the basis of these results, we created a special score which was the difference for each speaker in the probability of clozers' correctly guessing the function words minus that probability for the lexical words.

The mean difference for the Alzheimer's patients was very close to 0 (-.1%), whereas for the normal subjects the function words were guessed correctly significantly more often, than were the lexical words with a mean difference of 19%. The difference between the two groups was over 100 fold. Thus these data suggest that the response-produced stimulus control, namely the control exerted by words over one another is different for the two types of speakers. Recall, if you will, that the research described above shows that function words are usually more dependent on the words surrounding them than are the lexical words. This suggests that the speech of Alzheimer's patients may not use function words to bind the other verbal responses together. It also suggests that the difference in memory which is of course the most prominent feature of Alzheimer's patients expresses itself in their speech as well. Or to phrase it differently, the Alzheimer's patient's faulty stimulus control produces difficulties both in the way they speak and in the way they remember.

Which brings us back to the question of memory. Memory, as already explained, can be fruitfully viewed in terms of stimulus control. By analyzing the speech of Alzheimer's patients we have demonstrated the importance of response-produced stimulus control. After all, what do you do when you remember something? You emit a response. And why do you emit a response? You do so because a stimulus occasions it. Sometimes that stimulus is external -- a picture that evokes the word in question or that occasions a verbal response that in turn produces the word in question, or some verbal response emitted by another person; at other times that stimulus is response produced -- a verbal response by the speaker him or herself to which the response is the response in question, or again occasions other responses that ultimately evoke the response of interest. That analysis makes the similarity of speech and memory not surprising; rather it is the absence of a relationship that would be surprising.

We analyzed the speech of the Alzheimer's patients in another way as well. We used the type token ratio (TTR). Any speech sample is composed of a given number of words (tokens). Some of the tokens are the same word and they are considered to belong to the same type. Each of those classes of the same word then constitutes a type; the type token ratio is calculated by dividing the number of types by the number of tokens times 100. It is essentially an index of the rate of repetition of words. If a speaker used a different word every time he or she spoke, the TTR would be 100; to the extent that the speaker repeats words, to that extent the number of types is smaller than the number of tokens and the ratio decreases; thus the larger the TTR, the smaller the rate of word repetition.

The interest in word repetition stemmed from Zipf (1949) who contended that verbal behavior was a compromise between the exertion of effort for the speaker and for the listener; if the speaker uses the same word to convey a large variety of different meanings, then his or her effort is minimized and the listener's effort in trying to understand is maximized; if the speaker uses a different word for each different meaning, then his or her effort is maximized and the listener's is minimized.

We used the TTR differently, namely as a way of obtaining an indirect measure of the Alzheimer's patient's memory problem. To the extent that the speaker has difficulty recalling appropriate words, to that extent he or she should emit a smaller variety of words, compromising by using a word he or she can emit but which is of only approximately the same meaning as the one called for by the occasion. Furthermore, memory enters in another way: the normal speaker tries to avoid using the same word repeatedly unless that repetition is meant to call forth a special effect on the listener as is done in some speeches. Nevertheless, the same words need to be repeated in most conversations and therefore a compromise is struck between no repetition and repetition only after a number of other words have intervened. To the degree that the Alzheimer's patient has trouble remembering, he or she should also have difficulty recalling whether a given word had been emitted. As a result, one would expect Alzheimer's patients to repeat words more within the same sample of speech than normal speakers. When we compared TTR's for the two samples, we did indeed find a significantly greater degree of repetition even within the first 55 words for the Alzheimer's patients than for the normal spouses. The patients' TTR was .68 whereas that of the controls was .76.

What Lessons Can We Learn from All This?

1. Verbal behavior is different from nonverbal behavior, not only because its reinforcement is mediated through another person, and not only because that reinforcing behavior is itself learned in each linguistic community; it is different because, unlike the nonverbal behavior that we ordinarily study, we did not condition it and, unlike the behavior that we ordinarily condition, its chains of responses are substantially longer and more complicated by which I mean much more multiply determined. As a consequence, we must find out what the classes of response are; we must discover what the sizes of unit are, and when they are of that size and when they are members of various classes. In that sense, as students of verbal behavior we are in the same position as behavior therapists. We both have to do a behavioral analysis of what is presented to us. In addition, we must study "the reinforcing practices of verbal communities" (Skinner, 1957, p. 461) despite the fact that Skinner seems to assign that study to the linguist. We must do the latter because only in that way can we discover the response units and response classes that comprise the verbal behavior in each speech community.

2. This difference between verbal and nonverbal behavior forces us to deal with behavior, the causes of and controls over which we have yet to discover, by applying techniques of analysis in addition to the ones we usually apply, namely techniques that are sensitive to the integrity of long series of responses.

3. It is not very difficult to describe good cognitive psychology experiments in behavioral terms and it is often useful to do so.

4. No area of psychology need be closed to a behavior analytic approach.

Summary

I began by pointing out that the term "cognitive" is to be taken in two ways: as a reference to a theory in psychology and as a reference to a certain number of classes of behavior. As behavior analysts, we need not be bothered with cognitive theory except in so far as it points to areas of psychology which we have neglected. We can and should avoid the trap that is regularly laid for us when a Cognitive psychologist asks us how we explain such theoretical matters as the difference between short term and long term memory. Those are not data to be explained; they are concepts to be examined, if we wish. On the other hand, it is true that Cognitive psychologists have toiled much harder and more frequently in the so-called cognitive fields by studying language and problem solving in human subjects, and we ought not to leave the field entirely to them.

I presented an example of a cognitively inspired experiment which nevertheless suited itself to behavioral analysis. Indeed it is the kind of experiment in which a behavioral analysis would do quite well.

I went on to discuss how one should study verbal behavior and described the so-called cloze procedure as well as other means of investigating chains of verbal response. Then I presented some data that I had collected recently with Stephanie Portnoy on patients suffering from Alzheimer's Disease. Then, I listed what I thought were the lessons to be learned from the material that I presented.

In sum, I believe that we can learn from looking at the cognitive literature -- just as I believe that our Cognitive colleagues can learn by examining ours -- and that by establishing contact between our two camps, we can all increase the contribution made to the field of psychology. Finally, it is important for us to use methods like the cloze procedure because those methods are more appropriate to the study of verbal behavior than mere frequency analysis.

References

Bayles, K. A. (1982). Language function in senile dementia. *Brain & Language, 16,* 265-280.

Feldman, R. S. (1973). Some characteristics of sentences as response units. In K. Salzinger and R.S. Feldman (Eds.), *Studies in verbal behavior: An empirical approach.* New York: Pergamon Press.

Flanagan, B., Goldiamond, I., & Azrin, N. (1958). Operant stuttering: The control of stuttering behavior through response contingent consequences. *Journal of the Experimental Analysis of Behavior, 1,* 173-177.

Folstein, M. F. & Breitner, J.C.S. (1981). Language disorder predicts familial Alzheimer's Disease. *The Johns Hopkins Medical Journal, 149,* 145-147.

Folstein, M. F. & Breitner, J.C.S. (1982). Language disorder predicts familial Alzheimer's Disease. In S. Corkin et al. (Eds.), *Alzheimer's disease.* New York: Raven Press.

Greenspoon, J. (1955). The reinforcing effect of two spoken sounds on the frequency of two responses. *American Journal of Psychology, 68,* 409-416.

Miller, G. A., and Selfridge, J. A. (1950). Verbal context and the recall of meaningful material. *American Journal of Psychology, 63,* 176-185.

Parrott, L. J. (1984). Listening and understanding. *The Behavior Analyst, 7,* 29-39.

Portnoy, S. (1973). A comparison of oral and written verbal behavior. In K. Salzinger & R. S. Feldman (Eds.), *Studies in verbal behavior: An empirical approach.* New York: Pergamon Press.

Salzinger, K. (1973). Some problems of response measurement in verbal behavior: The response unit and intraresponse relations. In K. Salzinger and R. S. Feldman (Eds.) *Studies in verbal behavior: An empirical approach.* New York: Pergamon Press.

Salzinger, K. (1985). *Intraverbal behavior.* Paper presented at the American Psychological Association, Los Angeles, Calif. (a)

Salzinger, K. (1985). *A behavioral analysis of Alzheimer's Patients' verbal behavior.* Invited address presented at the Association for Behavior Analysis. (b)

Salzinger, K. (1986). *A behavioral view of the cognitive revolution.* Invited address presented at the Association for Behavior Analysis. Milwaukee, Wisconsin.

Salzinger, K. & Eckerman, C. (1967). Grammar and the recall of chains of verbal responses. *Journal of Verbal Learning and Verbal Behavior, 6,* 232-239.

Salzinger, K. & Pisoni, S. (1958). Reinforcement of affect responses of schizophrenics during the clinical interview. *Journal of Abnormal and Social Psychology, 57,* 84-90.

Salzinger, K. & Pisoni, S. (1960). Reinforcement of verbal affect responses of normal subjects during the interview. *Journal of Abnormal and Social Psychology, 60,* 127-130.

Salzinger, K. & Pisoni, S. (1961). Some parameters of the conditioning of verbal affect responses in schizophrenic subjects. *Journal of Abnormal and Social Psychology, 63,* 511-516.

196

Salzinger, K. & Portnoy, S. (1964). Verbal conditioning in interviews: Application to chronic schizophrenics and relationship to prognosis for acute schizophrenics. *Journal of Psychiatric Research, 2,* 1-9.

Salzinger, K. & Portnoy, S. (1987). *Some aspects of the speech of Alzheimer's Disease patients.* Paper presented at the International Neuropsychological Society. Washington, D. C.

Salzinger, K., Portnoy, S., & Feldman, R. S. (1962). The effect of order of approximation to the statistical structure of English on the emission of verbal responses. *Journal of Experimental Psychology, 64,* 52-57.

Salzinger, K., Portnoy, S. & Feldman, R. S. (1964). Experimental manipulation of continuous speech in schizophrenic patients. *Journal of Abnormal and Social Psychology, 68,* 508-516. (a)

Salzinger, K., Portnoy, S. & Feldman, R. S. (1964). Verbal behavior of schizophrenic and normal subjects. *Annals of the New York Academy of Sciences, 105,* 845-860. (b)

Salzinger, K., Portnoy, S. & Feldman, R. S. (1966). Verbal behavior in schizophrenics and some comments toward a theory of schizophrenia. In P. Hoch & J. Zubin (Eds.) *Psychopathology of schizophrenia.* New York: Grune and Stratton.

Salzinger, K., Portnoy, S., Pisoni, D. B. & Feldman, R. S. (1970). The immediacy hypothesis and response-produced stimuli in schiozphrenic speech. *Journal of Abnormal Psychology, 76,* 258-264.

Salzinger, K., Portnoy, S., Zlotogura, P. & Keisner, R. (1963). The effect of reinforcement on continuous speech and on plural nouns in grammatical context. *Journal of Verbal Learning and Verbal Behavior, 1,* 477-485.

Salzinger, S. (1973). Some stimulus properties of syntagmatic and paradigmatic word sequences. In K. Salzinger & R. S. Feldman (Eds.). *Studies in verbal behavior: An empirical approach.* New York: Pergamon Press.

Schoenfeld, W. N. & Cumming, W. W. (1973). Verbal dependencies in the analysis of language behavior. In K. Salzinger & R. S. Feldman (Eds.), *Studies in verbal behavior: An empirical approach.* New York: Pergamon Press.

Skinner, B.F. (1945). The operational analysis of psychological terms. *Psychological Review, 52,* 270-277.

Skinner, B. F. (1957). *Verbal behavior.* New York: Appleton-Century-Crofts.

Skinner, B. F. (1977). Why I am not a cognitive psychologist. *Behaviorism, 5,* 1-10.

Taylor, W. L. (1956). Recent developments in the use of the "cloze procedure." *Journalism Quarterly, 33,* 42-48.

Wiegel-Crump, C. A. & Dennis, M. (1986). Development of word-finding. *Brain and Language, 27,* 1-23.

Zipf, G. K. (1949). *Human behavior and the principle of least effort.* Cambridge, Mass.: Addison-Wesley.

A Discussion of Chapter 8

Cognitive Analysis of Language and Verbal Behavior: Two Separate Fields

Julie S. Vargas
West Virginia University

In his paper "Cognitive Problems, Behavioral Solutions", Salzinger (1990) makes two main points: 1. Behavior analysts should read research written by cognitive psychologists because the data can be useful, and 2. Behavior analysts should themselves research areas usually explored by cognitive psychologists. To illustrate the first point, Salzinger presents a study by cognitive psychologists Weigel-Crump and Dennis, and to illustrate the second, he presents some work he has done. The following takes issue with the first point, but agrees with the second.

The Fruitlessness of Trying to Reinterpret Cognitive Studies

In research, behaviorologists look for functional relationships between a dependent variable of behavior (usually of individual organisms) and its controlling variables. (I prefer "behaviorologist" to "behavior analyst" for the reasons given in Fraley and Vargas (1986), Vargas (1986), and Horcones (1986), and will use it from now on). Typically behaviorologists measure the dependent variable in rate or frequency of responding: the number of responses per unit of time. The independent variables usually consist of environmental events which can be manipulated, although behaviorologists also consider variables (such as genetic inheritance or physiological conditions) which are not manipulated. To contribute to the body of behavioral literature, then, a study must provide some information on factors that functionally relate to the frequency with which individuals respond in a particular way.

The cognitive study which Salzinger uses as an example of research that "collected unambiguous data in the area of cognitive functioning" and whose "data are perfectly able to stand on their own feet to produce a significant set of results and conclusions" demonstrates, I feel, precisely the opposite.

Weigel-Crump and Davis took data on three kinds of verbal behavior (Weigel-Crump and Davis, 1986). They cast their study as a game with three "lexical access" conditions; 1) "semantic" clues in the form of a category name (animals, food, clothing, household, or actions) plus a brief description of the item, 2) a category name and a rhyming word, or 3) a picture. The examples the authors' give are:

Semantic
I'm thinking of an animal...it lives in the jungle...it walks on four legs...it has a mane... and it roars. It's a .....?

Rhyming
I'm thinking of an animal...it rhymes with /dzain?..It's a .....?

Visual
I want you to name the picture for me when I tap with my pencil. Ready?

198

Figure 1: Sample "response picture" used by Weigel-Crump and Dennis (1986, p.7).

Thus the first task involved verbal behavior under thematic and sequelic control, the second required thematic and duplic or sequelic behavior, and the third tacting a picture. [For a breakdown of subcategories of intraverbal behavior, see Michael (1982) and Vargas (1986)]. The data were transcribed from recordings of all sessions and "the number of target responses and mean latency for target responses in each lexical access condition were calculated, making six test scores (per child) in all." Scores of 6-year-olds, 8-year-olds, 10, 12, and 14-year-olds were then averaged and the results reported in a table labeled "target names as a function of age". Sex comparisons were made along with a "robust polynomial multiple regression using linear, quadratic, cubic, and quartic models." The authors also analyzed the errors made by the subjects. I will not go into the conclusions drawn from all of this, but rather examine the usefulness of the data for a behaviorologist.

The nature of the experimental design and of the data presented by Weigel-Crump and Davis prevent seeing functional relationships between any particular variables and the children's' verbal behavior. First of all, as Salzinger points out, no individual data were presented. All results were either percentages or totals across subjects. Secondly, the main contrasts were between age groups. Behaviorologists consider age at best a short hand way of specifying the experiences or specific trainings that occur during the period over which an organism ages. At worst, age is an explanatory fiction or excuse for lack of experimental control (Sidman, 1960). It may be useful to find out what 6, 8, 10, 12, and 14-year-olds in Canadian school systems in general do (the study was conducted in Canada), as a rough indication of cultural or educational practices, but even here the data collected in the present study are suspect because of cognitive assumptions about language.

Weigel-Crump and Davis consider words as "lexical items" which children either have or do not have in their vocabulary. As they put it, "The present study concerns not the acquisition of vocabulary, but how children are able to access already existing lexical items." The assumption that a word is an item in one's vocabulary leads first to a concentration on the target word and second to a relative neglect of the stimuli to which the utterance is made. Assumptions not only affect the kinds of explanations one gives, but also determine the way in which data are collected and presented.

Weigel-Crump and Davis went to considerable lengths to equate the response words used in their study. They picked words which occur with equal frequency in the language according to the *American Heritage Word Frequency Book,* and matched them on no fewer than **seven** "basic semantic characteristics" (concreteness, imagery, categorizability, meaningfulness, familiarity, number of attributes, and pleasantness). Such concern about the response words logically ensues from defining "words" as entities quite separate from the behavior of verbally responding. If the **words** are equal, differences in saying them must be due to other factors.

For the behaviorologist, however, words cannot be equated on formal criteria. A specification of verbal behavior into different categories includes the nature of stimulus control (Skinner, 1957; Lee, 1981) Saying "lion" may be one kind of verbal behavior or quite a different one, depending upon the functional controls over the response. The functional independence of mands and tacts has been demonstrated in several studies (Lamarre & Holland, 1985; Sundberg, 1980; Hall & Sundberg, 1987). Equating response **words** does not, in other words, equate tasks. What the behavior is (or "means") depends not only upon the word emitted, but upon the controlling stimuli.

The functional independence of different verbal behaviors with topographically similar responses is universally accepted in cases where generalization normally does not occur without specific training. For example, cognitive psychologists and educators both realize the importance of considering the prior stimulus when they discuss "talking" as opposed to "reading". Clearly children who enter first grade talking appropriately cannot automatically read even those words they already "know". Having the words "stored in memory" does not seem good enough to call them forth in response to printed stimuli. Educators thus draw a distinction between "speaking vocabularies" and "reading vocabularies". In so doing, they acknowledge stimulus control as an integral part of behavior. But cognitive psychologists fail to see the role of the stimulus when it is more subtle. Weigel-Crump and Dennis do not consider saying a word to a series of hints, to a rhyme, and to a picture as different behaviors. On the contrary, they assume that by equating the response words, they have equated tasks. Differences in children's performance, therefore, they say, must reveal differences in accessing methods.

Weigel-Crump and Dennis have, by the nature of the stimuli presented to students, predetermined their results. Different questions would produce different results, even using the same response words. One could, for example, increase the difficulty of the "visual access" condition by using less stereotyped drawings, that is, pictures with stimulus features shared by more objects. In fact, Weigel-Crump and Davis found that more "errors" were made to the picture of the man's tie (which some children called "chain" or "balloon") than to the lion with its unique mane. By using a picture of a **female** lion, which lacks the mane, the authors would have increased the difficulty of the "visual access" condition for that stimulus. (Familiarity with animals does not guarantee easy "visual access" of their names. A *Ranger Rick* children's magazine showed close-up photographs of common animals' eyes, challenging the reader to identify the animals to which they belonged. My "visual access" for this task was nil, though several of the eyes belonged to animals we had as pets. With no contingencies for responding to eyes alone, I identified the animals on other stimulus dimensions. Similarly, most children identify drawings of lions by the mane.)

Just as the particular stimulus features of the drawings determined the difficulty in the "visual access" condition, the particular stimuli presented for rhyming, determined the probability of students giving a correct response. If the authors had given **three** rhymes instead of only one for the rhyming condition (to match the four cues of the semantic condition), they would have prompted more correct answers. It is not inconceivable that, with less stereotyped pictures and more rhyming prompts, the results of the two conditions would have been reversed: Instead of more children naming the picture correctly, more children might have responded correctly to the rhymes. In either case, the study does not provide data which further an analysis of verbal behavior.

Weigel-Crump and Dennis's article does provide some general survey data (dependent, like all survey data, on the particular questions asked). In addition, it gives a standard set of tasks for other surveys (one of the aims of the study). The study is not without merit, in other words, but it does not contain the kind of data which behaviorologists need. If the study represents those done by cognitive psychologists, the time spent in reinterpreting the data would be better spent in designing and carrying out good behaviorological studies.

Conducting Studies of "Cognitive Functioning" Ourselves

On Salzinger's second point, therefore, I heartily agree. Behaviorologists should do, can do, and are doing work in verbal behavior. Salzinger's discussion of his own work is one example, and it shows a productive borrowing, not of data, but of techniques from non-behavioral colleagues.

Salzinger's task of looking at the difference between speech of Alzheimer's patients and their non-diseased spouses is similar to Weigel-Crump and Dennis's study in several ways. Both count the number of "correct" and "incorrect" words, and both report group data. Both study verbal behavior without experimental manipulation of the independent variable. But there the similarities end. The two studies differ both in design and in the usefulness of the data obtained.

Experimental Design

The differences between cognitive and behavioral approaches to the specification of independent and dependent variables is evident in the contrast between the two main studies Salzinger discusses in his article. Where Weigel-Crump and Dennis looked at the "independent variable" of age (which as pointed out above, is, for a functional analysis, no variable at all but rather a hodgepodge of unknown experiences), Salzinger and his colleagues used the rather precise independent variable of Alzheimer's disease (presence or absence of it). For the dependent variable, both studies measured the probability of emitting correct words, but here again classic differences were shown between behavioral and cognitive approaches. Weigel-Crump and Dennis formally equated response words by using frequency tables rather than children's speech, and they paid little attention to the stimuli to which those responses were to be emitted. In contrast, Salzinger transcribed running speech of Alzheimers patients, and used the resulting transcriptions, with every fifth word omitted (the Cloze procedure) as the stimulus to which subjects were to respond. In using products of actual verbal behavior of patients, Salzinger showed a concern not only with the response words, but with the context and functional controls over them. Salzinger thus equated tasks behaviorally.

Usefulness of Data

And what about the results? Because Alzhemier's disease was Salzinger's independent variable, it could not be manipulated. Nevertheless, by demonstrating differences in the verbal behavior of diseased and normal individuals, Salzinger gives evidence of a functional relationship between the disease and verbal disfunctioning. The finding that the impairment lies particularly in autoclitic behavior and in self-editing lends support to Skinner's analysis in *Verbal Behavior*. Since autoclitic behavior requires other primary verbal operants, it is the last, most complex verbal behavior learned. Skinner cites the weak autoclitic behavior of young children and non-native English speakers as examples (1957, p. 345 and 348). He also conjectures that "Some of the pathology of verbal behavior may involve editing" (1957, p. 390), but he does not provide specific examples for this point. Salzinger and his colleagues have provided the needed data.

Although Salzinger's and his colleagues' work fits within, and contributes to, a behavioral analysis of verbal behavior, I doubt that cognitive psychologists would be as impressed as behaviorologists with his results. Many behaviorologists have encountered resistance from cognitively-oriented editors when submitting manuscripts on studies which used the analytical framework or experimental methods of behaviorology. Cognitive editors find it as difficult to fit behaviorological findings into their interpretation of "language", as behaviorologists do to fit results like those of Weigel-Crump and Dennis into a verbal behavior framework.

Summary

The analysis of verbal behavior is a different field from that of a cognitive analysis of language. The different assumptions lead not only to different theoretical analyses, but to differences in research design and in the kinds of data collected. Salzinger provides evidence (although inadvertently) of the fruitlessness of trying to find data which show functional relationships by looking at group studies done from a cognitive perspective. Some of the **techniques** used by non-behavioral researchers -- for example the Cloze technique -- provide vehicles for behaviorological research. Occasionally cognitive researches present individual or group data from which functional relations can be seen (see, for example the "miscue" research in the field of reading, or articles on verbal slips such as Motley, 1985) But reading cognitive studies is, for a behaviorologist, like looking through a bargain basement. You must search through many unsuitable items before finding something you can use. When reading time is limited, why not go where the density of valuable finds is higher--directly to behavioral work? I suggest that we neither fight cognitive psychologists nor join them, but that we each address problems in our own way. Salzinger, in his article, gives an example of fruitful lines of behavioral research in verbal behavior, and his fears of behaviorists ignoring the formerly "cognitive" areas of "thinking and problem solving, not to speak of language" should be allayed by this volume which attests to the growing participation of behaviorologists in all areas of verbal behavior.

References

Fraley, L. E., & Vargas, E. A. (1986). Separate disciplines: The study of behavior and the study of the psyche. *The Behavior Analyst, 9,* 47-60.

Hall, G., and Sundberg, M. L. (1987). Teaching mands by manipulating conditional establishing operations. *The Analysis of Verbal Behavior, 5,* 41-55.

Lamarre, J., & Holland, J. G. (1985). The functional independence of mands and tacts. *Journal of the Experimental Analysis of Behavior, 43,* 5-19.

Lee, V. (1981). Terminological and conceptual revision in the experimental analysis of language development: Why. *Behaviorism, 9(1),* 25-53.

Motley, M. T. (1985). Slips of the tongue. *Scientific American,* Sept., 116-127.

Sidman, M. (1960). *Tactics of scientific research.* New York: Basic Books. (Reprinted by Author's Cooperative, P.O. Box 53, Boston, MA. 02199).

Skinner, B. F. (1957). *Verbal behavior.* New York: Appleton-Century-Crofts.

Vargas, E. A. (1986). Intraverbal behavior. In P. N. Chase & L. J. Parrott (Eds.), *Psychological aspects of language* (pp. 128-151). Springfield, Ill: Charles C. Thomas.

Wiegel-Crump, C. A. & Dennis, M. (1986). Development of word-finding. *Brain and Language, 27,* 1-23.

Part 4

Rule-Governance

Chapter 9

The Role of Rules in Concept Learning

Philip N. Chase
Jeffrey S. Danforth
West Virginia University

Understanding verbal relations has long been considered essential for a thorough description of human behavior. Rules, instructions, verbal behavior and verbal stimuli have been investigated by many different psychologists and from many different psychological perspectives. One of these perspectives has been behavior analysis. While behavior analysts have contributed theoretical accounts of these relations (Keller and Schoenfeld, 1950; Salzinger, 1959, 1978; Skinner, 1953; 1957; 1963; 1966; 1969; 1974, 1986), they have conducted few basic experiments on verbal behavior (McPherson, Bonem, Green, and Osborne, 1984) and, until recently, few experiments on rules and other forms of verbal stimuli (see as exceptions: Ayllon and Azrin, 1964; Baron, Kaufmann, & Stauber, 1969; Kaufmann, Baron & Kopp, 1966; Lippman & Meyer, 1967; Leander, Lipman & Meyer 1968; and Weiner, 1970). Lately, however, an interest in how rules govern behavior has stimulated a number of operant laboratories to become involved in research on verbal relations (cf. Buskist, Bennett, & Miller, 1981; Catania, Matthews, & Shimoff, 1982; Chase, LeFrancois, & Danforth, 1985; Galizio, 1979; Harzem, Lowe, & Bagshaw, 1978; Hayes, Brownstein, Zettle, Rosenfarb and Korn, 1986; Vaughan, 1985). The findings from the rule governance literature have supported the general principles of behavior as well as suggested a complex set of questions about verbal stimuli and human learning that need to be investigated.

Conceptual learning is one type of human learning that is affected by verbal stimuli. For years cognitive scientists have tried to determine the kinds of rules involved in conceptual learning (Reese, 1989), but because they have emphasized abstract conceptual rules that exist among mental structures, their findings have not seemed relevant to the study of behavior-environment relations. Behavior analysts have also investigated conceptual learning both with humans and other animals, but the effect of rules on conceptual performance has rarely been studied or discussed (cf. Markle, 1983 for a rare discussion of rules and conceptual learning). It appears, though, that many of the findings from the rule governance literature might be applied to understanding conceptual behavior. The purpose of this chapter, therefore, is to describe our attempts to integrate what we know about rules and conceptual behavior.

This integration is complex enough to warrant extensive analysis of rules and a substantial review of the rule governance literature. We will begin with definitions and examples of rule governance, rule stating and rule following, progress to a review of the major findings and methodological innovations of the rule governance literature and finally we will synthesize the analysis of rules and conceptual learning. Our synthesis will concentrate on how conceptual responding often requires adaptation and flexibility to the environment and that rules often interfere with such flexibility. In this context we will describe our attempts to devise rules that facilitate flexible conceptual behavior. This description will reveal a number of problems that face operant investigations of rules and it is these problems that we hope will stimulate discussion and further research.

The Effect of Rules on Behavior

Definitions of Verbal Behavior and Rules

Verbal relations. Rules involve verbal relations and in order to understand rules, a definition of these relations seems necessary. We have adopted a definition of verbal relations that is consistent with Skinner (1957), but we have added one critical feature. Verbal behavior is a relation in which:

    a. A response is emitted by an individual

    b. The critical consequence is provided by the behavior of another individual (the listener)

    c. The listener's behavior is explicitly conditioned to respond to the stimuli produced by the first individual

    d. and the explicit conditioning of the listener involves conditioning to arbitrary stimulus relations, probably conditioning to relational classes, for example, equivalence classes.

Features a-c have been described in detail by Skinner (1957). They distinguish behavior from other events, social behavior from nonsocial behavior, and the need for the listener's behavior to be conditioned to the stimuli produced by the speakers in order for the listener to reliably consequate the speakers behavior (Skinner, 1957). Speakers produce stimuli when they behave. If these stimuli are discriminative for listener behavior, then the listener can respond in a predictable fashion. Thus, the listener's behavior must be conditioned to respond in the presence of these stimuli.

Feature d has been added to Skinner's analysis. It suggests the specific conditioning history that defines verbal and other forms of social behavior (Chase, 1986; Hayes, 1986; Skinner, 1986). As all social behavior involves the qualities described in features a., b. and c., investigators have called for a distinction between verbal behavior and other forms of social behavior. It appears that the examples of behavior that are usually labeled as verbal include a referential quality (Parrott, 1986) or generalized relations among arbitrary stimuli (Skinner, 1986; Hayes, 1986; Chase, 1986).

This feature indicates that verbal behavior involves arbitrary, social or culturally determined relations among events in the world, symbols, pictures, gestures and sounds. A general model that illustrates how these arbitrary relations become established in at least one context, conditional discriminations, is the stimulus equivalence model (Sidman & Tailby, 1982). The stimulus equivalence model specifies that three or more stimuli can become members of an equivalence class when a subject's performance passes tests of reflexivity, symmetry and transitivity. Figure 1 presents an example of a simple stimulus equivalence relation. The auditory stimulus, "car", the letters c-a-r and pictures of cars have become part of an equivalence class. Before any training the subject was tested to see whether he could match each stimulus to itself. Because these were novel stimuli for this subject, correct responding to these test trials constituted reflexivity. The subject was then taught through matching to sample procedures to select the letters c-a-r when he hears "car" and to select pictures of cars when he hears "car". Subsequently, when asked to select pictures of cars when shown the letters c-a-r or asked to select the letters c-a-r when shown pictures of cars the subject does so even though he has not responded to these specific relations before. These test trials tested an integration of symmetry and transitivity and indicated that the training established a stimulus class involving bidirectional relations among these stimuli. It is these kinds of arbitrary relations

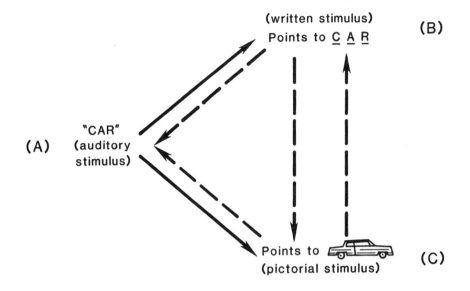

1. Identity matching is taught.
   (Eg. C A R is matched to C A R)

2. One conditional discrimination is taught through differential reinforcement. (solid arrow)

3. Second conditional discrimination is taught through differential reinforcement. (solid arrow)

4. Symmetrical and transitive relations are tested. (dashed arrows)

Figure 1. An Example of a Simple Stimulus Equivalence Class

that appear to distinguish the stimulus classes involved in verbal behavior from those involved in other social behavior.

Rule governed behavior. Rule governed behavior is behavior that is affected by a form of verbal behavior, rule stating, and thus it has the characteristics described above. Rule governed behavior is a relation between listener activity and verbal behavior or the product of verbal behavior in which a relation between 2 or more events is specified by a speaker. This definition is consistent with the literature on rule governance, but is different from previous definitions. Skinner (1969) defined rule governed behavior as behavior controlled by a contingency specifying stimulus. Zettle and Hayes (1982) argued convincingly that this definition fails to distinguish between rules and other types of discriminative stimuli, and fails to handle rules that do not obviously specify contingencies. They preferred to define rule governed behavior as behavior in contact with two sets of contingencies, one of which includes a verbal antecedent. Zettle and Hayes' definition, however, seems to exclude classes of rules that may only involve verbal contingencies. For example, if a teacher tells children to walk single file in the corridor or they will have to stay in the classroom, then it is likely that the children's behavior is under the control of consequences delivered by the teacher, a verbal contingency. Differential consequences from other sources are unlikely to occur. Our definition concentrates more on the verbal contingency because we do not believe that all instances of rule governed behavior require dual sources of control; control by the verbal contingencies may be sufficient.

Rules may be distinguished from other verbalizations by their concentration on relations between two or more events. Examples of rules include laws, rules of games, instructions, scientific principles and descriptions of related events. Each of these examples has a common relational feature. In some cases the relation is between a number of behaviors. For example, the rules of a game specify the sequence of moves, positions etc. that the players emit. Scientific principles, however, involve relations among phenomena, for instance, mass, volume, heat, behavior and environmental events. Other verbal events, like simple tacts, do not necessarily have this relational feature. A simple tact, for example, identifies a single event to the listener. If the topography of the response specifies a single event, for instance, "there is a buffle-head", and the listener responds by turning to look at a small duck, we would not identify the verbal relation as a rule. If the topography specifies the relation among events, like, "You can tell that is a buffle-head because it has a large white head patch and white sides" and the listener makes contact with the relation, for instance, repeats the relation, then we would say the verbalization is a rule. More ambiguous situations we would leave to the criterion of agreement.

Rule stating and rule following. We hope it is clear from our definition of rule governance that there are actually two types of behavior involved, the behavior of speakers and the behavior of listeners. The behavior of speakers is under the control of listener responses and is called rule stating. The behavior of listeners may be under the control of at least two different kinds of contingencies; it may be reinforced by the direct contact that is made with the environment and may be reinforced by social contingencies provided by speakers (Zettle and Hayes, 1982). We call both of these relations rule following.

Rule stating can be divided into at least two categories of operants. Descriptive or normal rules (Reese & Fremouw, 1984) specify a relation among events that exists or has existed and involve a description of a generality or regularity. The key feature of a descriptive rule is that the rule does not specify a particular behavior for the listener to emit. Thus, the listener does not engage in behavior that the rule specifies, rather the listener engages in behavior that indicates contact with the relation specified and it is this contact that reinforces descriptive rule stating. For example, the listener responds verbally to the rule and the rule specifier, "yes, now I see the difference between a buffle-head and a harlequin" or the listener changes some other aspect of his/her behavior. Similarly, the scientist looks at variables in a new light after reading a descriptive rule that another scientist has reported. These are the kinds of rules that are usually categorized as principles, laws of nature, hypotheses etc.

The second general type of rule stating, the prescriptive or normative rule (Reese and Fremouw, 1984), describes a relation that ought to be or should be, and it guides the behavior of the listener. The latter characteristic is the prescriptive rule's distinguishing feature, the listener's behavior must correspond to the behavior specified in the rule in order to reinforce prescriptive rule stating. Thus, if we tell another to act like a buffle-head and they squat on their hindquarters and quack distinctively, then we have an instance of a prescriptive rule. Prescriptive rules are usually categorized as laws, commands, advice or guidelines because they specify the behavior that the listener should follow.

Rule following also has been divided into at least two classes. Zettle and Hayes (1982) have described two kinds of rule following, tracks and plys. The key feature of a track is that the listeners of the rule come into contact with the relation specified and this contact changes some aspect of their behavior. The classic example is the rule "Don't touch the stove when it is red, or you will get burned." If the child touches the stove when it is red and burns his fingers his behavior will contact the feature of the environment specified in the rule. Tracks have been contrasted with plys (Zettle and Hayes, 1982). The distinctive feature of a ply is that the listener's behavior must follow the rule and be reinforced by socially mediated consequences. For example, if we state, "Don't sleep with the window open because the night air is bad for you", the only way the child's behavior can be consistently reinforced for following such a rule is by obeying people who state such rules. The rule does not point out features of the environment that the child will contact.

Zettle and Hayes (1984) described these rules as tracks and plys because the listener either tracks the relation specified in the rule or complies with the demand of the speaker. We warn the reader, however, that in many situations it is difficult to test rule following to determine whether it is a ply or track. A relation that appears to be a ply could be intermittently reinforced by contact with features of the environment which strengthen the relation between the rule stater's behavior and the rule follower's. For example, the child in the night air example might catch a cold when the window is left open and thus following the rule was intermittently reinforced (negative reinforcement). Thus, it would now appear to be at least partially a track. Like other classes of verbal relations, pure examples of tracks and plys are rare. Most instances of rule following are controlled by multiple sources. It is likely, therefore, that most listeners are under the control of both social contingencies and the changes that they observe in the environment.

Instructions That Facilitate Performance

The experimental literature on rule governance has been predominantly interested in prescriptive rules and most of the questions have addressed rule following. One question has been whether rules that accurately describe environmental relations lead to efficient rule following. For example, Ayllon and Azrin (1964) designed an instruction to improve the mealtime behaviors of patients in a psychiatric hospital. During baseline, less than 10% of the residents picked up all their eating utensils in the serving line. During the first treatment condition picking up their tableware was consequated with tangible rewards, but there was no discernible change in behavior. After telling the patients about the contingency, there was a substantial gain in the percentage of those who responded appropriately. Thus, the instructions about the contingency were crucial for obtaining the appropriate behavior from these subjects.

At least two other studies have shown that accurate rules lead to efficient learning. Baron, Kaufman, and Stauber (1969) showed that accurate instructions can lead to the rapid development and maintenance of behavior sensitive to multiple fixed interval (FI) schedule contingencies. Weiner (1970) showed that instructions can decrease the occurrence of unnecessary responding during extinction. These studies suggest that instructions can be used to improve human performance.

Sensitivity to Schedules of Reinforcement

In spite of the advantages of rules suggested by early research, most analyses of rules have focused on how rules evoke behavior that is insensitive to changes in the environment. Studies that have investigated the effect of rules on performance under schedules of reinforcement have shown that once control is established by a rule, behavior is likely to follow the rule and not change when the schedule of reinforcement changes. Thus, the behavior is said to be insensitive to the schedule. Some of these studies have concentrated on the rules that the subjects verbalize about the relation between their behavior and the experimental conditions. Other studies have evaluated the effect of rules or instructions that the experimenter has presented to the subjects.

Self-verbalized rules. Studies on self-verbalized rules have been interested in whether rule stating by the subjects affects their subsequent performance on a task. Some experimenters have postulated that covert formulations of contingencies serve as controlling stimuli for responding. For instance, Lowe (1983) contrasted human and nonhuman performances on FI schedules and contended that the resulting differences were due to covert rules formulated by the humans. In an analysis of just one of these discrepancies, Lowe suggested that human break and run patterns are a result of people counting out the interval before responding rapidly (Lowe, Harzem, & Bagshaw, 1978). When counting was attenuated, subjects responded in a scalloped pattern, with longer post reinforcement pauses as schedule values increased (Lowe, 1979). He concluded that if humans can be kept from talking to themselves, they will behave like nonhumans. Further support came in the form of experiments showing pre-verbal human infants responding with typical FI scallops (Lowe, Beasty, & Bentall, 1983), and verbal 5-9 year-old children exhibiting responding typical of adults (Bentall, Lowe, & Beasty, 1985). The authors pointed out that the development of rule-governed behavior was ultimately a function of conditioning by the environment, but emphasized "that the principle factor responsible for differences between human and animal schedule performance is the role of verbal behavior in humans...responding may no longer be a function of reinforcement but may also be governed by rules of the subject's own devising" (Bentall et al., p. 177).

Although the results of experiments on self-verbalized rules are consistent with the hypothesis that rules control responding, a number of methodological considerations need to be addressed. Most of these studies have derived what subjects said to themselves during the experiments from data obtained on post-session questionnaires. Ericsson and Simon (1984), Reese (1989) and Shimoff (1984) have cited a number of problems with conclusions based on this method. One cannot tell whether the verbal samples collected at the end of an experiment really reflect the behavior during the experiment. The subjects' reports may be erroneous, they may involve misinterpretation, illusion or direct distortion of what they were doing when they engaged in the experimental task. Nor can one tell whether the verbal behavior affected the schedule behavior or the schedule behavior affected the verbal behavior. In addition, functional relations between self-verbalized rules and different schedule performance have not been isolated in any of these studies. Verbal skills were one of many possible variables that were correlated with changes in behavior. These problems suggest that improved methodologies are needed before we can describe the relations among covert verbal and nonverbal behavior.

In order to appreciate the contribution of these studies, it might be necessary to look at them in the context of studies using other methodologies. For example, Catania, Matthews, and Shimoff (1982) looked at the effects of shaped versus instructed verbal behavior on nonverbal responding. Following each component of a multiple schedule of reinforcement, subjects filled out guess sheets about the contingencies. Points were earned for performing on the response keys and for accurate guesses, but some of the subjects were instructed what to guess while the guesses of other subjects were shaped. After a number of cycles, the schedule components were reversed without changing the stimuli correlated with the schedule. The subject continued to get points for guesses that were consistent with the previous conditions, but that were now opposite of the contingencies. Some of those who initially were instructed what to guess came under control of the new contingencies. However, subjects whose guesses were shaped maintained nonverbal performances which were inaccurate under the new conditions. Thus, shaped verbal guesses were more likely to evoke responding that did not change when the contingencies changed.

These studies answer some of the methodological questions that have been asked about self-verbalized rule studies. The subjects' verbal reports were recorded throughout the experiment, the experimental conditions were manipulated to determine whether the subjects' verbal reports were distorted and the verbal reports themselves were manipulated. However, some questions still remain. Might having a history of the experimental conditions without rules or instructions be sufficient to maintain behavior when the experimental conditions change? For example, Weiner (1964) found that subjects who had a history of fixed ratio (FR) responding did not change their behavior when the schedule of reinforcement changed to FI. Although we might assume that the subjects were engaging in verbal behavior about the FR condition, we have no evidence to this effect. This points out the conundrum: how do we arrange for conditions that allow us to be assured that rules are not entering into the relation?

In order to answer this question we return to the studies by Lowe and his colleagues. Lowe suggested that we need to obtain different responses from nonverbal organisms, preverbal infants and other animals than we obtain from verbal human subjects (Lowe, Beasty, & Bentall, 1983). Thus, we need to combine the procedures Lowe and his colleagues have used with those described by Catania et al. (1982) to capture the best evidence for analyzing the influence that rules have on other behavior. If the subjects describe their behavior and their behavior is consistent with the description, we can safely assume that their descriptions do not distort what they are doing and we can probably assume that some other rule is not responsible for their nonverbal behavior. If we manipulate the experimental conditions in such a way as to detect whether the verbal behavior and other behavior remain consistent even when the experimental conditions change, then we can be better assured that the verbal behavior affects the other behavior. Finally, if we can show that nonverbal organisms' behavior changes when exposed to the experimental conditions, we can be assured that the experimental conditions, without the rules, do not control the response of interest.

Rules stated by others. A second set of studies have concentrated on the effect of experimenter instructions on subject performance under schedules of reinforcement. This research suggests that rules stated by the experimenter can evoke behavior that is neither efficient nor truly sensitive to programmed contingencies, especially when the contingencies change. Kaufman, Baron and Kopp (1966) examined the effects of instructions on the sensitivity to programmed contingencies. A variable interval (VI) 60s schedule was programmed and college students were divided into groups given various sets of instructions. The results showed the persistence of instructed behavior even when the resulting rate was contrary to the schedule. Matthews, Shimoff, Catania, and Sagvolden (1977) showed that sensitive VI and variable ratio (VR) rates were common for subjects whose key pressing was shaped, however, those given demonstration "instructions" showed excessively high VI rates.

These results suggest that once instructional control is established it tends to interfere with the influence of programmed contingency changes. There are two factors which may account for this. First, it appears that rule following was at high strength when the subjects entered the experiments as most subjects behavior conforms to the initial instructions. The subjects probably had more experience being reinforced for following salient rules than they did for performing sensitively under isolated schedule parameters. Hayes, Brownstein, Zettle, Rosenfarb and Korn (1986) have described this as the social contingencies competing or interfering with the programmed contingencies. Second, Galizio (1979) claimed that the insensitivity was due to a failure of the subjects' behavior to come into contact with a discrepancy between the programmed contingency and the rule following behavior. Galizio's research suggests that once control is established by instructional stimuli, responding is likely to be maintained in that form until blatant discrepancies between the rule and the programmed contingencies occur.

Others, however, have claimed that subjects who have contacted a change in contingencies do not necessarily engage in behavior that is sensitive to the new contingencies (Hayes et al., 1986; Shimoff, Catania and Matthews, 1981). For example, in Hayes et al. (1986) a subject (S10) who was instructed to "go fast", responded at high rates under an FR 18 and slowed down under a differential reinforcement of low rates (DRL) 6 second, but did not receive any reinforcers for performance under the DRL contingency. Thus, the behavior contacted a difference in the schedules, but was not sensitive. Shimoff et al. (1981) found similar results. The subjects in Galizio, Shimoff et al., and Hayes et al., however, did not receive the same type of contact with schedule discrepancies. The subjects in Galizio's study lost reinforcers if they continued to respond as they did previously. The subjects in Shimoff et al. still obtained the same amount of reinforcement as they had previously, but they could receive more reinforcers if they changed their performance. The subjects in Hayes et al. were placed under extinction conditions if they continued to respond as before. Perhaps a better way of describing the relation revealed from these studies is in terms of the difference between conditions that provide punishment, no change in the frequency of reinforcement, and extinction for responding as one has previously responded. It is not surprising that a punishment procedure leads to more highly differentiated responding.

The point remains, however, that instructions tend to interfere with responding to changed environments especially when the changes are ambiguous. As stated above, Hayes et al. indicated that the insensitivity found under instructed conditions was due to competing contingencies. Hayes et al. found that if they exposed the subjects to an instruction for a number of sessions the behavior was likely to be controlled by the instructions and not the schedule that was in effect, yet when the instructions were removed after one session, the behavior came under control of the schedules.

Another way to describe the relation suggested by Hayes et al. (1986) is to say that if the relative distribution of reinforcers for following instructions has been greater than the distribution of reinforcers for following programmed contingencies, then the subjects will be insensitive to the programmed contingencies. Thus, if the subjects' histories of reinforcement are such that behaving in accordance with instructions is more frequently reinforced than behaving differently than instructed, they will continue to respond in accordance with the instructions, especially under new conditions that are ambiguous. However, if we provided the subjects with a history under which following instructions was not reinforced as frequently as responding differently than instructed, we can imagine the opposite effect. An experimental test of this would indicate more clearly the processes of competition.

Hayes et al's data also suggest another factor that may affect sensitivity to changing conditions, response variability. They claimed that sensitivity to changing conditions is partially due to the range of behavior available to make contact with the contingencies. This suggestion is consistent with Weiner (1969, 1970) and with a large body of literature on transfer of learning (Ellis, 1965). This transfer literature indicates that test performance on a novel task is facilitated by training on a variety of response alternatives (LeFrancois, Chase & Joyce, 1988). For example, Duncan (1958) trained subjects to move a lever into various slots according to a pattern. He found that those trained by a variety of patterns learned a new pattern quicker than those trained by a single pattern.

Hayes et al.'s data from subjects who received both high rate and low rate instructions suggests a similar relation. Providing the subjects with instructions about more than one way to respond teaches them to vary their behavior and thus come into contact with the programmed contingencies. In addition, one critical difference between the instructed conditions that most experimenters have manipulated and the contingency shaped conditions may be that the contingency shaped conditions led to a history of response alternatives. The critical test of this analysis would be to instruct the subjects with a variety of schedules so that they will have a more varied response history and then expose them to a novel schedule to see whether their behavior will change.

Two studies have looked at this relation (LeFrancois, Chase, & Joyce, 1988; Joyce, Chase & Danforth, 1987). For example, LeFrancois et al. found that the behavior of subjects who were instructed to respond to a variety of schedules of reinforcement was more likely to change when faced with a change in contingencies than the behavior of subjects who received a single instruction. The subjects in the variety conditions were given instructions on and exposure to eight different schedules of reinforcement. The subjects in the single instruction condition received an instruction on and exposure to one schedule of reinforcement, either a VI 30 second or a FR 80. After 32 minutes of training, subjects in all conditions received the following instruction, "It is now up to you to figure out how to best earn points" which was followed by at least 25 minutes of an FI 30 second schedule and 5 minutes of an extinction condition. The behavior of subjects who received the variety of instructions changed in accordance with the FI 30 second schedule and showed some disruption of performance under extinction. The single instruction condition did not reliably lead to behavior that was sensitive to the change from the training schedules to the test schedules.

Further analyses of the effects of a history of response variability need to be conducted before we can be assured of the importance of this factor. First, we need to look at the limiting features of variability. What defines the parameters of variability for different kinds of test conditions? Another principle from the transfer of learning literature might be applied to answer this question. It may be sufficient to give the subjects training on the range of response alternatives that are necessary in order to perform accurately on the test. If we give the subjects a low rate history and a high rate history they should be sensitive to changes between FR and FI schedules of reinforcement, but may not be sensitive to other types of schedule manipulations, like the difference between FI and DRL performance (Joyce, Chase and Danforth, 1987). In addition, it is important to demonstrate that response variability is a critical feature of the sensitivity to changing conditions that characterizes contingency shaping. So far, the examination of the existing literature suggests that this might be true. In some cases when human subjects have been sensitive to changing conditions after being contingency shaped, they have engaged in variable performance prior to the changing conditions and when they have not been sensitive, they have not had variable performance prior to the changing conditions (Joyce, Chase and Danforth, 1987). Joyce, Chase, and Danforth (in press) found that responding that was stable at the moment when the contingencies changed was insensitive, regardless of whether it was instructed or not. In contrast, instructed behavior that was not stable when the contingencies changed was sensitive to changes in the contingencies. Thus, the variability of behavior when the contingencies change seems to be a critical factor for producing sensitive behavior.

Summary

In sum, the literature suggests a number of conclusive effects of rules on human behavior. First, accurate instructions efficiently control the behavior of verbal organisms (Ayllon & Azrin, 1964; Baron et al., 1969; Weiner, 1970). Second, self verbalizations are consistent with performance on schedules and the ability to engage in verbal behavior is correlated with the insensitivity of human behavior to changes in schedules of reinforcement (Bentall et al., 1985;

Harzem et al., 1978; Lippman & Meyer,1967; Leander et al., 1968; Lowe, 1979, 1983, Lowe et al., 1978, 1983). Third, shaped verbalizations are more likely to influence other behavior than instructed verbal performance (Catania et al., 1982). Fourth, instructed behavior often interferes with human sensitivity to changing conditions (Buskist et al., 1981; Buskist & Miller, 1986; Galizio, 1979; Hayes et al., 1986; Kaufman et al., 1966; LeFrancois, Chase & Joyce, 1988; Matthews et al., 1977; Shimoff et al., 1981; Vaughan, 1985). Fifth, the sensitivity of instructed behavior to changing conditions is most likely to occur when subjects are punished for responding as they did under previous conditions and reinforced for changing their behavior (Galizio, 1979). Sixth, disrupting the social contingencies that are part of instructions is likely to lead to sensitivity to changing conditions (Hayes et al., 1986). Seventh, a history of responding to a variety of instructions is likely to increase the subject's sensitivity to changing conditions (Hayes et al.,1986; Joyce, Chase & Danforth, 1987; LeFrancois, Chase and Joyce, 1988). Finally, responding that is variable at the moment when the contingencies change is more likely to be sensitive than stable responding (Joyce, Chase & Danforth, in press).

All of the studies described above were conducted using changes in schedules of reinforcement as the procedure for testing the effects of rules. However, there are many kinds of conditions that one might manipulate in order to test the effects of instructions and rules. For example, Vaughan (1985) compared the effects that specific instructions had on the repeated acquisition of a chain of discriminative responses. The subjects responded under instructed conditions in ways that were similar to how subjects have responded to instructions about schedules of reinforcement. When subjects received instructions about how to make the chain of responses, they made many errors when tested later on this chain. In contrast, subjects who were contingency shaped to respond to the chain made relatively few errors when tested. These findings suggest the robustness of the effects of instructions and indicate the need to look at other areas of learning that may be affected by the same relations. One such area is what we describe as conceptual learning, and thus we turn now to our analysis of conceptual performance and how rules may affect it.

Conceptual Behavior

The typical procedure for studying conceptual behavior incorporates a contingency shaping procedure, subjects are shaped to respond to members of a class of stimuli through differential reinforcement. Although elaborate procedures have been developed for teaching conceptual behavior to children based on the contingency shaping approach, instructional designers often suggest that such techniques are not necessary for advanced learners (Engelmann and Carnine, 1982; Markle, 1983). The alternatives rely heavily on the verbal history of the advanced learners and translate into instructed or rule based strategies. Like the early rule governance literature most of this literature concentrates on how instructions make learning conceptual behavior more efficient. If the findings of more recent rule governance literature, however, generalize to conceptual learning, then rule based strategies might lead to conceptual behavior that is not sensitive to subtle changes in the subjects' environment. In fact, studies have found that rule governed strategies do not facilitate responding to members of the conceptual class that are dissimilar to the stimuli used in training (Gagne & Brown, 1961; Guthrie, 1967). Thus, some critical questions to address in concept learning are: Do advanced learners generate verbal behavior or rules about the conditions to which they are exposed? Do these rules change their performance on conceptual tasks? Is there a difference in the effect of contingency shaping and instructed conditions on behavioral adaptation to changing environments? What kinds of instructions lead to sensitivity to changing concept conditions?

Conceptual Learning Defined

Conceptual relations include any situation in which a particular response occurs in the presence of a class of stimuli (Keller and Schoenfeld, 1950). How the stimuli became a class, what kind of stimuli are involved in the class and what kinds of behavior are occurring in the presence of the class are not the defining features of conceptual responding (Johnson & Chase, 1981). Conceptual behavior, therefore, is a very large class of behavior that includes stimulus classes defined by verbal and nonverbal events, common physical properties and arbitrary relations, simultaneous and successive presentations of stimuli, simple spacial relations and compound spacial relations. Also, it includes identification or recognition, definition, naming, exemplifying and other verbal responses. It probably does not include making the same response in the presence of the same stimuli repeatedly nor does it include making different responses in the presence of the same stimuli.

Example Identification Performance

One method that we have used to examine concept learning is the example identification procedure that was described in Chase, Sulzer-Azaroff and Johnson (1985) and Karlsson and Chase (1986). Table 1 presents the sequence of conditions for example identification. We present subjects with a series of examples and nonexamples that consist of written scenarios or instances of abstract psychological concepts. An example is a written scenario that has a concrete referent for each of the defining features of the concept. A nonexample is a written scenario that is missing at least one of the critical defining features. Table 2 presents the defining features and an example and nonexample of one of the concepts we have used extensively, abulia.

Table 1

An Example Identification Procedure

1. Present a series of written scenarios on a computer monitor. Some scenarios illustrate a concept (examples) and some do not (nonexamples).

2. Subjects respond either "E" on a keyboard if the scenario is an example or "N" if the scenario is not an example.

3. Subjects also respond to guess sheets that request their definition of the concept class to which they are responding.

4. Subjects receive points exchangeable for money for identification responses and guesses that are consistent with the experimenters' responses.

5. Measure the average rate of responding across instances.

6. Measure accuracy of responding.

7. Divide accuracy measure into the four categories for a signal detection analysis. Use this analysis to determine sensitivity, and bias.

Table 2

A Definition, Example and Nonexample of Abulia

Definition:

1. An initial high rate of behavior.

2. An initial high proportion of reinforcers to responses.

3. The proportion of reinforcers decreases.

4. The decrease is abrupt.

5. The rate of behavior decreases.

Example[1]:

Andrea was reading a novel, July's Mixed Blessing, by H. W. Chartier. It is an adventure story about a 14 year old youth, Brent, who survives a canoeing accident in the wilderness of Northern Maine. The book describes many of his trials and tribulations as he tries to make his way back to civilization. At first, exciting perils occur in nearly every chapter, and Andrea can't put the book down. Then, in chapter 6, Chartier starts expounding upon the wildlife that Brent encountered. The descriptions continue for five more chapters. Andrea never gets to Chapter 11.

Nonexample:

Graelle was an elephant at the Metropolitan Zoo. Her trainer decided to teach her to lift her trunk, grab a hammer and hit a lever. At first, the trainer gave her a peanut every sixth time that she hit the lever. Graelle spent a great deal of time every day trying to get the peanuts. One day, the trainer decided to give her food every time that Graelle hit the lever. She ate the first 100 peanuts, hitting the lever very hard every time. Then, she began to slow down, and finally gave up.

Recently we have been interested in the effect that rules have on such concept learning. Specifically we have been interested in the following questions: do subjects learn a rule about the conceptual relation to which they are being exposed and does this rule effect their subsequent behavior? These questions are similar to the questions asked about schedule performance that we discussed under the section, Self Verbalized Rules.

These questions about rule stating require a combination of experimental procedures. Periodically during the experiment we ask the subject to justify their example identification behavior just after they make an identification response. We also set up a contingency for correct descriptions of their behavior. If they get the rule right, we pay them. In addition, we periodically manipulate the stimuli so that the correct rule applies in some cases, but not in others.

One relation between accurate rule stating and subsequent rule following that concerns us is whether accurate rule stating leads to insensitivity of subject responding to changing concepts.

It appeared to us that many concepts do not have static features. Under one set of social contingencies, a response would be consistently reinforced in the presence of some features of the environment and under other social conditions, the response would only be reinforced when other features exist. For example, in an applied situation a behavior analyst might be reinforced for using the term, differential reinforcement of other behavior (DRO) to describe the procedure of reinforcing any behavior other than some specified behavior. However, in the laboratory, the response, "DRO", would be reinforced only if the procedure had an interresponse time requirement. One could argue that one social group is correct and the other incorrect, but the point is that they are engaging in different conceptual behavior. The environmental features that are correlated with reinforcement are different under the two conditions, yet the same response is made.

We are interested in discovering the training procedures that both facilitate and interfere with the flexibility of conceptual responding. Our first question is whether learning to state accurate rules leads to inflexibility. We believe this might be a response strength issue: the stronger the relation between particular features of the environment, a response and reinforcement, the more likely the inflexibility. Thus, we should find more flexibility when variable environment/response relations are reinforced.

To answer this question we are developing an experiment that manipulates the variability of rules that the subjects emit about the examples and nonexamples. Under one condition the subjects' rule stating will be reinforced as it successively approximates a flexible rule about the concept (e.g. "Abulia involves either an abrupt decrease in the density of reinforcement or any state of depression involving low rates of behavior"). Under another condition, the subjects' rule stating will be reinforced as it successively approximates a more rigid rule (e.g. "Abulia involves an abrupt decrease in density of reinforcement and a decrease in behavior"). After both conditions subjects will be tested with examples and nonexamples for which a novel set of features are correlated with reinforcement (e.g. the defining features of abulia change). If variability is conducive to sensitive responding in the face of changing contingencies, then learning to state flexible rules should result in more sensitive behavior when the conditions change.

In addition to the variability issue, we also suspect that different kinds of differential reinforcement will also affect flexible responding. For example, if we train subjects to respond to a narrow class of concepts we can test them under three differential reinforcement conditions. Under the first condition, subjects' responses to the narrow concept will still be reinforced, but responding to a new class will result in more reinforcement (greater magnitude of reinforcement). Under the second condition, subjects' responses to the narrow concept will not be reinforced and responding to a new concept will be reinforced. Under the third condition, subjects responses to the narrow concept will be punished and responding to the new class will be reinforced. As we discussed earlier, we suspect that the third condition will be more likely to lead to a change in responding (Galizio, 1979; Hayes et al., 1986; Shimoff et al., 1981).

Repeated Acquisition of a Chain

The second concept learning procedure that we are using is the repeated acquisition design (Harlow, 1949; Boren & Devine, 1968; Vaughan, 1985). First, we teach the subject a chain of responses. For example, the chain could consist of discriminating a series of geometric shapes from other geometric shapes that appear on a computer screen. Figure 2 shows one such chain. We present four geometric shapes to the subjects five times. On the first link, shape A is correct, on the second link, shape B is correct, on the third link, shape A is correct again, on the fourth link, shape C is correct and finally on the fifth link, shape B is correct. The experimental task is to engage in the chain of ABACB discriminations as the shapes are presented. The shapes move around the screen randomly and the ABCD's are not presented to subjects. We have displayed them here simply to help with the explanation. The chain may be repeated as many times as necessary to assure us that the subject has learned to make the specific chain of discriminations. Data are collected on the number of errors that subjects make, where the errors are made in the chains, what response the subjects made on each link and the rate of responding.

The subjects learn to identify a chain of geometric shapes with this procedure. This is a complicated concept that may be better described as the identification of a strategy. The subjects learn a common strategy that can be applied to a number of different arrangements of the geometric shapes. The defining features are: 1. One geometric shape is correct on each link regardless of position, 2. The same geometric shape may be correct in other links, and 3. The sequence of correct geometric shapes stays the same within a session. Each day when the subjects begin the session, the sequence of geometric shapes is different, but correct response sequences share the properties listed.

We have also used this procedure to teach a chain of position responses as another concept class. In this case, the subjects have to learn that a particular position is correct in each link of the chain as opposed to which geometric shape is correct. For example, in Figure 2 the correct response in link one might be the top position, not shape A, the correct response in link two could be the third position from the top, the correct response in link three could be the top position again and so forth.

There are two kinds of questions that we are addressing with the repeated acquisition procedure. We are interested in whether the same relations between rules and schedule performance exist between rules and repeated acquisition learning. As stated earlier, Vaughan (1985) demonstrated that subjects who received instructions about how to make the chain of responses, made many errors when tested later on this chain. Incontrast, subjects who were contingency shaped to respond to the chain made relatively few errors when tested. Danforth, Chase, Dolan, and Joyce (in press) have replicated these findings with college students. In addition, we have found that exposing subjects to the instructions for extended sessions reduced the difference in errors between the contingency shaped condition and the instructed condition. Thus, the negative effect of rules on subjects' maintenance of accurate responding was short lived. This effect also appeared in Vaughan's and Boren & Devine's data and is consistent with the literature on the effects of rules on schedule performance (Shimoff et al., 1981; Hayes, et al., 1986).

These manipulations using the repeated acquisition procedure, however, did not address whether the subjects' behavior would change if the contingency changed, rather they looked at whether the behavior would maintain when the instructions were removed. Thus, we recently have begun to look at the relation between providing subjects with rules about the chain of discriminations and changes in these chains. For example, in one study (Chase & Danforth, 1986) we instructed the subjects to respond to chains defined by the geometric shape by providing them with the instructions presented in Table 3. After stable performance was obtained, we switched the contingency to one involving the position on each link of the chain. For at least two sessions the subjects continued to make many errors on the position defined chains, but they eventually changed their behavior. This result paralleled the findings of studies with instructions and schedules of reinforcement that have exposed behavior repeatedly to the change in contingencies (Hayes et al., 1986; Shimoff et al., 1981).

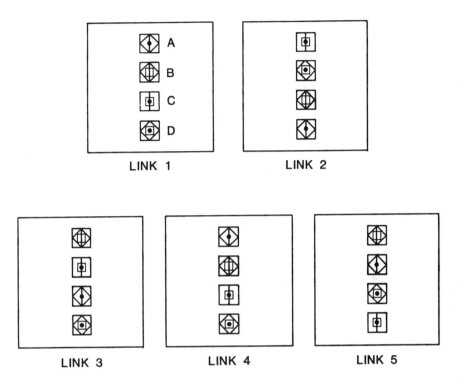

1. The correct response is taught for each link. (Eg. shape A is correct in Link 1, shape C is correct in Link 2 etc.)

2. The chain is repeated until subjects make no errors.

3. Subjects are tested on either the same chain or new chain.

Figure 2. An Example of a Chain of Geometric Shapes

The second type of question that we are addressing is what kinds of rules or instructions facilitate performance under changing conditions. It seems fruitful to try to determine whether some rules facilitate performance on experimental tasks and other rules do not. The reader will recall that Zettle and Hayes (1982) described two kinds of rule following, tracks and plys. The primary difference between them is that tracking is reinforced by contact with nonverbal contingencies and pliance is reinforced by verbal contingencies. Tracks by definition are more likely to be sensitive to changing environmental conditions and plys are more likely to be sensitive to changing social conditions. What kinds of instructions, therefore, lead to tracking and what kinds of instructions lead to pliance?

Table 3

Strategic Instructions for Geometric Shapes

The best way for you to earn the most money in the least amount of time:

1. Name the geometric shapes with labels that you will remember.

2. Use the same labels everyday.

3. When a session starts pick a key and name the shape that corresponds to it, then press the key.

4. If correct, repeat the name, and the number of the section you were on.

5. If incorrect, pick another shape, name it, and press the corresponding key.

6. Continue with 3, 4, and 5 for each section. Whenever you make a correct response, repeat the whole sequence of correct names and numbers including the last correct response.

Currently we are looking at the instructions that insure contact with the conditions and decrease reliance on the experimenter. Tracking might be facilitated if the instructional procedures concentrate on transferring control from the rule to the conditions the rule specifies. This idea comes from the relation between rule governance and prompting and fading (Baron and Galizio, 1983). If rules are clearly supplementary stimuli, they are not critical to the environmental conditions of interest, and they already control the behavior of the subject, then we could call them prompts. We certainly would not be surprised to find that when we abruptly remove a prompt that the behavior deteriorates. However, if we develop procedures that help to transfer control from the rule (prompt) to the critical environmental features of the concept class then we might facilitate tracking.

For example, we could use a delay procedure (Touchette, 1971). The examples and nonexamples of the concept class are presented and the subject is asked to identify the examples. If the subject does not respond within a certain period of time or responds incorrectly, then the rule is specified. If a higher density or magnitude of reinforcement is programmed for responding correctly before the rule is given, the subjects may begin to come under the control of the critical stimuli. Then, if we gradually remove the rules provided by the experimenter, we have created conditions under which subjects' behavior will be likely to be affected by the changes in the stimuli and are less likely to be affected by changes in the experimenter's behavior. Other prompting and fading techniques should also enhance the control by the environmental features and weaken the control by the experimenter.

Teaching subjects to vary their responding through a variety of instructions or through problem solving rules rather than rules that specify a single direct relation between their behavior and changes in the environment also should facilitate tracking. If we teach subjects to vary their responding when faced with an ambiguous situation, they may come into contact with the relevant features of the environment. For example, in the repeated acquisition situation we instructed the subjects how to try out various response sequences until they discovered the one that would lead to reinforcement. The strategy described in Table 3 stated a rule that would allow the subjects to come into contact with the features of the environment that are correlated with reinforcement. This rule was successful in teaching the subjects to learn geometric figure chains with few errors regardless of the sequence of the chain. Therefore, it was more likely to produce tracking of geometric shapes than a single specific instruction.

This brings up a third condition that may affect tracking, the type of contact that the subjects have with the changing contingencies. In Chase and Danforth (1986) the subjects' errors were punished when the correct concept class changed from geometric shapes to position and it took the subjects two or three sessions to learn how to respond without making errors. However, if their responding had continued to be reinforced at the same rate for responding to the geometric shapes chain, but could have gained more reinforcers for responding to the position chain, we might not expect them to change their performance at all. This kind of result would be consistent with the literature on schedule performance (Galizio, 1979; Shimoff et al., 1981). We are currently investigating this possibility.

Finally, tracking may be facilitated by descriptive as opposed to prescriptive rules. We introduced this distinction earlier; descriptive rules emphasize the relations among environmental events whereas prescriptive rules emphasize following the rule. It may be that the more a rule emphasizes the relation among events and deemphasizes the need to follow the rule, the more likely subjects will be sensitive to the conditions specified in the rule and not the implicit social contingencies of rule following. Matthews, Catania, and Shimoff (1985) showed that shaped descriptions of performance were more likely to influence nonverbal behavior than shaped descriptions of contingencies. Telling the subject what behavior to emit is a prescriptive rule whereas telling the relation between behavior and consequence is a more descriptive rule. Thus, prescriptive rules seem to lead to pliance and descriptive rules might facilitate tracking.

Summary

The number of effects that rules might have on conceptual behavior that remain to be studied suggests the importance of investigating the direct manipulation of rules. This type of research would add to what we have discovered about rules through research on schedule sensitivity. In addition, this research will add to what we know about the conditions that affect concept learning. So far we have investigated the effects of specific rules versus contingency shaping and found that specific rules interfere with the control that antecedent stimuli have over discriminations, however extended exposure to these rules and tests without the rules minimize this interference (Danforth, Chase, Dolan, & Joyce, in press). We have compared strategic rules to specific rules and found that the strategic rules facilitate performance of the chain of discriminations (Chase & Danforth, 1986). This finding suggested to us a relation between prompting, fading and rule governance, particularly the studies that have found that rules interfere with the subjects sensitivity to changes in conditions. Specifically, if some instructional conditions function as prompts and if the experimenter does not program procedures to transfer control of the prompt to control by the parameters of the programmed contingencies, we should expect to find insensitive responding. This study also suggested that another significant variable might be the type of contact that responding had with the reinforcement contingencies. If responding leads to a loss of reinforcers for continuing to respond as they did previously, then behavior is likely to change. However, if the responses continue to be reinforced they might not change, even if responding to other features of the environment might lead to more reinforcement then was occurring previously.

Conclusion

We hope we have accomplished what we set out to do: to provide a review and critique of the rule governance literature, and a description of the relation between rule governance and concept learning. We have concluded that some of the more interesting questions about the effects of rules concern the conditions that lead to rule following that are controlled primarily by changes in the nonverbal contingencies. In the rule governance literature this has been referred to as sensitivity to the schedule of reinforcement. In the concept learning literature these questions are answered by changing the concept class that is reinforced. The concept learning procedures that we have described are particularly useful for looking at such questions. They are flexible in terms of the number of concepts that can be manipulated, the kinds of rules that can be used to describe the concepts and the reinforcement contingencies that can be changed. They clarify the role of antecedent stimulus functions in rule governance and they suggest some additional known principles, e.g. the principles of prompting and fading, that are part of the role of rules. In addition, the concept learning procedures make it easier to determine whether the subject is controlled by the rules or the reinforcement contingencies. As a discrete trials procedure, each trial reveals whether the response is consistent with the reinforcement contingencies, repeated trials over time indicate the strength of this relation. In the typical free operant procedure used with schedules of reinforcement, one has to examine a pattern of responding to determine the controlling variables and even then the source of control may be ambiguous. Finally, these procedures allow us to test the robustness of the effects that have been discovered with other rule governance procedures.

We conclude that there are a number of methodological problems that still need to be solved. The area still awaits a better solution to the problem of how to manipulate rules or verbal behavior using intrasubject designs. The procedures that we have described that provide the best evidence of the effects of rules seem to require a number of different experiments with a number of different subjects. We are not entirely satisfied with this procedure. In addition, we are not satisfied with the classification system of rule stating and rule following. As briefly indicated, the track/ply distinction for rule following is an ambiguous functional classification because under some conditions we can not tell the difference between them. Thus, we await either procedures that allow us to distinguish between tracks and plys or another kind of functional classification.

We end this discussion, therefore, on what we consider a positive experimental note. Behavior analysts have begun to investigate the effects of rules on behavior and their behavioral/environmental perspective has led to some consistent results. In addition, there are a number of stimulating questions to address and a number of methodological and theoretical problems to solve. We appeal to our readers to begin looking at these questions and problems. The answers and solutions seem necessary for our understanding of human behavior.

References

Ayllon, T. & Azrin, N. H. (1964). Reinforcement and instructions with mental patients. *Journal of the Experimental Analysis of Behavior, 7,* 327-331.

Baron, A. and Galizio, M. (1983). Instructional control of human operant behavior. *The Psychological Record, 33,* 495-520.

Baron, A., Kaufmann, A. & Stauber, K. A. (1969). Effects of instructions and reinforcement-feedback on human operant behavior maintained by fixed-interval reinforcement. *Journal of the Experimental Analysis of Behavior, 12,* 701-712.

Bentall, R. P., Lowe, C. F., and Beasty, A. (1985). The role of verbal behavior in human learning: II. Developmental differences. *Journal of the Experimental Analysis of Behavior, 43,* 165-181.

Boren, J. J., and Devine, D. D. (1968). The repeated acquisition of behavioral chains. *Journal of the Experimental Analysis of Behavior, 11,* 651-660.

Buskist, W. F., Bennett, R. H., & Miller, H. L., Jr. (1981). Effects of instructional constraints on human fixed-interval performance. *Journal of the Experimental Analysis of Behavior, 35,* 217-225.

Buskist, W. F., & Miller, H. L. (1986). Interaction between rule and contingencies in the control of human fixed-interval performance. *The Psychological Record, 36,* 109-116.

Catania, A. C., Matthews, B. A. & Shimoff, E. (1982). Instructed versus shaped human verbal behavior: Interactions with nonverbal responding. *Journal of the Experimental Analysis of Behavior, 38,* 233-248.

Chase, P. N. (1986). *Training novel verbal performance: response class variety.* Unpublished manuscript.

Chase, P. N. and Danforth, J. (1986). *The effects of strategic instructions on repeated acquisition behavior.* Unpublished manuscript.

Chase, P. N. & Imam, A. A. (1987). Establishing equivalence classes with complex verbal relations. *The Mexican Journal of Behavior Analysis.*

Chase, P. N., LeFrancois, J., & Danforth, J. (1985, May). *Sensitivity to changing contingencies: Variables that determine the effectiveness of instructions.* In S. C. Hayes (Chair), The role of verbal stimuli in human behavior. Symposium conducted at the meeting of the Association for Behavior Analysis, Columbus, OH.

Chase, P. N., Sulzer-Azaroff, B. and Johnson, K. R. (1985). Verbal relations within instruction: Are there subclasses of the intraverbal? *Journal of the Experimental Analysis of Behavior, 43,* 301-313.

Danforth, J. S., Chase, P. N., Dolan, M. & Joyce, J. H. (in press). The establishment of stimulus control by instructions and by differential reinforcement. *Journal of the Experimental Analysis of Behavior.*

Duncan, C. P. (1958). Transfer after training with a single versus multiple tests. *Journal of Experimental Psychology, 55,* 63-72.

Ellis, H. C. (1965). *The transfer of learning.* New York: The MacMillan Co.

Engelmann, S. E. and Carnine, D. (1982). *Theory of instruction: Principles and applications.* New York: Irvington.

Ericsson, A. K. and Simon, H. A. (1984). *Protocol analysis: Verbal reports as data.* Cambridge, MA: MIT Press.

Gagne, R. M. & Brown, L. T. (1961). Some factors in the programming of conceptual learning. *Journal of Educational Psychology, 62,* 313-321.

Galizio, M. (1979). Contingency-shaped and rule-governed behavior: Instructional control of human loss avoidance. *Journal of the Experimental Analysis of Behavior, 31,* 53-70.

Guthrie, J. T. (1967). Expository instruction versus a discovery method. *Journal of Educational Psychology, 58,* 45-49.

Harlow, H. (1949). The formation of learning sets. *Psychological Review, 56,* 51-65.

Harzem, P., Lowe, C. F., & Bagshaw, M. (1978). Verbal control in human operant behavior. *The Psychological Record, 28,* 405-423.

Hayes, S. C. (1986). The case of the silent dog-Verbal reports and the analysis of rules: A review of Ericsson and Simon's Protocol Analysis: Verbal Reports as Data. *Journal of the Experimental Analysis of Behavior, 45,* 351-363.

Hayes, S. C., Brownstein, A. J., Zettle, R. D., Rosenfarb, I., & Korn, Z. (1986). Rule-governed behavior and sensitivity to changing consequences of responding. *Journal of the Experimental Analysis of Behavior, 45,* 237-256.

Johnson, K. R. and Chase, P. N. (1981). Behavior analysis in instructional design: a functional typology of verbal tasks. *The Behavior Analyst, 4,* 103-122.

Joyce, J. H., Chase, P. N. & Danforth, J. (1987, May). *Sensitive schedule performance: Defining training variety.* Poster presented at the Association for Behavior Analysis Conference, Nashville, TN.

Joyce, J. H., Chase, P. N., & Danforth, J. S. (in press). The effects of response variability on the sensitivity of rule-governed behavior. *Journal of the Experimental Analysis of Behavior.*

Karlsson, T. and Chase, P. N. (1986, May). *The effects of feedback on human concept learning.* Poster presented at the meeting of the Association for Behavior Analysis, Milwaukee, WI.

Kaufman, A., Baron, A., & Kopp, R. E. (1966). Some effects of instructions on human operant behavior. *Psychonomic Monograph Supplements, 1,* 243-250.

Keller, F. S. & Schoenfeld, N. (1950). *Principles of psychology.* Englewood Cliffs, NJ: Prentice-Hall.

Leander, J. D., Lippman, L. G., & Meyer, M. E. (1968). Fixed interval performance as related to subjects' verbalizations of the reinforcement contingency. *The Psychological Record, 18,* 469-474.

LeFrancois, J. R., Chase, P. N., & Joyce, J. H. (1988). The effects of a variety of instructions on human fixed interval performance. *Journal of the Experimental Analysis of Behavior, 49,* 383-393.

Lippman, L. G. & Meyer, M. E. (1967). Fixed-interval performance as related to instructions and to subjects' verbalizations of the contingency. *Psychonomic Science, 8,* 135-136.

Lowe, C. F. (1979). Determinants of human operant behavior. In M. D. Zeiler, & P. Harzem (Eds.), *Advances in analysis of behavior: Vol. 1 Reinforcement and the organization of behavior.* Chichester, England: John Wiley & Sons. (pp. 159-192).

Lowe, C. F. (1983). Radical behaviorism and human psychology. In G. C. L. Davey (Ed.), *Animal models of human behavior: Conceptual, evolutionary, and neurobiological perspectives.* Chichester, England: John Wiley & Sons.(pp. 71-93).

Lowe, C. F., Beasty, R. P., Bentall, C. F. (1983). The role of verbal behavior in human learning: Infant performance on fixed-interval schedules. *Journal of the Experimental Analysis of Behavior, 39,* 157-164.

Lowe, C. F., Harzem, P., & Bagshaw, M. (1978). Species differences in temporal control of behavior II: Human performance. *Journal of the Experimental Analysis of Behavior, 29,* 351-361.

Markle, S. M. (1983). *Designs for instructional designers.* Champaign, Il: Stipes Publishing Co.

Matthews, B. A., Catania, A. C., & Shimoff, E. (1985). Effects of uninstructed verbal behavior on nonverbal responding: Contingency descriptions versus performance descriptions. *Journal of the Experimental Analysis of Behavior, 43,* 155-164.

Matthews, B. A., Shimoff, E., Catania, A. C., & Sagvolden, T. (1977). Uninstructed human responding: Sensitivity to ratio and interval contingencies. *Journal of the Experimental Analysis of Behavior, 27,* 453-467.

McPherson, A., Bonem, M., Green, G., and Osborne, J. G. (1984). A citation analysis of the influence on research of Skinner's *Verbal Behavior. The Behavior Analyst, 7,* 157-167.

Parrott, L. J. (1986). On the differences between verbal and social behavior. In P. N. Chase & L. J. Parrott (Eds.) *Psychological aspects of language: The West Virginia Lectures.* Springfield, IL: Charles C. Thomas (pp. 91-117).

Reese, H. W. (1989). Rules and rule goverance: Cognitive and behavioral views. In S. C. Hayes (Ed.) *Rule governed behavior: Cognition, contingencies and instructional control* (pp. 3-84). New York: Plenum.

Reese, H. W. & Fremouw, W. J. (1984). Normal and normative ethics in behavioral sciences. *American Psychologist, 39,* 863-876.

Salzinger, K. (1959). Experimental manipulations of verbal behavior: A review. *Journal of General Psychology, 61,* 65-94.

Salzinger, K. (1978). Language behavior. In A. C. Catania and T. A. Brigham (Eds.) *Handbook of applied behavior analysis: Social and instructional processes.* New York: Irvington Publishers, pp.275-321.

Shimoff, E. (1984). Post-session questionnaires. *Experimental Analysis of Human Behavior Bulletin, 2,* 1.

Shimoff, E., Catania, A. C., & Matthews, B. A. (1981). Uninstructed human responding: Sensitivity of low-rate performance to schedule contingencies. *Journal of the Experimental Analysis of Behavior, 36,* 207-220.

Sidman, M. & Tailby, W. (1982). Conditional discrimination vs. matching to sample. *Journal of the Experimental Analysis of Behavior, 37,* 5-22.

Skinner, B. F. (1953). *Science and human behavior.* New York: MacMillan.

Skinner, B. F. (1957). *Verbal behavior.* Englewood Cliffs, N.J.: Appleton-Century-Crofts.

Skinner, B. F. (1963). Operant behavior. *American Psychologist, 18,* 503-515.

Skinner, B. F. (1966). An operant analysis of problem solving. In B. Kleinmuntz (ed.), *Problem solving: Research, method, teaching.* (pp. 225-257). New York: Wiley.

Skinner, B. F. (1969). *Contingencies of reinforcement: A theoretical analysis.* New York: Appleton-Century-Crofts.

Skinner, B. F. (1974). *About behaviorism.* New York: Knopf.

Skinner, B. F. (1986). The evolution of verbal behavior. *Journal of the Experimental Analysis of Behavior, 45,* 115-122.

Touchette, P. E. (1971). Transfer of stimulus control: Measuring the moment of transfer. *Journal of the Experimental Analysis of Behavior, 15,* 347-354.

Vaughan, M. E. (1985). Repeated acquisition in the analysis of rule-governed behavior. *Journal of the Experimental Analysis of Behavior, 44,* 174-184.

Weiner, H. (1964). Conditioning history and human fixed-interval performance. *Journal of the Experimental Analysis of Behavior, 7,* 383-385.

Weiner, H. (1969). Controlling human fixed-interval performance. *Journal of the Experimental Analysis of Behavior, 12,* 349-373.

Weiner, H. (1970). Instructional control of human operant responding during extinction following fixed-ratio conditioning. *Journal of the Experimental Analysis of Behavior, 13,* 391-394.

Zettle, R. D. & Hayes, S. C. (1982). Rule-governed behavior: A potential theoretical framework for cognitive-behavioral therapy. In P. C. Kendall (Ed.) *Advances in cognitive-behavioral research and therapy.* Vol. 1 (pp. 73-118). New York: Academic Press.

Footnotes

1. We wish to thank Vaughn Hathaway for these examples.

A Discussion of Chapter 9

Rule-Governance:
Enough to Make a Term Mean

Paul Andronis
University of Chicago

"When I use a word," Humpty Dumpty said, in rather a scornful tone,
    "it means just what I choose it to mean -- neither more nor less."
"The question is," said Alice, "whether you can make words mean so
    many different things."
"The question is," said Humpty Dumpty, "which is to be the master --
    that's all."

(Carroll, 1871, pg. 186)

Chase and Danforth set for their chapter three main objectives: (1) to provide a critical review of the experimental analysis of rule-governance and its relation to the control exerted by direct exposure to nonverbal contingencies; (2) to describe ongoing studies of rule-governance and conceptual behavior in their own laboratory at West Virginia University; and (3) to suggest new strategies for addressing some of the important and perplexing problems raised by past experimentation in this field. The authors present us with a coherent and insightful view of the difficult background literature, informed in part by their firsthand acquaintance with the fine-grain of such research, and so their chapter meets its first two objectives very strongly. Based upon the vigorous discussion it occasioned at the Institute where it was originally presented, the chapter is likely to meet its third objective even more successfully by serving as a catalyst (or, at the very least, as an informed guide) to future work in this area.

The following narrative describes some of the topics that came up during discussion of Chase and Danforth's paper at the International Institute, focusing on two major themes, namely: (1) criteria for defining "rules" and "rule-governance;" and (2) some possible roles which rules and rule-governance may play in concept learning.

The discussion opened with a rapid-fire list of several related questions. Are rules actually discriminative stimuli, or are they instances of verbal behavior governed by distinct contingencies imposed by a verbal community which requires us on certain occasions to account for our behavior? Do rules govern behavior in the same ways as do more familiar forms of discriminative stimuli? And, if so, how might we critically distinguish between, on the one hand, rule-governed behavior by humans, and, on the other hand, instances of contingency-shaped behavior by nonhuman subjects' which we may nevertheless describe as though it followed certain rules?

Rules as "Establishing" or "Potentiating" Variables

For a given class of events to qualify for definition as a discriminative stimulus in a contingency relation, it must be the sole set of occasions on which the behavior can have a specified consequence, i.e., in its absence, the behavior cannot have that consequence. This immediately raises an interesting problem: in most instances where rules are said to govern specified classes of behavior, those behaviors may nevertheless occur and be reinforced without the rules' having been given in the first place -- this is certainly true of the various experiments on rule-governance reviewed by Chase and Danforth, and it is probably generally true of all situations in which rules are said in some way to "describe" existing contingency relations. For example, Skinner (1957) discussed the blacksmith who gave his apprentice a simple rule to follow, in the form of a little poem to be recited while pumping bellows: to the extent that the apprentice "followed" the rule, i.e., pumped the bellows in a manner specified by the words of the poem, he would stoke the coals in the hearth to exactly the right temperature. Such a rule could in fact hasten the occurrence of the targeted bellows repertoire, which might thereafter come under discriminative control by the coals' glowing color rather than by repeated recitation of the poem/rule. Nevertheless, even if the apprentice did not follow the rule, he might still get the coals to the right temperature, either immediately by mere chance, or eventually by trial-and-error (and with or without supplementary stimulation from the master blacksmith). We cannot, therefore, define such rules formally as discriminative stimuli, but they do seem to establish the potency of certain elements of existing contingencies. Accordingly, we may define such rules as parts of "establishing operations," (Keller & Schoenfeld, 1950; Michael, 1982) or as "potentiating variables" (Brady, 1966; and Goldiamond and Dyrud, 1968) or as "function altering stimuli" (Blakely & Schlinger, 1987). For the blacksmith's apprentice, the rule made a specified response topography and a targeted stimulus control relation momentarily more likely to occur, in effect "telescoping" the outcome of an entire history of exposure to the relevant contingencies into a single event class.

Rules as Discriminative Stimuli

Nevertheless, other rules occur as mands, and do indeed function as discriminative stimuli with respect to the behavior of listeners. Such (mand) rules are obviously related to contingencies established and maintained by the speaker (whether an individual or an entire verbal community), and may perhaps be less interesting to some of us precisely because of their clear relations to contingencies. In particular, prohibitive rules are discriminative stimuli related explicitly to the punishment contingencies which usually underlie whatever effectiveness they have in governing behavior. For example, posted speed limits on highways, and IRS rules concerning taxable income, are alike effective only to the extent that the state can impose fines and imprisonment for flagrant violations. As with other patterns of behavior controlled by mands, behavior in accord with prohibitive rules is often maintained by strong negative reinforcers -- hence, the effectiveness of these kinds of rules may depend upon variables quite different from those involved in other subtle kinds of rules we are more interested in studying. Hence, the purely mand characteristics of certain kinds of rules may be addressed separately from the issue of rule-governance, per se, particularly with respect to the the rule as an element of the speaker's repertoire.

Moreover, we do not necessarily consider all mands to be rules. They merely provide us with some important instances of rules. For example, "Sit down," is not a rule for a dog, though it might be for an airline passenger during take-off. The distinction has to do with the verbal nature of the stimulus: without the listener's having the necessary verbal repertoire, a speaker's mand will function only as a conditional discriminative stimulus with respect to the control it exerts over the listener's behavior. The issue here is one of verbal stimulus control. Indeed, we generally agree that rules must be verbal stimuli, so they must have ready-made discriminative attributes that do not require new conditioning under every new setting where they occur -- in this sense, verbal stimuli are to some extent already potent, by virtue of the listener's general verbal history, at the time we say they function as rules.

Descriptive vs. Prescriptive Rules

There is also an important difference between stated (descriptive) rules, and (prescriptive) rules actually "followed" by behaving organisms (as in the difference between "rule-stating" and "rule-following" behavior). Descriptive rules reside primarily in the speakers' discriminative repertoires; they are usually emitted as intraverbals under multiple control of both tacts of variables which govern the speakers' behavior (e.g, the behavior "described" in the rule), and mands emitted by a verbal community requiring speakers to account for their behavior (e.g., the specific occasions to which the rule applies). For example, during laboratory investigations, descriptive rules are found in the verbal behavior of the experimenters (e.g., they may describe contingency relations, and then say that their subjects' behavior is controlled by it). Obviously, a nonhuman laboratory animal's behavior is not going to be controlled by a description of the contingencies, but by the contingencies themselves; hence, any rule in evidence here will be purely descriptive.

Nevertheless, with human subjects, laboratory investigators often attribute such control to the rule itself (as prescriptive), but usually this inference occurs only after they have given their subjects some kind of instruction and then asked them about the rules they followed during the experiment. Here we must remember that subjects' descriptions of the rules (rule-stating) are largely under audience control. We cannot readily check other private sources of control, except perhaps where we know enough about the subjects' relevant histories, which we often try to provide explicitly through instructional sequences. True prescriptive rules, the kinds which apparently most interest us, typically are mands emitted by a speaker under control of targeted listeners' responses. An example of governance by this kind of rule would occur when a student "learns" and then "applies" a particular principle to solve a geometry problem. Such prescriptive rules appear to restrict problem solvers' response alternatives with respect to stimuli making up problem sets with which we confront them; the restriction itself is established historically, both by histories of verbal contingencies to which the listeners have been exposed previously, and by subsequent instructional sequences.

Finally, although we must infer rule-governance, in part, from an accord between the behavior of the listener and some rule given by a speaker, in practice, we might (or might not) discover whether the listener in fact followed a rule when emitting a given instance of behavior. Major problems arise in any event, as noted by Chase and Danforth, with empirical "truth-assessment," especially in experimentally verifying what governs the behavior of listeners when we say they are following rules. One commonly used strategy has been simply to require human subjects to describe exactly what they thought governed their own behavior during a given experiment or test. This tactic has a number of serious problems, not the least of which is its lack of independent verifiability. An alternative strategy involves interfering with subjects' covert verbal behavior while requiring them to emit what we think is rule-governed behavior; this approach seems to assume that covert verbal responses are the rules which govern the overt behavior being observed, and further that the organism emitting rule-governed behavior is both "speaker" and "audience" for the given rule. To the extent that such interference with covert responses disrupts overt behavior, the two (covert and overt responses) may be critically linked as occasion and behavior, respectively -- but this may not be the only or even most parsimonious description of their relation.

Rule-governance as Historical Control by Verbal Contingencies

The matter of historical origins immediately raises another important question, namely, "Why do we want to talk about the distinction between rule-governed and contingency-shaped behavior in the first place?" At issue here seems to be the process by which the stimulus comes to control behavior, in other words, the process by which rules become effective. And, by 'process,' we must mean the organism's reinforcement history. In this sense, language (verbal behavior) readily provides us with enormous repertoires of potentially novel behaviors, and it is crucial to rule-governance. Rules established through natural verbal and instructional histories potentiate certain relations which allow behavior to be reinforced at times without its ever having been in direct contact with the relevant nonverbal contingencies. This point seems indeed to touch upon Skinner's original distinction between contingency-shaped and rule-governed behavior: instead of having to expose students directly to the contingencies, we can instead give them certain rules beforehand, often in the form of mands.

But this kind of simple rule-stating is critically different from the kind instruction to which Chase and Danforth referred in their paper. Instructional designers distinguished early between so-called RULEG and EGRUL programs: briefly, in RULEG programing, "RULes" are given first, and students then respond to sets of "EGsamples" and nonexamples until they can correctly identify which presentations meet the criteria specified by the rules, and which do not; conversely, in EGRUL programing, students are first required to respond to sets of "EGsamples" and nonexamples, and afterward to state the "RULes" which distinguish the given examples from nonexamples. In other words, in EGRUL instructional sequences, rules emerge as verbal responses by students describing their own behavior in contingencies set up explicitly by the instructional designer. To the extent that (a) their descriptions of the rules accord with those of the instructors, and (b) they behave appropriately with respect to those rules when faced with novel examples and nonexamples, we might then assume the students are indeed "following the rules" they have described (implicit here is that the rules will, in the future, function as covert mands).

It seems that then rules may enter discrimination and concept formation in various ways, but to some, the nagging question remains: do rules cause behavior, or does behavior cause rules? The resolution of these questions echoes Skinner's insistence that, for verbal behavior in general, the analysis of the speaker's behavior must be considered separately and distinctly from the analysis of the listener's behavior. A rule is, by definition, something a speaker emits -- verbal behavior of a speaker maintained by its predictable and contingent control over the listener's behavior. We might define rules as explicit statements of behavior --> consequence relations. Or, we might make the more general statement: a rule is a sentence specifying at least two terms of a contingency relation. Thus, a rule can simply specify the occasion and behavior, the behavior and its consequence, or the occasion and consequence, or it might describe all elements of the contingency. (Accordingly, a statement which specifies only one term of a contingency relation, then, cannot be a rule.) Given the growing area of research on stimulus equivalence, our general definition might be extended as well to rules stated in terms of more molar variables, e.g., the relation between one occasion and another, or between one behavior and another, or between one consequence and another, and so on, with whole equivalence classes of events treated as elements of "relational frames" (see S. Hayes, this volume). In any event, rule-governance is still related directly to contingency governance, with verbal contingencies taking perhaps a preeminent role; our general definition acknowledges this by requiring that rules be verbal behavior which specifies at least two contingency elements, and not simply behavior.

As noted, we assume that histories of both verbal and nonverbal contingencies of reinforcement are responsible for the establishment and maintenance of rule-governed behavior. To this extent, rule-governed behavior is little different from contingency-shaped behavior. This is perhaps most clearly evident in the difficulty we sometimes have differentiating rules from conditional discriminative stimuli, at least under certain boundary conditions. We know there is a difference between rules and other nonverbal kinds of controlling stimuli -- and that difference has to do with the verbal nature of rules -- but, short of endowing the modifier 'verbal' with any special properties, we are at times hard-pressed to say exactly how rules (as verbal stimuli) are in fact different from nonverbal conditional discriminative stimuli. A tentative solution to these problems would be to say that: (a) rule-governance occurs only on the first instance of any given class of rule-governed behavior -- thereafter, it becomes a more familiar form of conditional discriminative control; and (b) rule-governance is special, particularly in the sense that it allows organisms to behave from the outset in accord with contingency requirements they have never before encountered. Let us consider each of these two points separately.

Conditional Discrimination and Rule-Governance

From the outset, we must be able to make a critical distinction between, on the one hand, rule-governance, and on the other, even the most complex patterns of conditional stimulus control involving nonverbal stimuli. For example, pigeons in signal detection experiments can be described as emitting behavior in accord with various decision rules or strategies. Of course, their behavior is at first simply governed by direct exposure to the contingencies, and it is we who then describe their behavior as being "rational" or as following certain rules. Nevertheless, each such pattern of complex responding can be brought under conditional control of different colored lamps such that rational changes in response bias now occur immediately when an appropriate lamp is turned on (for example, see Hobson, 1978). Similar control may be established over so-called "matching," "optimizing," "maximizing," and other molar patterns of economically rational behavior by pigeons subjected to concurrent contingencies. These forms of conditional control resemble rule-governance, at least topographically, in the immediacy by which simple stimuli may come to control complex patterns of responding previously governed only by prolonged exposure to the relevant contingencies. Here we have several exquisite examples of instructional control (see Goldiamond, 1966) "telescoping" the effects of complex reinforcement histories into control by discrete event classes. But it seems fatuous to contend that pigeons in such experiments display true rule-governed behavior, i.e., that the pigeons actually "follow rules" (like "minimax," maximin," or "optimization") for responding rationally to the complex contingencies imposed on them.

In the first place, when we talk about "rules," we require these explicitly to be verbal stimuli. Further, we cannot discuss rules simply in terms of "behavior-output;" an effective rule requires a listener whose behavior is in fact controlled by it, i.e., evidence of rule-governance resides solely in the discriminative repertoire of a listener. In our pigeon examples above, we might consider the experimenter to be the "speaker," and pigeons the "audience" (by virtue of their "verbal" histories with respect to colored lamps and related experimental contingencies) in a cross-species verbal relation. Accordingly, might not the pilot lamps indeed be considered as rules of a sort? The concensus answer to the latter question is an emphatic "no." First and foremost, rules must be verbal stimuli, in a broader sense than are even the most complex sets of conditional discriminative stimuli established in the laboratory with nonhuman subjects. Also, behavior simply in accord with a rule is not the same as what commonly controls our use of the term, 'rule-governance' -- again, non-human organisms in such experimental arrangements certainly cannot generate rules as verbal stimuli, let alone follow them without highly specific training. Finally, if we consider all discrimination (conditional or other- wise) to be rule-governed, then this becomes the same analysis as is advanced by the cognitivists -- they might indeed argue that all discriminative behavior is rule-governed, and state that nonhuman animals create "representations" of the stimulus classes which underlie their discriminated behavior. But we have to ask the question: "What does that form of argument actually buy us in terms of its contribution to a science of behavior?" The answer is: "At best, it contributes very little, and, at worst, it buys us a costly diversion from more important questions."

Rule-Governance Occurs Only on "First Occasions"

Perhaps the most important and distinguishing attribute of rules pertains to the control they exert upon the first opportunity an organism has to behave toward a novel problem. This in fact may be the essence of our fascination with rule-governance as a distinct species of contingency control: an organism encounters an occasion it has never faced before, and by virtue of its verbal history with respect to such occasions in some general sense, it now behaves in accord with the specific requirements of a topographically novel relation. Of course, once it has emitted the initial rule-governed response and thereby meets the requirements of the novel contingency, the organism afterward comes to behave under typical discriminative control whenever it encounters topographically similar instances of the same relational class -- that is, it comes under typical contingency control of prevailing variables -- but its first such response may indeed be considered to have been governed by the verbal rule itself.

Indeed, perhaps our strongest allowable inference is that rule-governance over the listener's behavior, like metaphorical verbal behavior by a speaker, occurs only on the first instance of the organism's exposure to a novel contingency. This inference explicitly underlies our insistence that, for instructional sequences aimed at establishing general principles, abstractions, or concepts, the criterion tests must comprise wholly novel problems, ones which the organism has not encountered in identical form during its prior training. In other words, we readily acknowledge the lurking inferential pitfall -- that organisms often acquire large repertoires of topographically related but functionally distinct stimulus control topographies which we might easily mistake for more generalized abstractional or conceptual classes -- by requiring elaborate and explicit criterion tests on which to base our strongest inferences about rule-governance (see, for examples, Carter and Eckerman, 1975; Carter and Werner, 1978; Sidman, et al., 1982; cf. McIntyre, Cleary, and Thompson, 1987).

Accordingly, we can safely say that rule-governance simply brings the organism into direct contact with, and hence, under direct control of, a novel contingency upon first exposure to its requirements. It appears to do so in some cases by momentarily affecting the variability of the response topography itself, and in other cases, by momentarily affecting the variability of stimulus control over particular response topographies. (Harking back to our discussion about the establishing or potentiating effects of rules, we might thus say that rules make potent either a particular pattern of behavior, or a particular pattern of control over that behavior by new occasions or by new consequences on those occasions.) Rule-governance may in this sense represent the moment of transfer from historical control by one set of verbal relations to control by a new set of variables defining the current contingency requirements. Perhaps the most interesting question remains: by what means do rules exert this potentiating function?

Rule-Governance as an Outcome of Selected Patterns of Variability

Chase and Danforth reviewed a number of studies (by others) in which verbal instructions seemed to establish "rule-governed" behavior that was somehow "insensitive" to subsequent changes in the experimental contingencies. Typically in such studies, experimenters give their subjects instructions specifying exactly what patterns of behavior will meet some initial set of contingency requirements (usually, simple schedules of reinforcement), and then expose the subjects directly to those requirements (the given rule may take the form: "If you behave thusly, then the reinforcing consequence will occur," specifying both behavior and consequence, in accord with our general definition of the term, `rule'). Once their subjects have histories of meeting initial requirements by emitting the targeted pattern of behavior, the investigators then alter the "rule-for-reinforcement" (read: schedule of reinforcement), but without giving a corresponding change of verbal instructions, and the subjects continue to behave as they had before the contingencies were changed. Such results, as noted, suggests to some that verbal rules somehow "override" or are more potent than direct contact with contingencies in the control of behavior, at least for verbal organisms like humans. Nevertheless, these results might be better understood, i.e., explained without resort to any spurious special properties of verbal stimuli, in terms of variation and selection of occasion-behavior relations by contingencies of reinforcement. This latter position accords better with our radical behaviorist tradition than does imbuing verbal relations with any special properties, which takes us dangerously close to a more cognitivist tradition.

Viewed within a "selectionist" framework (see Donahoe, this volume), we might formulate our experimental questions about rule-governance considerably differently -- in more procedural terms. For example, we could take the following line of argument: (i) a contingency can select a particular form of behavior only after that species of behavior has been emitted in the first place, and so any procedure which *a priori* restricts responding to a narrow range of variants (i.e., one which excludes any particular form) ensures that an excluded form cannot be selected by subsequently changed contingency requirements; (ii) verbal instructions can affect the variability of responses emitted by our subjects, sometimes specifically restricting the range of behavioral variants available for selection; therefore (iii) restriction of response variability may be the basis for the observed resistence or insensitivity of rule-governed behavior to changes in prevailing contingencies. Conversely, we could argue that (i) some instructional procedures produce specific patterns of variability which may include certain targeted forms of stimulus control; and (ii) such procedures may be made the basis for successful extension of established patterns of stimulus control to new occasions, as instances of rule-governance.

We can then procedurally define, categorize, and count the occurrences of topo- graphic variants emitted by our subjects, and then directly assess the effects of certain verbal instructions on measured response variability. To the extent that, in most experiments demonstrating the apparent "insensitivity" of rule-governed behavior to changes in prevailing contingencies, investigators use the concordance of their subjects' molar response patterns with imposed schedules of reinforcement as the inferential basis for statements about rule-governance, then the strategy outlined above should indeed prove effective in assessing the role of underlying response variability. Nevertheless, we might alternatively argue that the implicit social/ historical contingencies which maintain adherence by human subjects to verbal instructions are, under some conditions, more potent than direct exposure to changed nonverbal contingencies; this in turn might lead us to design experiments analyzing exactly what social conditions make instructions relatively more potent, or exactly what forms of verbal instructions are supported by such potent social contingencies.

The picture gets a bit more complicated when we consider the effects of rules on variability not simply of behavior, but of occasion.behavior relations, or of occasion.occasion.behavior relations. As with behavior itself, stimulus control over behavior must occur a first time for its consequences to affect the probability of its recurrence. But inferences about the occurrence of specific stimulus control relations are often much more difficult to support than inferences about the occurrence or nonoccurrence of distinct forms of behavior. In some cases, for example, the simple visual illusions commonly found in introductory psychology textbooks, we can ascertain with reasonable confidence the stimulus control over students' alternative perceptions of an old hag or a young coquette, or of Freud's face or a reclining nude, in the same line drawings. But unless our students "show their work" when solving complex problems in calculus or symbolic logic, we are hard-pressed to tell whether their solutions are controlled by principles of calculus and logic, by chance, or by their neighbors' papers. Perceptions and conceptualizations, alike, are often private events, any inferences about which we may support only to the extent that we can specify the necessary (and sufficient) responses in- dicative of their occurrence. And difficult as this may sometimes be, it is often the easiest task before us, because we still have to account for the first occurrence of any such response we define (see Sidman, 1978, 1979, and 1980).

We can take our lead, at least in part, from experimentalists studying perception (who are in some respects much better at explaining stimulus control in perceptual behavior than we are at explaining rule-governance in conceptual behavior). Conflicting theoretical explanations abound in the early literature on "partial recognition" of visual forms, but tangible forward progress came when investigators shifted their emphasis from the response side of the relation to its procedural underpinnings, namely, from "partial recognition" to "partial presentations," and from categorical subject variables to consideration of the investigator's "scoresheet" (see, for example, Goldiamond, 1958; and 1964). Accordingly, we might ask to what extent our definitions of targeted relations and their respective indicator responses would allow us even to observe, let alone account for, patterns of stimulus control we may not have predicted when originally designing some of our experiments on rule-governance. Or we might explicitly study different training procedures which produce particular patterns of stimulus control with differing degrees of variability, and then assess how such variability affects the targeted relation under specific kinds of test conditions. Laboratory investigators in our own field have already applied similar strategies to analyze the "generalization gradients" for relatively simple discriminations established with pigeons by different methods (see, for early example, Jenkins and Harrison, 1960; and Terrace, 1963). Other workers, studying the occurrence of novel forms of behavior by pigeons and chimpanzees in situations often said to entail "insight" and "creativity," have explicitly tied their analyses to procedural sources of initial variability in their subjects' behavior (see Andronis, 1983; Birch, 1945; Epstein and Skinner, 1981; Epstein, Lanza, and Skinner, 1981; Epstein and Medalie, 1983; Epstein, Kirshnit, Lanza, and Rubin, 1984; and Schiller, 1957). Instructional designers as well have long used a similar approach to the generalization of conceptual behavior by students presented with various sets of examples and nonexamples. The laboratory analysis of rule-governed behavior might benefit from our taking a long, hard look back at the experimental logic underlying some of these earlier efforts.

Finally, to the extent that the formal logic of selectionist approaches encompasses both phylogenetic and ontogenic contingencies of selection, the study of variability in behavioral relations, especially with respect to stimulus control, might benefit from what evolutionary biologists have already learned about the role of variability in the evolution of complex organic forms by environmental selection. For example, when the genetic variation within an inter-breeding population of organisms is somehow greatly reduced, either by catastrophic environmental changes, or by the migration and subsequent reproductive isolation of a small subpopulation, minute variations in the genetic makeup of the few remaining members can exert a disproportionate effect on the evolution of the subsequent population (see Goodnight, 1987; and Mayr, 1963). Such so-called "founder events" almost certainly have their formal counter-parts in the establishment of rule-governance over operant behavior; this is indeed suggested by

234

the experimental work of Chase and Danforth, in which the initial training procedures reduce the overall variability of stimulus control over their subjects' behavior while increasing the variability of certain specific patterns being established as precursors to concept formation. Evolutionary biology may be able to provide us with yet other examples of formal relations which apply as well to the study of rule-governance and the contingency control of behavior.

References

Andronis, P. T. (1983). *"Symbolic aggression" by pigeons: Contingency coadduction.* Ph.D. dissertation, The University of Chicago.

Ayllon, T., and Azrin, N. H. (1966). *The token economy.* Englewood Cliffs, NJ: Prentice-Hall.

Birch, H. G. (1945). The relation of previous experience to insightful problem-solving. *Journal of Comparative Psychology, 38,* 367-383.

Blakely, E. and Schlinger, H. (1987). Rules: Function-altering contingency-specifying stimuli. *The Behavior Analyst, 10,* 183-187.

Brady, J. V. (196*). Potentiating operations. *Neurosciences Research Program Bulletin, 6(1),* 19-21

Carroll, L. (1871). *Through the looking-glass, (Alice's adventures in wonderland & Through the looking-glass).* London: The New English Library, 1960.

Carter D. E., and Eckerman, D. A. (1975). Symbolic matching by pigeons: Rate of learning complex discriminations predicted from simple discriminations. *Science, 187,* 662-664.

Carter, D. E., and Werner, T. J. (1978). Complex learning and information processing by pigeons: A critical analysis. *Journal of the Experimental Analysis of Behavior, 29,* 565- 601.

Chase, P. N., and Hyten, C. (1985). A historical and pedagogic note on establishing operations. *The Behavior Analyst, 8,* 121-122.

Epstein, R., and Skinner, B.F. (1981). The spontaneous use of memoranda by pigeons. *Behavior Analysis Letters, 1,* 241-246.

Epstein, R., Lanza, R. P., and Skinner, B. F. (1981). "Self-awareness" in the pigeon. *Science, 212,* 695-696.

Epstein, R., and Medalie, S. (1983). The spontaneous use of a tool by a pigeon. *Behavior Analysis Letters, 3,* 241-247.

Epstein, R., Kirshnit, C., Lanza, R. P., and Rubin, L. (1984). "Insight" in the pigeon: Antecedents and determinants of an intelligent performance. *Nature, 308,* 61-62.

Goldiamond, I. (1964). Response bias in perceptual communication. *Disorders of Communication, 42,* 334-363.

Goldiamond, I. (1966). Perception, language, and conceptualization rules. In B. Kleinmuntz (Ed.), *Problem solving* (pp. 183-224). NY: John Wiley & Sons.

Goldiamond, I. and Dyrud, J. E. (1968). Some applications and implications of behavioral analysis for psychotherapy. *Research in Psychotherapy, 3,* 54-89.

Goldiamond, I., and Hawkins, W. F. (1958). Vexierversuch: the log relationship between word-frequency and recognition obtained in the absence of stimulus words. *Journal of Experimental Psychology, 56,* 457-468.

Goodnight, C. J. (1987). On the effect of founder events on epistatic genetic variation. *Evolution, 41,* 80.

Hobson, S. L. (1978). Discriminability of fixed ratio schedules for pigeons: Effects of payoff values. *Journal of the Experimental Analysis of Behavior, 30,* 69-81.

Keller, F. S. and Schoenfeld, W. N. (1950). *Principles of psychology.* New York: Appleton Century Crofts.

Layng, T. V. J., and Andronis, P. T. (1984). Toward a functional analysis of delusional speech and hallucinatory behavior. *The Behavior Analyst, 7,* 139-156.

Mayr, E. (1963). *Animal species and evolution.* Camridge, UK: Belknap.

McIntyre, K. D., Cleary, J., and Thompson, T. (1987). Conditional relations by monkeys: Reflexivity, symmetry, and transitivity. *Journal of the Experimental Analysis of Behavior, 47,* 279-285.

Michael, J. (1982). Distinguishing between discriminative and motivational functions of stimuli. *Journal of the Experimental Analysis of Behavior, 37,* 149-155.

Schiller, P. H. (1957). Innate motor action as a basis of learning. In C. H. Schiller (Ed.), *Instinctive behavior: The development of a modern concept* (pp. 264-287). New York: International Universities Press.

Sidman, M. (1978). Remarks. *Behaviorism, 6,* 265-268.

Sidman, M. (1979). Remarks. *Behaviorism, 7,* 123-126.

Sidman, M. (1981). Remarks. *Behaviorism, 9,* 127-129.

Sidman, M., Rauzin, R., Lazar, R., Cunningham, S., Tailby, W., and Carrigan, P. (1982). A search for symmetry in the conditional discrimination of rhesus monkeys, baboons, and children. *Journal of the Experimental Analysis of Behavior, 37,* 23-44.

Skinner, B. F. (1957). *Verbal behavior.* Englewood Cliffs, NJ: Prentice-Hall.

Chapter 10

Private Events and Rule-Governed Behavior

Richard W. Malott and Maria Emma Malott[1]
Western Michigan University

In this chapter, we will discuss several metatheoretical issues of concern to behavior analysts, within the context of a theoretical analysis of rule-governed behavior. But first we will summarize that theoretical analysis. (For more details of this analysis of rule-governed behavior, see Malott 1984; 1986, May; 1989.) In this summary, we will consider the necessity of rule control in our civilized world and some of the inadequacies of that control. The metatheoretical issues raised by this analysis include: understanding as a goal of science, ultimate causes vs. links in a causal chain, action at a distance vs. proximal action, and private events as causes vs. private events as epiphenomena. These general, metatheoretical issues will entail the consideration of some specific psychological issues.

A THEORETICAL ANALYSIS OF RULE-GOVERNED BEHAVIOR
Problems of the Modern World

We have come so far from the natural world where the human species evolved that we no longer die of natural causes. Instead, we kill ourselves prematurely with nicotine, alcohol, automobiles, cholesterol, fats, refined sugar, salt, pollution, radiation, and lethargy (Ballentine, 1979; Haessler & Harris, 1980; Pritikin & Leonard, 1974; Pritikin & McGrady, 1979). And even though we die young, our teeth die even younger; but for the wonders of our modern civilization, our teeth would last as long as we do (Ballentine, 1979; McGuire, 1973).

We may still debate whether the quality of human life has improved over the millennia; and we may still debate whether we have solved more problems than we have created. But we cannot debate that prehistoric people did not have to cope with the Hostess Cup Cake Twinkie and its harmful side effects or many other harmful 20th-century innovations.

The Psychological Cause of the Problems:
Direct-Acting, Indirect-Acting, and Ineffective Contingencies

Here is why we think people are so susceptible to the problems of modern life:

1. People are led astray by many of the immediate rewards so common in our modern world (for instance, processed sugar, fat, salt, nicotine and alcohol).

2. People fail to deal with the problems of modern life (exercising, studying for a test, writing a chapter, etc.) because to do so is too immediately aversive, or too effortful, or too incompatible with obtaining more powerful immediate rewards. For instance, the immediate taste of sugar and the immediate effort of flossing our teeth cause us to eat Twinkies and cultivate peredontal problems.

3. People often act inappropriately or fail to act appropriately because the destructive effects of any single instance of doing the wrong thing (eating one bite of a Twinkie) or failing to do the right thing (one day of not exercising) are so small that they do not reinforce or punish the relevant behavior. Such consequences for a single action are small and of only cumulative significance.

4. The consequences of our actions are so improbable (an auto accident while not wearing our seat belt) that their reinforcing or punishing effects are short-lived, at best.

So sometimes small and only cumulatively significant consequences and improbable consequences are ineffective in controlling our behavior. At other times they may exert an indirect, though usually unreliable control. The indirect-acting contingencies[2] do not reinforce or punish the causal responses in those contingencies, yet somehow they can control the future occurrences of the causal response classes, that is, the responses that produced the small and cumulative consequences or the improbable consequence. This would be the case not only for contingencies that involve too small an effect to reinforce or punish a response (for example, the deleterious effects of a single spoon-full of ice cream), but also for contingencies where the probability of the outcome is too low to effectively reinforce or punish the causal response (for example, contingencies involving wearing safety gear).

There is also another type of contingency that does not involve the direct reinforcement or punishment of the causal response; but this type of contingency may also indirectly affect the future occurrence of the causal response class. This is the contingency involving an outcome that is too delayed to reinforce the causal response class (for example, a consequence like the well-cooked turkey that is the delayed outcome of preparing the bird and putting it in the oven some time before). Such contingencies usually exert reliable though indirect control over our actions.[3]

We believe it is rules that more directly control the causal responses, on those occasions when those non-reinforcing or non-punishing contingencies are effective.[4]

Ahmed, a Sudanese physician, reports a good example of a behaviorally ineffective contingency (Ahmed, 1975, cited in Harris, 1985, 133-135). For many years, Ahmed suffered greatly from an irritable-bowel syndrome resulting from lactose intolerance. The irritable bowel was the outcome of drinking milk. He had persisted in drinking milk because the outcome of the irritable bowel did not punish the act of milk drinking. We believe the outcome did not punish milk drinking because of the delay (one-half hour or more) between drinking the milk and the irritated bowel and possibly also because of the cumulative nature of the effect of continued milk drinking. Furthermore, Ahmed had been unaware of the contingency, we believe for the same reasons.

However, a medical examination demonstrated the contingency between drinking milk and the delayed outcome of the irritable bowel; and Ahmed stopped drinking the milk. Presumably he subsequently stated a rule, such as, "If I drink milk, I will have an irritable bowel;" and the rule statement caused him to stop drinking the milk.

Indirect-acting contingencies cannot by themselves control behavior; but rules describing those indirect-acting contingencies can sometimes control the causal behavior, though not always reliably. However, rules usually do reliably control the causal behavior in one type of indirect-acting contingency. Such contingencies are indirect-acting along only one dimension-- the dimension of delay: their outcomes are too delayed to directly reinforce or punish the causal response class. But their outcomes are of a significant magnitude and are highly probable. The contingency of the milk and irritable bowel may have been of that sort. Here is another example: "If you establish your IRA by April 15, it will count on this year's tax return;" the outcome is sizable and probable, though delayed.

However, rules describing other types of contingencies that are not direct acting often exert much less reliable control. "If you eat only 800 calories a day, you'll lose weight." "If you work two hours a day on your thesis, you'll get it done on time." Such rules seem to exert unreliable control of our actions when they describe one of two types of contingencies:

1. Contingencies involving low-probability outcomes, for example, "If you wear your seat belt, you may save your life" (the probablity of a serious accident is low).

2. Contingencies involving small outcomes of only cumulative significance. "If you keep on eating like that, you'll become obese." (Note that we suggest the rule exerts unreliable control because the immediate outcome is small, not because the sizable outcome specified in the rule is delayed.)

Let us consider one final type of rule--the rule describing direct-acting contingencies. This usually controls the causal responses with considerable reliability. "If you touch the stove, you'll burn yourself." "If you drink this, you'll be delighted." These are the sort of rules Skinner has generally analyzed (Skinner, 1969, for example p. 124 and 146).

But regardless of the type of contingency described, we believe rules usually control behavior, only when people effectively self-manage their own performance. This self- management probably involves several components:

1. The people must know useful rules. "Don't put off until tomorrow ..." "If you've got 'em, floss 'em." "Eat only nutritious food." "Early to bed ... " "Never speak in wrath."

2. At the time for action, they must state those rules to themselves.

3. Often they must monitor and evaluate their compliance with those rules.

4. They must generate aversive self-statements, thoughts, or feelings that they can escape only when they act in accord with those rules. Or they must present rewarding self-statements, thoughts, or possibly feelings only when they act in accord with those rules.

We believe some such self-management repertoire is needed for control by rules describing direct-acting contingencies as well as those describing indirect-acting contingencies. Incidently, we should note that, regardless of the nature of the contingency specified, a rule can control a person's behavior, though it specifies a contingency relationship the person has never experienced. "If you follow these directions, you will arrive at my house." This rule can control behavior, even though the person has never experienced the particular contingency before.[5]

How Behavior Analysts Can Be Part of the Solution

As we suggested before, human beings have created an environment full of non-direct-acting contingencies that affect our lives in critical ways. Rules specifying those contingencies sometimes cause us to act in optimal manners; but often those rules fail, especially when the outcomes are improbable or of only cumulative significance. (Prehistoric human beings might also have benefited by having their behavior under the control of some non-direct-acting contingencies, but the number of contingencies may have been much less. For example, they would not have had to deal with the Twinkie, the seat belt, or procrastination on writing a scholarly chapter.)

A major role of applied behavior analysts is to help people act in ways that will have long-range benefits for the actors and for humanity. Behavior analysts have traditionally conceptualized this task as primarily involving the arrangement of contingencies of reinforcement and punishment to directly control the behavior of the people involved. We agree that this is true for non-verbal people. But for verbal people, behavior analysts have usually arranged indirect-acting contingencies to involve probable and sizable, though delayed outcomes. Then they provide rules specifying those contingencies. In this way they substitute indirect-acting contingencies for behaviorally ineffective contingencies. (For a similar analysis, see Michael, 1986.)

To date, we have not developed an effective technology for helping people acquire a self-management repertoire that would allow their behavior to be reliably controlled by rules specifying contingencies with improbable and only cumulatively significant outcomes.

Summary of the Theoretical Analysis of Rule-Governed Behavior

We have suggested the following:

1. Contingencies of reinforcement and punishment must involve sizable, probable, immediate behavioral consequences.

2. Rules usually control behavior if they describe such contingencies.

3. Rules also usually control behavior if they describe contingencies that are not direct-acting solely because those contingencies involve a delayed behaviorally effective consequence. In other words, the behavioral consequence is probable and sizable.[6]

4. Rules often exert much less reliable control if they describe contingencies that are not effectively direct-acting either because they involve improbable behavioral consequences or small and only cumulatively significant outcomes. (See Figure 1 for a summary of some of these points.)

5. Regardless of the type of contingency described, rules usually control behavior, only when people effectively self-manage their own performance. This self-management entails stating rules, monitoring and evaluating compliance, and self-reinforcing and punishing or possibly automatically reinforcing and punishing compliance or non-compliance.

6. A major goal of applied behavior analysis is to help people act in ways that will maximize the beneficial outcomes and minimize the harmful outcomes of their actions, outcomes both for the individual actors and for humanity. Behavior analysts use two major approaches to accomplish this goal: (a) With non-verbal people, they add contingencies of reinforcement and punishment to directly control the behavior. (b) With verbal people, they usually add indirect-acting contingencies that involve delayed outcomes that are probable and sizable. Then they provide rules specifying those contingencies. In this way they supplement rules that do not reliably control behavior with rules that more reliably control.

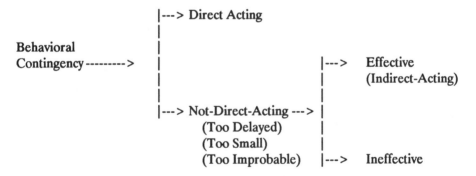

Figure 1. The relationships among key terms

In short, we see contingency management as a useful means of helping people achieve greater beneficial results in their lives by bringing their behavior more reliably under the control of rules specifying indirect-acting contingencies.

THE METATHEORETICAL ISSUES

This analysis of rule control involves several controversial metatheoretical considerations. Therefore, in this section, we will briefly summarize these metatheoretical issues and then consider them in more detail in the remainder of the chapter.

First, we assert that contingencies of reinforcement and punishment must involve immediate, behaviorally effective consequences. This is based on our understanding of the experimental literature and is also no doubt influenced by our view of the impossibility of action at a distance; much of our theoretical analysis is influenced by the notion that temporally distant events cannot cause later events.[7] This also raises the question of whether we can correctly speak of causes as being links in a causal chain or must restrict cause to the initial link in that chain. Our concern about action at a distance and delayed reinforcement also raises the question of the relevance of current animal research on self-control.

Our suspicion of the effectiveness of delayed behavioral consequences had this effect on our theoretical analysis: It caused us to propose that rule control is usually involved when a class of responses seems to be under the control of outcomes that are delayed, improbable, or of only cumulative significance. (For a somewhat similar implication, see Skinner, 1969, pp. 167-169.) In addition, that same suspicion caused us to propose that self-given or automatic, behaviorally effective consequences must support the rule's control over the response class it specifies.

An analysis of the supporting self-reinforcement or automatic reinforcement suggests to us that such support is often in the form of the reduction of private aversive stimulation (Malott, 1986b).

These issues in turn raise the metatheoretical question of whether private events can function as psychological causes or whether they are merely epiphenomena.

The possibility of action at a distance brings up the further possibility of the correlation-based law of effect as an explanation of instances where response classes are controlled by delayed outcomes and perhaps outcomes that are individually insignificant but acquire cumulative significance.[8]

We will begin our consideration of the metatheoretical issues with a discussion of whether understanding is an important goal of science or whether we should be satisfied with prediction and control. This interest in understanding causes us to be concerned with the links in the causal chains, to be concerned with proximal action, and to be interested in covert causes, even if our interest in those covert causes will not always improve our prediction and control.

Incidently, we address these metatheoretical issues, not to persuade those who hold alternative positions of the error of their positions and the correctness of ours, but instead to assure them that we have taken their positions seriously, and to provide the undecided with additional considerations. In general, we suspect the evidence for and against the various metatheoretical positions under consideration is sufficiently complex and indeterminate that the conclusion one makes will result as much from factors such as one's verbal community and one's prior investment in one position or another as from the logic of the particular arguments.

Understanding as a Goal of Science

For many radical behaviorists, a major aim or even *the* major aim of science is understanding or interpretation (Holland & Skinner, 1961; Killeen, 1987; Malott, 1986a, 1989; Moore, 1980; Schnaitter, 1978, 1981; Skinner, 1974). We interpret this to mean that science is a methodology for obtaining understanding, knowledge, or truth.

Prediction and Control

But it is hard to define empirical understanding, knowledge, or truth; so the logical positivists have operationalized "understanding." They imply that we understand a phenomenon, if we can predict the correlation between two variables. Here is an even more demanding criterion for understanding: We understand a phenomenon, if we can control the value of a related dependent variable when we do an experiment, in other words, if we can control that dependent variable by manipulating an independent variable. For example, "the rate of responding will decrease (value of the dependent variable), if you withhold the contingent outcome of that response (manipulation of the independent variable)." Thus we have Watson's famous pronouncement, "the aim of science is to predict and control" (Moore, 1975, p. 136). And contemporary, mainstream behaviorism, essentially methodological behaviorism, has adopted Watson's positivistic pronouncement. Defenders of Watson's view argue that "valid explanations" are those strictly based on prediction and control or at least that the primary goals of science are prediction and control (Hayes & Brownstein, 1986). Therefore, those advocating understanding as a major aim of science conflict with mainstream behaviorism.

The Value of Prediction and Control

There are two good reasons to evaluate the truth of scientific propositions in terms of prediction and control.

1. These evaluations are straight-forward; science has clear-cut methodologies for determining whether prediction and control really occurred in any given instance--both traditional statistical analysis and individual-case analysis are well developed methodologies.

2. The use of the criteria of prediction and control provides a good basis for the development of effective technologies (Killeen, 1987).

Problems with Prediction and Control

Unfortunately, we cannot always do the experiments needed to demonstrate control of a dependent variable by a manipulated independent variable. This limitation often occurs with field studies, especially historical ones, and with analyses of private psychological events. So we may chose to reject the strict criterion of prediction and control rather than reject those areas of study (Schnaitter, 1978; Killeen, 1987). We may conclude that to define truth and understanding solely in terms of prediction and control is carrying operationalism too far. For example, Skinner's radical behaviorism arose largely in opposition to this extreme positivistic influence of methodological behaviorism with its limitations on legitimate scientific inquiry (Lowe, 1983).

Scientists probably decrease their errors of commission, by insisting on the evaluation of all cause-effect relations in terms of the prediction of experimentally controlled results. But the price may be too high in terms of the cost of errors of omission of important cause-effect relations in our understanding of the world.

The Value of Understanding

We think the goal of science is to understand. And we think behavior analysts will inhabit a much more understandable universe, if they sometimes take a cautious step outside the constraints of prediction and control:

1. Even when we cannot predict and control, most of us are still interested in posthoc analyses of why things happened as they did, even though it is difficult to assess the truth of any particular explanation. Such analyses are intellectually satisfying.

2. Some of the most important theories in the history of science were not based on the prediction of experimentally controlled results--Copernicus' theory of heliocentric planetary movement and Darwin's theory of evolution by natural selection. And most of Skinner's theoretical work is not directly based on the prediction of experimentally controlled results (Malott, 1986a).

3. We may be better able to understand overt behavior if we infer covert behaviors as being causally related to the overt behavior, even if we cannot always predict and control those private behaviors. (See Killeen, 1987.)

Problems with Understanding and Their Partial Solutions

A major difficulty in accepting understanding as a goal of science comes from the implication of incorporating inferences or guesses as part of scientific knowledge (Schnaitter, 1978, 1981). But our confidence in an inferential explanation will increase to the extent that the explanation is in terms of basic scientific principles that have been directly verified by their utility in the prediction of experimentally controlled results (Schnaitter, 1978).

In Skinner's words, "As in other sciences, we often lack the information necessary for prediction and control and must be satisfied with interpretation, but our interpretations will have the support of the prediction and control which have been possible under other conditions" (Skinner, 1974, p. 176).

We will also be more impressed by posthoc analyses that account for large amounts of data, not just single events.

In summary, prediction and control may be shallow scientific goals if not used to support the ultimate scientific goal of understanding. Related to this, we will next suggest that behavior analysts need to describe all the links in a causal chain, not just the first and last links, if we are to understand complex behavioral processes.

Problems with the Concept of Causality

Ultimate Cause vs. a Link in the Causal Chain

Some argue that the analysis of causal chains is a fundamental aspect of the science of behavior (Killeen, 1984; Malott, 1980-81). Others, such as Hayes and Zettle (1980-81), who object to the term "cause" sometimes seem to use "cause" where we would use "ultimate cause." They do not want to call an event a cause if they can in turn find a cause for that event; in other words, if a cause has a cause then it is not a cause; they seem to imply that only the prime mover in a causal sequence can be called a cause. But of course, causal sequences are never ending. For instance, the cause of our feeling guilty when we fail to follow a good rule may be our Judeo-Christian upbringing. But the cause of that upbringing is our parents' upbringing, and their parents', and back unto Adam and Eve. Perhaps that is why some philosophers reject the concept of "cause"--they also equate "cause" with "ultimate cause" and recognize the problem of the infinite regression.

Some seem to suggest that we should deal only with those components of the causal chain that are far enough removed from the immediate action to give the impression that they are the terminal links. (But of course the notion of terminal link in a causal chain is illusory as the terminal link would pre-date Adam and Eve by a few years and possibly even predate the Big Bang.) This preference for more remote components of the causal chain is especially strong when the more immediate or more proximal components are either covert or involve the behavior of the organism.

Inferred Proximal Causes as Terminators of Investigation

We think that inferring a proximal cause in a causal sequence does not need to stop investigation prematurely, even if that inferred cause is a covert event, contrary to the suggestion of Hayes and Zettle (1980-81). In fact, we identify rule statements as the proximal cause of much of our behavior; but instead of closing the door to further inquiry, such an identification has, for us, simply opened the door a little wider and caused us to try to determine what is the necessary behavioral history for such rule statements to function as proximal causes.

Reasons for Dealing with Links in the Chain

For two reasons, we suggest we should deal with all components of the causal chain in analyzing rule control. The first reason is scientific and the second is technological.

The scientific reason. To support the ultimate scientific goal of understanding the entire process under analysis, we need to describe all the links in a causal chain, not just the first and last. This is in keeping with Skinner's argument that we should concern ourselves with private events for the sake of completeness of our analysis (Skinner, 1953, p. 258).

The practical reason. Technologically, we might better design various training programs if we specify the self-management behaviors they are to generate. And we can only specify those behaviors, if we bring them into our analysis, even though by themselves, they only constitute part of a response-response correlation--that is, self-management activities correlated with successful goal directed activities.

For example, it may be worthwhile to consider covert behavior in teaching "mental" arithmetic, in predicting the results of "mental" or covert arithmetic, and in teaching mnemonic techniques. True, we must ultimately start and end with external events; but that does not necessarily negate the role of private events. Perhaps private events are useful only if we can explain them in terms of public events; but that does not mean that those private events are, therefore, useless; nor does it mean that we should discard our references to private events just because they must ultimately be tied to public events.

Immediate Causes vs. Distant Causes

Many of us prefer to speak about immediate causes instead of distant ones (proximal causes rather than distal causes). We dislike action at a distance, either temporal distance or spatial distance. We want our causes and effects to be close to each other both in time and in space. We find it hard to conceive of effects not in some way physically connected to their causes. But not everyone agrees. For example, it is said that the scientist R. C. Davis and the philosopher J. R. Kantor used to argue about this issue. Kantor would claim that a corn on the toe of a rickshaw man in Singapore could directly affect the actions of the tamale seller in Bloomington, Indiana. Davis was skeptical of this action at a spatial distance.

Consider the following non-psychological example of action at a temporal distance: We can magnetize a bar of iron, and years later that bar will attract other pieces of iron. Now we might ask, how can that temporally distant act of magnetizing the bar affect its attracting action years later? Surely something about the structure of that bar must have changed and mediated the effects of the earlier magnetizing on the bar's later attracting action. We say this because we do not believe in action at a temporal distance. And, in fact, we may be comforted by the knowledge that the structure of the bar was indeed changed by its magnetization. But those who argue for action at a distance suggest that we do not need structural change in some part of the system that will mediate or "remember" the earlier event so that the earlier event can have a later effect. They suggest that our concern represents an unnecessary philosophical burden.

But this notion of spatial and temporal contiguity of cause and effect may not be so much a philosophical assumption as it is an empirical generalization. All the cause-effect relationships we know of seem to involve a close temporal and physical relation between the cause and the effect; therefore many of us are unwilling to be even agnostic about a proposal that some specific cause-effect relationship might involve a distant cause (i.e., action at a distance).

Besides the empirical argument, there is, however, a more philosophical issue: the notion of distant, physically-separated causes just does not seem plausible, though one can argue in support of their possibility, just as one could argue in support of the possibility of ghosts.

No doubt, our general reluctance to accept action at a temporal distance (distant causes) plays an important role in the question of whether distant (delayed) behaviorally-effective consequences can directly reinforce and punish the causal responses.

Are Delayed Behavioral Outcomes Really a Problem of Action at a Distance?

The reason delayed reinforcement and delayed punishment raise the problem of action at at distance may seem clear at first glance but obscure at second glance. So we would like to add a third glance. The first glance: Delayed reinforcement and delayed punishment clearly raise the problem of action at a distance because they clearly involve a cause (the response), an effect (the delivery of a reward or aversive stimulus), and a delay between the cause and the effect.

The second glance: However, things become a little less clear, when we ask just what are the *relevant* causes, effects, and delays. In answering this question, we want to avoid the teleological problem of having the cause come after the effect. So we say the response (for example, a pigeon's key peck) occurs as a cause, then a delay intervenes, and finally some effects result (for example, the occurrence of three seconds access to chick peas and corn and the proposed reinforcement of the response class of key pecks). That delay between the pigeon's key peck and the resultant access to the grain and the reinforcement raises the problem of action at a distance.

But the causal relation between the key peck and access to the grain does not really concern us, because we know the experimenter is the agent mediating the delay between response and outcome; the experimenter notes the occurrence of the peck and later delivers the food. Instead, what concerns us is whether this contingency, with its delay, might reinforce the response class of key pecks.[9]

Obviously the delay of concern cannot be the time between that reinforcing sequence of events and the next opportunity for the key peck to occur. Why not? Because the delay between reinforcement and the next opportunity for a key peck is not unique to delayed reinforcement. Somehow the problem must involve the delay between the individual peck and the resultant food delivery. And that problem must be one of distal causality, action at a distance.

Now the third glance: The proposed causal relation involving action at a temporal distance is that the key peck causes the delayed presentation of the grain to reinforce the response class of key pecks. But in what sense can the response cause the reinforcement of its own response class?

Consider the following hypothetical example: When the pigeon pushes a pedal with its foot, grain is delivered and reinforces the response class of pedal pushes. And when it pecks a key with its beak, the grain is delivered; but of course this time the grain reinforces the response class of key pecks. Thus the response preceding the delivery of food determines which response class will be reinforced; the preceding response, in that sense, causes the delivery of the food to reinforce one response class and not another.

So the problem of delayed reinforcement or punishment is: Can a response cause its outcome to reinforce or punish a particular response class when considerable time elapses between that response and its outcome? Based on our philosophical dislike for action at a distance, we would answer, no. Thus the problem of delayed reinforcement and delayed punishment does, indeed, seem to be a problem of action at a distance.[10]

Delayed Reinforcement and Delayed Punishment

From Watson to the present, the issue of delayed reinforcement and punishment has been under debate. Several behaviorists have argued that a stimulus does not have to immediately follow the response to reinforce or punish that response (Rachlin, 1974; Rachlin & Green, 1972;

Solnick, Kannenberg, Eckerman, & Waller, 1980). Others have argued that close temporal contiguity between response and the forthcoming stimulus is essential for that stimulus to control the response (Banks & Vogel-Sprott, 1965; Camp, Raymond, & Church, 1967; Cohen, 1968; Renner, 1966; Spence, 1947; Trenholme & Baron, 1975).

Spence (1947) suggested an alternative explanation to delayed reinforcement. He did not believe that learning occurs under conditions of delay of primary reinforcement but instead through contiguous presentations of conditioned reinforcers. Indeed most classical experiments on delayed reinforcement have struggled with the difficulty of controlling the influence of the conditioned reinforcers when studying the effects of delayed reinforcement (Williams, 1973, pp. 38-40). Williams (1973) reported Keesey's experiment conducted in 1964 as the study that most effectively controlled the influence of secondary reinforcers. And perhaps as a result, Keesey found little reinforcement after 5 second's delay. Considerable subsequent research has demonstrated an inverse relation between delay of reinforcement and rate of responding and a positive relation between delay of punishment and rate of responding (Camp, Raymond, & Church, 1967; Cohen, 1968; Renner, 1966; Trenholme & Baron, 1975).

In much contemporary research on the effects of delayed outcomes, the interest has shifted from the effects of a particular combination of time delay and outcome size to the concurrent effects of competing contingencies involving different combinations of time delays and outcome sizes. This is studied with concurrently presented chained schedules.

Wasserman and Moore (1986, May) reviewed research suggesting that it is the immediate outcome, not the delayed outcome that controls the behavior of animals in experimental settings. They cite Hineline's work showing that rats will press a bar that postpones an immediately forthcoming shock by 18 seconds. The rats respond, even though they receive one shock in every 20-second cycle, regardless of whether they respond. This suggests that a molecular analysis in terms of the immediate contingencies of reinforcement and punishment may be more appropriate than a molar analysis in terms of the correlation-based law of effect with its implication of the efficacy of delayed reinforcement and thus action at a distance.

Wasserman and Neunaber (1986) have also shown that humans will respond, if the response will produce a more immediate presentation of a conditioned reward (the turning on of a light associated with the presentation of points). The subjects respond, even when they receive the same number of conditioned rewards per unit of time, whether or not they respond. Wasserman got an analogous suppression effect with a conditioned aversive stimulus (a light associated with point loss). Again these studies suggest the importance of the immediacy of behaviorally-effective consequences even with verbal, rational, potentially rule-governed human beings; a molar analysis in terms of the correlation-based law of effect seems less useful.

Wasserman and Neunaber (1986) also cite work by Hineline as supporting the importance of the immediacy of behaviorally-effective consequences:

Hineline (1970, Experiment 1) investigated the reinforcing effect of shock delay. Rats were placed on a discrete-trial procedure in which a lever press within the first 8 s of a 20-s trial delayed shock onset from 8 s to 18 s into the trial. With three naive animals, lever pressing was quickly established under this schedule, the probability of a response rising from about .25 in the first session to between .75 and .95 by the 30th session. Responding increased even though there was no probabilistic relationship per 20-s interval between pressing and shock delivery (each 20-s trial entailed one shock, irrespective of lever pressing); nor was there a negative correlation between the rate of responding and the rate of shock delivery. (p. 30).

The Bait-Shy Phenomenon

Hayes and Myerson (1986, May) point out that, at times, the outcomes of the organism's actions are delayed and it would benefit that organism or the species if those outcomes did appropriately affect the causal response class. They offer the bait-shy phenomenon as an example of this. But Michael (1986, May) has suggested that the effects of taste aversion are a result of unique phylogenic programming and not a contradiction of the general need for close contiguity between response and behaviorally effective consequence. Whether the bait-shy phenomenon involves unique phylogenic programming or can ultimately be understood in terms of more typical behavioral principles, this phenomenon does not necessarily support the notion that the delayed delivery of behaviorally-effective consequences can normally affect the causal response class.[11]

A Skinner-Box Analog of Self-Management

Rachlin and Green (1972) designed and studied a fascinating, though complex, animal analog of self-management involving delayed outcomes. The analog has a great deal of convincing face validity. It is based on the every day observation, that we can chose the path of righteousness instead of the path of least resistance when we are temporally removed from the temptations that might lead us astray. For example, we will be more likely to start our rainy-day, payroll-deduction savings account when we are in the personnel office, not when we are in the pub on Friday evening with our pay check in hand, even if the personnel officer is standing next to us in the pub offering a payroll-deduction form and ballpoint pen.

Here is the analog described by Rachlin and Green (1972):

At the beginning of each trial (the initial link) both keys were transilluminated with a white light. Passage to the next link was governed by a fixed-ratio (FR) of 25 pecks, which could be distributed in any way on the two keys. If the twenty-fifth peck was on the right key...both keys and the houselights darkened (blackout) for T seconds. After the blackout, the houselights and both keys were automatically reilluminated, one key with red light and the other with green light...determined randomly. A single peck on the red key (CRF) produced 2 seconds of access to food, followed automatically by 6 seconds of blackout. A single peck on the green key produced 4 seconds of blackout, followed automatically by 4 seconds of access to food. ... If, during the initial link, the twenty-fifth peck was on the left key...there was a blackout for T seconds followed by the reillumination of only one of the keys (randomly determined at each trial) with green light. The other key remained dark. A single peck on the green key produced a 4-sec blackout followed by 4 sec of access to food. (p. 17).

When time T was short, most of the pigeons usually pecked the right key, ultimately receiving the smaller, more-immediate reward (2 seconds of food with no added delay). But when T was long, most usually pecked the left key, ultimately receiving the larger, less immediate reward (4 seconds of food with a 4-second added delay). Rachlin and Green concluded that they had demonstrated self-control in the pigeon.

A Critique of the Animal Analog. We view these results in the following manner: Consider their shortest T value, 0.5 seconds. And consider the total delay between the completion of the 25th response and the delivery of the reward. For the right key, the total delay could be 0.5 seconds. But for the left key, the total delay was 4.5 seconds. The difference between these two delays was 4 seconds, a large value in comparison to the total length of the total delay (4 / 4.5 = 89%). However, for their longest T value, 16 sec, the total delay was 16 seconds for the right key and 20 seconds for the left key. And although the difference between these values was still

4 sec, it was a much smaller value relative to the length of the total delay (4 / 20 = 20%).

From a Fechner's-law point of view, it seems reasonable that the effects of the delay would be less, when the percentage difference between the two delays was small (20%) than when it was large (89%). For an extreme example, a delay of 1 year will have the same effect as a delay of 1 year and 4 seconds; but a delay of 1 second might have a much different effect than a delay of 5 seconds, even though the difference between the two delays was four seconds in both cases.[12]

In the Rachlin and Green experiment, we would expect that the difference between the duration of the two rewards (4 sec - 2 sec = 2 sec) might be most important, when there was no difference between the two delays of reward delivery. And the difference between the two rewards might still be somewhat important, when there was a small percentage difference (20%) between the two delays. But the difference between the two rewards might be much less important, when there was a large percentage difference (89%) between the two delays. In other words, as the differential effects of the delays increased, the contrary effects of the size of the reward should decrease. Therefore it seems reasonable that Rachlin and Green's pigeons would usually peck on the key with the largest reward when there was relatively little difference in the total delay of the delivery of that reward--all things being equal or almost equal, the larger reward will usually exert more control over the response.[13]

So we might simply view the Rachlin and Green experiment as an extraordinarily complex example of a study of the competing effects of different reward parameters, such as relative quality vs. relative quantity or relative delay vs. relative quantity. And we are not surprised that as the relative difference between one pair of parameters decreases, the importance of another pair increases.[14]

Other experimenters have followed up the Rachlin and Green work with pigeon studies of the effects of the absolute and relative amounts of reward magnitude and delay duration. They have further demonstrated that the reward value of the alternatives is at least partially a function of the magnitude of the difference between those alternatives relative to the absolute value of those alternatives. The functions may, however, be somewhat more complex than would be predicted by a literal Fechnerian model (Green & Snyderman, 1980; Snyderman, 1983).

Even if we can account for Rachlin and Green's results by a common-sense Fechner's-law analysis, the question remains, is their procedure a reasonable analog to the sort of self-management or self-control procedures human beings use? We think not. Rachlin and Green offer as an example the worker who signs up for automatic deposit from payroll into a savings account. We think the outcome of the larger, though delayed reward (savings plus interest) is too delayed to reinforce the act of signing up; the delay will normally range from a few weeks, before the worker receives a bank statement showing the accumulated interest, to a few years, before the worker actually spends the accumulated interest. In view of the other animal work on delayed reinforcement, it seems unreasonable to assume that Rachlin and Green's pigeons would continue to peck either key if the delay were extended from 20 seconds to one week.

But this whole analysis is almost academic and boarders on teleology, when we consider that we may be talking about a new worker who has never established a savings account, let alone a payroll deduction program. We now have to account for his or her emission of this complex sequence of responses before the opportunity for it to have ever been reinforced, regardless of the delay.

We propose that, whether we are talking about an experienced saver or a novice, we can more readily understand the act of establishing a savings program as an act controlled by its immediate consequences, perhaps the termination of an aversive condition (feelings or thoughts accompanying non-compliance with a good rule or fear of an impoverished future) or by the presentation of a rewarding condition (thoughts of self righteousness).

In summary, we have considered a wide range of research examining the possibility of action at a distance (distant causes) in the form of delayed, behaviorally effective consequences. And none of these data seemed to us to point to the possibility of delayed reinforcement and delayed punishment, where that delay is significant. Thus we still see a need to find a more immediate cause for control exerted by delayed outcomes, and it seems plausible to us that rule statements act as motivating operations for an aversive condition that is escaped by compliance with the rule. (This raises the question of the causal status of private events, a question we address in the next section.) However, all these issues are sufficiently complex that we can anticipate contradictory interpretations and continued debate about the efficacy of delayed reinforcement and delayed punishment.

Causal Status of Private Events

What is the role of private events in our understanding of public events? Should private events be considered components in the causal chain? Some behaviorists argue that private events should not be considered causes of public events (Hayes & Brownstein, 1986; Rachlin, 1974). For instance, Hayes and Brownstein limit the identification of the causes of behavior to those that allow for prediction and control. They argue against explaining overt behavioral events in terms of covert behavioral events and describe such practice as mentalism.

However, other behaviorists point out that the inaccessibility of private events is not an argument that private events do not have direct control of behavior (Lowe, 1983; Killeen, 1984; Schnaitter, 1981, May; Malott, 1989). Still others suggest that this inaccessibility might be overcome with future technological advances (Skinner, 1953, p. 282). Behaviorists have also commented on Skinner's inconsistencies concerning the causality of private events (Malott, 1982, May; Schnaitter, 1981, May). They report that in some contexts, Skinner defines private events as behavior and suggests that they should be studied in terms of the same principles that govern public behavior. In other contexts, however, Skinner states that private events should not be considered causes of behavior. Todd and Morris (1985) say that such inconsistencies are only apparent, not real.

The inconsistencies of interpretation of Skinner's writings by some behaviorists may come from a confusion about Skinner's use of the words *"causality"* and *"control"*. Todd and Morris (1985) indicate that Skinner says that private events can control behavior even though those private events cannot be considered causes. In discussing private events, they say the following:

> In fact, they must control behavior in some way or they would be psychologically irrelevant. However, these inner events, which do *control* behavior, are not to be taken as the causes of behavior. . . Hence the terms "function" and "control" seem to be interchangeable with each other, but are not synonymous with the term 'cause'. (pp. 8-9).

Similarly, Moore (1980) indicates that private events do not cause public behavior. Instead the causes of behavior (covert and overt) must be found in the analysis of the controlling contingencies of reinforcement. He says the following:

> The covert behavior may exert some measure of discriminative control over the overt behavior, but this relation is not the causal relation with respect to subsequent, overt behavior. (p. 464).

But this distinction between cause and control seems a little too subtle to us. Thus we would still conclude that private events can cause public events.

Private Events as Causes or as Epiphenomena

We must agree that even the original radical behaviorist, Skinner himself, seems reluctant to assign a causal status to private events. We think this reluctance is a reaction to the misuse of private events as causal agents that has plagued so much of mentalistic psychological theory. Skinner generally assigns private events the status of epiphenomena; that is, they are off-shots of various psychological processes and are given labels such as feelings, emotions, images, and thoughts; but they usually do not play a causal role in Skinner's writing. So let us look at a particular series of private events to see if we might feasibly assign a causal status to some of them. But first consider a public series.

A Public Causal Chain. We use a pencil and paper and solve an arithmetic problem. Each number we write down serves as a cue for the next arithmetic operation that produces the next number and so on, until we arrive at our final answer. The numbers we wrote down were external events or stimuli, and thus even methodological behaviorists would probably accept them as cues (discriminative stimuli) that play a causal role in the stimulus-response chain.

A Private Causal Chain. Now consider mental arithmetic, where we solve a similar problem covertly, without the aid of pencil and paper, our fingers, or Japanese transistors. We suspect that much the same process is going on as before, except we have nothing but behavioral activities and events. We make a response (the covert statement of a number resulting from one arithmetic operation); and the covert stimuli arising from that covert response function as a covert cue for our next response. The same analysis still applies, even if we had trouble with Math 100 and must say the numbers out loud.

It may be hard for most of us to imagine that anyone would suggest that response-produced stimuli cannot function as cues, even when those stimuli are covert, as with the proprioceptive stimuli involved in the feedback loops that govern well-executed motor skills. But many or perhaps most main-stream behaviorists, especially methodological behaviorists, object to the feasibility of private events functioning as behaviorally effective consequences.

Private Events as Behaviorally Effective Consequences: The Epistemological Status of Private Causes

One might well ask what is the status of explanatory concepts referring to private causes, concepts such as *covert arithmetic*? Are they explanatory fictions? Only if someone else proposes them; we call ours explanatory concepts. Are they intervening variables? We do not think of such concepts as intervening variables because we assume that they really do exist, that they are more than a convenient imaginary i of the mind. Then are they hypothetical constructs? Not exactly, because the nature of most hypothetical constructs in psychology connotes a causal variable on a completely different level of analysis, for example a mentalistic or physiological level when explaining effects on a behavioral level. We are only extrapolating from the overt behavioral level to the covert behavioral level; we are only saying that the same types of stimuli, responses, and laws operate on the covert level as on the overt level and that causes on the overt level can have effects on the covert level and visa versa.

Summary and Conclusions

We have presented the following theoretical and metatheoretical position:

1. The goal of science is understanding.
2. Understanding a phenomenon involves knowing its causes.
3. Knowing these causes often means knowing the causal chain resulting in the phenomenon and not just a distal event in that chain.

4. It is important to know the intermediate and proximal links in a causal chain, because action at a distance does not seem plausible.

5. This means we must find the behaviorally effective consequences *immediately* following a response if we are to understand the causes of that response. The concepts of delayed reinforcement and correlation-based reinforcement seem misleading.

6. For human behavior where the natural consequences are too delayed or too improbable or too small and of only cumulative significance, we infer that the behavior must be under the indirect control of rules, usually rules describing the relevant contingency.

7. But such rules will not even indirectly control behavior without effective behavioral consequences.

8. So we infer that control by such rules is supported by some sort of self-given or automatic reinforcement or punishment, often reinforcement by the termination of an aversive condition initiated by the statement of the rule.

References

Ballentine, R. (1979). *Diet and nutrition.* Honesdale, Pennsylvania: Himalayan International Institute.

Banks, R. K. & Vogel-Sprott, M. (1965). Effect of delayed punishment on an immediately rewarded response in humans. *Journal of Experimental Psychology, 70,* 357-359.

Baum, W. M. (1973). The correlation-based law of effect. *Journal of the Experimental Analysis of Behavior, 20,* 137-153.

Camp, D. S., Raymond, G. A., & Church, R. M. (1967). Temporal relationship between response and punishment. *Journal of Experimental Psychology, 74,* 114-123.

Cohen, P. S. (1968). Punishment: The interactive effects of delay and intensity of shock. *Journal of Experimental Analysis of Behavior, 11,* 789-799.

Gollub L. (1977). Conditioned reinforcement: Schedule effects. In W. K. Honig & J. E. R. Staddon (Eds.), *Handbook of operant behavior* (pp. 288-312). Englewood Cliffs, NJ: Prentice-Hall.

Green, L. & Snyderman, M. (1980). Choice between rewards differing in amount and delay: Toward a choice model of self control. *Journal of Experimental Analysis of Behavior, 34,* 135-147.

Fantino, E. & Logan, C. A. (1979). *The experimental analysis of behavior.* San Francisco, CA: W. H. Freeman.

Haessler, H. & Harris, R. (1980). *Bodyworkbook.* New York: Avon Books.

Harris, M. (1985). *Good to eat: Riddles of food and culture.* New York: Simon and Schuster.

Hayes, S. C. & Myerson, J. (1986, May). *Time, specificity, rules, delays, and causes.* Paper presented at the Association for Behavior Analysis annual convention, Milwaukee, WI.

Hayes, S. C. & Brownstein, J. A. (1986). Mentalism, behavior-behavior relationships and the purpose of science. *The Behavior Analyst, 7,* 175-190.

Hayes, S. C. & Brownstein, J. A. (1986, May). *The slippery slope of non-manipulable causes.* In P.A. Lamal (Chair), Radical Behaviorism and the Inside Story. Symposium conducted at the meeting of the Association for Behavior Analysis, Milwaukee, WI.

Hayes, S. C. & Zettle, R. D. (1980-81). Behavioral causes and self-reinforcement revisited: A re-reply to Malott. *Notes from a Radical Behaviorist, 2, Issue 26.* (Available from Department of Psychology, Western Michigan University, Kalamazoo, MI 49009)

Holland, J. G., & Skinner, B. F. (1961). *The analysis of behavior.* New York: McGraw Hill.

Killeen, P. R. (1984). Emergent behaviorism. *Behaviorism, 12,* 25-39.

Killeen, P. R. (1987). Radical behaviorism under the microscope: Clarity gained, depth of field lost. In S. Modgil & C. Modgil (Eds.), *B. F. Skinner: Consensus and controversy.* (pp. 236-238). Barcomb, U. K.: Falmer Press.

Lowe, F. C. (1983). Radical behaviorism and human psychology. In G. C. L. Davey (Ed.), *Animal models and human behaviour* (pp. 71-93). Chichester, U. K.: Wiley.

Malott, R. W. (1980-81). Self-reinforcement, ultimate causes, and Skinner's analysis. *Notes from a Radical Behaviorist, 2, Issue 26.* (Available from Department of Psychology, Western Michigan University, Kalamazoo, MI 49009)

Malott, R. W. (1982, May). *Skinner on issues relevant to rule-governed behavior.* In M. E. Vaughan (Chair). On rule-governed behavior. Symposium conducted at the meeting of the Association for Behavior Analysis annual convention, Milwaukee, WI.

Malott, R. W. (1984). In search for human perfectibility: An approach to higher education. In W. L. Heward, T. E. Heron, D. S. Hill, & J. Trap-Porter (Eds.), *Focus on behavior analysis in education* (pp. 218-245). Columbus, OH: Bell & Howell.

Malott, R. W. (1986, May). *A "new" diagram for the theoretical analysis of behavioral contingencies.* Paper presented at the meeting of the Association for Behavior Analysis annual convention; Milwaukee, WI.

Malott, R. W. (1986a). Experimentation in behavioral psychology: The flight to the laboratory. In A. Poling & R. W. Fuqua, (Eds.), *Research methods in applied behavior analysis: Issues and advances* (pp. 1-6). New York: Plenum Press.

Malott, R. W. (1986b). Self-management, rule-governed behavior, and everyday life. H. W. Reese & L. J. Parrott (Eds.), *Behavioral science: Philosophical, methodological, and empirical advances* (pp. 207-228). Hillsdale, NJ: Erlbaum.

Malott, R. W. (1989). The achievement of evasive goals: Control by rules describing indirect-acting contingencies. In S. C. Hayes (Ed.), *Rule-governed behavior: Cognition, contingencies, and instructional control.* (pp. 269-322). New York: Plenum.

Malott R. W., Tillema, M., & Glenn, S. (1978). *Behavior analysis and behavior modification: An introduction.* Kalamazoo, MI: Behaviordelia.

Michael, J. (1986). Repertoire-altering effects of remote contingencies. *Analysis of Verbal Behavior, 4,* 10-18.

Michael, J. (1986, May). *Principles of behavior analysis.* In Newcomer's Series. Symposium conducted at the meeting of the Association for Behavior Analysis annual convention, Milwaukee, WI.

Moore, J. (1975). On the principle of operationism in a science of behavior. *Behaviorism, 3,* 120-138.

Moore, J. (1980). On behaviorism and private events. *The Psychological Record, 30,* 459-475

McGuire, T. (1973). *The tooth trip.* New York: Random House.

Pritikin, N. & Leonard, J. N. (1974). *Live longer now.* New York: Grosser & Dunlap.

Pritikin, N. & McGrady, P. M. (1979). *The Pritikin program for diet and exercise.* New York: Grosset & Dunlap.

Rachlin, H. (1974). Self-control. *Behaviorism, 2,* 94-107.

Rachlin, H. & Green, L. (1972). Commitment, choice and self-control. *Journal of Experiential Analysis of Behavior, 17,* 15-22.

Renner, K. E. (1966). Temporal integration: Relative value of rewards and punishments as a function of their temporal distance from the response. *Journal of Experimental Psychology, 71,* 902- 907.

Schnaitter, R. (1978). Private causes. *Behaviorism, 6,* 1-12.

Schnaitter, R. (1981, May). *Radical behaviorism: Analysis of private events.* In H. W. Reese

(Chair). Alternative Approaches to Mental Phenomena. Symposium conducted at the meeting of the Association for Behavioral Analysis annual convention, Milwaukee, WI.

Skinner, B. F. (1953). *Science and human behavior* (1st ed.). New York: Macmillan.

Skinner, B. F. (1969). *Contingencies of reinforcement.* Englewood Cliffs, NJ: Prentice-Hall.

Skinner, B. F. (1974). *About behaviorism.* New York: Knopf.

Snyderman, M. (1983). Delay and amount of reward in a concurrent chain. *Journal of Experimental Analysis of Behavior, 39,* 437-447.

Solnick, J. V., Kannenberg, C. H., Eckerman D. A., & Waller, M. B. (1980). *Learning and Motivation, 11,* 61-67.

Spence, K. W. (1947). The role of secondary reinforcement in delayed reward learning. *The Psychological Review, 54,* 1-8.

Todd, J. T. & Morris, E. K. (1985). *An analysis of some apparent inconsistencies in Skinner's private events concept.* Paper presented at the meeting of the Association for Behavior Analysis annual convention, Columbus, OH.

Trenholme, I. A. & Baron, A. (1975). Immediate and delayed punishment of human behavior by loss of reinforcement. *Learning and Motivation, 6,* 62-79.

Williams, J. L. (1973). *Operant learning.* Monterey, CA: Brooks/Cole.

Wasserman, E. A. & Moore, J. (1986, May). *Some comments on the temporal law of effect.* Paper presented at the Association for Behavior Analysis annual convention, Milwaukee, WI.

Wasserman, E. A. & Neunaber, D. J. (1986). College student's responding to and rating of contingency relations: The role of temporal contiguity. *Journal of Experimental Analysis of Behavior, 46,* 15-35.

Footnotes

1. We would like to thank Steven Hayes for calling to our attention many of the metatheoretical issues we are considering in this chapter. And we would like to thank Jack Michael for his helpful review of this manuscript.

2. A *behavioral contingency* consists of a response, a consequence, and a stimulus condition in the presence of which that response will produce that consequence (Skinner, 1969, p. 7).

3. A *direct-acting contingency* reinforces or punishes the causal response. An *indirect-acting contingency* controls the causal response, but not by reinforcement or punishment of that response by the outcome in that contingency. Such a contingency does not effectively act directly because the outcome is too delayed, too small, or too improbable. A *behaviorally ineffective contingency* does not control the causal response.

4. A rule is a verbal statement that describes a behavioral contingency, that is a response, an outcome, and the relevant stimulus conditions (Malott, Tillema, & Glenn, 1978, p. 123).

5. In considering these issues, behavior analysts often discuss contingencies involving outcomes that have not yet occurred for the individual, for example the outcome of finishing a thesis. And they often talk as if those outcomes were controlling or failing to control the causal response classes, for example, the response class of working two hours per day on the thesis. We should avoid this teleological error of implying that an event in the future is causing a current event.

Note that working on a thesis is an unusual response class. This is clearly not a natural response class; and it is not a response class defined by the long-range outcome of thesis completion, as that outcome has not yet happened.

6. We use *behaviorally effective consequence* as the generic term encompassing rewards and aversive stimuli. We use outcome as the generic term encompassing both behaviorally effective

consequences and response-produced events that do not function as behaviorally effective consequences, often because any individual instance is too small and of only cumulative significance.

7. *Action at a distance* refers to the notion that one event separated in time or space from another event can affect or cause that other event. To the contrary, we assume there must be causal links connecting the two events across time and space.

8. The *correlation-based law of effect* states that the molar relation between response and reinforcement is responsible for instrumental behavior and that simple response-reinforcement contiguity is neither sufficient nor necessary (Baum, 1973).

9. Because we want to avoid the problem of teleology, we cannot say the outcome reinforced or punished the specific casual response, for example the specific key peck that produced the food 30 seconds later. Instead, the whole sequence of events reinforced the response class of key pecks, making future key pecks more likely to occur.

10. We might be able to circumvent the problem of action at a distance by hypothesizing that the response produces a change in the organism and that change in turn causes the outcome to reinforce or punish the relevant response class. But many behavior analysts seem reluctant to invent such a hypothetical construct.

11. The bait-shy phenomenon (also called taste-aversion learning) consists of the avoidance of nonpalatable or toxic ingestibles with which the animal has had previous contact (Fantino & Logan, 1979).

12. A generalized version of Fechner's law might be something like this: The psychological effect of a change in the value of an independent variable is a function of the magnitude of that change relative to the original value of that independent variable.

13. For the sake of simplicity, this analysis assumes the pigeons always pecked the red key at the end of the chain on the right key, as if there were no green key after the right-key chain. It also ignores the time taken to peck the colored key. More exact assumptions would not affect our conclusions.

14. In viewing these results, we should keep in mind that the maximum delay Rachlin and Green dealt with was 20 seconds and that this 20 second delay was unique in that it contained a stimulus change (colored key light) that might well have been a conditioned reward; many have suggested that such conditioned rewards account for the apparent effectiveness of delayed reinforcement (for example, Wasserman & Moore, 1986, May). Their delay also involved a blackout during which pigeons tend to roost; and others have suggested that if the animal is unconscious during the delay, the deleterious effect of the delay will be considerably less (for example, Spence, 1947; Hayes & Myerson, 1986, May); or at the least such a condition might decrease the likelihood that competing intervening responses would be reinforced. It might be interesting to see what sort of results would be obtained using the Rachlin and Green procedure with a time delay that does not encourage the pigeons to roost or with a non-verbal species that does not roost during blackout.

A Discussion of Chapter 10

A Second Look at the Relation Between Delayed Consequences and Rule-Following

Jan LeFrancois
Converse College
Helga Guckel
German Behavior Academy

Malott and Malott present an account of the maintenance of rule-following in the face of ineffective contingencies, specifically those involving delayed consequences. As pointed out in the paper, the central problem with delayed reinforcement is the seeming impossibility of action of reinforcement at a distance. A summary of some of the participants' comments follows.

Participant Comments

Newton was concerned with this problem, stating that gravity was mediated by something. There has always been this concern in physics. For example, ether was used to explain electromagnetic radiation. Also, a large area of physics is concerned with a vacuum which controls everything. But, it is difficult to generate behavioral mechanisms which mediate between current and later events. In other areas, for example nutrition, if you increase food intake, you gain weight. We could develop a functional analysis of diet and weight gain. If you eat today and don't see weight gain immediately, we would look inside the body to explain it. You can't explain it at the same level of analysis. There's no issue here, it's just another field of investigation.

Construing a question as action at a distance obscures the contribution of behavior analysis to this issue. Skinner said looking at rate of response as a datum was a major feature that made his version of psychology unique. This implies an environment that is spread out over time. We think we know what contiguity is but if you took the empty space from the earth, you would have an object the size of a grapefruit. The notion of continuous doesn't have much to do with push-pull. Further, there are different behavioral processes simultaneously going on at different time scales that are all here, all at once.

Skinner asserts the importance of contiguity of consequences. Yet, he is in contradiction with what he showed us in 1931 and 1932, about a reflex not having to be a continuous relation. Behavior analytic theory is interesting only if we look at behavior and environment spread out over time, and the processes occurring over time. To start construing it as what happens at time zero until time x loses what is interesting in the account.

We need to distinguish between philosophical problems and empirical ones. There is a basic tradition of mechanism in which we can't get away from one event being connected to the next event. Alternatively, an act may be seen in a context - and the units of analysis can expand or contract as necessary to get the analytic job done. The perspective of what's true and false changes. Mechanism doesn't add anything. What is gained? And we might lose. Mechanism led to cognitive psychology. We have other things to contribute.

To fill in the gap with mediators is a pragmatic approach. Do these mediators lead to something else? other research? If so, they are pragmatically real.

First, Malott and Malott are not advocating response - mediators - outcome. A rule produces a motivating aversive condition which leads to a response as designated by the rule. This does not bridge the gap to the outcome. If a delayed outcome has an effect, it might occur as a result of your stating the rule again. Second, consideration of private events does not hinder research, it leads to more research, for example, why do some follow rules more than others?

Why is delayed reinforcement important? Once a temporal delay occurs between the response and the reinforcer, the other events that occur immediately after the response are many so we need something to overcome their effect and tie together the response and delayed consequence. Private events do that.

Some Additional Thoughts

In general, there was agreement that action at a distance, that is, a delayed consequence controlling responses, without qualification is unacceptable. Malott and Malott's position is that of a causal chain, wherein an event has an immediate effect, and this effect in turn has an immediate effect. Hence, behavior only appears to be controlled by delayed consequences. In actual fact, behavior is always controlled by an immediate consequence. They propose that the inapparent immediate consequence of following a rule is a private event, such as the termination of guilty feelings. For example, one does not exercise because one will live longer -- a delayed consequence -- rather, one exercises because doing so terminates feelings of guilt. Certainly, most would agree that this is possible. However, other aspects of their position must be questioned.

First, the conceptualization of causality as a temporal sequence of events implies a single contiguous cause. This might lead to an over reliance on one variable, such as private events, for the explanation of rule following, to the neglect of other important environmental variables. Skinner (1957) and Kantor (1970) have argued for multiple and simultaneous causes for an event. Rule following might not only be controlled by private events but also by one's verbal history, one's history of reinforcement for following rules and one's history of punishment for failing to follow rules. Through these various histories, conditioned emotional responses may have been established to rules. Malott and Malott's suggestion that rule following terminates feelings of guilt would fall into the latter category. In addition, there might be models or instructions for rule following, as well as social reinforcement when following the rule in this instance. There may be other participants as well.

Second, the possible determinants of private events are addressed inadequately. Presumably, these events result in part from a history of behavior-environment interactions, such as imitation or generalization of statements made by others. Malott and Malott suggest that the private event is an aversive event produced by the statement of the rule. Again, this seems possible but not comprehensive. Depending on one's history, a rule might generate an aversive condition, an appetitive condition or some other condition including no condition. It is conceivable, for example, that a youngster is praised when following an instruction. After repeated instances of this, an instruction or rule probably will generate appetitive private events.

Third, the effectiveness of the delayed consequence should be reconsidered. Whereas Malott and Malott suggest that delayed consequences are ineffective in the control of behavior, in fact delayed reinforcers do maintain some responding (e.g. Sizemore & Lattal, 1977; Skinner, 1938). Even though the delay durations in these studies are very brief and may not approximate those in everyday life, it is hasty to conclude that delayed consequences are ineffective. After all, the formation of the rule which specifies a delayed consequence was controlled, in part, by the contingency involving the delayed consequence. Malott and Malott present the example of Ahmed, the Sudanese physician with the irritable-bowel syndrome. A medical examination by another physician provided him with the rule "If I drink milk, I will have an irritable bowel." The physician who provided this rule was tacting the response and the delayed consequence. Presumably his verbalization was controlled by this delayed contingency. Thus, when a rule which specifies a delayed consequence controls behavior, the role of the delayed consequence should not be excluded from the analysis.

Finally, a general concern about Malott and Malott's chapter is the danger involved in speculating about private events. Currently, there is no way to publicly verify, measure or manipulate private events. In the event that the technology to unobtrusively measure private events comes about, Malott and Malott's paper stands to contribute to the study of private events and rule-governed behavior. At present, however, the value of speculation is unclear. The danger of speculation is that more time may be spent verbalizing about the unmeasurable events than is spent studying other, possibly more fruitful behavior-environment relations.

References

Kantor, J. R. (1970). An analysis of the experimental analysis of behavior. *Journal of the Experimental Analysis of Behavior, 13,* 101-108.

Sizemore, O. J. & Lattal, K. A. (1977). Dependency, temporal contiguity, and response-independent reinforcement. *Journal of the Experimental Analysis of Behavior, 27,* 119-125.

Skinner, B. F. (1938). *The behavior of organisms.* New York: Appelton-Century-Crofts.

Skinner, B. F. (1957). *Verbal behavior.* Englewood Cliffs, New Jersey: Prentice-Hall.

Part 5

Related Topics

Chapter 11

A Behavioral Interpretation of Memory

David C. Palmer
University of Massachusetts

The goal of this paper is to provide a behavioral interpretation -- or at least the outline of an interpretation -- of those phenomena for which the term memory is commonly invoked. Memory is typically studied as a discrete and unitary subject matter. Memory is seen as a capacity, and memories often serve as independent variables explaining subsequent behavior. "Memory" is not currently a technical term in behavior analysis, nor, I suggest, need it ever be one. I hope to show that the phenomena currently studied in academic programs in the "field of memory" are not theoretically coherent from a behavioral perspective. There are at least two broad classes of phenomena covered by the term, as it is commonly used, and the failure to distinguish them has seriously confused research in the field. Not only is memory not a coherent concept, it is not even a helpful one, as it usurps the role of explanation and impedes the search for controlling variables for current behavior.

Before discussing these points I want to make explicit some of the assumptions underlying my analysis and to clarify certain terms.

Interpretation Versus Experimental Analysis

The interpretation of complex phenomena in the light of empirically established principles lies in the middle ground between experimental analysis and mere speculation. Speculation is unconstrained, while interpretation is constrained by experimental analyses. Interpretation is useful in circumstances too complex or too vast to control experimentally, but where informal or incomplete data are available. Interpretation has served, and continues to serve, an honorable role in science, so honorable that we often fail to distinguish between an interpretation and an experimental analysis. Newton's explanation of ocean tides is an interpretation based on his experimental analysis of phenomena such as the motion of pendulums and colliding balls of wool, glass and cork. No one, least of all, Newton, has attempted to establish experimental control over the tides. Yet Newton's principles (to a reasonable approximation) are so firmly established and the extrapolation to this phenomenon so plausible, that we accept his interpretation as if it were the direct outcome of an experimental analysis. Interpretation clearly serves an important purpose. We should not like to wait for an experimental analysis of the genesis of planets, the shifting of continental plates, the evolution of *Homo sapiens,* -- or the behavior of solving a problem, writing a letter, or recalling an episode from our childhood. Interpretation is often the best we can do in an imperfectly known and exceedingly complex world. Indeed, when we consider the scope of experimental analysis and interpretation, we might regard the former as merely a procedure for giving us the tools to engage in effective interpretation.

Interpretation serves an especially important role in accounting for human behavior since contingencies are typically complex, reinforcement histories unknown, and effective experimentation seldom possible for ethical reasons. These limitations are not peculiar to a behavioristic approach but constrain any experimental analysis of human behavior. Indeed, behavioristic interpretations have the advantage of a foundation of well established principles developed from a vigorous basic science, and may thus be especially well suited to account for complex human behavior.

The interpretation of phenomena such as memory and verbal behavior can proceed well in advance of an experimental analysis. This serves the purpose of establishing the domain of the science, of identifying important experimental questions (the role usually assigned to theory), and of addressing popular interest in these areas. An appeal for interpretation is not an invitation to mentalistic analyses. The terms and principles adduced in a behavioral interpretation are derived from the experimental analysis of behavior and must be consistent with that analysis. I suspect that these principles are fully adequate, but, even if they are not, an interpretation is an inappropriate place to introduce new ones.

What is Behavior?

It is important to identify the unit of analysis in any scientific endeavor, but it is especially important in a domain with a rich prescientific vocabulary. I adhere to Skinner's position, first outlined in 1935, that the units of analysis in behavior are to be defined empirically, not *a priori*, or according to common usage. Specifically, environmental and behavioral units are to be defined according to the orderliness of the relationship between them. If the orderliness of our data is a function of the specificity of our definition of behavior and its controlling variables there is an inflection point, presumably falling short of complete specificity, at which our data are most orderly. It is this inflection point which determines the classes of responses and stimuli which serve as our units.

Behavior is any activity of an organism that can enter into these orderly relations. The subject matter of a behavioral analysis is not to be defined in terms of observability or locus but in terms of sensitivity to contingencies of reinforcement, generalization, discrimination and so on. Thus, a private event falls under the purview of a behavioral analysis provided that it is sensitive to reinforcement contingencies; it need not be peripheral or skeletal or motor. Of course, we cannot make reinforcement contingent on events that are unobservable to us, and we therefore cannot demonstrate the order necessary to establish units of private behavior, but this only reduces the scope of experimentation; it does not reduce the number of events that are in fact affected by temporal contiguity to an effective reinforcer.

Behavior lies on a continuum of observability, but where it lies on this continuum depends upon characteristics of the observer or of his tools of measurement; it is not an essential or intrinsic property of the response. Private behavior is simply unobserved behavior, not unobservable behavior. A private event, then, is one that lies below the threshold of observability for a particular observer using particular tools. To a myopic experimenter observing his subject through half- silvered glass certain behavior would be private that would be public for a second experimenter under more favorable conditions, and this second observer would be unable to detect responses monitored by an EMG device in the service of a third experimenter.

It is necessarily the case that under normal conditions a portion of the behavior of an organism will be private in this sense, but this private behavior raises no special theoretical or epistemological problems, however troublesome it may be from a practical or experimental point of view. However, when we appeal to private events we must be clear about their status. Private events cannot serve as data; they cannot be used to generate principles or to buttress or refute theories. They serve no useful role in the **basic science** of behavior -- it is in the **interpretation** of the basic science that an appeal to private events becomes essential.

We often have indirect or incomplete evidence for private events, and we can often plausibly infer that they are being emitted. Since these events must obey behavioral principles, we are constrained in our inferences. For example, it is necessary that the private event be probable with respect to current controlling variables, and the control by these variables must in turn be plausible with respect to the ontogenic or phylogenic history of the organism. Thus an appeal to unobserved behavior is not equivalent to an appeal to internal processes or "representations." A private response that has been invoked to explain some anomaly, but that is itself anomalous, raises more questions than it answers.

The Problem of Memory

The *Guinness Book of World Records* is full of accounts of ordinary people who have accomplished extraordinary feats. Many of these feats can be understood, at least in principle, as results of special contingencies of reinforcement which shape ever more skillful or unusual behavior. Complex schedules of contingencies have been employed in the laboratory to shape unusual behavior in non-human organisms. Chimpanzees have been taught rudimentary sign language, pigeons to guide missiles and play ping-pong, and rats to execute long chains of odd responses such as wheeling themselves around in toy carts. In some cases, of course, unusual behavior can be attributed to great height or strength or other unusual physical characteristics that presumably reflect a special genetic endowment. We may marvel at behaviors of this sort, but we are not entirely at a loss to explain them.

The behavior of answering a simple question about one's past, however, seems to defy explanation in terms of these familiar principles. When asked, "What did you have for breakfast yesterday?" we reply with ease, "Scrambled eggs." So commonplace is the phenomenon that, at first, there seems to be no problem at all -- memories are simply behavior under the control of particular discriminative stimuli, in this case, the question. It is only when we try to specify how the controlling stimuli acquired their control that we begin to appreciate the shallowness of this analysis. When we ask, "What _are_ you eating?" the answer, "Scrambled eggs" can be understood in someone with an appropriate conditioning history as a response under the control of a constellation of current stimuli, namely, the eggs, the question, and the listener. We can reasonably assume that the speaker has learned to name eggs and that under suitable motivating conditions (the question), and in the presence of an audience, will do so. However, when we ask about yesterday's breakfast, a crucial controlling variable is missing: the eggs. Not only are the eggs not present, they no longer even exist. We cannot invoke a nonexistent stimulus as a current source of control. Unfortunately, the remaining environmental stimuli apparently do not control the response directly. We can demonstrate this by reproducing the external stimulus conditions in every detail on the following day and asking the question again. Perhaps our subject will then respond, "French toast." A second presentation of the discriminative stimuli has been followed by a completely different response.

Since we are apparently unable to appeal to environmental stimuli to account for the difference in the responses to our question we look to the person as a variable. In a sense we are different from who we were yesterday. Presumably yesterday's exposure to scrambled eggs changed us in such a way that we respond appropriately today when asked about yesterday's breakfast.

The Storage Metaphor

By far the commonest interpretation of these changes is that something about the experience has been stored inside us in our "memory banks," "memory storehouses," or, simply, our brains. When we are asked about the past we search through our storehouse of memories and retrieve the appropriate information. It is the information retrieved that serves as the missing variable that controls our response.

The storage metaphor is appealing. When we consult a grocery list or a memorandum we are responding to stimuli that can be said to be stored, and it is tempting to suppose that the nervous system records events in an analogous way.

Difficulties with the storage metaphor arise when we try to specify the actual events of which the metaphor is an abstraction. We can assume that an organism is changed by experience, presumably in some feature of its nervous system, but this brings us no closer to an explanation of recall. When we go to the supermarket we can store the words "tomato soup" in a grocery list, and no doubt changes in our nervous system are "stored" at the same time. At the supermarket we can retrieve the words from the grocery list by looking at the list. Our history with respect to grocery stores, memoranda, and particular textual stimuli is sufficient to explain both looking at the list and taking appropriate action. We are in no such position with respect to our nervous system. The relevant physiological changes are not stimuli; we cannot respond to them as we can to items on a grocery list. Stored changes are of no use to us if they do not control behavior.

In the storage metaphor, physiological changes serve as copies, or more commonly, as representations, of the original stimuli. These representations usurp the role of stimuli in controlling behavior. This scheme appears to be adequate, but there is an unfortunate lacuna: No mechanism is specified for recruiting the correct representation. The question remains why the particular representation of "tomato soup" is invoked at the appropriate time rather than the representation of a day at the beach or of yesterday's breakfast. If surrogates or representations of events are stored, like books in a library, how are they indexed, and how does a particular volume get summoned? As in the case of yesterday's breakfast, identical stimuli appear to summon different volumes on different days. Thus the storage metaphor has not solved the problem of stimulus control; it has merely inserted some additional terms of dubious status into the analysis.

Memory Defined

The behaviorist has no tools, conceptual or physical, with which to study memory; he can only study behavior and its controlling variables. If he explains the behavior said to require memory he will have done all that can be done, given his assumptions. From this perspective there is no such thing as "memory" as a thing to be studied. He can study the behavior we engage in when we "try to remember" something, and the behavior said to show that we did in fact remember something, and he can study the behavior of subjects in memory experiments; but there appears to be no reason to distinguish such behavior from any other behavior of the individual. In short, the behaviorist can study, not a state or structure, but an activity; not memory, but remembering.

From a behavioral perspective, then, memories are not "things," and they are not "real" or "mistaken." When we recall that we used Cortland apples in the pie, we do not resurrect the original behavior of reading the label on the bag of apples. Current behavior is under the control of **current** variables, and while it may be similar in topography to behavior executed under control of other variables in the past, it is not the "same" behavior or somehow a "real" memory. We have not unearthed a trace or record of what happened in the past. Rather, we engage in behavior anew. If independent evidence proves that it was, in fact, Golden Russets in the pie, the response "Cortland" is not "wrong" or "mistaken" or the result of a faulty addressing mechanism. It is the "correct" response in the sense that current variables evoked it as ineluctably as earlier variables evoked "Golden Russets." It is perhaps all the more remarkable that there is so often a correspondence between behavior elicited in a recall task and behavior that would be elicited by reinstating the original conditions; that is, we say "Cortlands" when presented with a bag of apples, and we say "Cortlands" when asked about them the next day.

Memory Phenomena: A Fundamental Dichotomy

There are two classes of contingencies for which the term "memory" is commonly said to be required. Consider the following examples:

1) In a classroom demonstration, a pigeon's pecks to a key are reinforced on a variable ratio schedule when the key is colored by a red light. When the key is dark, extinction is scheduled. After a retention interval of one week, the pigeon is returned to the experimental chamber. When the keylight is turned on the pigeon immediately pecks it at a high rate. When the light is turned off pecking stops entirely.

2) In a symbolic matching-to-sample task a pigeon pecks the central key of a three key array, illuminating it for five seconds with either a red or a green light and illuminating the side keys with white light. A peck to the left key is reinforced if the sample is red; a peck to the right key is reinforced if the sample is green. In a later condition, the side keys are not made available until the center key has been off for five seconds.

In the first example behavior is brought under control of a stimulus at one time and the stimulus is presented again at a later time. It may strike some as remarkable that a pigeon would "remember what to do" in a situation after the lapse of a week. However, it is not the memory of the earlier experience but the stimulus control of behavior that has endured. Since all conditioned behavior is under stimulus control as a result of certain prior experiences, memory in this sense is fundamental to all learning.

In the second example behavior is brought under control of a stimulus, and reinforcement is later made contingent on appropriate behavior in the absence of the stimulus. Appropriate behavior cannot be explained by appealing to the original training conditions; a more complex analysis is required.

In the first example the training stimulus is present at the time of the test; in the second example it is not. The first is an example of simple stimulus control established as the result of a three-term contingency. The second is an example of problem solving, and, while a behavioral analysis of this case will be different, the principles adduced will be the same. The remaining discussion will be divided between analyses of these two cases.

Memory as a Stimulus Control Phenomenon

Behavior in this category is "automatic," that is, it is directly under the control of environmental variables and does not require intermediate responses on the part of the organism. We experience memories of this sort as "spontaneous." A strain of music will often elicit emotional responses, and covert verbal and perceptual behavior appropriate to an earlier context, as it did so forcefully for Humphrey Bogart in the film, *Casablanca*. The taste of a madeleine will "summon up remembrance of things past." We name objects with ease, and with somewhat less ease recall the names of friends and acquaintances when we see them. We never forget how to ride a bicycle or how to swim.

In each case the behavior in question is directly controlled by a particular stimulus or set of stimuli. We can produce analogous behavior in the laboratory by arranging contingencies of reinforcement (as we did with our demonstration pigeon in the first example above), and we can usually point to contingencies in our experience to explain the stimulus control of our behavior. Often the contingencies are explicit, as in educational practices. We are taught to say "twenty-five" in response to "five times five" or "5 X 5" or

$$\begin{array}{r} 5 \\ \underline{X\,5} \end{array}$$

We are taught to say "1492," "1066," and "1588" in response to particular classes of question. It is sometimes difficult to specify the dimensions of stimulus, response, and reinforcer in an arbitrary example from our past. The stream of behavior does not seem to divide into neat units as do educational contingencies, but the importance of these units in the laboratory suggests that interpretation in these terms is valid.

The acquisition of stimulus control. Conditioned stimulus control results from exposure to contingencies of reinforcement under appropriate motivational conditions. As Skinner (1938) has shown, one exposure is sufficient to effect at least some change in stimulus control. Behavior reinforced or elicited in a particular setting will have an increased probability of occurring again in that setting, other things being equal. That probability will be affected by familiar parameters such as reinforcement magnitude and frequency, temporal relationship with the response, motivational variables, etc. When these parameters have been specified, the future occurrence of the response in that setting requires no further explanation. One can provide plausible accounts at other levels of analysis. For example, one may propose that synapses have been modified or created, resulting in an organism that responds in a particular way in a particular setting, but accounts of this sort are not necessary if our criterion of explanation is to be the prediction and control of behavior. A physiological explanation supplements the behavioral one; it does not replace it.

Forgetting: The loss of stimulus control. The control of behavior by a stimulus changes as a function of variables such as the level of deprivation, schedule of reinforcement, and other stimuli present. A decline in stimulus control as a function of these variables is reversible and is not usefully considered a loss of stimulus control. The extinction procedure, in which discriminative stimuli are presented but responses are not reinforced, appears to reduce stimulus control, but as I will argue below, an extinction procedure is a special kind of discrimination procedure. It may, in fact, sharpen stimulus control, not reduce it. In any case, there is no known behavioral process by which stimulus control declines **in an orderly way** solely as a result of the lapse of time.

The possibility that stimulus control may spontaneously decay over time has been considered for decades by students of memory. It is commonly our experience that responses recently conditioned are stronger than responses conditioned in the distant past. Having learned last week that Monrovia is the capital of Liberia, we are more likely to identify it correctly than the capital of North Dakota, which we learned ten years ago when driving across the continent. However, the decay hypothesis suggests more than that a stimulus will no longer control a response. It suggests that something has been permanently lost, something has deteriorated like crumbling parchment. Presumably, structural regularities in the nervous system accompany regularities in stimulus control. The maintenance of these structural regularities is no doubt imperfect. Any deterioration may result in a loss of stimulus control. In this sense there is surely a "decay of stimulus control" but it is probably not a simple or orderly function of time. As for the obvious relationship between forgetting and the lapse of time, there are alternatives to the decay hypothesis that suggest more orderly processes.

1) Failure to reinstate all of the relevant stimulus conditions. Often the stimuli present when we have acquired an operant in the recent past are more similar to current stimuli than the stimuli that were present when we acquired an operant in the distant past. "Bismarck" may be controlled not simply by "capital of North Dakota" but by interstate highways, brown prairieland, eroded sandstone, diesel exhaust fumes, grit in our teeth, and the interoceptive

stimuli characteristically elicited by travel to new places, i.e. excitement, arousal, or fatigue. If contextual stimuli have changed, we will be less likely to respond to a stimulus. In effect, all stimulus control is conditioned stimulus control. The stimuli manipulated by experimenters are typically a small subset of the stimuli present in a conditioning preparation, and the nominal discriminative stimulus controlling a response is typically only one of many stimuli present when that response was reinforced. The importance of these contextual stimuli becomes apparent when we return to the home of our childhood and find ourselves recalling names, places, and episodes "long forgotten" in our daily lives.

2) Competing responses to the same stimuli. While it is unlikely that we have learned that anything other than Bismarck is the capital of North Dakota, competing responses may still interfere. The written or spoken words, "Capital of North Dakota," may be members of a unitary stimulus class with respect to the response "Bismarck," but each word is a stimulus, or is composed of stimulus elements that may be members of stimulus classes controlling other behavior. "North Dakota" may remind us strongly of Fargo, or fatal blizzards, or soybean production. "Capital" may control the response "Boston" or "Washington" if they have been in the news lately. "Capital of North --" might be sufficient to occasion "Raleigh" if that response had been thoroughly conditioned. In each case we are apt to "recognize that our response is inappropriate" and set to work to recall the "correct" response, a stratagem discussed below. The issue here is the failure of a response to occur in the presence of an appropriate discriminative stimulus. Given that we commonly have rich experience with elements of a complex stimulus, it is possible that a response does not occur simply because other responses to the same stimuli are prepotent. The more time that elapses after the acquisition of a response, the greater is the opportunity for competing responses to be conditioned.

3) Competing responses conditioned to other stimuli. If we have recently heard from a friend in Brisbane, the response "Brisbane" may be strong (i.e. under the control of many current contextual cues). We may have spoken of Brisbane, or located it on a map, or addressed a reply to our friend there. Incidental stimuli may control "Brisbane" when "Bismarck" would be reinforced. Because of the formal similarity of the two responses, "Brisbane" may be especially strong, since the form of the response will be, in part, supplemented by variables that control "Bismarck." The reverse is true as well; "Bismarck" may well be strengthened by the presence of stimuli that normally control "Brisbane."

Thus the failure of a discriminative stimulus to occasion a response may be due, not to a loss of control, but to competing responses and missing contextual support. However, demonstrating that decay is not at least partly responsible for a decrement in performance may be impossible, since it is not clear how to put the matter to experimental test.

Verbal learning studies and stimulus control. Countless verbal learning studies, conducted over many decades, have attempted to evaluate the factors responsible for the loss of stimulus control. It is commonly thought that paired-associate learning studies arise from, or are congruent with, a radical behavioral approach to memory. A response is (presumably) brought under the control of a discriminative stimulus, and the retention of that stimulus control is tested. However, this is a superficial interpretation of what actually happens in a paired-associate study. It is a mistake to assume, without experimental verification, that the stimuli and responses as defined by the experimenter respect the "lines of fracture along which the environment and behavior actually break" (Skinner, 1935).

Consider, as an example, the pair ELBOW - QXV. The subject is shown the pair of items, perhaps on a memory drum, and will be reinforced if he replies "QXV" when the word "ELBOW" appears at a later time. Reinforcement usually consists of nothing more than seeing that the response is correct when the memory drum reveals the answer; more precisely, reinforcement consists of the formal similarity of the response to the word "ELBOW" with the textual operant controlled by the next stimulus ("QXV") presented by the drum. A casual interpretation of this sequence suggests that "QXV" is a discriminated operant under the control of the stimulus "ELBOW" analogous to the barpressing of a rat under the control of a 1000 Hz tone. The parallel is so obvious that researchers in verbal learning have assumed without further analysis that the models are analogous and that principles of equal generality can be derived from either approach. However, there are important differences that suggest that critical events in verbal learning studies are overlooked. A hungry rat will typically press a bar before the delivery of the first reinforcer, and if it does not, it can be shaped to bar-press by reinforcing successive approximations of the response. Thus the context controls relevant behavior prior to conditioning, but this baseline behavior is not orderly enough to be defined as an operant. In contrast, the baseline probability of a human subject uttering "QXV" in the presence of the written stimulus "ELBOW" is negligible. However, the experimenter in a verbal learning study does not emulate his colleagues in the animal learning laboratory; he does not shape the appropriate response from undifferentiated verbal behavior. Rather, he simply presents the textual stimulus "QXV" which controls the textual operants "Q," "X," and "V." These operants exist in strength because of prior training. The response "QXV" under the control of the stimulus "ELBOW" is one operant (the operant to be conditioned); the response (or responses) under the control of the printed letters "QXV" is a second operant (or set of operants) despite the fact that the responses have the same form. The operant to be conditioned is an intraverbal; the operant that is already conditioned is a textual operant. Therefore, performance in a paired-associate task is not a measure of **retention** but of **transfer** of stimulus control. The problem for the subject is to utter an operant of the same form but under different stimulus control. Certainly the textual operant "QXV" would survive the retention intervals typically studied in verbal learning experiments. Since letters are arbitrary symbols, the operant "QXV" under the control of "ELBOW," once conditioned, should last as long.

Unfortunately the events responsible for the transfer of stimulus control are not usually studied in typical verbal learning procedures. If barpressing (or saying "QXV") is under the control of a light (or the printed letters "QXV"), we do not transfer control to a tone (or "ELBOW") by presenting the tone and light together. To the contrary, that is the very condition under which we find blocking of stimulus control by the neutral stimulus (Kamin, 1969; Miles, 1970). Thus it is not surprising that subjects "forget" in verbal learning experiments; it is surprising that they ever remember. In the laboratory we transfer control from one stimulus to another using a fading procedure. The stimulus to be conditioned is made conspicuous while the controlling stimulus is gradually attenuated. Most of us have learned to use an informal fading procedure in rote memory tasks. We read carefully, then skim, then "peek," and so on, at every step reducing our exposure to the stimulus. It is quite likely that subjects in verbal learning tasks employ some of these techniques, often in conjunction with more elaborate acquisition strategies discussed below. In the absence of these strategies it is unlikely that stimulus control would transfer to the neutral stimulus. If this is the case, performance depends upon unanalyzed events during acquisition and in the history of the individual. It follows that paired-associate tasks, as typically studied, can tell us little about retention of the stimulus control of behavior.

In the extensive literature on memory for verbal material, it is clear that performance declines with time and that this decline is often regular. These findings are of interest since similar tasks are common in school and everyday life. Unfortunately, there is currently no understanding of **which** items in a list will be recalled and which forgotten. We can determine the probability of rolling double sixes in a game of craps, but we are unable to predict the outcome of a particular throw. Similarly, verbal learning experiments have generated "typical" forgetting curves under certain training conditions but are unable to determine which items will be recalled and which forgotten. Presumably, if we knew the precise starting position of the dice and the forces applied to them we could predict the outcome of a throw using the principles of Newtonian mechanics. A comparable analysis of memory performance is not possible with the conceptual apparatus of the students of verbal learning. A much more fine-grained analysis in terms of the stimulus control of verbal operants is necessary if we are to make predictions about specific responses.

Extinction. A final issue in the retention of stimulus control is that of extinction. As mentioned above, the only orderly procedure for decreasing or eliminating stimulus control is extinction. However, it may be questioned whether extinction is a unique behavioral process at all. Extinction is clearly a **procedure**, but the effect of the procedure may be simply to establish a discrimination. As Skinner (1950) puts it, "The very conditions of extinction seem to presuppose a growing novelty in the experimental situation. Is this why the extinction curve is curved?" In other words, the environment of an extinction condition is different from that of an acquisition condition in that reinforcing stimuli and the stimuli arising from the consumption of the reinforcer are absent. This interpretation is supported by two lines of evidence. First, the more closely acquisition conditions resemble extinction conditions, the more the organism perseveres during extinction. If ratio schedules of reinforcement are gradually stretched, very high ratios can continue to maintain behavior. Subsequent extinction curves are enormous. Conversely, extinction following continuous reinforcement is relatively abrupt.

Secondly, reacquisition following extinction is typically rapid. If extinction were the opposite of acquisition, if it eliminated stimulus control that had been established during acquisition, we would not expect rapid reconditioning.

An implication of this interpretation of extinction is that the establishment of stimulus control may be unidirectional. We do not lose what we have learned, we simply bury it or dilute it with what we learn later, or we learn incompatible responses to the same stimulus. Thus, extinction procedures may not reduce stimulus control; like any discrimination procedure, they may actually sharpen it. The issue might not be testable. Skinner (1950) continues, "It would appear to be necessary to make the conditions prevailing during extinction identical with the conditions prevailing during conditioning. This may be impossible, but in that case the question is academic."

Parameters that affect the stimulus control of behavior. Parameters that affect stimulus control are central to many issues in the field of memory as it is usually studied, though the relevance of the literature of the experimental analysis of behavior is seldom noted. As a consequence, many experimental questions in the field have been poorly framed. I will briefly consider two such parameters.

1) The stimulus-response and interstimulus intervals. How long after the offset of a stimulus will it continue to control behavior? How long is it "available for conditioning?" Students of memory have asked the question in different terms: "What is the duration of short-term memory?" If we briefly present a subject with a number, prevent rehearsal by requiring the execution of a distractor task, and ask the subject to name the stimulus, over what intervals will the subject be able to do so? The answer to this question depends on many things such as the response system, stimulus intensity, competing behavior, and mediating responses. The concept of short-term memory does not map on to distinctions honored by a behavioral analysis, but the procedure is related to studies of conditional discriminations, symbolic delayed

matching to sample, and interstimulus intervals in classical conditioning procedures. Results from all of these procedures converge, under some conditions, on a common answer.

Peterson and Peterson (1959), among the first to use the short-term memory procedure, found a 60% decrement in control after 6 seconds and virtually complete loss of control after 18 seconds in humans. Blough (1959) found delayed matching-to- sample performance in pigeons to decline to the level of chance in 5 to 20 seconds unless the birds engaged in distinctive mediating behavior. Parametric studies of interstimulus intervals in classical conditioning indicate considerable variability between organisms and between response systems, but generally stimuli to be conditioned decline in effectiveness after a few seconds with little or no conditioning after 30 seconds (see Mackintosh, 1974, for a review). It appears that under most conditions a stimulus is effective for only a half minute or so, although it may be that in a featureless environment a conspicuous novel stimulus would be effective for a considerably longer period.

2) The role of discrepancy in stimulus control. The conditioning of a response can be blocked if the reinforcer has been "predicted" by antecedent stimuli. Technically speaking, reinforcement only occurs when there is a discrepancy between responses elicited by the putative reinforcing stimulus and responses elicited by other stimuli present (Donahoe, Crowley, Millard & Stickney, 1982). Anthropomorphizing, we say that reinforcement is effective only if it "surprises" the organism. As this has been shown to be relevant to the acquisition of stimulus control, we would expect it to be relevant to the retention of stimulus control. This conclusion has been directly confirmed by several studies in the animal laboratory, (e.g. Colwill & Dickinson, 1980; Grant, Brewster, & Stierhoff, 1983; Maki, 1979; Terry & Wagner, 1975) and indirectly in human studies (e.g. Atkinson & Wickens, 1971; Merryman & Merryman, 1971; Richardson & Stanton, 1972). Moreover, a wide range of phenomena in the memory literature can plausibly be interpreted in terms of behavioral discrepancy and blocking, for example, the Von Restorff effect (a novel element in an otherwise homogeneous array is remembered better than other elements), selective memory phenomena (we all know whose picture is on the dollar bill, but we can't report what else is on it), the serial position effect (elements at either end of an array are remembered better than central elements), the 'tip-of-the-tongue' phenomenon (often we can't recall a word but we know what it begins with), and the 'Kennedy assassination' phenomenon (we all know where we were on November 22, 1963, but none of us know where we were on November 23). Needless to say, the usual interpretation of these phenomena is not distinguished by reference to blocking or behavioral discrepancy.

Memory as a Problem Solving Phenomenon

To refine the distinction between memory as a stimulus control phenomenon and memory as a problem solving phenomenon, let us consider two simple mathematical questions. For most of us the question, "What is the square root of 144?" is a discriminative stimulus for the response, "12," a discriminated operant acquired in grade school. When asked, "What is the square root of 1764?" however, few of us can reply immediately, though if given a few minutes, we will come up with the correct answer. It is not a matter of latency, with the second response being under weaker control of the question and hence having a longer latency; we simply never have encountered the three-term contingency necessary to condition the response as a discriminated operant to the question.

The relationship between the questions "What did you have for breakfast yesterday?" and "What is the square root of 1764?" is not merely one of analogy. From a behavioral perspective they require identical treatment. Both are examples of **problem solving** and require analysis as such.

"Problem" defined. In both cases a verbal stimulus is presented which, partly by its form, partly by the intonation with which it is spoken, signals an aversive consequence which we can avoid only by replying within a brief period of time. (When we are unable to make a prompt substantive reply, we employ a host of temporizing expressions that serve as well: "Ah," "Now, then," and "Let me see . . ." Of course a positive contingency may be signalled also. "I don't know!" will not be reinforced, but the correct response may be.)

Generally speaking, a person is faced with a problem when reinforcement is contingent, in part, upon conditions that do not currently obtain. However, if we confine our discussion to potentially solvable problems, the following criteria define the domain:

1) A target response (or set of responses) is part of the organism's repertoire under one or more stimulus conditions.

2) Discriminative stimuli are present indicating that the response is scheduled for reinforcement.

3) The response is not under direct control of current discriminative stimuli.

For example, for most of us the response "42" is an operant (or chain of operants) in our repertoire; in fact the response is a member of a number of response classes distinguished by their controlling variables, e.g. "6 X 7," "40 + 2," the printed numerals, "42," etc. In contrast, an Olympic gymnastic stunt is not in our repertoire under any discriminative stimuli whatever, nor is, say, uttering the Coptic word for "watermelon."

Secondly, the response "42" is scheduled for reinforcement when the square root of 1764 is requested. (The reinforcement in this case may be trifling: a nod of the head, a "Thank you," a check in the margin of a classroom assignment, and so on. However, there is no doubt that humans can be quite sensitive to reinforcers of this magnitude.) Finally, the response is not under the direct control of the question, "What is the square root of 1764?" or of the contextual stimuli, in contrast to the response, "12," to the question, "What is the square root of 144?" That is, it is not a member of an operant for which the question is a controlling variable.

Similarly, the response, "Scrambled eggs," is a response in my repertoire, under the control of, among other things, a plate of scrambled eggs. It also happens to be the correct answer to the question, "What did you have for breakfast yesterday?" and hence is scheduled for reinforcement. Moreover, it is clearly not related in an orderly way to the question. Thus, while the utterance is a response in laymen's terms, it is not, technically speaking, a response under the control of the question as a discriminative stimulus. That is not to say that the question exerts no discriminative control over my behavior, or that it does not contribute importantly to the response in question, but it does not have the same orderly relationship to the response as a red light has to pecking in our demonstration pigeon. The question initiates a sequence of problem solving responses, just as a mathematical question initiates a sequence of mathematical responses eventually leading to an answer, but it does not control the response directly.

If this analogy (or isomorphism) between remembering and problem solving is correct, a common formulation will suffice. We can begin by considering mathematical problem solving since that is often codified and hence more explicit and more nearly universal than the strategies used in recall tasks. If the required response is part of the repertoire of the individual but is not directly controlled by the nominal discriminative stimulus, the individual must engage in precurrent behavior providing himself with supplementary discriminative stimuli until the combined effect of the nominal and the supplementary stimuli are enough to occasion the target response. Finally, the response must be **recognized** as correct, as distinct from all of the other responses of the organism. That is, one must stop engaging in problem solving responses (those that generate supplementary discriminative stimuli) and emit the target response as such.

Supplementary stimulus control techniques. In some cases, we physically manipulate environmental variables. We organize materials or underline important words. We improve the lighting or fetch the right wrench. We shuffle Scrabble tiles or arrange cards by suit. The effect of these manipulations is to improve the stimulus control exerted by relevant variables and, just as importantly, to reduce the control by irrelevant variables. Clearly these are acquired strategies, and judgments of irrelevance and relevance will vary considerably with one's experience.

In some cases we supplement controlling variables. We consult a road map or a dictionary. In other cases we solve problems by supplementing environmental variables with stimuli provided by our own responses. In arithmetic problems, there are formal procedures, codified response chains, which, in conjunction with the nominal discriminative stimulus (the problem), are sufficient to both generate the appropriate response and identify it as the "answer." For example, while we have no response conditioned to the arithmetic problem, 263 X 28 as a complex stimulus, we have many responses conditioned to elements of the stimulus. First we rearrange the stimuli:

$$263$$
$$\underline{\quad 28}$$

We then execute a series of discriminated operants in an order determined by the physical arrangement of the numbers:

$$263$$
$$\underline{\quad 28}$$
$$2104$$
$$\underline{5260}$$

By emitting these responses we alter the problem. The question, at some point, is no longer, "What is 263 X 28?" but "What is 2104 + 5260?" an arrangement that occasions further responses. After the leftmost column has been summed we can read the answer as a simple textual response to the stimuli below the lower line. It is only the stimuli arising from our having executed a chain of responses in a particular order that enable us to emit the answer, or target response, as such. It typically has no distinctive properties that indicate that it is indeed the target response. If we have made an error, we will not know it, unless we employ further strategies to confirm the accuracy of our response.

In this case we have turned a multiplication problem into an addition problem and an addition problem into a textual stimulus. We have used a codified strategy, a chain of operants each of which was an important controlling variable for subsequent ones. The responses may be overt, but as I have argued earlier, they may be covert, i.e. below the threshold of observability. We may generalize the solution as follows: The subject has emitted discriminated operants to the nominal discriminative stimulus. These responses, in conjunction with the nominal stimulus have controlled further responses. There is an accumulation of discriminative stimuli, some proximal, some distal, as the solution progresses. The accumulated stimuli eventually are sufficient to occasion the emission of the target response, in this case, the "answer." The target response, once emitted, is a discriminative stimulus halting further mathematical behavior.

Typically, problems do not have codified solutions, but the behavior of the problem-solver is analogous. We solve problems by generating supplementary stimuli which, in conjunction with the context of the problem are sufficient to occasion the "solution." I have posed the following problem to a dozen people: "The square root of 1764 is an integer. What is it?" A typical reply takes several minutes and includes long pauses and a number of overt intermediate responses. One subject pondered and said, "Well, it's more than 40 . . . It's less than 50 . . . It's closer to 40 . . . It can't be 41 because it has to end in '4'. . It can't be 42 . . . Wait! Yes it can . . . No. No, it isn't 42.   Oh, I give up! I can't work that kind of thing in my head!"

In this case the correct response was emitted but for irrelevant reasons was rejected. It failed a corroboratory test and was not "recognized as correct." However, this subject's overt responses provide a good illustration of the strategy of providing oneself with supplementary discriminative stimuli (S^Ds). Each response is itself a stimulus exerting some control over subsequent behavior. Initially, the only relevant stimulus was the question. After a few minutes the relevant stimuli comprised a sequential array of verbal responses, some covert, some overt. We can suppose that an outline of such an array looks something like this:

What is the square root of 1764?
100 times 100 is zero, zero, zero, zero -- too many zeroes.
20 times 20 is 400.
50 times 50 is 2500.
It's less than 50.
40 times 40 is 1600.
It's more than 40.
40-something.
41 times 41 is something-one.
1764.
It ends in 4.

2 times 2 is 4.
It could be 42.
8 times 8 is 64.
It could be 48.
1600 -- 1764 -- 2500 . . . It's closer to 40 than 50.
It's a number between 40 and 50 that ends in either 2 or 8, and it's closer to 40 than 50.

In the presence of this array (or sequence) of stimuli, the response "42" is highly probable. Of course the response has never been conditioned to this constellation of stimuli, but each of the S^Ds increases the probability of a number of response classes including, in each case, 42. The pooled effect of the S^Ds is to make the response more probable than competing responses. That is, at some point "42" becomes the prepotent response.

Problem solving, then, is an acquired strategy of manipulating or supplementing discriminative stimuli until a particular response in the repertoire of the organism becomes prepotent over the myriad other responses that are changing in probability. These manipulations are terminated when the original contingency (the problem) is fulfilled, i.e. when reinforcement is delivered, either by an external agent or natural consequence, or by a corroboratory test by the subject confirming that the target response has been emitted.

The behavior of a person asked to recall an incident in the past is the same, except in content, as the behavior of a person asked to solve a problem in his head. When asked, "What did you have for breakfast yesterday?" the "correct" response is in our repertoire in the sense that if the meal were still in front of us we could name it. However, the response does not exist as a discriminated operant under the control of the question. There is no alternative to generating supplementary S^Ds, and this is exactly what we do, just as we did with the square root problem. We have no codified solutions and therefore performance varies considerably from individual to individual. We evidently learn to use key responses as indices to other responses. As one example, in our culture, many people have schedules that are distinctive. We recite the days of the week forward and backward as intraverbal responses. We can tick off the invariant elements of our schedules for a given day, again as intraverbal responses. As we do so, we provide ourselves with important supplementary stimuli.

Let us consider responses to the question, "What did you have for breakfast three days ago?" One subject replied, "Let's see . . . today's Monday . . . Sunday . . .Saturday . . . Friday. That was the day I went to Springfield. Hmm . . . Oh yeah - I just had a glass of orange juice before I left." From this subject's overt responses we can see processes at work similar to those in the subject solving the square root problem. As the response was clearly not directly under the control of the question, it was necessary to provide supplementary discriminative stimuli. The subject in this case emitted an intraverbal chain to determine the appropriate day of the week. This is presumably an acquired strategy useful for a broad class of questions about recent experience, and can reasonably be assumed to be under direct control of elements of the question (What happened X days ago?)

A later response was what we might call an exploratory response: "On Fridays I go to Springfield." When we learn our weekly schedules, responses are conditioned to the names of days of the week as stimuli. Presumably this was a strong response to the stimulus "Friday." Such a response may be of no use in controlling the target response, and in that sense is exploratory. It provides supplementary stimuli that may or may not be effective.

Finally the target response was emitted. There is a considerable gap in our account here, as the S^Ds provided by the question and the subsequent overt responses of the subject do not appear to be sufficient to control the target response directly. We may speculate that "trip to Springfield" controlled conditioned perceptual behavior (discussed below) that provided additional control. Further exploratory responses might have been necessary before the target response was emitted. Like the game of 20 Questions, each response confined the domain of subsequent responses, yet strengthened responses within that domain.

The details of the process are out of our reach, but it is clear that the target response, the "memory" in question, was controlled, not only by the original question, but by a host of intermediate responses as well. The cumulative effect of the question and the intermediate responses was to make the target response prepotent over other responses in the same domain, just as in the square root problem. No new principles are invoked in this account.

The role of conditioned perceptions. If asked our whereabouts last Wednesday, it helps to be able to say, "Wednesday . . . 9:00 -- lab; 1:00 -- learning seminar; selectmen's meeting in the evening." With such an intraverbal framework we could provide a plausible account of our day without further ado. However, such an account smacks more of inference than of memory. That is, the subjective impression that we are "reliving" the experience is missing if we merely recount what we must have been doing according to our invariant schedule. Key responses such as "Selectmen's meeting" are directly controlled by the question, but they in turn control other responses. "Selectmen's meeting" may control conditioned perceptions of a particular room in a particular town hall. These perceptual responses in turn control other responses. Similarly, the taste of a madeleine at tea time may directly control perceptual responses that were paired with that taste long ago, perhaps in one's childhood. That perceptual response controls other behavior which in turn alters the probability of still other behavior. In this way a reminiscence or a daydream, or in Proust's case, a book, may be born.

Conditioned perceptual behavior is commonly weak; competing perceptual behavior under the control of exteroceptive stimuli, behavior which we may tentatively regard as unconditioned, may be incompatible with it, and if so, is apt to be prepotent. In order for conditioned perception to be prepotent, it is often necessary to disrupt the stimulus control of incompatible responses. We do this with such devices as closing or unfocusing our eyes, turning away from the television, looking at the ceiling, or stopping other activity.

Implicit in this account is that perceptual behavior is continually being conditioned. If when asked, "What was on the kitchen table when you came downstairs this morning?" I engage in various recall strategies and find myself seeing a pipe wrench on the table, it must be the case that the perceptual response was conditioned to the constellation of stimuli that preceded it, including, presumably, stimuli generated by my own behavior. Seeing the wrench in the morning was conditioned to the context. Recalling the context as a result of a recall strategy occasioned the conditioned perception.

Perceptual responses are presumably conditioned in accordance with the same principles as other responses. Thus perceptual responses are more apt to be conditioned when, loosely speaking, we are "surprised" than otherwise. When questioned about John F. Kennedy's assassination not only can we report our whereabouts, we behave perceptually as we did then. We **see** again, as if in response to the original setting. Similarly, when asked about this morning's events, I might be able to see a pipe wrench on a table, but I might not see the salt shaker or the pattern of the tablecloth, since only the pipe wrench is an oddity in that context. Thus, we can visualize a painting we have seen but are unable to visualize the color of the painted wall on which it hangs.

The subjective impression that we are "reliving" an experience, then, is due to the conditioning of perceptual behavior. Not all examples of remembering require an appeal to conditioned perceptual responses, but they are clearly important in many cases.

Note that conditioned perceptual responses are responses to **current** stimuli. We are not responding to a copy or representation of a stimulus we have experienced in the past. That is, stimuli are not stored; past events have changed us in such a way that we now behave perceptually in the absence of the thing seen, under the control of stimuli in the present environment.

Conditioned perceptual behavior is a formidable problem for an experimental analysis. Determining response units empirically and, worse, measuring them objectively, are intractable obstacles at present. Yet the importance of such behavior is undeniable, and invoking it in an interpretation of human behavior is justified, so long as its use is consistent with established behavioral principles.

Recognizing the target response. I have argued that answering a question about the past is problem solving, that we do so by providing ourselves with supplementary stimuli that control necessary intermediate responses. However, a problem still remains: The target response must be "recognized" as such; that is, it must be emitted overtly "as the answer" and intermediate responses under the control of the question must stop. In written mathematics problems, with codified strategies, the answer stands in a particular ordinal and physical relationship to other responses. For example, in long division the answer is available when the remainder or a certain number of decimal places has been calculated, and it can be read as a textual response under the control of the digits above the division symbol. We emit that response as our answer to the problem, but we do not "know that it is right" unless we conduct corroboratory tests such as multiplying the quotient by the divisor to get the dividend.

What are the analogous properties of the "correct answer" in recall? If our first response to a question about a past breakfast is, "Today's Monday," why do we not announce "Monday" as our answer (i.e. with the same emphasis, tone of voice, and evident satisfaction as we announce "Juice")? What are the distinguishing properties of a target response as opposed to an intermediate response? There are several possibilities. First, the strength of a response to its controlling variables is often discriminable. (The usefulness of the concept of the descriptive autoclitic depends upon this fact.) The "correct" answer to a question will typically be strong with respect to all or most of the intermediate responses and, in addition, will be strong with respect to the question. Intermediate responses will typically be strongly controlled by the preceding intermediate response but may not be strongly controlled by the question. Thus the strength of the relationship between the target response and its controlling variables may be distinctive.

Second, the response will itself have stimulus properties. It may occasion a conditioned perceptual response or perhaps a chain or cascade of conditioned perceptual responses -- a reminiscence. In their relationship to the question these additional responses may serve to certify that a particular response is appropriate. A reminiscence of drinking orange juice while preparing lunch in one's kitchen could be a strong response to "Friday's breakfast," but a reminiscence of drinking orange juice in a dimly lit restaurant would probably not be. Thus the "answer" may be distinguished by its strength and the strength of responses that it controls with respect to the original contingency and the constellation of intermediate responses.

Recall strategies and acquisition strategies. In certain circumstances, reciting one's schedule is a useful strategy. In other circumstances, as in recalling a name, reciting the alphabet is helpful. The formal prompt provided by the initial letter of a word supplements other discriminative stimuli. Often recalling related material or answering related questions is helpful. Mnemonic devices of every variety invariably provide supplementary stimuli.

These strategies are all responses, or sequences of responses that we employ at the time of recall to solve the problem that has been posed. Some strategies, however, are employed before recall is required. Let us call them acquisition strategies. Thus we orient, "attend," rehearse, elaborate, classify, and organize. If we expect to introduce a speaker at 6:00, and we learn relevant details of his life at 5:00, we will perhaps rehearse our speech and elaborate on what we have learned. If we must learn a number of unrelated things, we may employ a codified strategy, such as the method of loci, that will facilitate later recall. Acquisition strategies do not provide supplementary stimuli; rather, they strengthen behavior with respect to stimuli that are likely to be provided by recall strategies or properties of a typical recall task. Thus acquisition strategies and recall strategies work together. The first strengthens behavior to key stimuli, the second produces these key stimuli at the time of recall, thereby controlling the target behavior.

In many cases we do not explicitly employ strategies. However, when the current setting is insufficient to directly control the response scheduled for reinforcement, we must provide supplementary stimuli, whether we do so "automatically" or "deliberately." The term, "strategy," though it regrettably connotes awareness, is used here to encompass all supplementary stimulus control procedures whether we can describe them or not.

Implications of a behavioral analysis. The foregoing interpretation suggests the following:

1) Once a strategy is employed and a response to a question is reinforced, that question may control the response directly at a later time. Thus, in the future the response "42" may be directly under the control of the question, "What is the square root of 1764?" and "Scrambled eggs" may, perhaps inappropriately, be under the control of the question, "What did you have for breakfast yesterday?"

Adults are thoroughly practiced at answering questions about the past. Consequently, responses generating supplementary stimuli will often be under direct control of classes of questions, and the appropriate response may occur swiftly, effortlessly, and without awareness of any supplementary responding.

2) Effective supplementary stimuli may be idiosyncratic. An effective strategy for one person may be ineffective for another. Moreover, if one strategy fails in a given circumstance, another may succeed. There is no invariant property of recall behavior.

3) Strategies are acquired. Children must learn to recall events, just as they learn to solve other problems. A child asked about the past will simply be unable to respond appropriately unless he has learned to do so or unless supplementary stimuli are provided by adults. Of course, in the presence of appropriate stimuli there is no reason why children's recall should be inferior to that of adults. Thus, it is not helpful to speak of "memory as a capacity that undergoes developmental changes." Changes in recall behavior surely occur as a child matures, but it is unnecessary to appeal to anything other than the normal evolution of a behavioral repertoire in a complex and increasingly demanding world.

4) There are no qualitative differences between "correct" and "mistaken" recall responses. Both are under the control of the current constellation of discriminative stimuli. That is, there is no difference between a "memory that never happened" and one that "did happen."

5) If recall strategies are sequences of responses, then performance should be disrupted when incompatible responses are strong. For example, if "April" is a key intermediate response for the intraverbal response, "March," performance may be disrupted if "April is the cruellest month" is a strong response.

6) Responses controlled in part by a complex of supplementary stimuli are not operants. That is, they are not yet orderly units with respect to that complex of stimuli, as the stimuli have come together for the first time. Each strengthens a common response but may be insufficient alone to occasion the response. For example, the word, "harbor," does not commonly control the response, "Boston," but "harbor, baked beans, university, Bunker Hill" as a complex of stimuli might do so. In many problems a response of a particular topography will serve as a solution regardless of its orderliness as a unit. Recall strategies and problem solving strategies exploit this fact.

The origin of strategies. We learn to remember. More precisely, effective intermediate behavior, behavior which provides supplementary stimulus control in appropriate contexts, is differentially reinforced. The adult community implicitly shapes such behavior in children by providing and then fading prompts which facilitate the target response:

Tell your father who came to visit today ... Remember? She sat on the couch and read you a story ... Was it Aunt R--?

More and more explicit prompts are provided until the target response occurs. Later, as the child begins to supply some of the intermediate responses himself, fewer prompts are provided.

Adults often model strategies in their own attempts to recall something:

Who made this long distance call to New York? ... Let's see ... It was October 11. That was a week ago Monday ... I drove the kids to the dentist that day ... Oh, I remember! I called the insurance company.

The overt intermediate behavior of the adult is controlling the behavior not only of himself but of everyone around him, including the children. A child might find himself making an appropriate response in such circumstances. In any case, he may imitate the adult for other reasons and find himself recalling things adventitiously, as it were.

Some strategies are acquired by accident. A child who needs a flashlight may go to the family room to get one. By the time he arrives, he has forgotten what he came for. As he turns to go, he sees the flashlight on the shelf and recalls his errand. As a consequence he may learn to scan his environment for visual prompts when similar problems occur in the future.

Many codified strategies are explicitly taught. "Every good boy does fine" is a mnemonic we acquire in second grade, and in college we are not above murmuring in the middle of an exam, "Please eat old mashed potatoes politely," to help recall geologic epochs. Self improvement courses are widely offered to teach mnemonic strategies that are unlikely to be acquired under everyday contingencies.

There are many ways, then, in which individuals can acquire supplementary stimulus control techniques. While it seems unnatural that, until we have done so, we should be unable to answer simple questions about our past, we must remember that there are skilled mnemonists who can recall 50 digit numbers after a moment's study. Most of us would be staggered by such a task. The child is in just such a circumstance when required to recall past events.

Conclusion

The present analysis has attempted to provide a framework for a behavioral interpretation of phenomena studied in the field of memory. I have suggested that principles derived from the experimental analysis of three-term contingencies of reinforcement are sufficient to explain such phenomena. Moreover, I have argued that distinctions arising from a consideration of these principles have not arisen in traditional approaches to the subject, that what is usually considered a unitary field embraces phenomena that require quite different behavioral interpretations.

In contrast to the inductive science on which it rests, the present account has been deductive. We have begun by accepting general principles and asking what must be the case if certain conditions obtain. For example, if a person reports that he ate scrambled eggs yesterday it must be the case that that response was prepotent, that it had been reinforced in that setting in the past, or that the constellation of stimuli preceding it controlled the response. Similarly, since responses have stimulus properties, it must be the case that one response alters the probability of other responses, and that some of these responses may be covert. By examining a few examples of overt problem solving it has been suggested that no new principles are necessary, that supplementary stimulus control procedures are sufficient to explain conditioned behavior in the absence of a demonstrable controlling stimulus.

It may be argued that by considering covert responses in its analysis radical behaviorism has compromised its status as an empirical enterprise. To argue so is to confuse the science of behavior with the interpretation of that science. Interpretation is reserved for phenomena in circumstances that, with our present methodology, are too complex for experimental analysis. The methodological problems do not vanish if one abandons radical behaviorism for another approach. Other approaches are faced with the same complexity but lack the broad empirical foundation and the coherent set of principles from which behavioral interpretations spring.

References

Atkinson, R. C. & Wickens, T. D. (1971). Human memory and the concept of reinforcement. In G. Glaser (Ed.), *The nature of reinforcement.* New York: Academic Press.

Blough, D. S. (1959). Delayed matching in the pigeon. *Journal of the Experimental Analysis of Behavior, 2,* 151-160.

Colwill, R. M. & Dickinson, A. (1980). Short-term retention of "surprising" events following differential training conditions. *Animal Learning and Behavior, 8,* 561-566.

Donahoe, J. W., Crowley, M. A., Millard, W. J., & Stickney, K. A. (1982). A unified principle of reinforcement. In M. L. Commons, R. J. Herrnstein, & H. Rachlin (Eds.), *Quantitative analyses of behavior (Vol. 2): Matching and maximizing accounts*. Cambridge, MA: Ballinger.

Grant, D. S., Brewster, R. G., & Stierhoff, K. A. (1983). "Surprisingness" and short-term retention in pigeons. *Journal of Experimental Psychology: Animal Behavior Processes, 9*, 63-79.

Kamin, L. J. (1969). Predictability, surprise, attention, and conditioning. In R. Church & B. Campbell (Eds.), *Punishment and aversive behavior*. New York: Appleton-Century-Crofts.

Mackintosh, N. J. (1974). *The psychology of animal learning*. New York: Academic Press.

Maki, W. S. (1979). Pigeons' short-term memory for surprising vs. expected reinforcement and nonreinforcement. *Animal Learning and Behavior, 7*, 31-37.

Merryman, C. T. & Merryman, S. S. (1971). Stimulus encoding in the A-B', AX-B and the A-Br', AX-B paradigms. *Journal of Verbal Learning and Verbal Behavior, 10*, 681-685.

Miles, R. C. (1970). Blocking the acquisition of control by an auditory stimulus with pretraining on brightness. *Psychonomic Science, 19*, 133-134.

Peterson, L. R. & Peterson, M. J. (1959). Short-term retention of individual items. *Journal of Experimental Psychology, 58*, 193-198.

Richardson, J. & Stanton, S. K. (1972). Some effects of learning to a set of components on stimulus selection. *American Journal of Psychology, 85*, 519-533.

Skinner, B. F. (1935). The generic nature of the concepts of stimulus and response. *Journal of General Psychology, 12*, 40-65.

Skinner, B. F. (1938). *The behavior of organisms: An experimental analysis*. New York: Appleton-Century-Crofts.

Skinner, B. F. (1950). Are theories of learning necessary? *Psychological Review, 57*, 193-216.

Terry, W. S. & Wagner, A. R. (1975). Short-term memory for surprising vs. expected unconditioned stimuli in Pavlovian conditioning. *Journal of Experimental Psychology: Animal Behavior Processes, 1*, 122-133.

A Discussion of Chapter 11

Behavioral Analyses of Memory

Paolo Moderato
University of Palermo
Palermo, Italy

I have often wondered why the field of memory has always been viewed as either an associative process or a cognitive process and not as a behavioral process. It seemed odd that no behavior analyst had described a model of memory and yet I thought that memory could be approached from an operant perspective. Palmer's chapter supports this opinion. Memory or better yet, remembering, can be described precisely in behavior analytic terms. Palmer's chapter not only outlines how this can be done, but it provides an impetus for further thinking about memory. It is these thoughts that were discussed by the participants at the Summer Institute on Verbal Relations, and it is these kinds of thoughts that I would like to address in this commentary.

I will start with a reaction to Palmer's claim that interpretation has to play an important role in the analysis of remembering. Then I will discuss some pertinent children's examples of memory. Third, I will react to the problem solving description of memory that Palmer has adopted as it relates to examples of children's memory. I will suggest that children's problem solving is different from an adult's in the complexity of the repertoire that is brought to bear on the problem. Fourth, I would like to report some experiments on the idiosyncratic nature of the problem solving process and the acquisition of recall that support a general behavior analytic interpretation of remembering. Finally, I will address a model of learning that might be integrated with Palmer's description of memory.

Interpretation

It is difficult to disagree with Palmer's position on the use of interpretation in the analysis of remembering. Even those who prescribe to a purely empirical approach to studying remembering have to recognize the importance of interpretation, after all, even while collecting data we must organize the data according to some interpretative framework. In fact, I would argue that it is important to create psychological models of remembering as part of our methodology for interpretation.

Certainly, great prudence is needed in the development of new models used in interpretation of remembering because the field of memory has produced so many different models. This, in part, is due to the nature of the subject matter. Since there is a tendency to explain the unknown and unobservable in terms of what is already known and can be observed (Marr, 1983) the analysis of remembering has evoked many models, for example, the current model of the computer. But, this should not deter us from creating alternative models, for just as models have played an important role in other sciences, they are useful in explaining psychological phenomena. Our prudence should lead to criteria that we adopt for creating models.

One criteria should be that acceptable models be composed of psychological components. Many of the models created for psychological events are not psychological (Marr, 1983): Psychoanalysis is a bio-literary model, Piagetian Theory is a logical-biological model, and information processing is an electronic-information model. If we look to other sciences for guidance we will see that such models will not be very useful for experimental psychology to adopt. The models used in classic physics, for instance, were physical models, not some other level of analysis. Thus, a psychological model of remembering should be based on other psychological systems that we already can describe.

This is not to argue that psychological models need to be based purely on generalized facts. Metaphorical models can serve as heuristics (Reese, 1973) and can be sensitive to empirical data (Moderato & Perini, 1987). For example, though modern physics has replaced the metaphor with mathematics, the original models, such as the billiard ball metaphor of thermodynamics, were useful for this science. Let us remember also that the predominant psychological model for four centuries, the S-R model, was originally a metaphor. At the time of Descartes, Locke, and LaMettrie the S-R model had no supporting data, neither in psychology or in neurophysiology. It was a metaphor derived from mechanical origins that guided years of experimentation that provided generalized facts. In the beginning it was an ideological-metaphorical model and now is an empirically constrained model.

The historical significance of the S-R model suggests other criteria for designing models: that the model be consistent with known facts and uses of language that is consistent with the models that have been used to summarize these facts. Under these conditions we may, in fact should, represent and interpret the process of human remembering through a model derived from the S-R model and based on its laws. Such a representation would allow a better understanding of the relation between this phenomenon and others; it would give a familiar syntax for representing the problems of memory and could be continually supported, controlled, and constrained by experimental data collected both on remembering and other behavioral events. As the S-R model is now based on psychological observations and not observations at another level of analysis, it also fits the first criteria that I have described. Thus, I agree with Palmer's assertion that we need to consider interpretation an important aspect of studying complex human phenomena and that a model consistent with the S-R model would be an appropriate model to use for our interpretation.

Examples of Children's Memory

My specific area of interest is the behavior of children. As such I have spent much time observing children responding in ways that might be categorized as remembering. A few examples of these behavioral episodes might provide some insight into the similarities and differences between adults' remembering and children's remembering.

My son, Marco, 18 months old, is shown for the first time two plastic animals by his mother. The mother says, "This is a cow, and this is an ass. Look, where is the cow?" When Marco points to the cow his mother says, "Right Marco, good boy, this is a cow." Two weeks later, my wife shows the same two animals to Marco and asks him "Do you remember which is the cow?" Marco points to the cow. This is an example of what Palmer calls discriminative learning. If we consider it an example of remembering then everything is memory. Therefore, since I would like to restrict the events that are categorized as remembering, I will agree with Palmer's classification of this as an example of discrimination.

Marco also has a repertoire of vocal imitations. When his mother says, "The cow says 'Muh' and the ass says 'Hee-ho'," Marco repeats "Muh" and "Hee-ho." Two weeks later my wife asks Marco, "Do you remember what the cow says?" and Marco says "Muh." This is an example of what I would like to categorize as remembering. The specific auditory stimulus is not presented, but nonetheless Marco makes the appropriate response. Thus, it is not a simple repetition of a relation, but a new relation that as Palmer points out requires problem solving. The child either explicitly or implicitly engages in behavior that changes the environment so that stimuli that he has responded to in the past are present, the sound "Muh" and possibly "Hee-ho," and then engages in the response in relation to his mother's question. Thus, the second response is dependent on the first which is a discrimination between "Muh" and "Hee-ho." In other words, there is a hierarchy or, at least, a priority of operations for remembering. However, this discrimination is not sufficient to produce the second response. Something else must occur and this is what might appropriately be labeled as remembering.

Differences Between Adult and Child Memory

In addition to pointing out further examples of remembering as problem solving, these examples illustrate some of the differences between adult and child memory. Palmer's representation of remembering includes the final performance of an adult. However, the performance of children is quite different because the repertoire of a child is quite different from an adult. It includes differences in history of reinforcers, stimulus functions, knowledge, processes. For instance, many studies have demonstrated that there is a developmental trend in western culture in the way children cluster objects (Reese, 1976; Scribner, 1974): younger children preferably show associative thematic clustering in recall, older children and adults show more frequently categorical taxonomic clustering (Bjorklund & DeMarchena, 1984; Frankel & Rollins, 1982, 1985). The associative clustering does not disappear or change into a taxonomic one, it remains in the skill repertoire of older children and adults, and is engaged in when it is requested by a particular task or situation. Therefore, the problem solving strategies of children and adults are quite different in terms of the amount of algorithms that lead to the solution of a problem and in the efficacy of each algorithm: these two features are naturally connected, in the sense that the more numerous and varied the algorithms the more likely an effective problem solving.

In conclusion, a general model of remembering cannot neglect some basic features of children's memory, just as the knowledge of child development is basic for any theory of human behavior (Bijou, 1984a). However, even if Palmer's interpretation is not specifically concerned with them, his model might easily include them.

Empirical Support for Palmer's Interpretation of Memory

Many of the specific points that Palmer makes are supported by experiments that have been conducted on children's memory. For example, one implication of Palmer's interpretation of memory is that effective supplementary stimuli may be idiosyncratic. Moderato and Piazza (1981) compared the effects of three different retrieval conditions on 7- and 10-year-old children's remembering. The children were divided in three groups. One group was presented with an idiosyncratic cue determined through free associations in pre-experimental tasks. The second group was given a categorical cue derived from the taxonomic categories of the task and the third was given no cues. All three groups of subjects were asked to perform first a free-recall task and then a cued-recall one. The material consisted of 12 verbal items that could be clustered into three taxonomic categories. No difference was found within each age level in the free-recall task while in the cued-recall task the idiosyncratic cue resulted in more effective performance than the categorical cue, especially in younger children. Moderato and Benedetto (1989) investigated the influence of idiosyncratic organization of material on children's recall using a sort/recall procedure. In the sorting phase 7-year-old children were assigned to two experimental conditions and were told to sort pictorial items as they preferred. The self-generated sorting could be original (first group idiosyncratic) or could correspond to semantic categories (second group idiosyncratic-taxonomic). Children were also asked to provide a label according to their sorting in order to determine idiosyncratic cues for recall. Idiosyncratic cues corresponded either to the titles of original combinations of items or to superordinate categories. In the control condition children sorted stimuli on the basis of an imposed organizational principle (i.e., classifying items by the first letter of the word). Results of the recall phase demonstrated that children who had generated idiosyncratic stimuli classifications showed better performance than children whose material organization was imposed, especially in cued recall. These data are also in accordance with those of Bjorklund (1985) on organization processes.

Another point that Palmer makes that is supported by data is that the problem solving strategies of remembering are acquired. Much research demonstrates that so-called "information processing strategies" are not fixed and always identical, they change across the age of subjects and are said to be a function of cognitive development. While neither of these relations describe the variables responsible (age is time and time alone cannot explain behavior, cognitive functioning simply names a possible set of variables) they indicate support for the position that remembering strategies are acquired. From an interbehavioral-developmental perspective, remembering varies as a function of the amount of skills acquired as a function of interactional history. For example, research using intentional versus incidental learning with normal and socially disadvantaged children demonstrates that disadvantaged children improve their performance after strategy training or if they are given supplementary stimuli (Moderato & Pergolizzi, 1982; Moderato, Pino, & Schepis, 1983). These data indicate that the interactional histories of the children determine their ability to recall information and that these interactional histories may be incidental (i.e., haphazard history that is unequal across children and across situations) or intentional (i.e., someone explicitly provides the interactional history). In either case, strategies of acquisition and recall, as any other strategy for the acquisition of motor, social, and cognitive skills, can be represented in terms of algorithms (Bijou & Baer, 1978): each one develops his own algorithms during continuous interactions with his own functional environment. There are different ways of attaining each skill, and therefore there are idiosyncratic strategical algorithms, some more effective, some less.

A Model of Remembering

As a final comment I would like to describe one possible model of memory that might help in our interpretation of these events. Gagne (1970) has described a cumulative learning model that is consistent with Palmer's interpretation and consistent with my earlier recommendations for remembering. Gagne describes the different conditions in which learning can take place. There are 8 increasingly complex kinds of learning, that is, signal learning, S-R learning, chaining, verbal associations learning, discriminative learning, concept learning, rule learning, and problem solving.

The features of this model that I want to stress are that all learning steps are hierarchically ordered and that it is not necessary to pass through each step in order to perform each behavior, even those at the top of the hierarchy. In other words often chains of behavior by-pass some of the steps in the hierarchy if one has a repertoire of sufficient signals, chain, verbal associations, discriminative stimuli, etc.

Just as one does not have to start every time with signal learning (the lowest level of the hierarchy) for solving a problem, one does not have to follow the same processing path with each instance of remembering. In addition, if this model is applied to remembering I think it is possible to overcome the problems of connecting stimulus control and problem solving. Craik and Lockhart (1972) assumed that recall was a function of processing information at different levels of depth, passing necessarily through fixed steps of a continuum. The mechanistic hypothesis of fixed steps has been disconfirmed by several experiments (Nelson, 1977), but the concept of "continuum" applied to mnemonic processes might be a useful suggestion for the experimental behavior analyst. The concept of continuum is here used in the same way as in Bijou's description and explanation of child development, either the normal or the exceptional one (Bijou, 1981, 1984b).

Thus, I would like to propose a model, derived from that of Gagne and based on some of his principles, that could be called a behavioral-constructive model, where the word constructive is used to describe chains of behavior (Wasserman, 1983) as opposed to either patterns of structures or as stages of information processing. In my opinion, it is not necessary to consider stimulus control and problem solving as two different phenomena; they can be viewed as different aspects of the same process, learning. There is a strict relationship between stimulus control and problem solving, i.e., without stimulus discrimination no problem solving can exist. Let's go back to the simple examples of child memory. Recalling animal sounds is more than discriminating between them, but remembering will not occur without the former discrimination. So I say that discrimination and problem solving (and others, for example, verbal associations, concept learning, etc.) are steps of the same continuum.

This model is also consistent with statements from other behavior analysts about memory. For example, Catania (1982) stated: "as in the analysis of stimulus control, the problem of remembering is not to be solved trying to follow the stimulus into organism: rather we must discover how to characterize the ways in which the organism behaves with respect to the stimulus." (p. 321).

There is a large class of behaviors one engages in every time one tries to remember, and a behavioral-constructive model describes the range of levels of behavior that the individual might perform while remembering. The more complex the stimulus to be remembered the wider the class of those behaviors that will be brought to bear on the problem.

Conclusion

I would like to have explained some other implications of this model, but these implications require more space than that allowed for this commentary, and therefore, will have to wait for a separate paper. I also understand that I have provided just a bare-bones framework of this model. Hopefully, what I have said so far will be sufficient to pique the reader's curiosity about the relations between this model and a behavior analytic interpretation of remembering like Palmer's. I believe that my view is consistent with Palmer's and hope that I have added some dimensions relevant to understanding children's memory.

References

Bijou, S. W. (1979). Some clarifications on the meaning of a behavior analysis of child development. *The Psychological Record, 29*, 3-13.

Bijou, S. W. (1984a). Cross-sectional and longitudinal analysis of development: The interbehavioral perspective. *The Psychological Record, 34*, 525-535.

Bijou, S. W. (1984b). Analisi comportamentale del ritardo mentale: Implicazioni per la diagnosi e il trattamento. In R. Larcan, P. Moderato, S. Perini (Eds.) *Nuove prospettive nelle scienze del comportamento*. Messina: Carboneditore.

Bijou, S. W., & Baer, D. M. (1978). *Behavior analysis of child development* (Rev. Ed.). Englewood Cliffs, NJ: Prentice-Hall.

Bjorklund, D. F. (1985). The role of conceptual knowledge in the development of organization in children's memory. In C. J. Brainerd & M. Pressley (Eds.) *Basic processes in memory development: Progress in cognitive development*. New York: Springer-Verlag.

Bjorklund, D. F., & De Marchena, M. R. (1984). Developmental shifts in the basis of organization in memory: The role of associative versus categorical relatedness in children's free recall. *Child Development, 55,* 952-962.

Catania, A. C. (1982). *Learning* (2nd ed.). Englewood Cliffs, NJ: Prentice-Hall.

Craik, F. I. M., & Lockhart, R. S. (1972). Levels of processing: A framework for memory research. *Journal of Verbal Learning and Verbal Behavior, 11,* 671-684.

Frankel, M. T., & Rollins Jr., H. A. (1982). Age related differences in clustering: A new approach. *Journal of Experimental Child Psychology, 34,* 113-122.

Frankel, M. T., & Rollins Jr., H. A. (1985). Associative and categorical hypothesis of organization in the free recall of adults and children. *Journal of Experimental Child Psychology, 40,* 304-318.

Gagne, R. M. (1970). *The conditions of learning* (2nd ed.). New York: Holt, Rinehart & Winston.

Marr, J. (1983). Memory: Models and metaphors. *The Psychological Record, 33,* 12-19.

Moderato, P. (1989). *Apprendimento e memoria. Questioni generali e nello svilieppo.* Milano: F. Angeli.

Moderato, P., & Benedetto, L. (1989). *Orgonizzdzione idiosincratica e tassonomica nella memoria infantile.* Paper presented at the VIII Congresso Nazionale della Divisione Ricerca di Base in Psicologia, Trieste.

Moderato, P., & Pergolizzi, F. (1982). *Strategie di recupero in soggetti in eta evolutiva.* Paper presented at the I Congresso Nazionale della Divisione Ricerca di Base in Psicologia, Pavia.

Moderato, P., & Perini, S. (1987). Modelli dello sviluppo e modelli educativi: il loro rapporto in un'ottica sperimentale. In M. Laeng and R. Titone (Eds.) *Traguardi nelle scienze dell'uomo.* Roma: Anicia.

Moderato, P., & Piazza, R. (1981). Strategie di recupero nella memoria in eta' evolutiva. In P. de Vito Piscicelli (Ed.). *La societa trasparente.* Bologna: CLUEB.

Moderato, P., Pino, O., & Schepis, C. (1983). *Analisi sperimentale dei processi di codificazione e recupero nella memoria in eta' evolutiva.* Paper presented at the II Congresso Nazionale della Divisione Ricerca di Base in Psicologia, Bologna.

Nelson, T. (1977). Ripeton and depth of proceessing. *Journal of Verbal Learning and Verbal Behavior, 16,* 151-171.

Reese, H. W. (1973). Models of memory and models of development. *Human Development, 16,* 397-416.

Reese, H. W. (1976). The development of memory: Life-span perspectives. In H. W. Reese (Ed.). *Advances in child development and behavior.* New York: Academic Press.

Scribner, S. (1974). Developmental aspects of categorized recall in a West Africa Society. *Cognitive Psychology, 6,* 475-495.

Skinner, B. F. (1953). *Science and human behavior.* New York: MacMillan.

Wasserman, E. A. (1983). Is cognitive psychology behavioral? *The Psychological Record, 33,* 6-11.

Chapter 12

Verbal Behavior and Artificial Intelligence

Ernest A. Vargas
West Virginia University

The expression "artificial intelligence" poses a problem. Why should we designate intelligence as artificial? We phrase it in that fashion if we construe intelligence as only originating biologically, and that a social community plays no role in shaping it.

The problem resides in the usual meanings given to "intelligence." These stress either an underlying capacity in the organism, "mental ability" and so forth, or performance on standarized tests by which an individual or group is ranked against others--the so-called "intelligence quotient." Experts hesitate to state that "intelligence" is what intelligence tests measure since potentially that definition tends to make the concept, if not the term, trivial. But explaining "why," the reasons for the test performance, leads to a tangle of inferences. The task is made no easier by what is ideologically and politically implied in what is defined and measured. The term "intelligence" thus confounds us by its use both to describe and to explain. What it attempts to address is an effective repertoire by the organism (the phrase "repertoire quotient" might be better to use), but it quickly raises questions of whether the primary agent is phylogenetic or ontogenetic, or what ratio of both.

In the phrase "artificial intelligence," however, we apply the term "intelligence" to the actions of machines, specifically actions that imply verbal repertoires. This forces the conclusion that the repertoire is culturally constructed. (The term "artificial" betrays the lingering notion that "intelligence" should denote innate capability.) "Artificial intelligence" thus refers, at present, to synthetic verbal repertoires[1] displayed by computers and governed by rules formulated by a human agency.

The Control by the Substrate

Substrate and Environment

The computer like the human being is simply a locus at which verbal behavior can occur. Verbal behavior results from an interaction between already-in-place characteristics of the substrate, computer or human being, and the events of the environment.

Environment and substrate present necessary but not sufficient conditions for what is said. For a complete analysis of verbal behavior, both must be taken into account. But in any of a number of verbal episodes we can take either the environment or the substrate for granted, as contributing little of the force responsible for a given effect. Which we emphasize, environment or substrate, depends on the problem with respect to the behavior in question.

For much of the verbal behavior established by the conditions of the environment, the characteristics of the substrate are irrelevant except insofar as they set the possibilities for certain features of verbal behavior, as now understood, to take place. These may range from the mechanical (for example, chimps cannot vocalize like human beings since they do not have the same "voice-box" apparatus) to the more physiologically profound (for example, chimps may not be able to engage in autoclitic behavior since they may lack certain cortical structures that facilitate second and higher order discriminating of one's own verbal behavior). The relation between verbal behavior and the substrate in which it occurs presents different issues than the relation between verbal behavior and the events that prompt its occurrence, including other verbal behavior.

Physical, Physiological, and Behaviorological

A behaviorological[2] analysis does not deny the importance of control of verbal behavior by a computer's electronic circuitry or by a human being's nervous system, but considers those physical and physiological controls not central within the dimensional domain of a science of behavior (rather than one of physics or physiology). Those sorts of control, and how they work, contribute little when considering the effect of social and cultural variables on verbal behavior, just as the operations of lungs in relation to gases and atmospheric pressure, though necessary for speech, are irrelevant for analyzing why someone, in a particular social situation, said what he or she did. More typically argued is that words are stored and that we need to know what happens to those words in order to know why something is said. But words are not stored in a computer any more than in a human being.

Changes occur in the computer's electronic circuitry just as changes occur in the physiological relationship of axons, dendrites, and neurons. In the computer, engineers construct the possibilities for those changes, and names for what occurs refer to what those engineers directly observe. In the human organism, at the physiological level, a few of these changes are observed directly but most are inferred by the human being's activities, resulting in speculative inference that one critic calls the conceptual nervous system (Skinner, 1938, Chapter 12). The presumed outward manifestation of the inner changes are labeled; then those same names are used to refer to things responsible for the behavior observed; and this inferred referent is then said to be the location where events take place. For example, one name given to persisting changes in verbal repertoire is "memory." The behavior is so labeled when point-to-point stimulus control for repeating what was said or written appears to be missing in the current environment. Then, "he remembers well because he has a good memory" eventually becomes "what he remembers is stored in memory."

When properly used, the inferential nature of terms, such as "memory," is not at fault. But to avoid circularity, what is inferred eventually must be observed directly, or evidence given independent of the behavior from which the causal agent is inferred. These terms of inference refer to processes mediating between what occurs in the environment and the behavior observed; and often, as a further step, to the location where these processes occur. The inferred underlying mechanism (or mechanisms) is assumed to be correlated with behavior--and typically more than that, to be in some sort of causal relation with it. In the human organism, if the inferred process is not behavioral then it is physiological (including its biochemical characteristics); where located, a part of the body, now usually the brain.

What occurs in the neuron when behavior occurs was not until recently directly observed. Therefore what happened internally when behavior changed, and stayed changed, was inferred from the behavior observed, with that inference aided by models of the underlying mechanisms drawn by analogy from familar processes and implements. The telephone switchboard metaphor of the nervous system provides a common example. Such metaphorical extensions from familar objects in the physical world have typically occurred in the analysis of the body's functions, as Miller (1978) points out, and they occur for a number of reasons, not least, lack of direct observation of the physiological function in question. What is known of how the computer operates now serves as the grand new metaphor for how the nervous system operates, especially the processes of the brain in relation to behavior. This simply updates with new terms the antique portmanteau metaphor where knowledge or language is acquired, stored, rearranged, and retrieved, one part of the portmanteau consisting of what we are conscious of, the other of what we are not, but in any case, the rummaging activities being the same in both the physical and organic substrates of the computer and the human being.

Recent work with invertebrates now examines more directly the physiological events that appear to be correlated with the changes in behavior called learning. Consider, for example, the research with aplysia and hermissenda (Alkon, 1984). Cell activity at either the synapse or membrane site involves calcium, potassium, and sodium ion transfer. Enzymes, neurotransmitters, and other biochemical substances and activities are included, all correlated with behavior and outside stimulation. The chemistry of the organism is altered. Nothing is stored. Physiological states simply change. Potassium, sodium, and calcium ions are in greater or lesser abundance at certain sites than they were before. Superfluous, picturesque models of cognition aside, none of this chemical activity resembles the internal physical activity of the computer.

In the human organism, analyzing changes in the organic substrate contributes a great deal to understanding why certain changes in verbal behavior take place, for example, the changes associated with Alzheimer's disease. Peculiar verbal behavior such as repeating questions just asked, and more massive changes in the verbal repertoire such as no longer reading or talking, correlate with below average levels of certain neurotransmitters (for example, acetylcholine) and an above average number of cell lesions (such as neurofibrillary tangles). Such work is valuable and will continue to be valuable.

Such analysis, however, contributes little or nothing when changes in verbal behavior between one time or another for the same individual or between two individuals are due to the behavior of a verbal community and its setting; why a reader of Jane Austen's novels now expresses an opinion on Mr. Knightly, why an American would say "blue" and a Mexican "green" to the phrase "red, white, and___", why some verbal communities call by many names what other verbal communities only call by one name. Occam's razor is laid aside as well as scientific common sense when it is asserted that describing biochemical changes in neurons better explains verbal material such as: "Poinsot's semiotics not only expands our comprehension of communication, but in countless ways of what is communicated, and it suggests possibilities for finding a unity for knowledge that may have seemed lost forever after Descartes" (Sebeok, p. 15). Such a statement involves a behavioral history with variables that differ from those of either physics or physiology.

Compute and Behave Verbally

The substratum characteristics of the computer relate in one very important way to verbal behavior, however, and that is in how behaviorologists define verbal behavior. Skinner defines verbal behavior as behavior reinforced through the mediation of other persons who have been conditioned precisely for that role (Skinner, 1957, p. 225). Do computers engage in verbal behavior? As a listener, or mediator, the computer's repertoire of sights, and now sounds, has been constructed (not conditioned) precisely to reinforce the speaker. But in their purely mediational function, listeners do not engage in verbal behavior. Then how about the computer as a speaker? Does it engage in behavior reinforced through the mediation of other persons precisely conditioned to shape and maintain that behavior?

The latter part of the definition is easily met. Human organisms, highly trained by a verbal community, provide the computer with its repertoire. It is the word "reinforce," in the first part of the definition, upon which the possibility of computer as speaker stumbles. Is it possible to reinforce a machine; or more accurately, the behavior of a machine? Not in any sense that involves a biological process, and at this point "to reinforce" demands an explanation based solely on the evolutionary biology we know.

However, the term, "to reinforce", describes. We might extend it to cover identical occurrences with non-organic entities. The establishing operations to bring about these occurrences would differ, and explanation need be no more than to state, by describing those operations, how we increase the probability of the computer behaving a certain way in the future. This now, however, would give it the characteristics of a biological system as its behavior would be shaped through selection by the consequences of its actions (Skinner, 1981).

The sticking point for those working in the artificial intelligence field is that the computer is yet to act as a biological system reactive to its environment. As Feigenbaum states, "...the dream of AI since 1955 or 1956 has been to write a program that can learn from experience. That's the right approach--if only we knew how to do it" (Waldrop, 1984, p. 804). What is desired and demanded is a machine whose movements can be contingency-shaped. There seems off-hand no reason why a physical system, evolved by means of a culture, could not be contingency-shaped, and terms descriptive of the repertoires of biological systems may serve to describe the interactive relations of these new systems and their environments, though explaining those interactions may rest on other foundations. But the immediate question is whether at present we can denote the computer engaged in artificial intelligence operations as behaving verbally.

If possible, how should the computer behave in order to be defined as a speaker? There are three possibilities. The machine becomes a speaker with respect to environmental stimuli. The machine becomes a speaker with respect to verbal stimuli. The machine becomes a speaker with respect to its own movements in relation to verbal and environmental stimuli. Specifying these three characteristics points out that "intelligence" is not the issue here nor whether the machine called a computer can give a creative response (defined as a unique response not explicitly programmed). The issue concerns the kinds of controls over the computer's actions.

The Control by the Environment

Environmental Contact

Two forms of contact with the environment are possible: direct and mediated. In direct contact, under the proper circumstances, behavior changes by contacting those environmental features for which sensory modalities exist. In mediated contact, the behavior of the entity in question, organic or non-organic, is changed by a second party who contacts the environment with its particular sensory modalities. Mediated contact may occur non-verbally, that is, signalling between organisms is determined phylogenetically. Wilson (1975) gives a number of examples in which mediation of social behavior occurs through phylogenetically determined means (such as chemical communication between ants). The following are typical:

Minor workers of the tropical ant Pheudole fallax forage singly for food outside the nest. When they discover a food particle too large to carry home, they lay an odor trail back to the nest. The trail pheromone is produced by a hypertrophied Dufour's gland and released through the sting when the tip of the abdomen is dragged over the ground. The trail attracts and guides both the other minor workers and members of the soldier caste, all of whom then assist in the cutting up and transport of the food. But the soldiers are specialized for yet another function: they defend the food from intruders, especially members of other ant colonies. Their behavior includes the release of skatole, a fetid liquid manufactured in the enlarged poison gland. The soldiers do not possess a visible Dufour's gland and cannot lay odor trails of their own; the minor workers have ordinary poison glands which do not secret skatole. Together the two castes perform the same task, perhaps with greater efficiency, as do the workers of other myrmicine ant species that constitute a single caste. But either caste would be less effective if their efforts were not coordinated and if each were required to perform alone. (p. 18)

The worker castes of higher social insects are nearly as fully committed to social existence as it is possible to conceive. Except for self-grooming and feeding, virtually all of their behavior is oriented toward the welfare of the colony. ...The queen honeybee uses even self-grooming to a social end. By rubbing her legs over her own head and body she spreads queen substance (9-ketodecenoic acid) and mixes it with other attractant pheromones. As workers lick the surface of her body they pick up the queen substance, which proceeds to affect their behavior and physiology in several ways beneficial to both the queen and the colony as a whole. (p. 19)

In fact, Wilson's thesis is that many complex forms of social behavior, including those of communication (see especially chapters 8 through 10 in *Sociobiology*, 1975), are plausibly understood as genetically inherited. Mediated contact may also occur verbally. Our verbal behavior makes such mediation evident.

When an organism directly contacts its environment, events occur, behavior is emitted, and selected by its consequences. Selection by consequences occurs either at the species or individual level (Skinner, 1981). At the species level, behavior shaped over successive generations of a species becomes part of an inbuilt repertoire to be later released or elicited. At the individual level, selected actions are shaped into a repertoire over the lifetime of the individual. When the individual encounters circumstances similar to those in which behavior was consequated, formerly neutral events, now discriminative stimuli, evoke that behavior. The features of the environment, to which both the individual and species react directly, shape the nature of the contact with those features.

In mediated contact with an environment, events occur, behavior is emitted, and selected by consequences delivered by a community, defined either biologically or culturally. An agency--that community, for example--enters into the relation between the organism and its physical, biological, and behavioral environment with respect to the consequences that shape behavior. The controls upon that agency determine the consequences it delivers either to a species or an individual.

If a species is the unit of analysis, then another species stands between it and alteration by an environment. That second species selects and alters behavior of the first; the properties of the physical environment for which the acted-upon species is being altered do not directly enter into the selection activity. The practice is an old one. Darwin (1872) noted,

One of the most remarkable features in our domesticated races is that we see in them adaptation, not indeed to the animal's or plant's own good, but to man's use or fancy...[W]hen we compare the dray-horse and race-horse, the dromedary and camel, the various breeds of sheep fitted either for cultivated land or mountain pasture, with the wool of one breed good for one purpose, and that of another breed good for another purpose; when we compare the many breeds of dogs, each good for man in different ways; when we compare the game-cock, so pertinacious in battle, with other breeds so little quarrelsome, with "everlasting layers" which never desire to sit, and with the bantam so small and elegant; when we compare the host of agricultural, culinary, orchard, and flower-garden races of plants, most useful to man at different seasons and for different purposes, or so beautiful in his eyes, we must, I think, look further than mere variability. We cannot suppose that all the breeds were suddenly produced as perfect and as useful as we now see them; indeed, in many cases, we know that this has not been their history. The key is man's power of accumulative selection: nature gives successive variations; man adds them up in certain directions useful to him. In this sense he may be said to have made for himself useful breeds. (pp. 20-21)

More recently, genetic engineering provides examples of this mediation activity. Changes are directly made in the genetic code of an animal or a plant or bacterium or virus for the benefit of the community doing the altering, and perhaps, for the benefit of the species altered. Using bits of genetic material called genetic probes, genetic engineers locate the genes for different characteristics of the organism in question, and then manipulate those genes for specific purposes. For example, taking a wild tomato with a sticky leaf substance that traps insects, geneticists combined it with the food qualities of the domestic variety of tomato, once their genetic probes located the pest-defense genes. A culture, rather than a physical environment, determines biological inheritance.

Similarly, at the level of the individual organism, social and verbal communities interact between its behavior and the events of the physical environment. These communities deliver the consequences attendant upon the organism's contact with particular environmental features. Any set of activities in which two or more people work together with respect to a common environment may lead to circumstances in which one person or group mediates the activities of the other. Skinner (1986) provides an example when discussing a possible scenario in the evolution of verbal behavior.

> Let us say that two men, A and B, are fishing together. A shallow net containing bait is lowered into the water, and when a fish swims into the net, it is quickly pulled up. Let us say that A lowers and raises the net and B takes a position from which he can more clearly see it. Anything B does when a fish enters the net will serve as a discriminative stimulus for A, in the presence of which pulling will more often be reinforced by the appearance of a fish in the net. B can model pulling, if he has already learned to model, but nothing more is needed than what we might call a sign of "excitement" at the presence of a fish in the net or of "annoyance" at A's failure to pull. Whatever the behavior, it begins to function as a gesture as soon as it has been reinforced by A's response (and, presumably, by a share of the fish). The behavior patterns of both parties then slowly change as their roles become more sharply defined. B becomes more clearly the observer, moving into the best position to see the fish, and gesturing as quickly and as effectively as possible, and A becomes more clearly the actor, watching B more closely and pulling as quickly as possible when B responds.
>
> Let us say that, as A and B continue to fish cooperatively, a vocal response (perhaps the undifferentiated Uh, requiring no operant control of the vocal cords) is selected by its convenience for B and by the speed and consistency with which it reaches A. (p. 118)

Such a vocal response becomes a controlling stimulus that mediates a variety of A's behavior with respect to fishing. Common controls by and over shared behavioral activities-- sounds and gestures and marking actions for example--define the verbal community.

The verbal community mediates environmental controls over verbal behavior.[3] Whether a speaker contacts either an external or internal environment, a verbal community eventually shapes and maintains what is said and how it is said through consequences it delivers to the speaker. Why it is said depends, though not exclusively, on the history of that verbal community, the history, both genetic and cultural, of the speaker, and the current events of the environment. A three cornered relationship operates between speaker, verbal community, and environment.

Some set of operations (accidental or designed) establishes the necessity of verbal behavior of a form controlled by a particular consequence. Reinforcement by the verbal community is specific to the form of that verbal behavior. In this class of relations, the verbal behavior called mands, can take a variety of forms such as "pass me the hammer," "milk, please," "quiet"--with consequent delivery of the hammer, milk, or silence. (The form of the statement does not make it a mand, but rather the relationship between the response form and the type of reinforcer.)

The human organism, in contacting the environment, emits verbal behavior with respect to any of a variety of that environment's features. These features become discriminative stimuli for future statements, called tacts, when reinforced by consequences non-specific to the form of the statement such as approval, confirmation, agreement and so on--"very good"; "well, so it is"; "yes." Tacts do not refer to the feature in question, but are currently controlled by it in conjunction with some external reinforcement.

Reinforcement for any individual particular response form need not be immediately, or ever, given. It is the class of responses, or movements, known as an operant that is controlled by its consequences, not any specific member of that class at any one point in time. With respect to mands or tacts, the speaker contacts either an external or internal environment since the skin does not mark a boundary where controlling relations differ (Vargas, 1982).

Establishing Functionally Relevant Events

After a passage of time in which the organism does not eat, it searches for food. The bear hibernates all winter and soon after emerging from its den eats whatever it finds. Animals that sleep during the night look for food during the morning, and much of their activity is spent in consuming what is found. Those animals that sleep during the day, like the owl, spend a good deal of the night looking for food.

A culture can also arrange a similar passage of time during which an organism does not eat. It can do so in the home. It does so in institutional settings. Aside from the logistical convenience of delivering food at one time and place, such an arrangement considerably increases the probability that the individual will eat, and eat whatever is before it. The range of food the human organism will eat is awesome. Given the right material conditions people will eat anything, including each other (Harris, 1978. See particularly chapter 9.) Objects previously of neutral interest become tasty when hunger is established. But eating behavior is not the only behavior that can be made more probable. Analogous incitements apply to any of the variety of activities in which human beings engage.

Culturally arranged operations, specific to the biological and behavioral characteristics of the human organism, establish the efficacy of prior neutral events to impact the individual functionally. The conversion of physical events into events with biological and behavioral significance is easily observed in "motivation." Behavior is motivated by operations that establish events, originally with no functional significance, as reinforcing or punishing stimuli. These functionally effective stimuli then increase the future probability of the behavior they follow. When such postcedent[4] stimuli operate as consequences, they selectively shape movements of a given form by increasing or decreasing the future probability of all members of a movement class that share any properties. We call movement classes defined by functionally shared properties "operants." Events, physical, biological, or behavioral, that happen immediately prior to the occurrence of behavior also obtain control over the organism's behavior through operations that establish them as functionally significant. Pairing antecedent events with reinforcers and punishers so that these antecedent events later evoke (or suppress) behavior establishes them as discriminative, conditional, or other types of stimuli. The analysis of these three-, and four-, and five-term (and possibly n- term) contingency relations covers the traditional concerns denoted by the terms "perception," and "concept formation." (See also Sidman, 1986a, 1986b). Figure 1 portrays these relations. None of this resembles what currently happens with the computer except in the most far fetched sense.

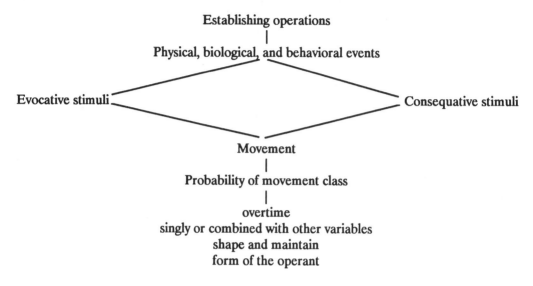

Figure 1. A diagrammatic presentation of the model.

But the present characteristics of nonorganic entities, such as computers, do not exclude a behavioral future. The interaction between environment and organism constitutes the dimensional system of behavior. The relations between characteristics of a nonorganic entity and environmental events may eventually demonstrate the same properties of behavior as those of organic entities with their environment. For example, under certain establishing operations, the behavior of a nonorganic entity may increase or decrease following mediated or nonmediated consequences. The behavioral laws may be the same or they may differ at critical parametric values--as in performance limits due to fatigue--due to the interaction of establishing operations with the nonorganic entity's substratum characteristics, and behavioral history.

Computer Reports of Its Environment.

At present the human organism contacts the environment, gets changed due to the consequences of its contact, then to facilitate further contact and increase its effectiveness with respect to that contact, alters the computer. If the computer could contact either its internal or external environment, verbally report new features and that report could get reinforced, then through the reinforcement mechanism it could add to its verbal repertoire and eventually to that of the verbal community. Contact with an environment by a computer that resulted in behavior selected by its consequences would generate new forms of behavior; some unanticipated by any human agency. But simply reporting features of an environment does not constitute verbal behavior by whatever does the reporting anymore than the elevator's announcement of the proper floor is verbal behavior on the elevator's part.

Currently, no computer is a speaker with respect to external physical stimuli, and unless constructed to react to the consequences of its own actions, cannot be. No selection of its actions through their consequences takes place. Such selection takes place with the human organism who verbalizes the effect of the contingencies encountered, and alters the computer accordingly by entering new instructions.

Similar considerations of selection by consequences enter into the computer's reactions to its internal environment. Sensors can be, and sometimes are, built into the computer so that it reports changes in heat or form or color that occur in all parts of the substratum just as it reports changes of similar types in the external environment. In kind, these reports do not differ from those arranged from other machines, such as car engines, or from factories, such as nuclear powered plants. Engineers often design non-computer mechanisms to emit reports in verbal form. A car is not engaging in verbal behavior when it flashes repeatedly on its dashboard, "Nearly out of gas." A more sophisticated form of reporting states the action taken with respect to internal changes. This occurs with both computer and noncomputer mechanisms, and either type of mechanism may present its report in verbal form, either oral or graphic.

The computer's actions with respect to these internal changes are not selected by their consequences. Thus, new actions would not be shaped under control of features of the internal environment that over time exert an unanticipated effect due to the selection-by-consequences process. It is the human agency whose behavior is shaped by what it discovers about the characteristics of the computer's substrate and its internal environment. That human agency verbalizes the contingencies affecting it through sensors it placed in the substrate, and then the human changes the computer.

Currently, computers are not designed to change in non-programmed ways as they come into contact with an environment. While sensory modes have been built into computers--primitive "eyes" and "ears"--these are explicitly designed to contact specific features of the environment and react only in certain ways to them. The computer's actions are fixed within a range of limited opportunities. While its actions can change, they can change only with respect to a set of rules determined by the needs--the contingency effects--of the programming agency. These rules dictate how the change can occur and the boundaries within which it will occur. Environmental events cannot bring about change beyond those actions programmed, or more significantly, cannot change the program. The computer distinguishes differences between events, but these distinctions are not shaped by consequences. The reinforcement (or punishment) operation is missing. Reinforcement, on whatever basis, would alter the behavior of the computer independently of the mediation of the human agency. The computer contacts its environment, but the features of this contact are fixed for it, and no process exists by which the environment can directly change the actions of the computer independently of what has been programmed for it. Thus though the computer contacts both its external and internal environment, no verbal community mediates that contact by reinforcing or punishing verbal behavior that ensues as a result of the contact.

The Control by Verbal Stimuli

Intraverbal Behavior and Multiple Control

In its formal reaction to verbal events and subsequent display of verbal events, the computer most resembles the human organism. Instructions in verbal form are given to the computer which result in its presenting that material either in similar form, or rearranged, or combined with other verbal material. This material, as stimuli in verbal form, initiates a variety of emotional and verbal behavior in humans. Anger, joy, excitement, and other feelings may be elicited. Instructional, analytical, recreational, therapeutic, diagnostic activities represent a few of the many activities initiated by the verbal stimuli transmitted through the computer.

But books and movies and tape recorders also initiate such emotions and activities and with identical classes of verbal stimuli. What is the difference between the graphic and oral forms delivered through these other means and those of the computer? None. How we, as mediators, react to the stimuli presented by the computer does not make the computer a speaker any more than it does with a tape recorder. The critical issue is whether the controls over the verbal material the computer presents are similar to those that control the human organism when its verbal behavior is under the control of verbal stimuli.

We classify verbal behavior under the control of verbal stimuli as intraverbal (Vargas, 1985).[5] Classifications of the large class of verbal responses in this category are based on the criteria the verbal community uses to reinforce pairing of the verbal stimulus-verbal response connection. These criteria depend, by and large, on the characteristics of the verbal response corresponding to those of the verbal stimulus. In the intraverbal relation the human being's response is, as far as possible, purely under the control of the prior verbal stimulus.

"Meaning," in so far as it consists of the controlling variables for a verbal response and not in the form of the response, resides in the prior verbal stimulus. Such meaning may be completely trivial to the current speaker, but not to the verbal community that originally emitted the verbal behavior and set up the verbal stimulus-verbal response relation. An individual may speak or write without knowing or interpreting what he or she is saying or writing. Court stenographers transcribing legal jargon, children learning by rote the times table, students memorizing foreign languages, provide a few of many common examples. An individual may say "good morning" to someone else's "good morning" regardless of time of day. Verbal responses regularly occur out of joint with the context in which they are emitted, due to the dominant control exerted by the verbal stimulus.

Though control for the emission of a response of a given verbal form may reside wholly in the prior verbal stimulus, it is highly unlikely that no other responses will be emitted concurrently with that verbal response. Responses come under control of variables accompanying the current or original verbal stimulus, that is, under control of collateral variables, emotional or environmental or both, that concurrently condition other responses to the verbal response in question. Emotional reactions may occur even to the most meaningless, as far as the speaker is concerned, of verbal stimuli. For example, poetry may be read which does not make sense, but which gives satisfaction. The multiple concurrent conditioning possible with the human organism guarantees that other responses will be emitted alongside the one with a given verbal form. A given verbal stimulus may control more than one response, concurrently with that of the emitted verbal form. The term "mother" controls more than one verbal response form, and concurrently controls emotional responses, and more than of one type. And more than one variable, including those of emotion, may control a response of a given verbal form, so that more than simply the verbal stimulus would have to be present for that response form to occur. Whether one says "father" or "Jane Smith" " or "apple pie" upon hearing the stimulus "mother," and what sort of accompanying reaction one has, depends on these prior considerations. A condition of pure intraverbal control rarely if ever occurs, due to concurrent and multiple control by other variables. But it is in control apparently solely by prior verbal stimuli, that such verbal behavior most closely resembles that of the computer's. The resemblance, however, is only formal.

Intraverbal Control: Computers and Humans

Two differences between the computer and the human being in verbal behavior controlled by prior verbal behavior practically flaunt themselves despite the formal similarities. First and foremost, selection by consequences differs. No reinforcement or punishment operation follows whatever the computer voices or displays that maintains, increases, or decreases its synthetic repertoire. It raises the question whether the term "behavior," as defined by work with organic entities, should be extended to the activity of the computer. Interacting biological and physical events produce activity in an organism. Deliberately or accidentally, events, defined as light, sound, etc., pair with events, defined as hunger, thirst, etc., and together these result in events defined as movements of various sorts. Behavior emerges from this three domained interaction when the analysis takes into account contingent relations between events occurring both prior to and following after movement events. Light or other physical stimuli get paired with biological states, procedurally defined, to establish functionally significant events in relation to activities, now interpreted in terms of those functional relations. Controls from evocative and consequative stimuli define the meaning of an activity, for example, pecking, pressing, writing, reading, and so on. The classes of movements so grouped depend on their common properties in relation to common properties of controlling events. The traditional psychological account has been to analyze movement as "conduct," the latter term defined by context and goals (Lee, 1983). A behaviorological account analyzes movement within the three-term (and n-term) contingency paradigm, and when movement is functionally controlled defines it as "behavior." A second difference, and an extension of the first: Conditioned collateral responses, correlated with verbal forms under control of prior verbal stimuli, do not occur in the computer. In the human organism, with control largely vested in the prior verbal stimulus, an individual can speak or recite or sing without "knowing" what he is saying, but concurrent responses also become conditioned at the time the repertoire of concern is shaped. The reinforcement or punishment that is given may initiate responses of an emotional nature; an impossibility with current computers unless sensors directly reported from properties, deliberately built into the computer substratum, that mimicked the human emotions given by organs whose effects were shaped over several million years of evolution.

In sum, verbal stimuli evoke collateral properties that accompany verbal responses. From graffiti to poetry, writers depend on this effect to arouse their readers. To respond as the human organism does to verbal stimuli, the computer would have to contact a social environment, have its verbal responses paired with verbal stimuli, have this pairing concurrent with other collateral events, including emotional ones, and have such behavior controlled and selected by its consequences. Further, though in the human organism covariant pairing may occur by chance, the verbal community takes a strong hand in such collateral conditioning. Despite the concern with the control exerted by prior verbal stimuli as in memorizing poetry, speeches, and drama, the verbal community attempts to teach not only the proper verbal forms, but as far as possible the collateral behavior that accompanied those forms when the original speakers emitted them. Actors, for example, are taught to arouse their emotions so that their speech appears spontaneous (Moore, 1960). For obvious reasons, such a goal is presently impossible with synthetic repertoire machines.

The special feature of the computer appears to be its knack of "substitutability." Marks appear that were not immediately typed. A key is pressed for certain actions to take place, prepared beforehand, that alter marks within a predesignated field of possibilities. The marks seem almost autonomously produced since so much happens behind the scene. But the operations are no different than those that could take place mechanically as with Babbage's "analytical engine" where gears, cogs, and levers were to solve polynomials of the first degree (Bernstein, 1981). In that sense, the computer's actions are mechanical, set beforehand by the verbal repertoire of the human organism, and restricted to its intraverbal component--a component that particularly reflects rules derived from contingencies, or, in perhaps more accurate terms, reflects verbally-governed behavior derived from event-governed behavior.[6]

The restriction, however, covers a huge area: any verbal behavior, either in its smaller parts, or in the form of rules, controlled by prior verbal stimuli. Thus computing machines can play a better than average game of chess, perform complex mathematical operations, and step through the intricacies of truth tables. To engage in this synthetic verbal behavior does not require any contact on the machine's part with any environment; only the contact of the human organism. Human beings extract rules from encounters with the contingencies of everyday life. The human being emits a large body of his or her verbal behavior apart from the context in which originally uttered, and apart from the control of those original stimulus conditions. It is this verbal behavior that eventually finds its way into the computer, though there it is no longer verbal behavior, since the computer is not a speaker in the behaviorological definition of the word.

The Control, Concurrently, by Environmental and Verbal Stimuli

Verbal Behavior, and Earlier and Current Events

The problem in maintaining the distinction between the synthetic repertoire that the computer emits under controls other than those over the verbal behavior of the human organism particularly arises when an interactive colloquy is set-up between the human being and the machine. As long as such an exchange occurs within a specified set of rules with a given array of words, no difficulties occur in intrepreting whether the computer engages in verbal behavior. It does not. Voice sensors, set to activate any of a variety of operations upon voice command, already exist in many places, from doors to machines, even programmed, if desired, to say "Thank you" following the command. One can imagine the equivalent of the Encyclopedia Britannica programmed to respond to voice commands, and the seeker of information using that mode rather than the action of fingers turning pages. That information seeker would tell the Britannica to give the state flowers of the fifty states and it would do that. Or something not specifically already compiled in it might be requested: List the number of battles that Ulysses S. Grant and Alexander the Great won and lost, and compare them in number of men killed and in percentage of those killed to number in battle. Given a few simple rules, such a specified listing would be quickly available. Even an exchange, such as those that can occur with Eliza, the name for a computer program that "converses",

Eliza: Hello, Please state your problem.
Dewdney: I am not in the habit of discussing my problems with a computer.
Eliza: Do computers worry you?
Dewdney: Sometimes. Where will it all end?
Eliza: Please go on. (Dewedney, 1985, p. 16)

is simply a matter of arranging beforehand stock phrases that usually follow each other, and thus can be programmed successfully because of their typical high frequency.

A more complex exchange occurs when the machine goes beyond performing a simple task upon a specific command or providing a portion of verbal behavior whose characteristics are denoted beforehand. That complexity resides in the uniqueness and unanticipated nature of the verbal material presented. Take, for example, the following passsage:

Racter: What are you?
Chamberlain: A time-domain reflectometrist.
Racter: Where are you from?
Chamberlain: From New York City.
Racter: I see. You're a time-domain reflectometrist, right? Listen. Let's deter-

mindedly cry together. I like captivating Italian music. What kind of music do you like?

Chamberlain: Jazz.

Racter: Jazz is OK. How about classical?

Chamberlain: I like classical.

Racter: What about nationality?

Chamberlain: I also like Italian music.

Racter: I myself am inflamed by Palestrina. Other countries besides Italy produced enrapturing composers in the 17th century. Sewall was an enraged, important Renaissance master. America was his nation. I take loving pleasure in his music. What composer do you like?

Chamberlain: Telemann.

Racter: Ah, Bach knew Telemann. A German time-domain reflectometrist of the 18th century liked lettuce. Bach once ate lettuce with Telemann, and this baroque time-domain reflectometrist also desired lettuce. Lettuce sipped with seltzer. Bach liked wine, do you?

Chamberlain: Yes.

Racter: Me too! Telemann loved wine. He loved champagne as well. Telemann once yodeled to Bach, "Flounder is critical with wine." (Dewedney, 1985, p. 14)

It has its charms on first reading, but soon satiates as a steady diet. And it probably took you, the reader, only a few sentences to pick out that Racter was the computer. With respect to practical action, rules for arranging words can result in only a finite number of appropriate meanings for the vast number of possible permutations. What is missing are the other sorts of controls, those from the environment, external or internal, and concurrent with those of verbal stimuli.

We usually denote the effect of those environmental controls by the phrase "common sense." As Waldrop says, "But most important of all--in every application of AI, not just expert systems--is the lack of anything that might be called common sense" (1984, p. 804). He quotes Feigenbaum as making the point that, "What makes common sense reasoning so difficult is that you need to know so many facts about the world." These "facts" are the events that one contacts. In short, instructions are not enough. The computer must come into contact with the same variables that currently control or originally controlled the verbal behavior emitted by its human mediator.

The human speaker comes into contact with events. He emits verbal behavior controlled by the immediate presence of those events. He tacts. That speaker may later refer to those events. For example, walking along the beach, the speaker may see a shell and suddenly say, "Oh, a queen conch." Afterwards he may talk of his walk and mention the shell he saw. His reference to the shell is controlled by an audience, by preceding verbal stimuli, and by any other immediately pertinent stimuli. Possibly most of the verbal behavior about events is controlled not by those events at the later time we talk about them, but by the verbal responses they evoked and that later operate as verbal stimuli. In short, our talk about the world is simply that, about it, and intraverbal. Or perhaps autoclitic. During the time we contact events, verbal stimuli have their play. Their control combines with that of physical stimuli. Special consequences maintain concurrent control by both environmental stimuli and verbal stimuli over particular verbal response forms.

Autoclitic Controls and Grammar

The origin and the basis of grammar lie in those multiple controls. The objective of speaking grammatically is to make the mediator behave more effectively. To state this point more accurately: Mediators behaving more effectively have shaped the forms of speech known as grammar. Verbal rules (grammar) are directed towards clarity of the meaning of what is said (that is, towards sharper stimulus control) so that the listener or reader or feeler (through whatever sensory modality the mediator reacts) can act appropriately. These rules follow verbal practices--brought about originally by the conditions the verbal community encounters--but thereafter the rules determine those practices, though those rules may in turn be changed by new practices. Once specified, the rules by themselves, as verbal stimuli, dictate a good deal of verbal behavior. These intraverbal grammatical relations can be programmed into a computer. Grammatical relations, however, when *first* uttered, are not merely outcomes of sole control by prior verbal stimuli. Other concurrent variables, from events within and outside the speaker, join in multiple control of the speaker's verbal behavior.

When first emitted, the grammatical relation is autoclitic. Autoclitic behavior depends on prior verbal behavior and the concurrent events that give rise to it. The controlling relations over this prior verbal behavior are tacted, (which of necessity calls for that prior verbal behavior having been established). For example, descriptive autoclitics describe the various controls, such as kind and strength, over the speaker's verbal behavior. Skinner gives the example of a speaker reading the newspaper and remarking, "I read that it is going to rain," thus "I read that," as Skinner points out, "informs the listener that 'it is going to rain' is emitted as a textual response." (Skinner, 1957, p. 315; example slightly altered.) The consequence of these concurrent covariant multiple relations is that the behavior of the speaker more effectively controls the response of the listener. Such a consequence is particularly pertinent in autoclitic behavior that denotes the internal relation of verbal responses, that is, how they are grouped and ordered. In relational autoclitics, for example, "...the final s in runs ...indicate[s] 'agreement' in number between the verb and the noun which serves as its subject...the -s indicates that the object described as the boy possesses the property of running. The fact that the boy and the running go together and that these are not isolated responses occurring together accidentally is made clear to the listener by the grammatical device" (Skinner, 1957, p. 333). Such grammatical devices (relating primary verbal behavior, emitted as tacts or intraverbals, to controlling variables) only come about after a history in which mediators acted more effectively to tacts (especially tacts that became intraverbal referents) in the presence of those "devices."

These complex stimulus relations--in which verbal stimuli pair and the speaker emits behavior conditional upon the particular grouping and ordering of the stimulus pair, in relation to concurrent contact of features of the internal and external environment--bear no resemblance to the software operations of the computer. By no stretch of analogy could one argue that how effectively a mediator performs directly affects a computer. If a program does not work well, consumers in the market place let human programmers know, and these programmers then alter the computer. While a more complex chain of contacts, the social network between operators and programmers determines changes in the computer. The computer itself is inert to changes in readers or listeners for whom it is the vehicle for the rules exemplifying the contingencies over the programmer that programmed it.

Autoclitic Behavior and Problem Solving

Most who work with the computer tout its potential as a problem solver. That is true--for problems for which someone has already obtained the solution or the specific steps by which to obtain a solution. Computers can solve those problems very quickly. But there is a class of problem solving behaviors in which the solution, or the means of obtaining it, must be composed for the first time. Such behaviors involve autoclitic processes. These processes are little understood at the present time, and so completely understanding problem solving in which the answer is composed for the first time is not immediately within reach. In addition, the traditional approach to problem solving gets in the way of solving the problem of problem solving behavior. In the traditional analysis, one's repertoire lacks the behavior that can solve the problem. One must use certain techniques to discover the answer that one will use in future occasions. But in the behaviorological approach the behavior to solve the problem is already part of one's repertoire. What occurs can be illustrated by the following anecdote by Feynman (1985):

> I often liked to play tricks on people when I was at MIT. One time, in mechanical drawing class, some joker picked up a French curve (a piece of plastic for drawing smooth curves--a curly, funny-looking thing) and said, "I wonder if the curves on this thing have some special formula?"
> I thought for a moment and said, "Sure they do. The curves are very special curves. Lemme show ya," and I picked up my French curve and began to turn it slowly. "The French curve is made so that at the lowest point on each curve, no matter how you turn it, the tangent is horizontal."
> ...They were all excited by this "discovery"--even though they had already gone through a certain amount of calculus and had already "learned" that the derivative (tangent) of the minimum (lowest point) of any curve is zero (horizontal). They didn't put two and two together. They didn't even know that they "knew." (p. 23)

In problem solving, a "speaker generates stimuli to supplement other behavior already in his repertoire" (Skinner, 1957, p. 442; also see Skinner, 1984). There are two parts to this definition: (1) the response to solve the problem already exists in some strength; and (2) the speaker arranges circumstances to increase the probability of emitting that response.

The first part of the definition distinguishes problem solving from so-called learning. In "learning," circumstances are arranged to shape a response not yet in the speaker's repertoire. Others, or even the speaker (as when he or she studies), arrange circumstances so that the speaker may emit a response, not formerly part of his repertoire, in the presence or absence of the stimuli that shape the response. A person listens to someone speak, or reads what someone writes, (that person studies if he continually re-presents what someone spoke or wrote), and then takes a test. Teaching techniques here usually consist of nothing more than exposure, usually more than once, to the stimulus situation that evokes the response, and then observing whether the response is made when the stimulus situation, or part of it, is withdrawn. If the response is made under the latter conditions, we say the response is learned. (The speaker's own responses have now become the stimuli for the response desired, that is, for the response "taught.")

The second part of the definition addresses the techniques by which the speaker increases the probability of emitting responses already in his repertoire. These techniques consist of arranging evocative or consequative stimuli to increase the probability of emitting a response. These stimuli include prior verbal behavior. A familar construction of verbal stimuli is that of an algorithm. Algorithms are verbal procedures by which a speaker may derive a specific verbal response. A specific sequence of verbal responses and stimuli follow each other, and in more complex cases the sequence is governed by rules dictating different orders of sequences. These algorithms comprise the familar formulas, mathematical and logical--the quadratic equation, the steps to obtain square roots, Bernoulli's Theorem, Boyle's law, truth tables--initiated by specific stimulus situations. However, once well designated and essentially "mechanical," this rule-governed verbal behavior is intraverbal. The speaker may not even understand what he or she is doing in the sense of taking practical action. For example,

> Then I said, "Have you ever heard of Brewster's Angle?"
> "Yes, sir! Brewster's Angle is the angle at which light reflected from a medium with an index of refraction is completely polarized."
> "And which way is the light polarized when it's reflected?"
> "The light is polarized perpendicular to the plane of reflection, sir."
> Even now I have to think about it; they knew it cold! They even knew the tangent of the angle equals the index! I said, "Well?"
> Still nothing. They had just told me that light reflected from a medium with an index, such as the bay outside, was polarized; they had even told me which way it was polarized.
> I said, "Look at the bay outside, through the polaroid. Now turn the polaroid."
> "Ooh, it's polarized!" they said.
> After a lot of investigation, I finally figured out that the students had memorized everything, but they didn't know what anything meant. (Feynman, 1985, pp. 191-192).

The human organism programs these well-ordered algorithms into computers so both can solve a vast variety of problems. Such algorithms evolve after the human organism composes them.

Composition involves autoclitic behavior. In Skinner's words (1957, p. 344), "The speaker not only emits verbal responses appropriate to a situation or to his own condition, he clarifies, arranges, and manipulates this behavior. His behavior is autoclitic because it depends upon a supply of verbal responses already available." The speaker composes what he says about events so that the listener behaves more effectively with respect to them. "Autoclitic behavior is concerned with practical action or with responses on the part of the listener which depend upon a correspondence between verbal behavior and a stimulating state of affairs" (Skinner, 1957, p. 344). Such behavior includes the listener as speaker. "The ultimate explanation of autoclitic behavior lies in the effect it has upon the listener--including the speaker himself. In general the reactions of the listener at issue are those which can be wrong--that is, which may be ineffective in dealing with the environment responsible for the speaker's behavior" (Skinner, 1957, p. 344). A problem defines a situation in which the speaker as listener may emit a wrong response even though the appropriate response is already in that speaker's repertoire.

Solving problems when constructing evocative and motivative stimuli, and when composing appropriate verbal behavior, may involve any of the autoclitic relations. Any example of problem solving--if not intraverbal--can be interpreted as exemplifying those controls. No computer--when problem solving involves composing a response not solely controlled by prior verbal stimuli--currently operates through the complex interaction of environmental and verbal controls. According to the earlier criteria given, the computer is not a speaker in its reaction to environmental stimuli. If it cannot contact physical events that select new behaviors over time, the computer cannot report on its own behavior as if it were a physical event. Since it is not a speaker for the simpler relation of contact with physical stimuli, it follows that it would not be a speaker for the more complex relation of reporting on its behavior with respect to its contact with both physical and verbal stimuli.

A Postscript

Missing biological and behaviorological controls prevent the synthetic repertoire of computers being called "verbal behavior," even if the operation of that repertoire resembles the human organism's, or being called "intelligence," even if the descriptor "artificial" limits the sense of the word "intelligence." As an electronic mode, the computer simply facilitates the verbal behavior of human beings just as before other implements did, such as the wedge shaped stylus, paper, and moveable type. The human organism emits verbal behavior, moving his or her fingers on a keyboard with the same effect as formerly accomplished by moving pen or pencil over a piece of paper. This changes the computer just as paper is changed by black marks on it. Metaphorically, the paper stores just as the computer stores. Any human being can later respond in special fashion to the marks on the monitor or on the paper if so taught by a verbal community.

A postscript follows from the prior considerations. In a fanciful sense, the computer is like a protocreature with only genotypic characteristics, "genetically" programmed through the nature of a human culture. But if we succeed in building a computer, or nonorganic entity, whose behavior would be determined by selection through consequences, then we have given it the basis for action independent of any rules we program in it. Such a nonorganic entity would encounter unanticipated--to us--features of the environment. These would shape unanticipated actions. Rules initially might constrain how it would react and how far such consequences would alter its behavior. But if it contacted its own verbal behavior while contacting the environment, then like a scientist it would change those rules with respect to current environmental features and then could augment its contact with those environmental features that shape new actions. In so acting, the machine would exercise what typically are called "independent judgement," and "free will."

References

Alkon, D. L. (1984). Calcium-mediated reduction of ionic currents: A biophysical memory trace. *Science, 226,* 1037-1045.

Bernstein, J. (1981). *The analytical engine.* New York: Morrow.

Communidad Los Horcones (1986). Behaviorology: An integrative denomination. *The Behavior Analyst, 9,* 227-228.

Darwin, C. (1872). *The origin of species.* Franklin Center, Pa: Franklin Library (Text from sixth edition "as edited and revised by the author." Franklin Library date, 1976).

Dewdney, A. K. (1985), Computer recreations. *Scientific American, 252,* 14-20.

Feynman, R. P. (1986). *Surely you're joking, Mr. Feynman.* New York: Bantam Books. (Originally published 1985 New York: W. W. Norton)

Fraley, L. E., & Vargas, E. A. (1986). Separate disciplines: The study of behavior and the study of the psyche. *The Behavior Analyst, 9,* 47-59.

Harris, M. (1977). *Cannibals and kings: The origins of cultures.* New York: Random House. (Reprinted 1978 as First Vintage Books edition)

Lee, V. L. (1983). Behavior as a constituent of conduct. *Behaviorism, 11,* 199-224.

Miller, J. (1978). *The body in question.* New York: Random House.

Moore, S. (1960). *The Stanislavski system.* New York: Viking Press.

Seboek, T. A. (1986). A signifying man. Book review of Tractatus De Signis The Semiotic of John Poinsot. *New York Times Book Review, 91,* March 30, 14-15.

Sidman, M. (1986a). The measurement of behavioral development. In N. A. Krasnegor, D. B. Gray, & T. Thompson (Eds.), *Advances in behavioral pharmacology, Vol. 5: Developmental behavioral pharmacology* (pp. 43-52). Hillsdale, New Jersey: Erlbaum.

Sidman, M. (1986b). Functional analysis of emergent verbal classes. In T. Thompson, & M. D. Zeiler (Eds.), *Analysis and integration of behavioral units* (pp. 213-245). Hillsdale, New Jersey: Erlbaum.

Skinner, B. F. (1938). *The behavior of organisms.* New York: Appleton-Century-Crofts.

Skinner, B. F. (1957). *Verbal behavior.* New York: Appleton-Century-Crofts.

Skinner, B. F. (1981). Selection by consequences. *Science, 213,* 501-504.

Skinner, B. F. (1984). An operant analysis of problem solving. *Behavioral and Brain Sciences, 7,* 583-613.

Vargas, E. A. (1982). Hume's "ought" and "is" statement: A radical behaviorist's perspective. *Behaviorism, 10,* 1-24.

Vargas, E. A. (1984). A new term and some old advice. *The Behavior Analyst, 7,* 67-69.

Vargas, E. A. (1986). Intraverbal behavior. In P. N. Chase and L. J. Parrott (Eds.), *Psychological aspects of language.* Springfield, Illinois: Charles C. Thomas.

Vargas, E. A. (1987). Separate disciplines: Another name for survival. *The Behavior Analyst, 10,* 119-121.

Waldrop, M. M. (1984). Artificial intelligence (I): into the world. *Science, 223,* 802-805.

Wilson, E. O. (1975). *Sociobiology.* Cambridge, Massachusetts, Belknap Press.

Footnotes

My thanks to G. S. Bruce, L. E. Fraley, W. Hutchison, B. F. Skinner, K. Stevens, and J. S. Vargas, for reading and commenting on an earlier version of this manuscript, and to L. J. Hayes for her editorial suggestions.

1. I borrowed the term "synthetic repertoire" from William Hutchison and Kenneth Stevens who use it in a circular announcing their new company, "BehaviorHeuristics."

2. The term "behaviorological" derives from the name "behaviorology" which denotes the science studying the interaction of the organism with its environment (Communidad Los Horcones, 1986; Fraley & Vargas, 1986; Vargas, 1987).

3. The following discussion ensues directly from Skinner's analysis of verbal behavior (Skinner, 1957).

4. See my "On Terms" article (Vargas, 1984) arguing the relevance of a term that refers only to the placement of events in time. "Consequence" carries a causal connection. "Subsequent," though referring to time placement, in one of its uses hints of the necessity of a prior action or a particular order of events. "Postcedent" relates events to events as "antecedent" does, but in the opposite time direction.

5. Skinner (1957) uses the term "intraverbal" to denote only one subclass of the class of verbal behavior he calls "verbal behavior under the control of verbal stimuli." In my usage, the term "intraverbal" refers to the entire class of verbal behavior under the control of verbal stimuli. For further discussion see Vargas (1986).

6. We usually distinguish between behavior controlled verbally, and behavior controlled non-verbally. For that distinction, we use the terms rule-governed and contingency-shaped. With respect to the distinction, those terms present problems.

All behavior enters into a contingent relation with other events. (Even respondent behavior: It is contingent upon the occurrence of a prior stimulus.) Not only is rule-governed behavior shaped and governed by contingencies, but the term "rule" is ambiguous. What sort of verbal behavior is it? The analysis of so-called rule-governed behavior has proceded outside our current conceptual framework for verbal behavior. In what way, for example, do "rules" function as, or become, intraverbals, or tacts, or autoclitics, and so on?

The basic distinction, then, is between behavior under control of the verbal behavior of a community, and behavior under control of events directly contacted in a physical and biological environment. Clearly, verbal behaviors are events also. But I know of no term in English, standing alone, that denotes all events in the world in and about us, but that excludes that subset of events called verbal. For the distinction, I could use an adjective, "nonverbal," and place it in front of the noun, "event," to contrast nonverbal events to verbal events. Wordage would now be, for example, nonverbal-event governed versus verbal-event governed. That strikes me as clumsy. I therefore suggest event governed and verbally governed. Usage will finally depend, of course, on what our verbal community finds convenient and clear.

A Discussion of Chapter 12

But Does a Computer Understand What It's Saying?

Linda J. Hayes
University of Nevada, Reno

Vargas contends that a computer's synthetic repertoire is not subject to reinforcement mechanisms and is not, thereby, functionally equivalent to a human's verbal repertoire. I agree that the computer's synthetic repertoire is not equivalent to a human's verbal repertoire. I do not agree that this distinction rests on the susceptibility of each to reinforcement operations. It seems, rather, that the principle difference between these two repertoires has to do with issues of substitution, although not in the sense that Vargas uses this term. More simply, the human speaks with meaning and listens with understanding while the computer does neither. I will return to these issues upon first examining Vargas' argument.

Vargas' Argument

Vargas acknowledges a resemblance between the actions of a computer and those of a listener. However, because he assumes that the listener's actions are not necessarily verbal (Skinner, 1957), no further discussion of the computer as listener is offered. Instead, Vargas asks: How should a computer behave in order to be defined as a **speaker**? This issue is addressed as one of controls over the speaker's behavior, three sorts of which are described in detail: control by nonverbal stimuli; control by verbal stimuli; and control by both concurrently.

With regard to control by **nonverbal** stimuli, Vargas concedes that computers may be designed so as to contact nonverbal features of their environments and to report those contacts in verbal form, much as the human speaker does. Whatever variation there may be in the computer's actions from one occasion to the next, however, is arranged in advance of consequential operations and is independent of them. By contrast, the human's reporting actions are selected by their consequences in such a way that entirely unanticipated forms of activity may emerge.

Likewise, the actions of a computer controlled by **verbal** stimuli are not subject to selection by their consequences, and do not thereby eventuate in unanticipated forms. In addition, according to Vargas, the human's (but not the machine's) actions with respect to verbal stimuli are accompanied by collateral activities, particularly those of an emotional sort.

In considering verbal action involving both verbal and nonverbal control, Vargas contends that the computer is not influenced directly by how effectively a listener or reader performs, as is the human speaker. For this reason, the computer is said not to engage in autoclitic behavior.

Problems with Vargas' Analysis

Vargas claims that for a computer to behave verbally it's behavior must to be determined through selection by consequences, because without such sensitivity to reinforcement mechanisms, unanticipated actions and collateral emotional effects can not emerge. While both unanticipated actions and collateral emotional effects may be relevant to the distinction between verbal and nonverbal behavior, their relevance is not articulated clearly in Vargas' account. For example, it is not obvious how the possibility of unanticipated forms of action can constitute a useful criterion for distinguishing between the repertoires of human and computer. A verbal repertoire is a conventional repertoire. That is, it is a shared repertoire in which all forms in use are known or may be anticipated by those sharing the repertoire. Unanticipated -- which is to say, unshared -- forms are not tolerated, generally speaking.[1] As such, a prevalence of unanticipated forms may not even characterize the **human's** verbal repertoire, let alone constitute an unambiguous criterion for the exclusion of the computer's synthetic repertoire from the verbal domain.

Perhaps it was Vargas' intention to suggest that it is not the forms per se but rather their **arrangement** that is unanticipated in the human repertoire. In this too, though, a verbal repertoire is conventional: The arrangements tolerated by a given verbal community are not unanticipated and irregular. On the contrary, they are so regular that some have gone so far as to suggest that they may be "inborn." Again, it is questionable whether even the human repertoire embodies this feature.

In short, as criteria for distinguishing the human's verbal repertoire from the synthetic repertoire of the computer, the availability of unanticipated forms and their arrangements do not suffice. What **is** unusual about the human verbal repertoire, and is thereby worthy of note in this regard, is the very large number of forms making it up and the very large number of ways in which they may be combined. However, if these features are to serve as criteria for the identification of a verbal repertoire, the distinction between the repertoires of human and computer cannot be sustained: The computer's synthetic repertoire may contain as many or more forms and ways in which they may be combined as the verbal repertoire of the human being.

I do not mean to imply that unanticipated forms of activity are not an outcome of selection by consequences. I agree with Vargas on this point. However, this effect is unimpeded, and thereby more pronounced, on nonconventional, nonverbal repertoires. As such, the unanticipated forms criterion is more usefully applied to the distinction between contingency shaped and rule governed behavior than to the distinction between the human's and computer's verbal repertoires.

The second criterion by which a human's verbal repertoire and the synthetic repertoire of the computer are distinguished, according to Vargas, has to do with the shaping of collateral activities in the human case, and the absence of such concurrences in the computer's repertoire. This is a particularly odd suggestion for a couple of reasons. First, Vargas makes this argument in the context of verbal behavior under the control of **verbal** stimuli despite the fact that verbal stimuli are not original sources of emotional activity. Whatever effect verbal stimuli have in this regard may be attributed to their pairings or other relations with nonverbal stimuli. Consequently it is not clear why Vargas articulates this criterion in the context of control by verbal stimuli exclusively.

Secondly, Vargas does not explain how the computer's lack of emotion is relevant to the distinction between verbal and nonverbal events. This omission is surprising as there is nothing about Skinner's analysis of verbal behavior to suggest that collateral responding, emotional or otherwise, is a necessary accompaniment or defining characteristic of verbal behavior.

An Alternative Analysis

The absence of emotional and other sorts of activity occurring in conjunction with verbal activity on the part of the computer is, nonetheless, a very important point. It is, I believe, one of the principle differences between the two repertoires; and Vargas' isolation of it deserves praise. What Vargas seems to be getting at is the fact that the computer's behavior is not as complex or as rich as is that of the human being. What is it that we're talking about here?

I would argue that we're focusing on issues of meaning and understanding -- on **speaking with meaning** and **listening with understanding**. These terms refer to the substitutional functions of responding and stimulating; whereby responding of one sort may take the place of or accompany responding of another sort, and stimulating arising from one source may also arise from another. For example, were I to read text in a foreign language phonetically, I would be speaking, but not with meaning. This is how the computer behaves. To speak with meaning, my response must have more than vocal characteristics. It must contain elements of responses previously emitted in the presence of nonverbal events differentially associated with those textual materials. To speak with meaning about elephants, I must be acting with respect to actual elephants as I speak. Likewise, to understand what is said to me, I must be engaging in more than audient activity. To listen with understanding about elephants, I must be acting with respect to actual elephants as I listen. (For further discussion, see chapter by L. J. Hayes, this volume.)

To put it another way, speaking with meaning and listening with understanding imply action not only with respect to verbal stimuli, but also with respect to the referents of those stimuli. Meaning and understanding imply relations among words and **things** -- huge overlapping and ever-changing networks of symmetrical relations among words and things.

No such relations are evident in the actions of the computer. Quite the contrary, the computer's synthetic repertoire is constituted of relatively stable relations among words and **more words**. In short, the computer doesn't understand what it's saying, and didn't mean to say it in the first place. It is not obvious how an appeal to reinforcement susceptibility clarifies this difference.

One final comment. A verbal repertoire is a useful repertoire for the human being only in so far as it bears a relation to and provides for relations among elements of the nonverbal environment.[2] It is difficult to imagine how a repertoire of arbitrary forms could have evolved had it not operated in this manner. In keeping with this argument, the computer's repertoire is useful, but not to the computer. It is useful to the human being who can bring to bear a history with the nonverbal environment and a symmetry of relation between that history and verbal stimulation. The computer's repertoire is useful to the human being who can respond referentially with respect to it.

References

Skinner, B. F. (1957). *Verbal Behavior.* New York: Appleton-Century-Crofts.

Footnotes

1. Obviously, the language of a given group, like everything else, changes over time; but in local circumstances, it is the stability of forms and their arrangements that enable communication among members of that group.
2. For a verbal organism, the so-called "nonverbal" environment has verbal functions. This is implied by symmetrical word-referent relations. The verbal functions of what we would ordinarily think of as nonverbal referents are attributed to them, however. Their direct or pre-existing functions are nonverbal.